# I LOVE IT WHEN YOU TALK RETRO

D0006601

## Also by Ralph Keyes

*The Quote Verifier*

*The Post-Truth Era*

*The Writer's Book of Hope*

*The Courage to Write*

*Chancing It*

*The Height of Your Life*

*"Nice Guys Finish Seventh"*

*· Sons on Fathers*

*We, the Lonely People*

*The Innovation Paradox* (with Richard Farson)

*Timelock*

*The Wit and Wisdom of Harry Truman*

*The Wit and Wisdom of Oscar Wilde*

*Is There Life After High School?*

# I LOVE IT WHEN YOU TALK RETRO

### Hoochie Coochie,

### Double Whammy,

### Drop a Dime,

### and the Forgotten Origins

### of American Speech

## RALPH KEYES

ST. MARTIN'S GRIFFIN ⚓ NEW YORK

Picture credits are as follows. (Those whose source is not credited are either in the public domain or are from the author's personal collection.)

© 2008 Jupiterimages corporation: 27 Rasputin; 29 gauntlet; 100 jib sails; 105 Duesenberg; 138 icebox; 140 breadbox; 164 logjam; 165 dovetail; 177 telegram; 184 boys playing marbles; 185 Erector set; 186 brass ring; 189 Punch & Judy; 217 Sad Sack; 238 juggernaut; 249 brass knuckles.

Harry S. Truman Library and Museum. 46 whistlestopping; 258 Buck Stops Here; 90 Wally Pipp. Courtesy Ted (a.k.a. BlackSoxFan); 94 Gorgeous George. Professional Wrestling Hall of Fame and Museum; 109 Tabloid. Wellcome Library, London; 153 Pet Rock. Courtesy Mike Harding, Montara Ventures; 158 Moxie song. Courtesy Ira Seskin; 160 Clara Peller. Wendy's International, Inc.; 193 Frank Merriwell. Stanford University Dime Novel and Story Paper Collection; 199 Queen for a Day. Courtesy Geraldine McConville-Holdsworth and Shawn Hanley; 211 Alphonse & Gaston. Courtesy Mort Walker; 235 Mae West. From Jon Tuska, *The Films of Mae West* (Secaucus, N.J.: Citadel, 1975), by permission of Jon Tuska; 257 Malaeska. Courtesy University of Oklahoma Press.

I LOVE IT WHEN YOU TALK RETRO. Copyright © 2009 by Ralph Keyes. All rights reserved. Printed in the United States of America. For information, address St. Martin's Press, 175 Fifth Avenue, New York, N.Y. 10010.

www.stmartins.com

The Library of Congress has catalogued the hardcover edition as follows:
Keyes, Ralph.
   I love it when you talk retro : hoochie coochie, double whammy, drop a dime, and the forgotten origins of American speech / Ralph Keyes.—1st ed.
      p. cm.
   Includes index.
   ISBN 978-0-312-34005-6
   1. English language—Terms and phrases.   2. English language—Idioms.   3. English language—Figures of speech.   I. Title.
   PE1689.K49 2009
   422—dc22

                                                                2008030157

ISBN 978-0-312-60640-4 (trade paperback)

First St. Martin's Griffin Edition: February 2010

10  9  8  7  6  5  4  3  2  1

*For my sons David and Scott,*

*who helped me with this book,*

*as they've helped me with so many things.*

# Contents

# A Note to Readers

This book can be browsed, read straight through, or used as a work of reference. It's written with all those possibilities in mind. I've tried to make the text as engaging as possible for those who wish to read it straight through. For ease of browsing in particular, key words and phrases are highlighted—principal ones in bold, the others in italics. All principal words and phrases are indexed at the end to make looking them up easier. Sources consulted are also listed at the end.

# 1. Talking Retro

When I play twenty questions people ask "is it bigger than a breadbox?" but I don't know what to say because I don't know how big a breadbox is and it really bothers me. Please help! How come everyone else knows stuff like this but not me??? Was I absent that day at school or what???

*—query to a website*

A list compiled every fall at Beloit College attracts much attention. This list gathers cultural references that might puzzle first-year students. "You sound like a broken record," for example, doesn't make much sense to a generation that grew up with iPod buds in their ears. Terms such as "stuck in a groove" and "flip side" could also be puzzling. Today's eighteen-year-olds may not know who Ma Bell is, why 1984 was a year to be concerned about, or how to get to Peyton Place.

*Watergate* is problematic too. Three decades after the break-in at that office complex in Washington, D.C., a South Carolina high school teacher asked students in her government class what "Watergate" referred to. Some had a vague idea that it had something to do with Richard Nixon. Others thought it referred to a fight between the British and Americans in 1789, or that it happened in the mid-1900s, or the late nineteenth century, and could have involved bribery, or the Clintons, or Vietnam, or possibly World War II.

And it isn't just not-so-current events that can be perplexing. In Ohio, thirty-one students in a Canton high school class were polled about their familiarity with everyday items barely a generation old. None knew what "45 rpm" referred to. One fifteen-year-old thought it might be a term for modem speed—the *rate per minute* perhaps. Another fifteen-year-old guessed that "45 rpm" referred to the rotations per minute of a car wheel. These teenagers were vaguely familiar with vinyl records ("You mean those giant black discs? My parents have some in the basement.") and rotary phones, because a few of their grandparents still used them. On the other hand, they could only speculate that a *fuzz buster* might be some sort of vacuum cleaner.

Not just young students but recent immigrants are liable to be puzzled when dated allusions come up. That's what a Harvard graduate student named Michele Gordon discovered when she surveyed twenty colleagues about their familiarity with common American expressions such as "Put your John Hancock there," "The buck stops here," and "You're not in Kansas anymore." Half of her subjects were native-born, half English-speaking students from countries such as Denmark, Switzerland, and Nigeria. Even when they realized what such expressions meant, her foreign-born subjects seldom knew why. Although most had heard the name John Hancock, none could say why his name was synonymous with signatures. As for not being in Kansas anymore, Gordon assumed that because *The Wizard of Oz* runs so often on television, her foreign-born group would be familiar with this expression and its meaning. She was wrong. Although some had a general idea that it meant one was no longer in a rural environment, they missed the broader connotation of leaving a provincial setting for one that's more cosmopolitan. None realized that this catchphrase came from a movie. One guessed that it originated in the Broadway musical *Oklahoma*.

The foreign-born participants in Gordon's study were taken aback by their lack of familiarity with these allusions. Some figured the references were likely to puzzle most Americans as well. But native-born participants did not find the expressions puzzling at all. Most found their meaning obvious. Asking about them was "a silly exercise" one told Gordon.

It wasn't. Even though American discourse is filled with references we assume "everyone's heard of," everyone hasn't. Those who were born after what's alluded to took place, who grew up in another country, or who simply don't know what it refers to, get left out in the conversational cold. After seeing "Ka-Ching" in a newspaper headline, an elderly New Yorker assumed this expression came from China and asked several Chinese acquaintances what it meant. Michele Gordon herself had no idea why "The buck stops here" refers to the final point of responsibility. (It comes from the old poker player's expression *pass the buck*, discussed in chapter 21.) Any one of us is liable to be puzzled by an allusion whose meaning presumably is clear to others but not to us. Even terms we commonly use aren't ones whose origins are always familiar. Who was Hobson and what was his choice? Why does *zipless* have sexual overtones? And what's the big deal about drinking Kool-Aid?

Think of this as *retrotalk*. Retrotalk is a slippery slope of puzzling allusions to past phenomena. Such allusions take the form of *retroterms*, verbal artifacts that hang around in our national conversation long after the topic they refer to has galloped into the sunset.* They are verbal fossils, ones that outlive the organism that made their impression in the first place. This could be a person, a product, a past bestseller, an old radio or TV show, an athletic contest, a comic strip, an acronym, or an advertisement long forgotten. To qualify as a retroterm, a word or phrase must be in current use yet have an origin that isn't current. Iconic individuals can be the source of retroterms. Leftover slang is a common part of retrotalk, and old jokes that left punch lines behind but not always the setup. ("Take my wife (please).") They're clear to those who are familiar with these phenomena, confusing to those who aren't. This distinguishes retroterms from idioms, which tend to be self-explanatory (e.g., "dig your own grave," "skate on thin ice") or easily deciphered ("born with a silver spoon in his mouth"). Retroterms have no intrinsic meaning. These words and phrases make sense only when one knows where they came from.

Relying on retroterms can be problematic. For those of a certain age, making reference to things past is so routine that they're seldom even aware of doing this. But it's painfully apparent to those who aren't familiar with dated verbal shorthand. Take my son Scott (please). When he was in middle school, Scott—who was born just after history's worst nuclear power disaster—asked, "Who's this Cher Noble I keep hearing about?"

Such verbal confusion is more than a mere curiosity for those who want to communicate with younger cohorts. Members of the media have a particular problem here. During just a few evenings of televised political coverage I've watched middle-aged news analysts allude to Hercule Poirot, Judge Crater, Apollo Creed, Popeye Doyle, Rain Man, Ponzi schemes, blue plate specials, and eighteen-and-a-half-minute tape gaps. Such allusions confirm shared experi-

---

*A related but distinct concept is that of *retronyms*, terms such as "snail mail" and "acoustic guitar" that need a modifier to distinguish them from newer versions such as "e-mail" and "electric guitar."

ences but create distance from those who didn't share them. When *Meet the Press* guest David Brooks said about Hillary Clinton, "In the first debate she's Emily Post, now she's Howard Beale"—referencing the late etiquette maven and the angry protagonist of the 1976 movie *Network*—he set himself apart from viewers born in the last three decades. Those who fall back on such references might as well hang a sign around their neck reading OLDER YAKKER AT WORK. NO ONE UNDER 50 NEED PAY ATTENTION.

Journalists, teachers, and communicators of all kinds run the risk of casually using dated allusions that draw blank looks. Tom Wolfe has lamented the fact that authors of his generation so often rely on imagery from a more agrarian era such as "bark up the wrong tree," "has blinders on," and "a hard row to hoe." Those phrases mean little to those who aren't familiar with that era. When a Florida teacher told her third graders that while visiting a century-old schoolhouse they'd learn to shoot marbles, churn butter, and hoe the ground, some snickered. "Isn't *'ho* a bad word?" asked one student.

This illustrates how the same terminology can mean different things to members of different generations. To parents *beta* is a videotape format that lost the marketing war to VHS. To their kids it's a software program being tested. To them *thongs* are an exciting type of minimalist underwear. To their mothers and fathers thongs are cheap sandals with a thingie that goes between the toes. *Hoody* to me is hoodlumlike behavior. To my sons it's a sweatshirt with a hood.

Discourse between members of different generations can be a minefield of perplexing allusions. To the annoyance (and disdain) of their offspring, parents and grandparents routinely use terms such as *icebox, tin foil,* and *dime store.* Those who use such retroterms don't necessarily mind that they're confusing to younger ears. Language is a potent weapon in the generational wars. Older folks often complain that they can't make head or tail out of what younger folks are talking about with all their slang. Well, duh. That's just the point. Kids everywhere shoot slang at their parents and always have. Parents retaliate with retrotalk.

For those words to make sense one must be familiar with the experiences that gave them birth. Just as slang can be self-consciously in-group talk, allusions are an effective way to confuse outsiders. Those who don't get the allusion clearly don't belong. One reason for using references known only to the cognoscenti is to distinguish insiders from outsiders. This has always been an important role of language among ethnic or geographic groups, and it is just as important today when generations collide. Retroterms and modern synonyms draw lines in the generational sand. Lipstick is what our ancestors wore. We use lip gloss. They used rouge, we use blush. They ate prunes, we eat dried plums. They got crew cuts, we get buzz cuts. They got VD, we get STDs. Very important distinctions, as you can see.

Although my original intention for this book was to explore the origins of dated allusions that might puzzle young people and immigrants, the more deeply I got into this project, the more I realized how many of the words and phrases I was investigating were ones whose origins weren't necessarily known to all. What made me realize this was how many I encountered that mystified me. In a *New York Times* column, Maureen Dowd referred to "Nosey Parker." Who he? To characterize those who naively believe that managed health care drives down medical costs, Dowd's colleague Paul Krugman used the expression "There must be a pony in there somewhere." Say what? Upon investigation, such puzzling allusions proved to have a clear historical root, and often a fascinating one (discussed more fully in the text). After chasing down their origins I found myself repeatedly musing, "So *that's* where that comes from!"

Along the way my book's scope broadened to include a wide variety of allusions in current use whose origins aren't always clear. It isn't meant to compensate for a spotty education. I'm assuming that most readers can recognize a *Mona Lisa smile* and know what it means to "meet your Waterloo." Shakespeare and the Bible are rich with retroterms I've mostly ignored on the assumption that their genesis is widely known. But assuming familiarity with a wide range of other terms is risky. Making sense of the many linguistic relics in our lexicon requires familiarity with events that left behind a verbal residue. This is what syndicated columnist Leonard Pitts discovered when he referred to *Mayberry* in a column. His editor, who grew up in a home without television, challenged Pitts's reference to a town she thought could make readers ask, "Where's that?"

That's the type of question this book strives to answer. In examining its contents, some may wonder, "What's *X* doing here? Or *Y*? Everyone knows what they refer to." But everyone doesn't. We're all familiar with some allusions but not others. (While serving as White House press secretary, Dana Perino confessed that she didn't know what the *Cuban missile crisis* referred to.) Which retroterms we know about and which we don't vary with the individual. That's why I've tried to err on the side of inclusiveness. But even familiar terminology may have an unfamiliar origin story. This book is full of those stories. They explain where such retroterms came from and why they've lingered in American discourse.

Although not a work of history as such, *I Love It When You Talk Retro* hits the high points: those allusions from our past that made a big enough impression to stick around. As Bill Bryson wrote in *Made in America,* "unless we understand the social context in which words are formed . . . we cannot begin to appreciate the richness and vitality of the words that make up our speech." That's why this book concerns itself with social history as much as word history. One can't be divorced from the other. Language reflects its times. Words, phrases, and allusions are excellent barometers of what mattered to us during a given period of history: what resonated, struck our fancy, or simply tickled our funny bone.

Americans love to play with words. Ever since the first *hotcake* was fried in bear grease, they've invented new terms with abandon, revised grammar on the fly, and continually moved concepts from one context to another. As visitors routinely discover, American conversation is filled with inventive terms and always has been. While visiting the United States in the early nineteenth century, an Englishman named Basil Hall discussed this topic with dictionary compiler Noah Webster. Webster was favorably impressed by the many new words Americans had coined. Hall was appalled. If a new word proved useful, asked Webster, why not add it to the lexicon? "Because there are words enough already," Hall responded, "and it only confuses matters, and hurts the cause of letters to introduce such words."

New circumstances demand new words, however, and Americans have always been up to the task of supplying them. A recurring question in this book is why some endure as retroterms while others don't. In their Darwinian struggle for survival, new terms that take hold are not necessarily the flashiest, most colorful, or most widely used. The only thing that really matters when a fledgling word or phrase is being auditioned is utility. Does it improve on an existing one? Has anything better come along to take its place? Perhaps most important, do we *like* the terms in question? That's why this book returns so often to the concept of *striking a chord.* Certain events, people, movie lines, or ad slogans linger in our collective memory. It's intriguing not only to identify them and explore their origins but to understand why they stuck around when others didn't. How is it that the comic strip characters *Alphonse and Gaston* left their names behind but the *Katzenjammer Kids* didn't? Why has boxing been the source of so many analogies and football so few? And what makes us rely on *sell the sizzle* long after we've forgotten who coined that expression?

Even though it's not always clear why some words and phrases gain traction while others don't, here are some guidelines. Lasting retroterms:

1. *Strike a chord.* For whatever reason, some terms just strike our fancy in a lasting way. This can be seen in TV ads that contribute catchphrases which do—or don't—stick around. "Flick my Bic" lasted for only a season, as did Alka-Seltzer's "I can't believe I ate the whole thing!" But "Where's the beef?" is still part of our national conversation more than two decades after Wendy's rolled it out, and Chiffon margarine's "It's not nice to fool Mother Nature!" has lasted even longer. Both struck a durable chord.

2. *Fill a void.* It is well known among lexicographers that words and phrases most likely to enter the vernacular fill a gap. They prove more useful as a form of verbal shorthand than any existing word. *Gerrymander* is one example, a term coined early in the nineteenth century to describe artfully drawn voting districts. (See chapter 5.) More recently, *Mrs. Robinson* has proved more economical and far more evocative than "an older woman who seduces a younger man," just as the forgettable movie *Mr. Mom* left its title behind in our lingo because those two words allude to a stay-at-home father better than any others that have come along.

3. *Excite strong feeling.* Intense emotion, fear especially, welds content into our brains. Ask any psychiatrist. Conveying a sense of dread, as director Alfred Hitchcock did so effectively so often, guaranteed that movies such as *Psycho* and *The Birds* would be a fertile source of lasting retroterms.

4. *Are fun to say.* A retroterm's life expectancy is helped immeasurably if it feels good on the tongue. *Cootie. Cha-ching! Rope-a-dope. Sizzle. Gong. Bimbo.* All these terms have endured in large part because they're just so gosh-darn fun to say. For someone's name to become iconic, it helps to roll smoothly off the tongue. "Kiplingesque" doesn't work very well. Nor does "Woolfian" or "Conradian." "Hemingwayian" is a complete nonstarter, and "Hemingwayesque" isn't much better. *Proustian* works just fine though, as does *Dickensian. Orwellian* works best of all and *Kafkaesque* nearly as well.

One problem retroterms present to those unfamiliar with them is a simple matter of spelling. Phonetics are no help. Quite the contrary. While researching this book I've seen references to "brass tax," "text's bad boy," "Mutton Jeff," and "Profit of God." In a *Blondie* comic strip, Dagwood holds a black platter, saying, "Look. Here's our old Guy Lombardo New Year's record." "Let's take it up to the attic and play it on the old Victrola," responds Blondie. Their teenage daughter Cookie overhears this exchange. When her brother Alexander asks, "Where are Mom and Dad?" Cookie says, "I'm not sure. They're going to play with some guy named Vic Trola who has lumbago."

Not all retrotalk takes place on a generational fault line, however. Some allusions can be perplexing to anyone of any age or station. Take "waiting for the other shoe to drop." I once asked a twenty-eight-year-old graduate of an Ivy League college if she knew the genesis of that common catchphrase. The woman didn't. My subsequent minipoll found she was not alone. Most of those whom I queried realized this phrase referred to an unresolved situation; but few knew why. Where did that allusion come from?

# 2. Story Lines

Two tenants of an apartment building are at loggerheads. One lives above the other. The upstairs man concocts a diabolical scheme to drive his downstairs neighbor insane. While going to bed one night, he drops a single shoe on the floor. His nemesis below waits for the other shoe to drop so he can go to sleep. As he waits, and waits, and waits, this man slowly goes mad. The next morning he's taken away by men in white coats. His fiendish neighbor upstairs had placed his second shoe on a chest of drawers, never dropping it to the floor.

That's one version of this story. In another, a traveler in the Alps is told there is only one room left at an inn, next door to a very light sleeper. The traveler agrees to take every care to be quiet in this room. When getting ready to retire, however, he nervously drops one shoe to the floor. Realizing that this probably has disturbed his next-door neighbor, he carefully removes his second shoe and places it gently on the ground. Early the next morning he is awakened by his neighbor pounding on his wall and shouting, "When are you going to drop the other shoe?" (A Canadian variant of this tale features two loggers in adjoining rooms of a North Woods cabin.)

Whatever the version, this story's allusion—**waiting for the other shoe to drop**—has become so commonplace that "the other shoe" alone is often used as a catchphrase. An executive coach advises clients that if they're not deft at dispensing praise, employees may consider it a prelude to criticism. They are "waiting for the other shoe."

## All Greek to Me

A second story based on footwear involves a Greek painter named Apelles. The first artist known to have painted a self-portrait, Apelles was the subject of many legendary tales during his lifetime in the fourth century BC. In the one most widely repeated, Apelles displayed some of his work outdoors, then hid nearby to eavesdrop on comments made by passersby. A cobbler who stopped to examine one of the paintings observed that a sandal worn by one subject lacked a loop. Apelles corrected his mistake and put the result back on display. Upon noticing this correction the critical cobbler was so pleased that he ventured another opinion: a leg was painted poorly. Upon hearing this comment, Apelles called out from his hiding place, "Shoemaker, do not go above your last!" (referring to wooden models of feet used by shoemakers). In the centuries since, **stick to your last** has come to mean not venturing beyond one's area of expertise. **Stick to your knitting** is a close cousin.

Another ancient Greek tale featured Gordius, the ruler of Phrygia in what is now Turkey. A onetime peasant, Gordius retained some of his country ways. These included securing his oxcart with a piece of rope tied in a knot so complicated that he alone knew how to untie it. Gordius's intricate knot excited fevered speculation among his subjects. A legend grew that whoever could untie it would rule all of Asia. Many tried but none succeeded. Then Alexander the Great came to town in 333 BC. After examining King Gordius's knot and being told what he stood to gain by untying it, the young warrior-king withdrew his sword and cut its tangled strands in half with a single stroke. Alexander subsequently added Asia to his vast domain. That is why **Gordian knot** refers to any intractable problem. (Because it resists reform, America's complex primary system for choosing political candidates has been called a "Gordian knot.") **Cutting the Gordian knot** suggests a swift, direct, and innovative solution to such a problem.

In what is now northwestern Greece and southern Albania, King Pyrrhus ruled a small country called Epirus. Pyrrhus was notorious for tolerating enormous casualties among his troops. After suffering a hideous loss of soldiers and officers while vanquishing the Romans in a 279 BC battle, Pyrrhus achieved verbal immortality by observing that one more such victory would do him in. Because Pyrrhus was so famous for "winning" wars at an enormous

price this way, any apparent success that costs too much is still known as a
**Pyrrhic victory**.

Dionysius was another ancient ruler, of Syracuse on the island of Sicily. A
mercurial sort, Dionysius was quick to anger, but also to repent (if he hadn't
already killed the object of his ire). His
methods were, to say the least, *inventive*.
A member of Dionysius's court named
Damocles once earned the King's wrath by
saying once too often that Dionysius was
a fortunate man. To show up such idle
talk, Syracuse's ruler mounted a feast for
Damocles, then seated the guest of honor
beneath a sword tied to a thread. It would
not take much for that sword to fall and kill
the man below. By this means Dionysius
hoped to convey how fleeting good fortune
can be. **The sword of Damocles**, therefore,

alludes to a situation whose outcome is uncertain. **Hang by a thread**, suggesting a precarious situation, also alludes to poor Damocles' evening beneath the
barely suspended sword.

## The Animal Kingdom

A black political columnist created a firestorm of controversy when she called
the fact that involuntary servitude brought Africans to America "the pony
hidden in slavery." This alluded to an anecdote beloved by Ronald Reagan. In
that story, a boy confronted with a mound of horse manure plunges in and
begins to dig with enthusiasm. Asked why he's doing so, the boy responds that
with this much manure, there's bound to be a pony inside. That story dates
back at least to the early 1960s, when my brother Gene heard it from a college
professor. Over time **there must be a pony in there** has come to signify sunny
assessments of gloomy circumstances.

A colonial-era American tale involves a white hunter and an Indian hunter
who join forces to shoot several crows and wild turkeys. When it comes time to
divide their catch, the white man gives his companion all the crows while keep-

ing all the turkeys for himself. The incensed Indian protests. "You talk all turkey for you," he says. "You never once talk turkey for me! Now I talk turkey to you." The Indian then takes his fair share of turkeys. This story was so popular in nineteenth-century America that **talk turkey** became synonymous with getting down to business. This evolved into *talk cold turkey* for blunt talk about difficult subjects, which in turn led to **cold turkey**—the abrupt cessation of drug use.

Unlike turkey, crow is a notoriously unappetizing bird. Stories involving crow consumption have fueled American humor for decades. For example: *If lost in the woods, (1) Catch a crow. (2) Boil for a week with one of your boots. (3) Eat the boot.* After the Civil War, those forced to admit an error were said to *eat boiled crow.* In 1885 an American magazine told its readers "To '**eat crow**' means to recant, or to humiliate oneself." It still does.

## PACHYDERMS AND SIMIANS

By legend, when a king in ancient Siam (now Thailand) wanted to make life difficult for someone, he gave that person an albino elephant. Because Buddha's spirit was thought to inhabit these rare pachyderms, the recipient could not make it a beast of burden. Nor could he sell this elephant. Instead, its new owner had to feed and house his huge white pet until he went broke. From this heritage grows our modern notion of the **white elephant**: any possession that's hard to dispose of, but too valued to dispense with.

An elephant of another color has an altogether different significance. This is the **pink elephant**, referring to preposterous elements of a story that require suspension of disbelief. Walt Disney's 1941 movie *Dumbo* includes a memorable "Pink Elephants on Parade" routine in which the protagonist accidentally consumes a tub of champagne. Bill Clinton got his elephants mixed up when he referred to an issue Democrats were avoiding as "the pink elephant in the living room." What Clinton apparently had in mind was **the elephant in the living room** (no color specified), a popular way of portraying problems everyone knows exist but no one wants to face. A series of ticklish questions posed to presidential aspirants during a debate were called "Elephants in the Room." This concept may have grown out of the "elephant jokes" that were popular half a century ago. (For Example, Q: How can you tell if there's an elephant in the room? A: You smell the peanuts on his breath.) The elephant-in-the-room notion subsequently became popular in substance abuse programs whose participants routinely confront family members' resistance to acknowledging that they have a problem.

At times this elephant gets confused with a corpulent gorilla. Then, reference is made to "the 800-pound gorilla in the room." That grows out of an old gag about a simian so large that no one will tangle with him. The most common version asks, "What does an 800-pound gorilla get?" Answer: "Whatever he wants." Alternatively, "Where does an 800-pount gorilla sleep? Wherever he wants." Or "When wrestling with a large gorilla, you don't quit when you're tired. You quit when the gorilla is tired." Exactly how large is this gorilla? Confusion reigns. I have seen all sorts of weights tossed about: 300 pounds, 350, 400, 500, 600, 900, 1,000, 2,000, 4,000, 8,000, 10,000, 9-zillion, and 800 tons. While discussing political heavyweights on *This Week*, ABC correspondent Cokie Roberts referred to 900-pound gorillas, her colleague Sam Donaldson to ones weighing a mere 300 pounds. Most often, however, the gorilla under consideration weighs 800 pounds. It is **the 800-pound gorilla**.

## Yarns

In a century-old English yarn, a woman is chosen as the happiest resident of her village. When town fathers arrive at her home to give this woman an award for her cheerful disposition, she disabuses them by opening a closet that contains skeletal remains of a former lover whom her husband killed. Every night, she tells the committee, her husband makes her kiss this skeleton in their closet. Is this why we talk of having a "skeleton in the closet"? It could be. But another possibility has to do with the fact that in nineteenth-century England the study of cadavers was severely restricted. As demand for corpses rose amid the growth of modern medicine, grave robbers sold bodies to doctors on the sly. After thoroughly dissecting such a body, doctors would keep its skeleton hidden from public view, in a closet, say. This alleged practice may have inspired the phrase **a skeleton in the closet**, referring to all manner of shady information kept under wraps, especially family secrets. The narrator of William Makepeace Thackeray's 1855 novel *The Newcomes* describes a visit to an English mansion whose housekeeper keeps extolling its various attractions. Finally his droll companion interrupts her to say, "And now, madam, will you show us the closet *where the skeleton is?*" Throughout the rest of his text Thackeray makes repeated reference to metaphorical skeletons in closets, asking at one point, "Have we not all such closets?"

Well before that, the narrator of an early-nineteenth-century American yarn recalled as a small boy being asked by a man with an axe if his father owned a grindstone. Told that he did, the man asked if the boy could rotate this stone and help him sharpen his axe. Flattered by this request, the boy turned the grindstone until his hands were blistered and the axe's blade was sharp. A school bell then rang and the axe owner—his mission accomplished—scolded the boy about being late for class and sent him off. Based on this dismaying experience, the narrator—Pennsylvania essayist Charles Miner—concluded, "Whenever I see a merchant over-polite to his customers, begging them to taste a little brandy and throwing half his goods on the counter, thinks I, that man has an axe to grind." Ever since then Americans have used the phrase **an axe to grind** to characterize someone whose actions are based on ulterior motives.

During America's Civil War, a newspaper sketch written by popular humorist Artemus Ward was called "A Hard Case." In that yarn a baby-faced fourteen-year-old is convicted of killing his parents with a meat cleaver. The judge asks if he has anything to say before being sentenced. "Why no," the boy replies. "I think I haven't, though I hope yer Honor will show some consideration FOR THE FEELINGS OF A POOR ORPHAN!" Ward's gag proved so popular that to this day **pleaded for mercy because he was an orphan** refers to unmitigated gall. In *Hooray for Yiddish*, author Leo Rosten called that plea a classic illustration of the Yiddish concept of *chutzpah*.

## Punch Lines

After listing various calamities that had befallen him recently, a sixty-something friend of mine concluded, "Other than that, I enjoyed the play." He assumed—correctly—that I was familiar with a one-line gag from an era when humor was testing the limits of taste: "Other than that, how did you like the play, Mrs. Lincoln?" (referring to the fact that Abraham Lincoln's wife accompanied him when he was assassinated while watching a play at Ford's Theater in Washington). With "Mrs. Lincoln" deleted, this has become a catchphrase that is often used to depict the obvious: **Other than that, how did you like the play?**

The punch line of many a joke is considered so well known that it can be dropped into conversations on the assumption that everyone knows the setup. This isn't always the case. When a *Minneapolis Star-Tribune* article included the line "And by the way, have you stopped beating your wife?" an outraged reader wrote to ask why the paper would pose such an off-the-wall question. It can be traced back to a 1914 book of legal humor that includes a joke about a lawyer who tries to badger a witness into answering "yes" or "no." "I can not do it," says the witness. "There are some questions that can not be answered by a 'yes' or a 'no,' as anyone knows." The lawyer challenges him to give an example. "Are you still beating your wife?" responds the witness. **Have you stopped beating your wife?** has since become the standard allusion to any question that can't be answered without self-incrimination.

Another punch line in search of a setup comes from an old joke featuring the sole survivor of a wagon train massacre who is discovered by rescuers with an arrow in his back. When asked if it hurts, the man moans, "Only when I laugh." Former Secretary of State Dean Acheson relied on this line when asked whether the verbal arrows aimed in his direction were painful. **Only when I laugh** subsequently provided the title for one novel, a song, and two movies.

Like those in this chapter, another set of allusions come from old stories and circumstances, but ones involving a key character whose name has become iconic.

# 3. The Name's Familiar

F rom 1568 until 1631 Thomas Hobson owned a stable in Cambridge, England. A hearty coachman who lived well into his eighties, Hobson rented some forty horses to Cambridge University students. These young men had a tendency to return Hobson's horses panting and covered with froth. As a result, his most popular steeds were getting worn out. To remedy this problem, Hobson came up with an ingenious solution. A returned horse went to the farthest stall of his stable, then moved up in turn. Customers could only rent the horse closest to the entryway (i.e., the freshest one). "This one or none" was his policy. Students sarcastically called that **Hobson's choice**, meaning no choice at all. When Henry Ford said Model T customers could have any color they liked, so long as it was black, he offered them a Hobson's choice.

## Human Icons

Human iconography takes various forms. In some cases "esque" is added to the name of a noted person (e.g., "Clintonesque"). In other cases "ian" serves the same purpose ("Machiavellian"). A real elite consists of those whose name alone is sufficient to make a point: the brilliant Albert Einstein, say ("He's no Einstein"), escape artist Harry Houdini ("a real Houdini"), or Attila the Hun. An unusually small man, Attila's name meant "little father." His methods were not paternal. While invading European settlements from 433 to 453, Attila's Huns shot volleys of arrows at the populace, threw nets over fleeing survivors, then finished them off with swords. Even though their leader is not known to have had political goals other than pillage and plunder, he is so associated with savagery that **to the right of Attila the Hun** is a common way to characterize extreme conservatives. It's an interesting commentary on those who use Attila's name this way that they equate radical conservatism with Hunlike cruelty.

Torquemada is another name used in the same spirit. This refers to Tomás de Torquemada, Spain's onetime head inquisitor. Although he himself apparently had Jewish ancestors, the Dominican friar's greatest achievement was helping persuade King Ferdinand and Queen Isabella to expel any Jew who wouldn't convert to Christianity. In 1492 it was so ordered. When not whispering in royal ears, Torquemada busied himself mangling the thumbs of "heretics" with thumbscrews, breaking their spines on the rack, and ordering them to be thrown alive into flaming pyres. At least a thousand Spaniards were killed this way during the Inquisition. In the centuries following his cruel reign, **Torquemada** became synonymous with anyone who treats others harshly. *New Republic* blogger James Kirchick once accused fellow blogger Glenn Greenwald of being "the Torquemada of the liberal blogophere."

Across the Atlantic, John Hancock of Massachusetts—a wealthy, flamboyant supporter of America's revolution—exclaimed, "There, I guess King George will be able to read that!" as he scrawled his name on the Declaration of Independence in mid-July 1776. Or so goes the legend. In fact, since no colleague joined Hancock on the day

he signed the Declaration, most likely he scrawled in silence. Nonetheless, as anyone can see on the document itself, Hancock's signature is first and extra-large. As the source of America's most famous autograph, **John Hancock** has lent his name to signatures of all kinds.

In 1787, a few years after Hancock signed the Declaration of Independence, Catherine the Great visited Ukraine. The governor of those newly annexed provinces made sure that the Russian empress's route passed freshly painted buildings, peasant huts decorated with flowers, and even some temporary structures erected in her honor. The enemies of this governor—Prince Grigori Potemkin—snarkily spread the story that he'd constructed entire villages out of cardboard to impress the empress. Ever since then **Potemkin village** or simply **Potemkin** has come to mean any setting with an impressive facade but no substance. Questioning the authenticity of a Web log, *Newsweek*'s Steven Levy called it a "Potemkin-like blog."

## Lowercased

Some twenty-six centuries ago, the head judge of Athens was named Draco. Under his aegis, unwritten, sometimes arbitrary laws were finally codified. Many crimes large and small, including petty theft, were now punishable by death. Three decades later Draco was replaced by a jurist named Solon, who relaxed the judicial code of Athens. Solon also introduced trial by jury. Draco's name is immortalized in the term **draconian**, meaning severe, while his more flexible successor is remembered when we apply the word **solon** to lawmakers.

Like these two Athenians, a unique group of human icons has had the first letter of their last name lowercased in common usage: sandwich, guillotine, martinet, and diesel (to name just a few). Nicolas Chauvin was another, a French soldier noted for his prowess on the battlefield and fanatic devotion to his country and its emperor, Napoleon Bonaparte. Chauvin's fervent patriotism became a source of ridicule, and he was caricatured in several plays as a character convinced that France and its one-time ruler could do no wrong. His name inspired an enduring term for mindless conviction about the superiority of some group: **chauvinism.**

During the Crimean War, the seventh Earl of Cardigan led a suicidal charge against Russian guns that was later immortalized by Tennyson's poem "The Charge of the Light Brigade." ("Theirs not to reason why, / Theirs but to do and die.") This is not what made Lord Cardigan's name immortal, however. What accomplished that feat was the type of sweater he wore throughout the 1853–56 Crimean campaign—a button-up model still known as a **cardigan sweater**. Lord Raglan, the leader of British forces in Crimea, favored a loose overcoat with ample diagonally set sleeves that are still referred to as **raglan sleeves**. In Raglan's honor we also sometimes talk about **raglan overcoats** or **raglan sweaters**.

Prior to the Crimean War, on Texas's Gulf Coast, a transplanted South Carolinian named Samuel Maverick was given four hundred head of cattle to settle a $1,200 debt. Maverick had little interest in ranching, and didn't even bother to brand his calves. As these cattle reached maturity, nearby ranchers began to call any unbranded cow "one of Maverick's." Eventually, in southwest Texas, *mavericks*—lowercased now—referred to unbranded cattle. This term subsequently was applied to independent human beings as well. They were, and are, **mavericks.**

## FUSSIN', FEUDIN'

Before the Civil War two extended families left Virginia's lowlands for a freer life in mountains to the west. One, the Hatfields, settled north of the Big Sandy River in what is now West Virginia. The other, the McCoys, set up a homestead to the south, in Kentucky. Over the years members of these two clans sometimes married and often squabbled. One dispute involved ownership of a pig. Another had to do with the impregnation of Roseanna McCoy, apparently by Johnse Hatfield. Throughout the 1880s Hatfields and McCoys engaged in an escalating feud. By the time these clans made peace in 1890, twelve Hatfields and McCoys had died at each other's hands. More than a century later their conflict still excites our imagination. Outdoor theaters re-create this feud. Tourists flock to its major locales. The **Hatfields and Mc-Coys** gave us a lasting parable for bitter conflict. Constantly feuding factions of the Democratic Party are routinely compared to the Hatfields and McCoys. So are bitter basketball rivals Duke University and the University of North Carolina.

### Immigrants

In mid-nineteenth century Edinburgh, a well-regarded whiskey was produced by the G. Mackay distillery. When comparing this product to inferior imitators, Scotsmen talked of "the real Mackay." In time this catchphrase was applied to products and people of many kinds. Scottish migrants to the United States and Canada brought that concept with them, and used it for anything considered authentic. Americans of other ethnic backgrounds soon took over the phrase, with spelling changed to **the real McCoy**. This process was accelerated by the fact that a popular turn-of-the-century prizefighter was known as Kid McCoy. Many stories circulated about this boxer, including one in which he floored a barroom drunk who questioned his legitimacy. "That's the real McCoy," this drunk was said to have conceded while rubbing his tender chin as he got up off the floor.

American palaver was heavily influenced by the post–Civil War influx of immigrants. In some cases disdain for such recent arrivals led to their being victimized by history. One victim was named Catherine "Kate" O'Leary. With her husband, Patrick, this Irishwoman settled on Chicago's West Side. After the sun went down on October 7, 1871, a fire erupted in the barn behind her home. Over the next several days this spreading blaze consumed a large proportion of the Windy City's buildings in what came to be known as the Great Chicago Fire. Some three hundred Chicagoans died in its flames, and ninety thousand were left homeless. According to hypercaffeinated press accounts the culprit was Mrs. O'Leary's cow, who had kicked over a lantern while being milked. Subsequent investigation discounted this allegation. Onetime insurance investigator Richard Bales, who has studied the Great Chicago Fire exhaustively, calls the cow-kicked-lantern story a "quintessential urban legend." Bales fingers two of O'Leary's neighbors as more likely sources of the fire. Nonetheless, **Mrs. O'Leary's cow** is such a familiar allusion that Brian Wilson could include a song by this title on his *Smile* album, confident that listeners would know what he was referring to

Another Irish-American, Mary Mallon, worked as a freelance cook in New York. From 1900 to 1907 at least twenty-two of her clients came down with typhoid fever. One, a young girl, died. When every guest who ate Mallon's food

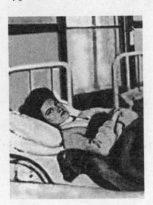

at a 1907 dinner party contracted typhoid, suspicion turned to the cook. It turned out that Mallon had suffered a mild case of typhoid as a young woman, though she no longer displayed its symptoms. Despite her promise to stop cooking and report regularly to health authorities, Mallon still plied her trade. For the next eight years typhoid victims cropped up wherever she worked. Of fifty people known to have contracted this disease from Mary Mallon, three died. In 1915 Mallon was confined to a hospital. After she died there twenty-three years later, an autopsy found live typhoid bacteria in her gallbladder. Forever after Mallon would be known by the name headline writers gave her: **Typhoid Mary.** That name reappears whenever symptom-free carriers of contagious diseases are discovered, literally or figuratively. Lamenting Walt Whitman's impact on aspiring writers, Garrison Keillor called him "the Typhoid Mary of American Lit: so much bad poetry can be traced back to him."

## Adjudicators

*Whist* was a popular card game in eighteenth-century England. The only problem was that players could not agree upon its rules. What was permissible in this forerunner of bridge depended on who was playing. In 1742 a barrister and whist tutor named Edmond Hoyle published *A Short Treatise on the Game of Whist*. This codification of whist's rules was so successful that its author went on to produce booklets on backgammon, chess, and other games. Over time his name became so associated with codified authority that **according to Hoyle** remains synonymous with well-established, widely accepted rules.

Emily Post played a similar role in the world of manners. In 1922 the Baltimore debutante, finishing-school graduate, and banker's wife published *Etiquette: The Blue Book of Social Usage*. This became an instant hit. After ten revisions, Post's book was in its eighty-ninth printing when she died in 1960. The secret of Emily Post's success was her reassuring tone. "Nothing is less important than which fork you use," Post told readers. Indeed, she said, if you can't decide which fork to use for a given dinner course, perhaps your hostess gave you too many to choose from. "Manners are a sensitive awareness of the feelings of others," Post concluded. "If you have that awareness, you have good manners, no matter what fork you use." Post reassured Americans that so long as they behaved in a way that made others feel comfortable, their manners were impeccable. Her radio program and widely syndicated column on etiquette made *Emily Post* a household name. This name continues to be so synonymous with proper deportment that **"What would Emily Post say?"** remains a way of judging the right thing to do in any social situation. MSNBC commentator Eve Tahmincioglu called thanking a job interviewer "an Emily Post moment."

## Censors

In 1818, retired English physician Thomas Bowdler published a collection of Shakespeare's plays that he'd edited for tender ears. "Those expressions are omitted," Dr. Bowdler explained in his introduction, "which cannot with propriety be read aloud in the family." This included profanity, all allusions to sex, and any references to God that Dr. Bowdler considered insufficiently reverent. In *The Family Shakespeare*, "Out damn'd spot" was revised to "Out crimson spot," Romeo and Juliet were a chaste young couple, and Ophelia's suicide became an accidental drowning. The bard himself, Bowdler was sure, would have approved. After completing this improvement of Shakespeare, Dr. Bowdler turned his attention to cleaning up Edward Gibbon's *Decline and Fall of the Roman Empire*, then had a go at the Old Testament. Although popular in Bowdler's time, the resulting bland gruel did not remain on very many bookshelves. His name did stick around, however, as a verb: to **bowdlerize**, or sanitize text with prudish editing. *Newsweek* called the profanity-deletion that Ken Burns did on his epic World War II documentary at the request of some television stations a "mini-bowdlerization."

Several decades after Thomas Bowdler's death in 1825, Anthony Comstock picked up his fallen standard. During the Civil War, Comstock had been deeply offended by the foul language and coarse manners of his fellow Union soldiers. In response he founded the New York Society for the Suppression of Vice. At its behest, in 1873 Congress passed the "Act for the Suppression of Trade in, and Circulation of, Obscene Literature and Articles of Immoral Use." The so-called Comstock Act forbade the mailing of "obscene, lewd, or lascivious" material. Anthony Comstock himself became a post office official charged with enforcing that law. Among other initiatives, Comstock called any magazine on the docket that dared to advertise condoms, and restricted the mailing of anatomy books that he considered too revealing. During his long crusade Comstock took credit for destroying 160 tons of "smut." After he criticized a George Bernard Shaw play that dealt with prostitution, Shaw warned that **Comstockery** was abroad in the land. This term—defined by my dictionary as "censorship because of perceived obscenity or immorality"—still refers to overzealous prudery. George Washington University law professor Jeffrey Rosen called attempts to censor Internet content "electronic Comstockery."

Although he limited his focus to the motion picture industry, Indiana's **Will Hays** carried on Comstock's work. Alarmed by their growing reputation for lasciviousness, in 1922 leading moviemakers hired this onetime congressman and postmaster general to clean up their act. Hays proved up to the job. Early on he created the **Hays code**, which proscribed any onscreen portrayal of illicit drug traffic, demeaning portrayals of the clergy, sympathetic treatment of adulterers, scenes of passion that might arouse moviegoers, lighthearted depictions of seduction, and any depiction at all of interracial romance, perverse sex, venereal disease, obscenity, or, of course, nudity. (*Tarzan and His Mate* was called to account for the latter.) According to an unfounded but widespread rumor, Hays subsequently banned any couple sharing a double bed onscreen unless the man had one foot on the floor. This led to a popular euphemism for heavy petting without consummation: *one foot on the floor*. (In Elmore Leonard's novel *Up in Honey's Room*, a woman tells a man visiting her apartment, "I'm not censored by the Hays Office, so you don't have to sleep with one foot on the floor.") During Will Hays's decades of cinema oversight the public enjoyed speculating about what might or might not "get past the **Hays Office**." Permissible onscreen behavior gradually broadened after its director retired in 1945, but the name **Will Hays** lives on as a symbol of puritanical, ham-handed censorship.

## Wretched Excess

Each era has individuals who symbolize arrogant wealth. **Marie Antoinette** was hers. Even if she didn't advise the hungry to eat cake (an old canard put in her mouth by enemies), Louis XVI's wife was such a haughty, frivolous spendthrift that it was widely assumed she had said this. When we call someone **the Marie Antoinette of _____**, it's usually to suggest she's imperious. Alternatively, we could call her **the Leona Helmsley of _____**. Before she spent eighteen months in prison for tax evasion, this New York hotel magnate was notorious for her snotty 1983 observation that "only the little people pay taxes." Helmsley had a personality that, to put it mildly, was less than warm and cuddly.

Her nickname—"the Queen of Mean"—became the title of a 1990 biopic. Helmsley was so associated with rich bitchiness that her name alone suggests arrogant wealth. A guest on NPR's *All Things Considered* once referred to "the Leona Helmsley world of CEO pay."

Long before Leona Helmsley sneered at the little people, another hotelier—César Ritz—had already contributed his name to the lexicon of wealth. The hotel chain founded by this onetime Swiss restaurateur during the early twentieth century represented over-the-top opulence in a time when Las Vegas was still a tiny desert town, and Miami a mosquito-infested swamp. That is why

**ritzy** still refers to sumptuous living, and **putting on the ritz** to a conspicuous display of one's wealth. This piece of post–World War I slang inspired a 1929 song by Irving Berlin and a 1930 movie called *Puttin' on the Ritz.*

That's exactly what Imelda Marcos did. A world-class shopper, the wife of Philippine dictator Ferdinand Marcos had a particular passion for footwear. In the course of her reign, Mrs. Marcos was said to have purchased some 3,000 pairs of size 8½ shoes, many of which were put on display (along with several hundred of her bras and girdles) after her husband was toppled from power in 1986. Mrs. Marcos defended herself as simply living out the dreams of the Philippines' poor. All of those shoes, she said, were a sign of "thanksgiving and love." Besides, Mrs. Marcos added, she owned only 1,060 pairs, not 3,000. The name **Imelda Marcos** is today synonymous with extravagant, unnecessary purchases. Rocker-activist Bono has said of his proclivity for tinted eyewear, "I'm the Imelda Marcos of sunglasses."

## Artists

In the paintings of Flemish artist Peter Paul Rubens, women who today might be considered candidates for gastric bypass do not hide their folds of flesh. Instead, they flaunt it wantonly. The painter obviously found his corpulent subjects alluring and invited viewers to concur. From Rubens's perspective even

Venus is a plump woman whose substantial behind flows over the bench she sits on. A famous 1638 portrait of the artist's young wife, Héléne, nude save for a fur draped over one shoulder, makes no attempt to divert the eye from her protruding stomach and thick thighs. That is why the term *Rubenesque* is a euphemism for "fat." Along with "voluptuous," "pleasingly plump," and "full-figured" (as well as the Yiddish *zaftig*), **Rubenesque** is one of the few terms available to describe heavy women without disdain. Queen Latifah is routinely called Rubenesque. Bette Midler has been called "gloriously Rubenesque."

With an entirely different sensibility, Norman Rockwell portrayed America as it wanted to see itself: a land of bucolic towns with smoke curling from chimneys, earnest citizens speaking their piece at town meetings, and extended families gathered for holiday meals. It takes a cold heart to examine a Rockwell painting without feeling nostalgia for this neighborly world. That world was largely a figment of Rockwell's idealized imagination, however. "I paint life as I would like it to be," he once said. The artist himself was an aloof loner who observed his Stockbridge, Massachusetts, neighbors closely but took little part in their activities. His paintings were Disney World in two dimensions. But—like Disney's Main Street, Ralph Lauren's ranch, and Martha Stewart's garden—Rockwell's vision tapped a deep vein of longing. He did this so effectively that the very term **Norman Rockwell** or **Rockwellian**, signifies an upright community with wholesome, friendly inhabitants and happy families celebrating Christmas and Thanksgiving. As film critic Roger Ebert pointed out however, "Not all holidays are by Norman Rockwell."

In upstate New York, Rockwell had a spiritual country cousin named Anna Marie Robertson Moses. Mrs. Moses was a farmer's wife who raised five children and buried another five. After she had to abandon embroidery in her seventies due to arthritis, Mrs. Moses took up painting. Her colorful if primitive portrayals of quilting bees, Christmas gatherings, and sleigh rides on country lanes appealed to a public hungry for simpler times. As "Grandma Moses," their creator appeared on television (including *See It Now* with Edward R. Murrow) and in major magazine layouts. On her one-hundredth birthday Cornell Capa took a picture that appeared on the cover of *Life* of the bespectacled, sprightly artist sitting in a rocking chair. The fact that Grandma Moses's success came at such an advanced age was inspirational for any older person who's ever wondered "Is it too late?" Long after her 1961 death at 101, the name **Grandma Moses** remains a synonym for unusually late blooming. An elderly shutterbug in Minneapolis calls herself "the Grandma Moses of photography."

## Seducers and Seductresses

Nicholas Rowe's 1703 play *The Fair Penitent* features a scoundrel named Lothario who seduces and abandons the female lead. This popular domestic drama was in continual production well into the nineteenth century, and the name of its male lead is still applied to men who behave like him. They are

**Lotharios**. Long before Lothario appeared on stage, a legendary lover named Don Juan was the subject of many a European tale. Some portrayed **Don Juan** as a selfish seducer. Others presented him as a romantic who genuinely cared about the many women he bedded. Since the early seventeenth century countless books, plays, and movies—including *Don Juan DeMarco* (1995) starring Johnny Depp—have kept his reputation alive as a lover nonpareil. "He's a real Don Juan," we still say. Or "He's no Don Juan." Unlike Don Juan, we know that there was an actual human being named Casanova. Giacomo Girolamo Casanova was a Bohemian writer, adventurer, and lover who lived in Venice. While touring Europe in the mid-1700s, Casanova fought one duel after another, usually over women. This man's allure to members of the opposite sex had as much to do with the attention he paid them, and their pleasure, as to his so-so looks. Although his name today suggests a heartless womanizer, **Casanova** remained friends with many ex-lovers. His remarkable life inspired books, plays, and movies, including *Fellini's Casanova* (1976). During Warren Beatty's womanizing heyday the actor was commonly called a Casanova (when not being called a Don Juan or a Lothario).

As Casanova romped through Europe, Russia's Catherine the Great busily modernized her country during the day, but felt no need to act like a lady at night. Instead, Catherine conducted herself like men of her time, taking one lover after another throughout her 1762–96 reign. Because she was considered quite attractive, and was generous with her lovers, Catherine had no shortage of men waiting for their turn in her bedchamber. At the age of sixty Catherine enjoyed one last affair, with a young nobleman who was nearly four decades her junior. "Our baby," she called him in a letter to longtime lover Prince Grigori Potemkin, adding, "[he] weeps when denied the entry into my room." This extraordinary record of romance made the name **Catherine the Great** memorable not just for the political prowess of this czarina but as an allusion to powerful women who see no reason to limit the number of men in their life. During an online discussion about an amorous female pharaoh in Egypt, one participant observed that "she was the Catherine of the Great of her day in more ways than one."

More than a century after Catherine's death, a low-rent Casanova named Grigori Yefimovitch Rasputin worked his wiles in Moscow. A coarse, uneducated religious mystic from Siberia, Rasputin mesmerized Czar Nicholas II's wife, Alexandra, by claiming he could cure their son's hemophilia. After insinuating himself into the czar's court, the "Mad Monk" seduced as many women as he could get his hands on there. Not the least part of what Rasputin had go-

ing for him was a rumored foot-long penis.·(A St. Petersburg museum has on display a mummified eleven-inch penis that it claims is his.) Pictures of the Mad Monk show a man with fly-away black hair, a long beard, and dark eyes that glow like pieces of coal in the moonlight. In late 1916 a group of Russian aristocrats laced Rasputin's wine with cyanide, shot him thrice, then stuffed the still-breathing monk beneath the ice of the Neva River, where he finally drowned. (Details of his assassination vary.) Since then Rasputin's name has lived on as synonymous with demented but powerful men who hold others in a hypnotic grip, women especially. Cult leaders who take licentious advantage of their followers are said to be **Rasputins**.

While Rasputin was seducing women in the Russian court, an exotic dancer named Margaretha Zelle plied her trade in Paris. Zelle's admirers and lovers included both French and German military officers. Toward the end of World War I, the French government charged this Dutch native with conveying military secrets to the Germans. During her trial she was said to have declared, "Harlot, yes. But traitor? Never!" After being convicted the forty-one year-old courtesan was put before a firing squad on October 15, 1917. Various accounts circulated about what Zelle did on the verge of being shot. In the most popular version she flung open her coat to reveal a naked body just as the fingers of twelve riflemen began to squeeze their triggers. Greta Garbo portrayed Zelle in a 1931 film, one of many movies and books devoted to this woman's story. Her stage name—**Mata Hari** (Malay for "sunrise")—lives on, representing any woman thought to use sexual guile to treasonous ends. Since serious questions have been

raised about Mata Hari's actual guilt, this is probably unfair. Be that as it may, her stage name is just one of many retroterms left over from World War I.

# 4. Fighting Words

ack in the day, kids routinely accused each other of being covered with *cooties*. A popular children's game consisted of folding pieces of paper into *cootie catchers*, then snapping each other's arms with their pincer-like points. Why cooties? Because that's what soldiers in World War I's verminous trenches called body lice, adapting *kutu*, the Malay word for louse. After the war American soldiers brought this term home along with their ribbons and medals. Kids liked the sound and the concept of **cooties** and took it over. ("Ooh. Cooties!") But it wasn't just kids. As Tom Cruise's behavior grew increasingly bizarre, a Hollywood agent said this movie star's reputation had been sullied by "the cootie factor."

A remarkable number of retroterms were born in the foxholes, trenches, and no-man's-land of combat. Whatever else they do, or don't, accomplish, wars have always been first-rate incubators of slang, allusions, and catchphrases. *Going ballistic. Bombshell. Bunker mentality. Marching orders. Saber rattling. Smoke screen. On the front lines. In the crosshairs. A shot in the dark.*

Until quite recently a wounded soldier whose intestines were being repacked or whose leg was being sawed off had to endure excruciating pain. In some cases he would be held down by comrades who first placed a lead bullet between his teeth to keep him from screaming. A character in Rudyard Kipling's 1891 novel *The Light That Failed* is advised, "Bite on the bullet, old man, and don't let them think you're afraid." Well into the age of anesthesia, **bite the bullet** referred to facing unpleasant realities, and still does.

This cross-fertilization of civilian and soldier talk has lasted for centuries, and reflects changing military tactics. For example, the tapered slits in medieval castles through which defenders could peek outside or shoot arrows were known as **loopholes**. Over time this came to mean a way to escape, including unintended exceptions to rules. As he leafed through a Bible on his deathbed, the heathenish actor W. C. Fields told a visitor he was "looking for loopholes."

Armor worn by medieval knights included leather gloves with metal plates called *gauntlets*. A knight who took offense could throw this glove at the feet of the offending party. If that man picked it up, their fight was on. Although no one has worn gauntlets for centuries, we still talk of someone's **throwing down the gauntlet** when issuing a challenge. To characterize Russia's increasingly provocative foreign policy under president Vladimir Putin, NPR's Moscow correspondent Gregory Feifer referred to "the new gauntlet the Kremlin has thrown on the world stage."

In pre-cryptography times confidential messages had to be obscured by creative means. One tactic was to write such messages in invisible ink between the lines of an innocuous letter. From this bit of derring-do we've retained the phrase **reading between the lines**, or looking for hidden meanings in messages of all kinds. In Walter Mosley's novel *Blonde Faith*, a man says of his elliptical exchanges with a woman, "The majority of our relationship was a dialogue that occurred between the lines."

During the late eighteenth century soldiers were expected to brush elbows as they marched. This meant they were *in touch*. Civilians adopted the antonym of this phrase to refer to situations in which they'd lost contact with one another. They were **out of touch**. In the same era, soldiers called extra pay for length of service *fogey*, or *old fogey pay* ( *fogey* being what they called invalid soldiers). That piece of military slang gave the rest of us **old fogey** for senior citizens. Also during the eighteenth century a soldier's knapsack began to be referred to as a *kit bag* or *kit*. When full it was called *the whole kit*. A few decades later Americans began talking of *the whole caboodle*, a phrase they adapted from *boodle*, or "the entire lot." Once combined they resulted in **the whole kit and caboodle**.

European military tactics at this time called for soldiers to move forward and back like ocean waves. Those facing the enemy fired their muskets, dropped back to reload, then worked their way forward once again. There they were **on the firing line**. Today this refers to anyone at the forefront of a volatile situation. (William F. Buckley's long-running televised interview show was called *Firing Line*.) More often we say simply **on the line**, meaning exposed, vulnerable.

One early type of musket was called a **blunderbuss**. This rifle often appeared in pictures of Pilgrims. Its flared muzzle left the firearm's name behind as an allusion to scattershot tactics. (A New York judge reprimanded a man for continually filing broad-spectrum lawsuits "blunderbuss fashion.") Since

muskets consisted of a firing mechanism called a flintlock, or *lock* for short, a wooden *stock* to brace against one's shoulder, and a long tube, or *barrel* through which the bullet traveled, **lock, stock, and barrel** came to mean "the entire thing"—what a future generation would call *the whole nine yards* (for reasons that have never been fully explained). Musketeers who kept their rifles half-cocked had trouble getting them to fire when pulling the trigger in a hurry, giving us the expression **go off half-cocked**, or ill-prepared. Like cannons, muskets had *pans*, depressions that held a small amount of gunpowder. If this powder flared up but didn't propel a bullet, the only thing accomplished was a **flash in the pan**. On the home front, *flash in the pan* came to mean a brief, ephemeral moment of achievement. ("His one good season was only a flash in the pan.")

Early cannons on warships were mounted on wheels so they could be rolled inboard for loading, then outboard for firing. In both cases it was essential to lash the cannon securely to the deck. Otherwise it was liable to roll around uncontrollably, especially in rough seas. During this extremely dangerous event sailors were at risk of being crushed against the ship's walls by the random path of that careening piece of iron. That is why we call human beings whose actions are unpredictable **loose cannons**.

Early in the eighteenth century artillerymen began to fire *grapeshot* from their cannons. This referred to grape-sized pieces of metal packed loosely in a canvas bag. Because they distributed so widely on impact, this so-called grapeshot killed or maimed many more enemy soldiers than a mere cannonball could. In the process, **grapeshot** came to signify scattershot activity, and it does to this day, as when author Ron Suskind referred to the "very broad grapeshot kinds of efforts" being used to fight terrorism.

Other expressions left over from early ordnance include **offhand**, or shooting without sighting down the barrel, and **blow your wad**, shooting after you'd stuffed a musket's barrel with powder and a wad of cloth but no piece of shot. **Keep your powder dry** went from protecting the integrity of one's gunpowder to *be prepared* in general.

By the time weaponry had advanced enough to warrant having rifle ranges, standing in the *pits* behind targets to mark and adjust them was not considered good duty. Over time soldiers, then civilians, began to use **the pits** to refer to anything they didn't like. ("That movie was the pits.")

## The Civil War

As Rear Admiral David Farragut led a U.S. Navy fleet through Mobile Bay during the Civil War, one of his lead ships hit a submerged mine, also known as a "torpedo," and foundered. When told that the ship behind his had halted for fear of being torpedoed, Farragut said, "Damn the torpedoes! Four bells! Captain Drayton, go ahead." Over time the last two sentences were converted into "full speed ahead!" or "full steam ahead!" Those who push forward without regard to obstacles are still called **Damn the torpedoes!** types.

Confederate sympathizers in the North came to be known as *copperheads*. Unlike a rattlesnake, which gives fair warning with its rattle, the copperhead is a sneaky sort of snake that strikes without notice. Before the Civil War its name had been slang for renegades of many kinds. Today **copperhead** characterizes anyone seen as a betrayer, particularly since Franklin Delano Roosevelt applied that term to those who undermined his New Deal legislation, then to isolationists who fought our efforts to join the struggle against Hitler.

As Confederate forces were about to lose the pivotal Battle of Gettysburg in 1863, a division of soldiers commanded by General George Pickett was ordered to attack Union soldiers massed on Cemetery Ridge. Pickett himself didn't think this was a good idea but followed General Robert E. Lee's orders. Withering artillery fire met his soldiers as they emerged from the woods and marched in formation across a half mile of open ground. Fewer than half survived. This suicidal gambit was the culmination of a decisive clash whose loss sealed the fate of the Confederacy. Nearly a century and a half later, **Pickett's**

**Charge** still characterizes doomed ventures of all kinds. When a Louisiana furniture dealer proposed that Caddo Parish secede from the state, one Caddo resident told a TV news reporter that this plan was no more likely to succeed than Pickett's charge did at Gettysburg.

## The Great War

The horror and futility of World War I were best captured by Erich Maria Remarque's novel *All Quiet on the Western Front*. Remarque's bitterly ironic title was taken from a phrase commonly used in military dispatches and civilian press coverage to indicate that combat was in abeyance along a six-hundred-mile front extending from the English Channel to Switzerland. After this novel was published in 1929, **all quiet on the western front** or **all quiet on** (fill in the blank) became a common catchphrase. A news report on tax forms was titled "All Quiet on the 1040 Front."

In its later stages, World War I (known then as the Great War) was one long stalemate interrupted by occasional carnage. Much of that war was fought by soldiers in trenches separated by a barren, ominous **no-man's-land**, a phrase we still use for any dangerous, desolate terrain. (During the Middle Ages, *no-man's-land* referred to an area outside London where the bodies of executed criminals were left to rot.) In occasional hair-raising moments, soldiers went *over the top*, scrambling out of their trenches to attack those in the facing trench. **Over the top** eventually took on a different meaning altogether: extreme, outlandish behavior. ("He gave an over-the-top performance.") Mostly, though, World War I's soldiers just hunkered down in the mud, puddles, and stink of eight-foot-wide slits dug in the ground. Nearly a century later, **trench warfare** still refers to hard-slogging conflict of all kinds. Those actually engaged in such conflict, or simply participating in demanding activity, are said to be **in the trenches**. By extension, anyone mired in a firmly held position is **entrenched**.

Wounded Great Warriors were transported in litters, or "baskets." The grim visage of a soldier who had lost both arms and both legs being moved this way inspired the term *basket case*. According to the U.S. Army's surgeon general, there were no such cases. His postwar denial did not prevent speculation about *basket cases* being hidden in homes and hospitals. Dalton Trumbo wrote a horrifying portrayal of one such casualty in his 1939 novel *Johnny Got His Gun*. Today **a basket case** refers to anyone who is totally out of commission, physically or emotionally. The traumatized survivor of a Manhattan bed bug infestation called those like herself "Exhibit A basket cases."

American soldiers in World War I called unqualified civilians who received military commissions *goldbricks*. This term originally referred to just what it sounds like: a brick of gold. In the late nineteenth century *goldbrick* more often referred to a piece of cheaper metal that con men painted to look like gold. Eventually this term referred to all manner of swindles. By 1918 *goldbrick* was applied first to unqualified officers, then to any soldier who didn't do his job. In time this noun became a verb, and that is how it is used today. To **goldbrick** means to shirk. The goof-off comic-strip character Beetle Bailey continually engages in **goldbricking**. A character in Richard Russo's novel *Empire Falls* says of disability collectors in her town "not one of these goldbricks was actually injured, but most at least had the decency to pretend."

. Other terms coined by World War I soldiers or popularized by them include: **cold feet** (a term originally used by fliers for anxious hesitation); **joystick** (also pilot slang, for the lever controlling an airplane's flight); **nosedive** (originally referring to a plane's rapid descent, then to anything that falls rapidly); **pipsqueak** (a type of artillery shell whose arc was thought to begin with a sound like *pip*, and end with a squeaky squeal; subsequently applied to ineffectual soldiers); and **dud** (an unexploded shell or, by extension, anything that doesn't live up to expectations).

Every war has its own way of referring to soldiers who break down during combat. In World War I this condition was called **shell shock** (in part because it was originally thought to result from shell-generated shock waves traumatizing the nervous system). When we want to say that someone is traumatized we commonly revert to Great War terminology and say that person is **shell-shocked**. This term evokes an image of a stunned, wide-eyed individual, someone, say, who has just been in a car crash. By World War II that condition was more euphemistically labeled **battle fatigue** or **combat fatigue.**

## World War II

Spain's 1936–39 civil war was used as a practice field by Nazis and Soviets looking ahead to a broader conflict. There, some areas held by loyalist Republicans were infiltrated by rebel Fascist sympathizers who stood ready to rise up when called upon. These disloyal citizens were said to constitute a *fifth column* ready to join the four columns of Fascists advancing on cities such as Madrid. Coined by one of Franco's generals in 1936, this phrase (*quinta columna* in Spanish) quickly caught on, especially after Ernest Hemingway titled a 1937 play *The Fifth Column*. Ever since then, **fifth column** has referred to any group that infiltrates another group to hasten its demise. Many Iraqi Shiites regard Sunni members of that country's police and army as a subversive *fifth column*.

After losing their investment in Republican Spain, the Soviets invaded Finland in 1939. The outmanned and underequipped Finnish soldiers threw gasoline-filled bottles topped with slow-burning rag wicks at Soviet tanks. They sardonically called these weapons *Molotov cocktails* in honor of Soviet foreign minister Vyacheslav Mikhailovich Molotov. Molotov was a longtime Bolshevik so loyal to dictator Joseph Stalin that he remained a steadfast apparatchik even after his own wife was imprisoned on trumped-up charges. Although he was the Soviet Union's foreign minister for thirteen years, his name is best remembered for the **Molotov cocktails** still thrown by insurgents around the world.

As war clouds thickened in the late 1930s, France built what it thought was an impregnable barrier on its border with Germany. This barrier consisted of concrete walls, bunkers, machine-gun emplacements, barbed wire, and miscellaneous other obstructions. It was named after France's minister of defense, André Maginot. The *Maginot Line* proved to be impregnable in the same sense that the *Titanic* was unsinkable. In 1940 German invaders simply bypassed this obstacle course as they raced across France's unprotected border with Belgium through the dense Ardennes Forest. Mere days after their assault began, Nazi soldiers were marching on French soil. Ever since then the term **Maginot Line** has alluded to futile ventures. The fence being built between the United States and Mexico to prevent illegal border crossing has been called a Maginot Line.

It took German forces only two weeks to reach the city of Dunkirk on France's northern coast. British soldiers who came to France's aid were pinned down on Dunkirk's beach. Prime Minister Winston Churchill issued a call for seaworthy vessels to cross the English Channel and help rescue them. Between May 26 and June 4 an armada of rowboats, lifeboats, fishing boats, dinghies, sloops, yachts, ferries, destroyers, minesweepers, and Dutch scoots succeeded in evacuating some 338,226 British and French soldiers while under constant German bombardment. This rescue effort is considered one of the most dramatic events in modern military history. Churchill called it the "miracle of Dunkirk." When Ronald Reagan was elected president in 1980, his aides announced plans for an "economic Dunkirk" to stimulate the economy with tax cuts and the like. That allusion is a two-edged sword, however. As Churchill never hesitated to point out, **Dunkirk** was in fact a defeat. When his team performed poorly, Marquette University's late basketball coach Al McGuire would call their efforts a "Dunkirk."

Hitler's Nazis shocked the world with the speed and brutal effectiveness of their tactics. These tactics were based on withering air attacks followed by rapid ground assaults in a relentless attacking style that came to be known as a *blitzkrieg* (German for "lightning war"). It did not take long for this word to be shortened to its first syllable. As early as November 1940, the *Nation* magazine noted that "the word that has received the greatest currency at home and abroad is *blitz*, used as both noun and verb." **Blitz** remains synonymous with swift, effective activity. In football, a rapid assault on the quarterback is known as a *blitz*. Politicians who mount well-funded campaigns characterized by saturation advertising *blitz* their opponents.

What made Germany's invasion of Norway unique was that it was done by invitation. The head of Norway's Fascist National Unity Party, Major Vidkun Quisling, asked Hitler to take over his neutral country. After helping plan that successful invasion, Major Quisling headed a puppet government. Soon after Nazi soldiers began patrolling Oslo's streets, the term **quisling** was being used generically to refer to traitors everywhere. In mid-1940, *Time* magazine felt no need even to capitalize the Norwegian's name when it reported, "South America becomes very quisling conscious." After being liberated Norway temporarily suspended its ban on executions so that Vidkun Quisling could be shot by a firing squad on October 24, 1945. His Dickensian last name has endured for over half a century to suggest a sniveling collaborator.

World War II's bombs were far more potent than those used in the First World War. Ones weighing several tons—powerful enough to destroy large complexes of buildings, what the British called "blocks"—were dubbed *blockbusters* by Royal Air Force (RAF) fliers. After the war, **blockbuster** was applied to many types of high-impact events, including bestselling books and box-office-smash movies. In 1951, with an unprecedented $7 million publicity budget, *Quo Vadis* was the first movie called a *blockbuster*.

Simulated bombing missions were called **dry runs** by World War II's pilots, a term we now use for dress rehearsals of all kinds. When actually flying missions, slow-moving bomber planes were subjected to shells fired from antiair-craft guns that exploded around them like fireworks. Originally called "ack-ack" after the sound it made, such ordnance was ultimately referred to as *flak* or *flack*, an acronym for the German *Fliegerabwer Kanone* or "aircraft defense gun." This ear-pleasing acronym caught on quickly as an allusion. ("Rumors were as thick as flack," reported *Time* magazine in early 1942.) Veterans used the term *flak* for any verbal barrage. Over time **flak** came to mean criticism, verbal fire. A president's press secretary takes a lot of flak.

Another phrase that American pilots picked up from RAF counterparts was *flying by the seat of your pants*, or navigating a plane by feel, without instruments. (Consistent with its British roots, this phrase originated as *fly by the seat of your trousers*.) We now use **seat-of-pants** to depict any sort of rough calculation or unaided activity. A 2005 management book is titled *By the Seat of Your Pants*. British fliers also gave us **Roger!** as a terse way to say "got your message" in radio exchanges. There is no more elaborate explanation for this term than the fact that "Roger" and "received" share the same first letter. "Roger" just sounds better. As the war went along, pilots began using this term in their everyday conversations, and after the war civilians followed suit, sometimes upgrading the expression to "**Roger that**."

A device invented before the war by Scotland's Robert Alexander Watson Watt used high-frequency radio signals to detect ships or airplanes at a distance, day or night, and in all weather conditions. Watt's invention may have saved London from being obliterated by Luftwaffe planes early in the war. Originally called a *radiolocator* by the Brits, with typical briskness Yanks re-dubbed this device *radar* (for *ra*dio *d*etecting *a*nd *r*anging). The only way planes could avoid detection by radar was to fly beneath the area of its surveillance signals, or **under the radar**—a term we now apply to stealth activity that is hard to detect. Related terminology includes **on your radar, on the radar screen, off the radar**, and **blip on the radar screen**.

Well beneath the radar, soldiers dug holes in which to hunker down. Great War soldiers called such mini-trenches *dug-outs*. One war later they became known as *foxholes*. According to a famous observation by a World War II chaplain, "There are no atheists in foxholes." After the war, **foxhole** was applied to defensive strategies of many kinds. Senator Russell Feingold (D-Wis.) once accused his party's leaders of being "foxhole Democrats" who were too timid to confront Republicans aggressively.

As in any war, World War II's soldiers produced lots of slang. Borrowing the longtime sailors' term for his hammock, **sack** became GI-speak for "bed." ("GI" itself is apparently an acronym for "Government Issue," though other explanations have been suggested.) To **hit the sack, sack out**, or **do sack time** meant going to bed. This slang outlasted the war. Then and now, **in the sack** implied that activities other than sleeping might be going on there. Other terms born in the barracks and battlefields of World War II include **goof off** (malinger), **snow job** (deception), **bum steer** (deliberate misdirection), **raunchy** (sloppy, dirty, disheveled), and **gizmo** (a generic term for any device without a name).

Relationship-ending letters received by soldiers from girlfriends or wives—usually explaining that they'd "found someone else"—have been known ever since as *Dear John* letters. According to Paul Dickson's *War Slang*, this term was popularized by a World War II–era radio program in which *Dear John* letters were read aloud. In *From Here to Eternity*, James Jones's 1951 novel set in prewar Pearl Harbor (where the author had served in the Army), one soldier says that in a tight sexual spot all a woman has to do is "holler rape and it would be Dear John, that's all she wrote." To this day any kiss-off is liable to be called a **Dear John** or a **Dear Jane**. In his memoir *Born Standing Up*, comedian Steve Martin mentioned a girlfriend who sent him "a gentle and direct Dear John letter" to let him know she'd taken up with a movie director. **That's all she wrote!** was what military mail clerks shouted after they finished handing out letters. First veterans, then civilians, adopted this phrase to refer to disappointing endings.

Although most World War II lingo adopted by civilians originated in the European theater, some came from Pacific combat as well. When attacking, Japanese soldiers uttered loud cries in unison, similar to the rebel yell of Confederate soldiers during the Civil War. A word they often shouted was *"Banzai!"* for "Long live!" or *"Tennoheika banzai!"* for "Long live the emperor!" Since so many of these noisy attacks proved to be fatal as well as futile, the term **banzai** today suggests a suicidal venture. (A motorcycle racer once said that although he hoped to race well, "I will not be going too banzai!") That suggestion applies even more to *kamikaze*—Japanese for "divine wind"—referring to the hundreds of fighter pilots who crashed bomb-laden airplanes into Allied ships as the war in the Pacific wound down. Long after Japan's surrender, **kamikaze** remained synonymous with futile, self-defeating activities. Politicians who run in elections they're unlikely to win are sometimes called *kamikaze candidates.*

The commander of a Marine battalion in the South Pacific, Colonel Evans Carlson, had been impressed by the team spirit he'd observed among a group of soldiers in China called the Chinese Industrial Cooperatives. Organized by New Zealander Rewi Alley, this group's motto was *Gung ho* ("working together in harmony," anglicized by Alley from *kung,* Chinese for "work," and *ho* for "together"). Colonel Carlson borrowed their motto for his Marines. In 1943 the victory of this battalion over Japanese forces on Makin Island was celebrated in a movie titled *Gung Ho!* That movie inserted this saying into public discourse, where it has stayed ever since, referring to aggressive enthusiasm. Over the years **gung ho** took on an odor of overzealousness. Nowadays calling someone "real gung ho" isn't necessarily a compliment.


## Korea

American soldiers captured by North Korean or Chinese forces during the 1950–53 Korean War were subjected to intense interrogation accompanied by sophisticated psychological efforts to replace their existing beliefs with Communist ideology. These tactics consisted of a combination of isolation, sleep deprivation, threats, torture, self-criticism sessions, and ceaseless "re-education." This process came to be known as *brainwashing,* a literal translation of the Mandarin words *xi nao* or "wash brain." The notion that they'd had their brains laundered was the only way shocked Americans could make sense of the fact that so many POWs publicly "confessed" to war crimes, and the fact that nearly two dozen of them chose not to come home at all. As cults grew more ubiquitous during the 1960s, the term **brainwash** became more common. Over time **brainwashing** took on broader significance, referring generally to any drastic change of beliefs under duress, or due to dubious indoctrination. Michigan Governor George Romney—who supported the war in Vietnam based in part on an upbeat assessment by American military officers during his 1965 visit to that country—later concluded that this briefing had in fact caused "the greatest brainwashing that anybody can get."

Although veterans typically bring back native terms from foreign countries where they fought, a single word seems to have made the voyage from Korea to the United States: *skosh.* This actually is an adaptation of a Japanese term, *sukoshi*, meaning "a small amount." American GIs first adapted this word as *skoshi*, then shortened it to **skosh**, or "a smidgen" (as in "I'll have just a skosh"). That term was already common back home when Levi Strauss bumped its exposure up a notch with a late-1970s ad campaign that promised bulging baby boomers "a skosh more room" in strategic points of their jeans.

The 1953 cease-fire agreement that ended hostilities between North and South Korea established a four-kilometer buffer zone between the two countries. This strip of land was dubbed a *demilitarized zone*, or *DMZ*. It now is home not only to a generous supply of landmines but an astonishing array of wildlife that has taken up residence in one of the few pieces of earthly land where human beings are loath to tread. **DMZ** is used generically in a variety of ways, usually referring to a location where feuding parties must cool down, a church, say, or counselor's office. The year after the Korean version was established, another *DMZ* was established at the 1954 Geneva Conference to divide North and South Vietnam.

Following this convention, President Dwight "Ike" Eisenhower warned that if a single country in Southeast Asia went Communist, others would follow. "You have a row of dominoes," he said; "you knock over the first one, and what will happen to the last one is that it will go over very quickly." Eisenhower called this "the 'falling domino' principle." Secretary of State John Foster Dulles relabeled his warning the **domino theory**. In time it came to be known as the **domino effect**. Ike turned out to be a bad soothsayer. Although some countries in Southeast Asia did go Communist, most didn't. Nonetheless, so many decision makers agreed with Eisenhower that fear of a *domino effect* dominated American foreign policy for decades. Today the term is used routinely to describe any situation in which one event leads to another. When bad weather forces the cancellation of hundreds of flights at busy airports, many of them connecting, airline officials fret that "a domino effect" of delayed and canceled flights will ensue.

## Vietnam

GIs fighting in Vietnam produced what *War Slang* author Paul Dickson called "a totally new slang—brutal, direct, and geared to high-tech jungle warfare with a rock 'n' roll beat backed up by the throb of chopper engines." Words we use now that were born or became common in the jungles of Vietnam include

**bust chops** (give a hard time); **fat city** (a good place to be); **on the line** (from *on the front lines*, or right up against it); and **turnaround time** (the period between cruises of an aircraft carrier in port).

The too-frequent phenomenon of soldiers killing officers in Vietnam came to be known as *fragging*. This derived from the most common method of doing that: rolling an armed fragmentation grenade, or *frag*, into an officer's tent as he slept. That term made its way back to the States, where it took on broader significance. **Frag** can now mean destroying pretty much anything, and among video game players it refers to temporarily killing another player.

Infantrymen in Vietnam were called, and called themselves, *grunts*. Presumably the very sound of that word suggests its origins: as a reference to someone close to the ground, doing menial tasks, grunting as he goes along. Since then this term has come to characterize any person engaged in entry-level work. Clerical workers commonly call themselves **grunts**. They do *grunt work*. In Vietnam, a synonym for *grunts* was *boonie rats*. That's because soldiers on the ground in Vietnam called the isolated areas in which they were fighting the **boonies**. This was short for *boondocks*, a term that originated among American soldiers fighting in the Philippines at the turn of the twentieth century. While there, the Yanks picked up *bundok*, the Tagalog word for "hinterlands," and transformed it into **boondocks**, a term they used to refer to any remote setting. **Boondockers** is longtime soldier slang for combat boots.

One might think that *boondoggle* is a close cousin to *boondocker*, but it's not. *Boondoggle* originally referred to the leather lanyards that Boy Scouts braided to gather their scarves or attach to their whistles. During the Great Depression conservatives disparaged public works projects by calling them *boondoggles* after a *New York Times* article reported that the unemployed were being taught how to make that ephemeral object. In Vietnam this word became soldier slang for meaningless missions. In time **boondoggle** came to characterize our futile involvement in Vietnam overall. That term has since been applied to a wide range of fiscal fiascos, ranging from Boston's "Big Dig" underground highway tunnel to shoddily built levees in New Orleans.

# 5. Stump Speech

**E**uropean settlers noted that Indian leaders stood on stumps of downed trees to address members of their tribe. This made so much sense that they adopted the practice themselves. By the mid-nineteenth century it was common to refer to political *stump speeches*, and to campaigning in general as *stumping it*. In an 1813 letter to John Adams, Thomas Jefferson referred to "stump Orators." Today **stump speech** refers to set pieces repeated ad nauseam by candidates for office, or anyone advocating a position. They are **stumping** or **on the stump.** We also say such advocates **lobby** when pushing their cause. That's because, since the early nineteenth century, special-interest advocates who accosted legislators in the lobbies of capital buildings came to be known as **lobbyists.** They **lobbied.** So do teenagers who *lobby* their parents for a later curfew.

American discourse is filled with terms borrowed from politics. When suggesting that a particular activity isn't for sissies, wimps, or shrinking violets, for example, we're likely to say, "It ain't beanbag." This is because, late in the nineteenth century, newspaper columnist Finley Peter Dunne wrote that a fanciful bartender named *Mr. Dooley* sagely observed, "Politics ain't bean bag. 'Tis a man's game; an' women, children, an' pro-hybitionists do well to keep out iv it." The operative phrase in this passage caught on and stuck around. We fill in the blank of "_____**ain't beanbag**" with whatever activity we think is best suited to the thick of skin. War, marketing, and cooking are just a few of the examples I've seen. None are considered *beanbag*.

Another phrase that jumped political fences and made its way into general conversation was put in play by Harry Truman. Explaining his decision not to run for re-election as president in 1952, Truman cited the advice of an old friend back in Missouri: "If you can't stand the heat, get out of the kitchen." After he said that, **take the heat** or *taking heat* became standard shorthand for being able to endure controversy and criticism. "He can take the heat," we'll say, or "She's taking a lot of heat."

Ten years after Truman left the White House, California Assembly speaker Jesse Unruh observed that "money is the mother's milk of politics." Unruh, a large, flamboyant figure known as "Big Daddy," put into cynical words what many already suspected. Time would confirm the truth of his observation. Few remember Big Daddy, but many are familiar with his famous seven words, a comment so renowned that reference to **mother's milk** alone is usually enough to evoke the extravagant amounts of money being spent on political campaigns.

Another form of political nutrition has to do with sausage. Senator Ted Kennedy (D-Mass.) once said of a Medicare bill, "Even a sausage maker would be offended by how this law was made." Why a sausage maker? Because he was referencing an old saying that grew especially popular during America's many political fiascos in the early twenty-first century: "If you like **laws and sausage**, you should never watch either one being made." Assuming we all got his point, *Washington Post* political editor John Harris once observed that he and colleagues "love to watch sausage getting made."

## Political Palaver

Much political terminology that we use today is rooted in past events, reaching as far back as the early nineteenth century, when Elbridge Gerry was governor of Massachusetts. A signer of the Declaration of Independence and onetime U.S. vice president, in 1812 Gerry presided over the redrawing of his state's congressional districts. His party designed these districts to favor themselves. Their results were, shall we say, *artistic*. A *Boston Gazette* cartoon portrayed one reconfigured district as being shaped like a dragon-salamander. It was called "the Gerry-mander: A New Species of Mon-

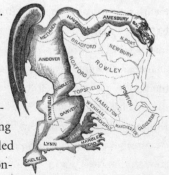

ster." This term caught the public's fancy. Converted to a verb, **gerrymander** is what we still call the tortured redrawing of electoral districts to favor those in power.

During the run-up to the Civil War an abolitionist politician named James Baird Weaver frequently held aloft a stained piece of ragged cloth when exhorting crowds in Iowa, telling them it had been worn by a local clergyman as his back was flogged raw for preaching to slaves in Texas. "I waved it before the crowds," Weaver later wrote, "and bellowed 'under this bloody shirt we propose to march to victory.'" Following the Confederates' surrender, Weaver and many other Union veterans continued to figuratively *wave the bloody shirt* when reminding northern voters why the war had been fought in the first place. Democrats accused Republicans like Weaver of demonizing them by **waving the bloody shirt**. This old expression still characterizes emotional allusions to past outrages. George W. Bush's constant evocation of 9/11 when justifying his anti-terror policies was often characterized as bloody-shirt waving.

After the war quite a few northerners traveled south to take part in Reconstruction. Many of them arrived with their belongings packed in a valise made of carpeting that was known as a *carpet bag*. Because so many Yankee entrepreneurs, hustlers, and do-gooders carried such a satchel, southerners called them all *carpetbaggers*. Today **carpetbagger** refers to anyone perceived as an interloper, especially in politics. When running for the U.S. Senate from states to which they'd recently moved, Robert Kennedy, Hillary Clinton, and Alan Keyes were all charged with **carpetbagging**.

Long after the Civil War ended, General William Tecumseh Sherman was pressured to run for president. He steadfastly refused. During one Republican convention, Sherman received a telegram telling him that like it or not he was about to be nominated. Sherman's son Tom later recalled his father's response to this telegram: "Without taking his cigar from his mouth, without changing his expression, while I stood there trembling by his side, my father wrote the answer, 'I will not accept if nominated and will not serve if elected.'" In the retelling, Sherman's resolute words were edited into a livelier statement of noncandidacy: "If nominated, I will not run. If elected, I will not serve." To this day any American politician who declines to run for a particular office is routinely asked if he or she will make a **Sherman statement** or a **Shermanesque** disavowal. Few do.

When General Sherman's brother John, then secretary of the treasury, returned to his Ohio farm in 1879 to court support for a U.S. Senate run, he said the purpose of his trip was "only to repair my fences." This gave birth to the catchphrase **mend my fences** as a euphemism for tending to political relationships. That phrase in turn was compressed to **fence-mending**.

Another Ohioan, William McKinley, addressed voters primarily from the front porch of his Canton home when running for president in 1892. McKinley's predecessor, Ohio native Benjamin Harrison, did the same thing from his front porch in Indianapolis. This successful approach—later adopted by yet another Ohioan, Warren G. Harding (is it something about Ohio?)—was semi-derisively called a *front porch campaign*. Since all of these candidates were elected, there was a limit to how derogatory this term could be. Nonetheless, Harry Truman later contrasted his own frenetic criss-crossing of the country in 1948 with the more placid *front porch campaign* style of Republicans. All manner of lethargic activity is still denigrated as a **front porch campaign**.

William McKinley's vice president, Theodore Roosevelt, had spent time cowboying in the Dakotas as a young man. While there he may have witnessed spectators declaring their willingness to challenge a professional boxer by throwing their hat into the ring. When announcing his intention to run for president, TR said he intended to "throw my hat into the ring." Ever since then it has been routine for American political candidates to say "I am **throwing my hat in the ring**," and sometimes to actually do so.

Roosevelt used the term *bully* the way kids a century later would say "awesome." When TR called the presidency a *bully pulpit*, he meant that it was a first-rate platform from which to advocate his positions. To him, "pulpit" was a noun, "bully" an adjective. Today **bully pulpit** is more likely to be used as a single phrase. In his *New Political Dictionary*, William Safire defines that phrase as "active use of the Presidency's prestige and high visibility to inspire or moralize." Because the term "bully" is typically misapprehended as referring to coercion, *bully pulpit* today has overtones of arm-twisting.

At the 1901 Minnesota State Fair, Roosevelt told listeners, "A good many of you are probably acquainted with the old proverb 'Speak softly and carry a big stick—you will go far.'" This adage fit the tough-talking TR so well that it endured throughout his presidency and well beyond in the phrase **big stick**

**diplomacy.** This refers to a foreign policy based on a calm national demeanor backed up by robust military force.

## From Harding to McCarthy

As the1920 Republican convention began, Warren Harding's handler Harry Daugherty was quoted as saying that its nominee for president would be chosen "in a smoke-filled room in some hotel." Even though it turned out Daugherty's prophetic words were put in his mouth by a reporter, the key phrase—**smoke-filled room**—became a lasting allusion to deal making out of public view. According to one news account, American clothing company executives consider the complicated, seemingly arbitrary tariffs imposed on imported apparel "a vestige of smoke-filled, backroom trade negotiations."

Harding, who liked to play poker and canoodle with his young mistress in a White House coat closet, is not considered one of our better presidents. He did contribute more terms and phrases to American parlance than is generally realized: **normalcy**, for one (by mistake; Harding meant to say "normality"), as well as **the founding fathers** for the revolutionary founders of the United States. Harding also popularized **bloviate** for verbose speechmaking.

Herbert Hoover was a tight-lipped Quaker not given to bloviation during his 1929–33 presidency. When he ran unsuccessfully for re-election, Democrats mocked Hoover for promising voters **a chicken in every pot**. Although Republicans did use a version of this slogan in 1928 (at times adding *"a car in every garage"*), Hoover himself made no such promise. The culinary part of that thought originated with King Henry IV of France, who said, "I desire that every laborer in my realm should be able to put a fowl in the pot on Sundays." Allusions are still made to the modern version of this promise (e.g., "car-in-every-garage prosperity").

Hoover's successor, Franklin Delano Roosevelt, surrounded himself with smart, well-educated advisers. This group came to be known as the *brains trust* ("brains" for obvious reason, "trust" alluding to companies that gathered many operations under one roof). This term was applied to FDR's advisers by a *New York Times* reporter after "brains department" didn't pass the president's phonetic test. Roosevelt also preferred a singular version: *brain trust*. Ever since his early years in the White House, any group of people who appear to be on the smart side are liable to be called a **brain trust**, those who belong to such a group **brain trusters**.

Soon after taking office, FDR gave a radio talk in which he assured listeners that his suspension of bank transactions would last only four days. This address was titled "An Intimate Talk with the People of the United States on Banking." A CBS radio executive advised Roosevelt to give his second radio talk a folksier title, something along the lines of *a fireside chat*. FDR took this advice. All the rest of his popular radio addresses—thirty in all, each one beginning "My friends" and delivered in a reassuring, almost intimate tone— were dubbed **fireside chats**. That term is still applied to soothing, intimate presidential talks (notwithstanding the fact that one of Jimmy Carter's less memorable televised addresses as president was given while wearing a cardigan sweater before logs crackling in a fireplace).

When Vice President Harry Truman became president after FDR died in 1945, the obscure machine politician from Missouri was considered little more than a seat-warmer. After being nominated for a full term by the 1948 Democratic convention, Truman set off by train to visit as many of America's communities as possible, blistering the "do-nothing Congress" in 356 speeches from his train's rear platform. Senator Robert Taft (R-Ohio) accused the president of "blackguarding Congress at whistle-stops across the country."

*Whistle-stops* referred to towns too small to merit regular train service. (Trains stopped there only when a passenger pulled a signal cord. The engineer would then blow his whistle to indicate that he'd got the message.) Enough voters lived in such settings that Taft's remark backfired. Truman and the Democrats took pride in Truman's successful **whistle-stop** campaign. **Whistle-stopping** be- came a common term referring to covering a lot of ground in a short period of time. British comedian Sacha Baron Cohen was said to be on a "whistle-stop publicity tour" as he promoted his movie *Borat* in the United States.

During the 1952 presidential campaign, a group of Republicans followed

Truman around as he campaigned for Democratic nominee Adlai Stevenson, holding constant press conferences to "refute" the president's assertions. They called themselves a *truth squad*. The GOP repeated this tactic when Stevenson ran against Dwight Eisenhower in1956, and again when John Kennedy took on Richard Nixon in 1960. The term **truth-squad** persisted into the following century, becoming a verb in the process. Now reference was frequently made to **truth-squadding**, or debunking the claims of an opposition candidate. An NPR show host once asked congressional correspondent Andrea Seabrook to "truth-squad" allegations about abuse of travel privileges by the House Speaker.

One target of Harry Truman's sharp tongue was Senator Joseph McCarthy (R-Wis.). At different times Truman called McCarthy a "guttersnipe," a "skunk," and "a pathological liar." When asked about a charge that he'd libeled Senator McCarthy, Truman responded, "Do you think that is possible?" The source of his ire was a balding man with dark jowls who served for a decade in the U.S. Senate before dying of acute alcoholism in 1957. Much of that time was spent pursuing the Communists whom McCarthy claimed had infiltrated every level of American society. Hearings he chaired brought one witness after another before his Permanent Subcommittee on Investigations to answer the question "Are you now, or have you ever been a member of the Communist Party?" Some wouldn't answer, citing the Fifth Amendment to the Constitution, which guaranteed their right against self-incrimination. Along with organized-crime figures who invoked the same right, these mute witnesses put **take the fifth** and **plead the fifth** on our linguistic map as a generic way of saying one would rather not discuss something. ("I'll take the fifth on that.") Then and now Joe McCarthy's frenetic pursuit of Communists was compared to an earlier hunt for "witches." (See chapter 7.) When not called a **witch hunt**, political persecution that involves dubious charges is routinely called **McCarthyism**. After an NBA referee was charged with fixing basketball games, a *Boston Globe* sportswriter worried that this man's colleagues might be "McCarthyized" in a process of guilt by association.

## The Eisenhower Era

Second only to Joseph McCarthy as a Communist-hunting senator was Richard Nixon (R-Calif.). As Dwight Eisenhower's running mate in 1952,

Nixon responded to allegations that he'd benefited from a "slush fund" of illegal donations with a dramatic televised address. Midway through his eleven-minute speech the vice-presidential nominee admitted that he had indeed accepted a gift, a black and white cocker spaniel given to his family by a man in Texas. Their six-year-old daughter Tricia named it Checkers. "And you know," concluded Nixon, "the kids, like all kids, love the dog, and I just want to say this, right now, that regardless of what they say about it, we're gonna keep it." This was quickly dubbed the *Checkers speech*. Those who liked Richard Nixon found his talk honest, forthright, and sincere. Those who disliked him thought it was smarmy, unctuous, and phony. History has tended to the latter assessment. Today the **Checkers speech** refers to any dubious statement of contrition. As a beleaguered Bill Clinton dribbled out admissions about his relationship with Monica Lewinsky late in his presidency, references to Nixon's 1952 speech were ubiquitous. *Dayton Daily News* columnist Mary McCarty advised Clinton to "take to the airwaves and deliver an appeal that out-checkers the Checkers speech."

During two terms in the White House, Dwight Eisenhower developed a reputation for being a cautious leader whose convoluted public comments made him seem tongue-tied. It therefore was quite a shock when, in his farewell address, Eisenhower lambasted an alliance of military officers and defense contractors whom he said had inflated the Pentagon's budget. "In the councils of government," warned Eisenhower, "we must guard against the acquisition of unwarranted influence, whether sought or unsought, by the military-industrial complex." Since the man delivering those words was a career army officer who hobnobbed with industrialists, this warning attracted an unusual amount of attention. Its key words—**military-industrial complex**—are still heard, often. In the process they have become a modular catchphrase in which a wide range of terms are substituted for "military." *Newsweek*'s Jonathan Alter characterized the many show business figures who support political causes as an "entertainment-industrial complex." In her book *Buy Buy Baby*, Susan Gregory Thomas called all the companies that sell early learning products a "toddler-industrial complex."

Eisenhower's successor, John Kennedy, was the best-looking man to occupy the White House since Warren Harding. Kennedy's thick head of hair and erect six-foot bearing seemed to symbolize the passing of a generational torch from his balding, modest-sized predecessor. In contrast to outgoing first lady Mamie

Eisenhower, JFK's glamorous wife, Jacqueline, stepped right off the pages of *Vogue*. Journalist Theodore White said the Kennedys gave the White House an aura of *Camelot*, alluding to Lerner and Loewe's 1960 musical by that title (whose closing lines were "Don't let it be forgot / That once there was a spot, / For one brief, shining moment / That was known as Camelot"). Even though JFK's White House turned out to be more dissolute cathouse than glamorous castle, the label stuck. Any presidential aspirant with even a hint of stride and dash—especially a Democrat with decent hair whose spouse has even a gram of fashion sense—still excites feverish speculation about a restoration of **Camelot**.

One of President Kennedy's first acts was to approve an invasion of Cuba by exiles under the direction of the Central Intelligence Agency. This invasion, at Cuba's Bay of Pigs, was an unmitigated disaster. Among the thousands who landed there, those not mowed down were herded into prison. To his credit, Kennedy took full responsibility for this fiasco. In subsequent years **Bay of Pigs** became a modern-day counterpart of "Waterloo" (from Napoleon's standpoint, anyway) as shorthand for disastrous undertakings. On an episode of the sitcom *That 70s Show*, one character warns another that his plan to get married will prove to be "your Bay of Pigs."

Late in his third year in office, JFK left Washington to shore up his shaky political base in Texas. While motorcading through Dallas with Texas Governor John Connally, Kennedy was assassinated. A sometime Communist named Lee Harvey Oswald apparently shot both men from a high window at the Texas Book Depository, killing Kennedy and wounding Connally. The next day Oswald himself was killed by a bar owner named Jack Ruby. How the alleged assassin could have successfully shot two men in a moving car at some distance has been debated ever since. Those who defend this conclusion subscribe to a **single-bullet theory**, in which one bullet from Oswald's high-powered rifle passed through both Kennedy's head and Connally's torso. Others speculate that a second gunman was hidden on a *grassy knoll* ahead of the motorcade. Although no conclusive evidence has ever confirmed this theory, **grassy knoll** became synonymous with nefarious plots hidden from view. An online clearinghouse for information about such conspiracies is called the Grassy Knoll Institute.

To the horror of Camelot's faithful, John Kennedy was succeeded by Vice President Lyndon Johnson. Kennedyites regarded Johnson as a vulgar, badly educated Texan who had been added to their ticket only to help carry his home state. The fact that LBJ liked to conduct conversations while seated on the Oval Office commode did nothing to dispel this stereotype. In Washington the shrewd onetime Senate majority leader was famous (or notorious) for having said that Representative Gerald Ford (R-Mich.) couldn't "fart and chew gum at the same time." Reporters bowdlerized LBJ's put-down to "Jerry Ford can't **walk and chew gum** at the same time." This version, already part of the vernacular, became a lasting allusion to those who can't even master the basics. In response to allegations that he wasn't the Senate's sharpest pencil, Jim Bunning (R-Ky.) told an audience, "I want everybody to look and see that I can walk and chew gum."

Other phrases that emerged from Lyndon Johnson's five years in the White House include *the Great Society*, *hearts and minds*, and *Nervous Nellies*—a term LBJ used to denigrate those who expressed reservations about the Vietnam War. The only one that could genuinely be called a retroterm is **credibility gap**, a euphemism for *lying* that first appeared in a 1965 newspaper headline and caught on quickly because LBJ's actions were so often at odds with his words. At one point White House press secretary Bill Moyers remarked that "the credibility gap . . . is getting so bad that we can't even believe our own leaks."

## Tricky Dick

There was something mesmerizing about Nixon's undistilled smarminess, rather like watching *Jerry Springer* in prime time. His Checkers speech was just one of many slippery gambits that earned Nixon the nickname **Tricky Dick**. A question often asked to demean the thirty-seventh president, and posed about many others since, was **"Would you buy a used car from this man?"**

No one contributed more terms to modern political discourse than Richard Nixon. In a speech during his first year in the White House, Nixon said, "And so tonight—to you, the great silent majority of my fellow Americans—I ask for your support." **Silent majority** subsequently became a popular catchphrase, referring to the many Americans who don't necessarily share their conservative views with pollsters or reporters. This group was thought to be concentrated in what Nixon liked to call **Middle America** (a phrase coined by journalist Joseph Kraft). Incorporating the Midwest and a few contiguous states, that setting later became known as the *heartland*.

Part of Nixon's stock in trade was blistering attacks on *Red China* and those who would appease its dictatorial leader, Mao Zedong. China's response was no less vehement. Among other things Mao charged that despite its nuclear arsenal the United States was a mere *paper tiger* with no real bite. Early in 1971, however, seven American table tennis players traveled to the People's Republic of China for matches with local counterparts. Their trip was widely viewed as paving the way for broadened diplomatic contacts between the United States and China. Nearly four decades later the phrase **ping-pong diplomacy** has come to characterize nonpolitical initiatives, such as sending a baseball team to Cuba, or earthquake aid to Iran, that might lay the groundwork for improved relations between estranged countries.

Ten months after America's **ping-pong diplomats** returned to the United States, Richard Nixon himself showed up in Beijing toasting Mao Zedong with glasses of rice wine. Because he had always been so adamantly anti-Communist, Nixon's visit to Red China stunned the world. But that very record was what allowed Nixon to shake Mao's hand without fear of being pilloried as "soft on Communism." Ever since then **Nixon-goes-to-China** has been the go-to allusion for a public figure who is best equipped to take a controversial step be-

cause of previous opposition to that step. When hawkish, pro-settlement Israeli prime minister Ariel Sharon ordered Jewish settlers to leave the Gaza Strip, references to *Nixon-goes-to-China* were ubiquitous.

---

### THE ORIGINAL 'GATE

During Richard Nixon's 1972 presidential race against George Mc-Govern, a group of men broke into Democratic National Committee headquarters on the sixth floor of Washington's Watergate complex. Five of them—equipped with bugging gear, cameras, and a walkie-talkie—were apprehended inside. Two days later White House press secretary Ron Ziegler dismissed this bungled venture as a **"third-rate burglary attempt."** In fact those arrested were a gang of so-called **plumbers** who had been assembled to, among other things, plug leaks to the press. They had broken into Democratic headquarters in search of information incriminating to its inhabitants. Because the aftermath of this crime caused such profound national trauma, and because those involved used such colorful tough-guy talk, the jargon associated with the Watergate break-in and its cover-up remained part of American discourse long after the plumbers and their supervisors had gone to prison and Nixon had left the White House in disgrace.

According to presidential counselor John Dean, during frantic attempts to cover up their involvement in the Watergate break-in, Nixon aide John Ehrlichman suggested that he *deep-six* a briefcase with incriminating documents. When Dean asked what that meant, Ehrlichman responded, "You drive across the river at night, don't you? Well, when you cross over the river on your way home, just toss the briefcase into the river." **Deep-six** turned out to be an old nautical term for throwing objects into the ocean's depths. (See chapter 9.)

Instead of tossing his briefcase into the Potomac, Dean placed its contents in a sealed envelope that he gave to acting FBI director L. Patrick Gray. Gray burned the envelope without opening it. Later he was subjected to intense grilling about his role in the Watergate cover-up by senators who were considering his nomination to become permanent FBI director. After it became clear that Gray's nomination was in trouble, John Ehrlichman (who went on to become a novelist) once again reached into his kit bag of vivid imagery when John Dean asked how he thought they should proceed. "I think we ought to let him hang there," Ehrlichman responded. "Let him twist slowly, slowly in the wind." This portrayal of Gray's doomed status was so evocative that **twisting in the wind** is still used for someone who has been left hanging.

Two weeks after Ehrlichman talked with Dean about Gray, Nixon gave top aides their Watergate marching orders: "I want you all to stonewall it, let them plead the Fifth Amendment, cover-up, or anything else." The term **stonewall** has outlived Nixon (who died in 1994) and to this day refers to those trying to hide transgressions. Its origins are unclear. One possible source is Confederate general Thomas Jackson, who earned the nickname "Stonewall" because he was said to have stood as firm as a stone wall during the first battle of Bull Run in 1861. *Stonewall* is also Australian cricket slang for a defensive strategy of blocking balls hit by opposing players, as if with a stone wall.

The discovery of audiotapes in which Nixon and his aides discussed how to cover up the growing scandal were said to constitute a **smoking gun**. Borrowed from detective stories, this term alluded to a just-fired gun clearly visible in the hand of a criminal. Today it refers more broadly to any conclusive evidence of wrongdoing. A website that posts incriminating documents is called www.thesmokinggun.com.

Perhaps the most enduring linguistic legacy of the Watergate episode was the application of **'gate** to other scandals such as *Irangate*, *Whitewatergate*, *Monicagate*, and *Nipplegate* (after Janet Jackson's breast was "accidentally" exposed during a Super Bowl halftime performance).

## Post-Nixon

During the early Democratic primaries of 1972, Edmund Muskie was the leading candidate to challenge Richard Nixon. Then, on a snowy day in New Hampshire, the tall, craggy senator from Maine choked up while protesting press attacks on his wife. Televised images of Muskie tearfully addressing a rally with snowflakes clinging to his eyebrows horrified American viewers. We didn't want a crybaby in the White House! In another time, of course, that moment would have earned him an immediate booking on *The Oprah Winfrey Show* and enthusiastic applause for his emotional candor. Back then, however, this single lachrymose episode effectively ended Ed Muskie's political career. Ever since, his name has become a common allusion when political figures choke up in public. During the 2008 presidential primaries, Republican Mitt Romney and Democrat Hillary Clinton both had misty-eyed episodes that the press dubbed **Muskie moments**. *New York Times* columnist Maureen Dowd said both were "doing the Muskie."

While running for president in 1976, Jimmy Carter told a *Playboy* reporter that he sometimes felt **"lust in my heart."** This surprising admission from the pious Democrat achieved lasting catchphrase status. *People*'s review of Norman Mailer's Jesus-based novel, *The Gospel According to the Son*, fretted that Mailer should have given his protagonist a bit of a sex life, "or at least a little lusting in the heart."

Witnessing Carter's 1980 race against Ronald Reagan was like watching Danny DeVito box with Muhammad Ali. During a televised debate, the one-time actor zinged his opponent with the well-rehearsed phrase **"There you go again."** After Reagan unleashed this patronizing remark, the smaller, less polished president just stood there with the stunned look of a third grader who's been shoved into a corner by a sixth grader. Reagan's putdown subsequently took on a life of its own. "There they go again," noted a *Newsweek* article about Republicans who shape their message for fervent followers.

Republican operatives worried obsessively about Carter unveiling a last-minute foreign policy initiative that would swing the 1980 election his way. "Let's be prepared for some *October surprise*," warned Reagan's running mate, George H. W. Bush. That concern has become common among challengers who face sitting presidents, and needn't even refer to something that takes place during October. An **October surprise** can be any event late in a campaign that changes its dynamics. This concept has achieved broader currency, referring to any unexpected occurrence with seminal impact. Skittish investors sometimes fret about *October surprises* on the financial scene.

When he ran for president himself in 1988, George H. W. Bush put a shaggy-haired thirty-seven-year-old named Lee Atwater in charge of his campaign. Although a hip rock guitarist in his spare time, Atwater was a ruthless political street fighter who created a template for negative campaigning. One of his most effective strategies was to approve attacks on Democratic nominee Michael Dukakis, Massachusetts' governor, based on convicted African-American murderer Willie Horton, who had terrorized a young married couple in Maryland while on furlough from a Massachusetts prison. One Republican ad featured a shadowy black figure in a revolving door meant to symbolize the "revolving door of justice" supposedly favored by Dukakis. In fact Dukakis had played no direct role in Horton's case or his state's furlough policy (which was signed into law by a Republican governor). Nonetheless, Atwater bragged that when it came to Dukakis, the Bush campaign would "make Willie Horton his running mate." After contracting terminal brain cancer in his early forties Atwater apologized to Dukakis for using tactics against him that smacked of racism. His legacy, however, was to show that such tactics *work*. The Willie Horton ad was instrumental in Dukakis's crushing defeat. After 1988, Republicans and Democrats alike increasingly used negative advertising based more on demolishing opponents than promoting themselves. When referring to strategies of that type, the name **Willie Horton** is routinely invoked. After being forced off the bench by public outcry over a decision he made, a federal appeals court judge warned about efforts to "Willie Hortonize the federal judiciary."

Bush himself tried to stay above his manager's bare-knuckles tactics. The Republican candidate came across as an amiable man of limited intellect who favored terms such as **deep doo-doo** and **the Big Mo** (referring to the momentum he felt his campaign had achieved). This contrasted with the Rhodes scholar mien of his 1992 opponent, Bill Clinton. Vulnerable to being seen as too liberal, Clinton seized an opportunity to suggest otherwise when soul singer Sister Souljah, following the internecine Watts riots, said, "If black people kill black people every day, why not have a week and kill white people?" Clinton rebuked the African-American musician. The fact that Jesse Jackson and other prominent liberal blacks criticized Clinton for this stand reinforced his credentials as a centrist. Since then, any politician who reprimands an apparent ally is said to have had a **Sister Souljah moment**. That singer's name also got verbed. When Bill Clinton later upbraided left-wing critics of his wife Hillary's Iraq war policy, a liberal blogger asked, "Are we being 'Sistah Souljah'd' already?"

Bill Clinton's main political problem was keeping his pants zipped when a *bimbo* was in the vicinity. *Bimbo* is a contraction of *bambino*, Italian for "baby." Although early in the twentieth century this term referred to men of loose morals, in the 1920s it switched genders. In the late 1980s comely young women caught in the arms of prominent married men were routinely called *bimbos*. During the 1992 primaries, Clinton's aides grew terrified about the prospect of so-called **bimbo eruptions**. What most concerned Clintonians was the possibility that a real-live **smoking bimbo** would appear on the nightly news with irrefutable evidence that she'd coupled with the candidate. Even those who realized this verbal alloy referred to a confirmed Clinton coupling didn't necessarily make the connection to *smoking guns* (see "The Original 'Gate" sidebar above). This term caught the public's fancy. We rather enjoyed the titillating image of a young woman with big hair and bigger breasts enjoying a postcoital cigarette while lying next to the man who would become our next president.

Smoking of another kind posed a bit of a problem for the Democratic nominee. When Clinton said he'd tried marijuana as a young man but **"didn't inhale,"** this transparent dodge instantly became a catchphrase signifying all manner of cockamamie evasion. After Republican operative Karl Rove defended himself against charges that he'd revealed the identity of CIA agent Valerie Plame, a commentary in *Editor & Publisher* magazine said his careful parsing of language "sounds like an I-did-not-inhale defense." That type of evasive, hair-splitting approach became known as **Clintonian** or **Clintonesque**.

# 6. From Levittown to Jonestown

**T**wo years after World War II ended, a convoy of trucks showed up in a potato field outside Hicksville, Long Island. Every sixty feet they dropped off prepackaged bundles of boards, bricks, shingles, and piping. Backhoes then excavated a twenty-five-by-thirty-two-foot trench beside each bundle. Cement trucks followed, pouring concrete into these rectangular trenches. After the concrete dried, successive teams of men raised trusses, laid bricks, nailed laths, shingled roofs, installed plumbing, strung electrical wires, put up drywall, and painted walls. Each such sequence produced a house. By 1951 17,447 virtually identical houses had been built this way. Buyers—veterans mostly, all of them white—could choose among six somewhat different designs. They paid no money down and assumed a monthly payment of $65 for their $6,990 homes.

The developer of these homes was a bluff, chain-smoking navy veteran named William Levitt. Levitt went on to build three more such assembly-line communities, in Pennsylvania, New Jersey, and Puerto Rico. Each was named *Levittown*. Americans who could afford custom homes were put off by the uniformity of these mass-produced houses—some 130,000 in all—and, by implication, those who bought them. Their apparent sterility was thought to typify stultifying suburban life in general. The fact that Levitt's developments mandated weekly lawn mowing, forbade fences, and even dictated what type of clothesline residents could use and when they could use it did nothing to dispel that stereotype. As a result, **Levittown** became shorthand for lockstep conformity.

To the horror of many, similar communities popped up all over the country after the war. In her 1962 song "Little Boxes," folk singer Malvina Reynolds bemoaned "Little boxes on the hillside / Little boxes made of ticky tacky." Ever since then **ticky-tacky** has been our preferred catchphrase for uniform homes and those thought to live in them. In the words of one blogger, "Forget trying to convince ticky tacky people that fossil fuel emissions contribute to global warming."

Throughout the 1950s an elite band of social critics looked askance at the conformity and anomie they saw in a society typified by suburban housing developments. The titles of some of their books—David Riesman's *The Lonely Crowd*, William H. Whyte's *The Organization Man*, and Sloan Wilson's *The Man in the Gray Flannel Suit*—became enduring catchphrases. Wilson's best-seller portrayed corporate executives whose passion to conform was symbolized by their matching single-breasted suits. This novel acquired its iconic title when the author's wife told his editor that her journalist husband was surrounded by "all those men in gray flannel suits" at Time-Life. The editor, Richard Simon, leaped on this phrase as the title of her husband's book, then himself donned a gray flannel suit to model for its jacket photo. Although few have read Sloan Wilson's novel in recent years, many still use the phrase **gray flannel suit** or simply **gray flannel** as shorthand for careful conformists. The *New York Times* once referred to the "gray-flannel style" of Hong Kong's chief executive Tung Chee-hwa, then headlined a profile of National Security Adviser Stephen Hadley "Cautious Man in Gray Flannel."

Postwar **organization men** who worked in corporate settings increasingly saw themselves as engaged in a *rat race*. This alluded to experiments involving white rats made to run unwinnable races on treadmills or in revolving wheels. As more and more human beings felt that they too were running in place, the phrase **rat race** became an allusion to fast-paced, overstressed, on-a-treadmill lives.

To unwind, those who felt caught up in rat racing bought **paint-by-numbers** kits. Introduced in the early 1950s, these popular kits allowed hobbyists to daub premixed oils into prenumbered sections of predrawn pictures—anything from a mournful circus clown to Michelangelo's *The Last Supper*. Judges at a contest for numbers painters were advised that "neatness" was the primary criterion for winning entries, and that "pictures should be painted strictly according to the numbered canvas." Long after number-painting sets had been taken to Goodwill, their name lived on to signify lack of imagination. According to playwright David Mamet, too many actors take a "paint-by-numbers" approach to their craft, ticking off emotions and character traits on a predetermined checklist. The terser phrase *by the numbers* dates back to World War I, when each procedure of routine tasks being learned by American soldiers was numbered. A **by-the-numbers** approach still alludes to doing exactly what one is instructed to do.

All was not backyard barbecues and number painting in the conformist 1950s. Well into that decade polio struck down American children by the thousands, as it had every summer since the First World War. In 1952 alone some fifty-eight thousand American children contracted polio, the worst year ever. Many of those lucky enough to survive ended up sitting in wheelchairs, lying in iron lungs, or walking stiffly with braces on their legs. To try to conquer polio, the National Foundation for Infantile Paralysis created posters of young victims wearing heavy metal braces and supporting themselves with crutches. These *poster children* headlined a "March of Dimes" campaign in which schoolchildren were urged to insert dimes in slots on small cards. One poster showed a before-and-after picture of a boy wearing, then not wearing, a neck brace. "Your dimes did this for me!" it read. In another, a dimpled little girl arose from her wheelchair. Its caption was "Look! I can walk again." The March of Dimes campaign made such a deep impression that decades after polio succumbed to Jonas Salk's discovery of a vaccine in 1954 we still use the term **poster child, poster boy**, or **poster girl** metaphorically, as when a *Washington Post* writer called Franz Kafka a "poster boy of twentieth-century alienation," and one at the *New York Times* referred to Newark, New Jersey, as a "poster child for inner-city decay."

The fifties were not nearly as one-dimensional as we like to imagine. In retrospect, counter-currents to conformity can be seen in the birth of rock 'n' roll, growing sexual candor, and what was then called "juvenile delinquency." Evan Hunter's 1954 novel *Blackboard Jungle* portrayed Rick Dadier, a young teacher in an inner-city high school struggling to teach rowdy delinquents who call him "Daddy-O." The riveting portrayal of classroom mayhem in a 1955 movie based on Hunter's book and its throbbing sound track featuring "Rock Around the Clock" by Bill Haley and the Comets made watching *Blackboard Jungle* an electrifying experience for teenagers, and an alarming one for their parents. This was an opening salvo in the youth revolt to come. More than half a century later **blackboard jungle** remains shorthand for beleaguered teachers and out-of-control students. When Bill and Melinda Gates began making grants to improve troubled public schools, *Newsweek* said they were "taking on the blackboard jungle."

The mother of all juvenile-delinquency films was called *The Wild One*. Loosely based on an actual incident in the late 1940s, this 1951 movie featured a motorcycle gang led by Marlon Brando that takes over a small town. The lasting impact of Brando's booted, leather-jacketed, visor-capped fashion statement can be seen on the streets of any American city (and some foreign ones as well). The movie's only memorable dialogue takes place when a woman asks Brando's character, "Hey, Johnny, what are you rebelling against?" "Whadda ya got?" mumbles Brando. More than half a century after it was released, *The Wild One* is still referred to, often, when one or more bikers gather. Although Brando rode a Triumph Thunderbird, the *Dayton Daily News* thought Harley-Davidson motorcycles stood for "an entire *Wild One* way of life."

Brando's bikers looked like scrawny Hell's Angels but talked like Bay Area hepcats. For a long time we didn't know quite what to call folks whose talk was rich with interjections of "man," and "cool" and "crazy!" One April day in 1958, *San Francisco Chronicle* columnist Herb Caen wrote about a group of goateed, beret-wearing poets and writers who recited poetry in smoky North Beach jazz clubs with bongo drum accompaniment. They called themselves *beats*, members of the *beat generation*. Caen called them *beatniks*. This was a play on the word *Sputnik*, what Russia called the space satellite it launched in 1957. In Russian the suffix *nik* means "one who." Variations on this theme eventually included *peacenik*, *neatnik*, *no-goodnik*, and *refusenik*. **Beatnik** itself largely disappeared along with bereted poetry reciters but still brings to mind a scruffy nonconformist who likes to read verse while someone beats on a bongo drum. The antonym to *beatnik* was **square**, or hopelessly unhip. Writer David Halberstam liked to call himself "a square from the fifties."

## Sex After the War

The sex education of many a postwar American teenager consisted of reading Grace Metalious's 1956 bestseller *Peyton Place*. "Betty's back arched against his arm as she thrust her breasts up to him," they read. "Her nipples were always rigid and exciting and full, firm flesh around them always hot and throbbing." In a pre-porn era, Metalious's potboiler about the randy residents of a small New England town was the hottest thing available over the counter. *Peyton Place* sold sixty thousand copies in its first ten days on the market. Over time, some twenty million copies were purchased, more than the combined sales of respectable authors such as Ernest Hemingway and Virginia Woolf. An estimated one in six Americans at least leafed through this book. *Peyton Place* was made into a 1957 movie with the same title, then a 1964–69 television series that featured serial bed-hopping. Today **Peyton Place** alludes to any setting where lots of illicit behavior is concealed by a thin veneer of respectability. The founder of a workshop for writers once observed that its constant shouting matches, near fights, and sexual static made it "the Peyton Place of writers' groups."

Reading Alfred Kinsey's *Sexual Behavior in the Human Male* (1948) and *Sexual Behavior in the Human Female* (1953) wasn't nearly as exciting as reading *Peyton Place*. Kinsey, a Ph.D. zoologist with a brush cut and a bow tie who taught at the University of Indiana, surrounded his titillating findings with statistics, tables, and impenetrable prose. Kinsey's research is no longer considered reliable because it was based on an unrepresentative sample of volunteer subjects. The zoologist apparently took liberties in reporting findings, encouraged assistants to copulate with each other's spouses before movie cameras, and concealed his own predilection for sleeping with members of both sexes behind a facade of detached scholarship. Kinsey's tolerant attitude toward voyeurism and pedophilia would raise eyebrows today. At the time, however, his heavily footnoted volumes—generically called the *Kinsey Reports*—gave us an excuse to talk about sex in the guise of discussing scholarship. No one was more instrumental in knocking down American sexual taboos. Alfred Kinsey validated that sex is okay, different kinds of sex are okay, variety in sex is okay too, and talking about sex in all its varieties is healthy. Today this sounds obvious, but in part that's because Kinsey helped loosen us up. And that is why the term **Kinsey** alone still evokes a quasi-scholarly acceptance of sexuality. To this day sex surveys are routinely called *Kinsey-like*.

Alfred Kinsey had a midwestern comrade-in-arms named Hugh Hefner who also toiled tirelessly during the fifties to conquer sexual taboos. The product of a repressed, puritanical upbringing outside Chicago, Hefner published the first issue of a magazine he called *Playboy* in 1953. After its debut, featuring what became a classic picture of Marilyn Monroe with nothing on but the radio (as she put it), Hefner strove—with some success—to make *Playboy* not just a nudie magazine but one that would transform American attitudes toward sex. Its strategy was to mingle busty, well-photographed naked women with substantial articles, stories, interviews, and ponderous essays by Hefner himself explaining the *Playboy philosophy* (essentially, if it feels good and hurts no one else, do it). More than half a century after Hefner became a magazine publisher, right-wing commentator Ann Coulter accused public schools of teaching an "amalgam of liberalism, feminism, Darwinism, and the *Playboy* philosophy."

Despite its efforts to be more than a mere skin mag, the terms *Playboy* bequeathed to American discourse had more to do with naked women than with thoughtful men. Because the Playmate of the Month was highlighted in a two- or three-page picture that folded out from the middle of the magazine, the term **centerfold**, or **foldout**, suggested women with melon-sized breasts and pea-sized brains. Onetime Playmate of the Year Anna Nicole Smith was sometimes referred to as *a centerfold*.

## Protesting

On October 1, 1964, a twenty-four-year-old University of California dropout named Jack Weinberg was arrested for handing out literature on the University of California's Berkeley campus. After Weinberg was placed in a police car, hundreds of students and sympathizers who surrounded that car, kept it from moving for thirty-two hours. Two months later nearly eight hundred protesters were arrested in Berkeley. When the *San Francisco Chronicle* sent an older reporter to cover this event, Jack Weinberg needled him by commenting, "We have a saying in the movement that you can't trust anybody over thirty." Weinberg himself made up this adage. It quickly became a youth movement credo. As baby boomers got further and further away from their third decade of life, **You can't trust anyone** fill in the blank became a multipurpose catchphrase.

The 1964 Berkeley protests came to be known as the Free Speech Movement. That movement kicked off what we now think of as "the sixties." In fact this era lasted from the midsixties to the midseventies (i.e., from the Berkeley protests to the end of the Vietnam War). Demonstrations were its essence, against the war in Vietnam especially. During the protest era, **warmonger** came to refer to one considered preternaturally disposed to settle disputes with firearms. *Warmonger* gave way to **peacemonger**, then to a wide range of other mongers ("scandalmonger," "rumormonger," etc.). Originating in the sixteenth century, this term referred to humbler pursuits of peddlers or tradesmen, as in "fishmonger" or "ironmonger." Undoubtedly we have many more types of *mongering* to come.

Singing was integral to protesting. At left-wing summer camps, on college campuses, and within protest movements, a good day of dissent was often capped with a rousing rendition of "Kumbaya." This song was based on a nineteenth-century spiritual sung by the Gullah, descendants of African slaves on the Sea Islands off South Carolina and Georgia. Its name means "come by here." Today that song's title evokes an image of earnest activists seated around a campfire holding hands and crooning their anthem with glistening eyeballs. Singer-actress Sara Ramirez once called her folky upbringing "very Kumbaya." In recent years **Kumbaya** has become synonymous with starry-eyed idealism. Reference has been made, for example, to "peace-loving, Kumbaya people" and "the Kumbaya wing of the Democratic Party." One stock analyst characterized unexpected talks between bitter rivals Microsoft and Novell as "a Kumbaya moment." Idealistic tendencies in general are sometimes called **Kumbayaish**.

A darker side of sixties–seventies movements came to light in early 1974 when nineteen-year-old newspaper heiress Patty Hearst was kidnapped in Berkeley by a self-styled revolutionary group called the Symbionese Liberation Army. Several weeks later Hearst showed up in San Francisco's Hibernia Bank brandishing an assault rifle while taking part in a robbery. She subsequently issued manifestos on behalf of the SLA under the nom de guerre "Tania." After being arrested in late 1975, Patty Hearst claimed she'd been coerced into taking part in SLA activities by psychological, physical, and sexual abuse. At the time this claim seemed outlandish. Since then there have been so many other cases in which the kidnapped ally themselves with their kidnappers that this phenomenon even has a name: **Stockholm syndrome**. That's because just a few months before Hearst was kidnapped, a Swedish criminal seized four Stockholm bank employees and held them hostage in a vault for over five days. Upon being freed the four had little bad to say about their captor and a colleague who joined him. One hostage subsequently married a man who'd kidnapped her. In the United States that type of conversion under duress is sometimes called **Patty Hearst syndrome.**

## Feminists and Fish

The heady days of early feminism are often recalled as ones in which skies glowed red from the flames of burning brassieres. In fact there is no evidence that any bra was ever burned in anger. This presumed rallying cry of liberated women can be traced to a 1968 protest against the Miss America pageant. Those involved were invited to discard symbols of restriction, such as brassieres. Although none went up in flames, so many other things *were* being burned at the time—flags, draft cards, overturned cars—that it wasn't hard to imagine blazing bras as well. This was an exciting thought. We're still so attached to this image that the birth of modern feminism is often called a **bra-burning** era, one that was filled with **bra burners.** Then and now avowals of respectable feminism are commonly introduced with "I'm no bra burner but . . ."

*Libbers* were often accused of being humorless neo-prudes. To refute that charge a jest was put in play, usually attributed to *Ms.* magazine cofounder Gloria Steinem. That jest was "*A woman needs a man like a fish needs a bicycle.*" Not exactly a knee-slapper, but you get the point. Steinem herself never claimed the epigram originated with her, and disowned authorship on more than one occasion. Apparently an Australian activist named Irina Dunn coined it in 1970, adapting a phrase she said she'd read in a philosophy text: "A man needs God like a fish needs a bicycle." This version had long been commonplace among atheists. **Like a fish needs a bicycle** remains in play, implying uselessness.

In the premier issue of *Ms.*, Jane O'Reilly wrote a much-discussed article on the awakening of feminist sensibilities. "American women are angry," wrote O'Reilly. "Not redneck-angry from screaming because we are so frustrated and unfulfilled-angry, but clicking-things-into-place-angry, because we have suddenly and shockingly perceived the basic disorder in what has been believed to be the natural order of things." Each litany of social outrages against women O'Reilly depicted was followed by the term *Click!* For a long time after this article was published, **Click!**—signifying a moment of recognition (sort of a

movement counterpart to the overhead lightbulb going on in comic strips)—
enjoyed wide currency, and it can still be heard on occasion. One review of a
memoir by feminist Susan Brownmiller referred to the "feminist 'click'" she
experienced at a **consciousness-raising group** in 1968. These once-common
feminist gatherings were alluded to in a 2007 account of a workshop for home
health aides that the *New York Times* characterized as a "quasi-consciousness-
raising group."

Although it was not a feminist tract as such, the 1973 publication of Erica
Jong's bestselling novel *Fear of Flying* was, and is, considered a milestone in the
sexual liberation of women. Among the many types of tryst that Erica Jong depicted, one in particular caught the reading public's fancy: a spontaneous, passionate, drawer-dropping, short-lived, guilt-free coupling that Jong termed
*zipless.* "Zipless," she wrote, "because when you came together zippers fell away
like rose petals, underwear blew off in one breath like dandelion fluff. Tongues
intertwined and turned liquid. Your whole soul flowed out through your
tongue and into the mouth of your love." To this day **zipless** can refer to any
transient event, as when *New Yorker* writer Jon Lee Anderson referred to an
abortive "zipless coup" in Iraq.

## Sages of Aquarius

In the summer of 1966, media maven Marshall McLuhan advised drug guru
Timothy Leary to come up with a slogan that would capture the public's imagination. After much rumination, six words popped into Leary's head as he was
taking a shower. "Dripping wet," Leary wrote in his 1983 autobiography, "with
a towel around my waist, I walked to the study and wrote down this phrase:
'Turn On, Tune In, Drop Out.'" The former Harvard professor had noodled
with variations on this theme for years, including "Turn On or Bail Out," and
"Drop out, turn on, tune in." The best sequence was not always clear, to Leary
or those recording his words. Sometimes the media reported that *turning on*
came first, sometimes *tuning in.* At times Dr. Leary himself would exhort listeners to *turn on and tune in,* and other times to *tune in and turn on.* In 1966 he
founded the League for Spiritual Discovery, calling it "a legally incorporated
religion dedicated to the ancient sacred sequence of turning on, tuning in, and
dropping out." This catchphrase did its attention-getting job. **Turn on, tune in,
drop out** became the mantra of drug-using members of the *counterculture.*

Others picked up the beat. An ad campaign for Squirt soda pop urged customers to "Turn on to flavor, tune into sparkle, and drop out of the cola rut." Evangelist Billy Graham conducted a European crusade on the theme of "Turn on [to] Christ, tune in to the Bible, and drop out of sin."

Some social dropouts began distributing flowers to startled passersby on the streets of cities such as Philadelphia and San Francisco. Flowers played an important symbolic role in this countercultural revolution. In the words of Scott McKenzie's 1967 hit song "San Francisco," "If you're going to San Francisco / Be sure to wear some flowers in your hair." When confronted by National Guardsmen carrying rifles during unruly demonstrations, protesters placed blossoms in the barrels of rifles pointed at them (at least until four anti-war demonstrators were shot dead by National Guardsmen at Ohio's Kent State University in 1970). Flowers were also a common component of hippie design: on posters, or the sides of Volkswagens. It was the era of **flower culture, flower children, flower power**. Those phrases still evoke a certain type of hip or post-hip person. Or not. As *Newsweek*'s Howard Fineman pointed out, even though she lives in San Francisco, Baltimore-born House Speaker Nancy Pelosi "is no flower child."

On a rainy weekend in mid-August 1969, an event occurred that many thought epitomized the sixties. This was the rock festival held on Max Yasgur's farm near Woodstock, New York, that attracted far more long-haired, bead-wearing, dope-smoking, candle-waving, mantra-chanting flower children than were expected—some four hundred thousand in all. News photos of mud-splattered revelers cavorting naked in the rain got America's attention. In the fevered imagination of straight and hip alike there must have been lots of *hanky-panky* going on in Woodstock's fields, kind of like mud wrestling with benefits. To participants themselves—in fact and in spirit—it presaged an idyllic life in the making. They considered this concert a gathering of youth tribes who practiced what they preached. It did not take long for *Woodstock* to refer not only to an event but to a state of mind. This wasn't just a rock festival but a show of generational strength. In the words of Joni Mitchell's tribute song "Woodstock," "By the time we got to Woodstock / We were half a million strong." This weekend was so tectonic-shifting that far more baby boomers later claimed to have been at Max Yasgur's farm than actually were. They wanted to be part of what came to be called **Woodstock nation**.

To many, peace, love, and brotherhood seemed just over the horizon in this era. Some thought it was an astrological age in which old bonds of repression were being broken and a freer life was not only possible but inevitable. This was the **Age of Aquarius**. The key stanza in the song "Aquarius" from the 1967 musical *Hair*—"This is the dawning of the age of Aquarius"—helped popularize that notion. Since war, enmity, and repression were at least as prevalent as peace, love, and brotherhood as the sixties became the seventies, this concept didn't last long. Through the wistful mists of memory, however, we still like to think of that period as an **Aquarian** era.

---

### WOLFE'S SIXTIES AND SEVENTIES

Tom Wolfe's 1968 book *The Electric Kool-Aid Acid Test* depicted novelist Ken Kesey and his Merry Pranksters (including journalist Hunter Thompson and novelist Robert Stone) as they rode on a Day Glo–painted school bus from the West Coast to the East, sipping LSD-laced Kool-Aid along the way. According to its flap copy, Wolfe's book portrayed "what is popularly known as *the hippy*." In doing so Wolfe popularized the notion that "you're either **on the bus**, or you're **off the bus**," part of the scene or hopelessly out of it.

At the top of his form, Tom Wolfe was a genius-grade coiner, purloiner, and popularizer of catchphrases. In mid-1970 Wolfe wrote a scathing *New York* magazine article about a fund-raiser for Black Panthers held at the posh Manhattan apartment of conductor Leonard Bernstein. It was titled "Radical Chic: That Party at Lenny's." Wolfe repeatedly hammered home his key catchphrase. "Radical Chic invariably favors radicals who seem primitive, exotic, and romantic," he wrote. "Radical Chic . . . is only radical in style; in its heart it is part of Society and its traditions." Although Wolfe succeeded in injecting that phrase into public discourse, it did not originate with him. *Radical chic* was coined by Seymour Krim in a 1962 essay criticizing the fashionable but superficial sympathy for black causes that he thought characterized *New Yorker* writers. As it became de rigueur for the likes of George Clooney and Barbra Streisand to moonlight as left activists, **radical chic** enjoyed a verbal renaissance.

In another 1970 essay, "Mau-Mauing the Flak Catchers," Tom Wolfe reported on the intimidation of public officials by black activists. "If you were outrageous enough," wrote Wolfe, "if you could shake up the bureaucrats so bad that their eyes froze into iceballs and their mouths twisted into smiles of sheer physical panic . . . then they knew you were the real goods. They knew you were the right studs to give the poverty grants and community organizing jobs to." The operative phrase in Wolfe's essay came from the name given Kenyan insurgents who resisted British colonial rule after World War II. Back then *Mau Mau* was strictly a noun. Today, in the United States anyway, it is more likely to be a verb used in the Wolfeian sense. **Mau-Mauing** is still applied to those who shake down bureaucrats by threatening to engage in disruptive behavior.

Tom Wolfe was instrumental in giving the post-Aquarian era its most enduring label. He accomplished this in a 1976 essay that called the 1970s "a period that will come to be known as the Me Decade." The white-suited author was right, of course, in large part because he worked hard to put his prediction on the demographic map. The unbridled narcissism that Wolfe (and many others) saw unleashed during the seventies led to its being called what he said it would be called: **the me decade.**

## Touching and Feeling

Those not in a position to turn on, tune in, or drop out during the Age of Aquarius or the Me Decade sometimes did the next best thing: they took part in the *human potential movement* (so called in recognition of psychologist Abraham Maslow, whose theories focused on the human potential to grow). This New Age antecedent incorporated sensitivity training, T-groups, encounter groups, and sundry other activities in which participants worked on touching, hugging, and being freer with their feelings. Such events were sometimes called **touchy-feely**. We still pin this label on that type of experience. Attempts to make military officers more aware of soldiers' needs have been disparaged as "touchy-feely."

The sixties and seventies were chock-full of genuine and self-described therapists who offered a smorgasbord of techniques for becoming looser, happier, and more self-actualized. California psychologist Arthur Janov believed that only by reliving early, primal feelings such as terror at sliding through our mother's birth canal could we hope to achieve emotional equilibrium. One technique Janov employed was having patients shout out that sense of panic. So-called *primal therapy* or *primal screaming* (the press's term, not Janov's) enjoyed quite a vogue for a time, attracting John Lennon, among others. Many of the songs on Lennon's album *Plastic Ono Band* grew directly out of his experience with Janov, leading some to call it his "primal." album. A rock band later called itself Primal Scream. When Howard Dean unleashed his famous shout during the 2004 presidential primaries, journalists predictably called it a **primal scream**. This confused younger cohorts. Why reference a rock group?

Human-potential therapies began to decline in conjunction with a book written in 1977 by journalist R. D. Rosen. That book was called *Psychobabble*. In it Rosen lambasted all the touching and feeling and primal screaming and its attendant jargon, or "babble." Few people read this book, but its title provided just the word detractors were looking for to belittle new forms of therapy. "Psychobabble" quickly became part of everyday discourse. Since most of those who used that term didn't even realize there was a book by this title, its author said he felt as though his own child had been adopted without his consent. "That's the last word I ever invent," R. D. Rosen vowed. Three decades after he coined it, the term **psychobabble** was more ubiquitous than ever, its origins less well known. Inevitably it became a verb as well as a noun. "Nobody wants to psychobabble through their birthday party," wrote columnist Ellen Goodman.

## Kool-Aid

San Francisco's sixties and seventies were filled not just with therapists galore but with a wide range of crypto-gurus who promised salvation along with counterculture. None did so more successfully than the Reverend Jim Jones, founder of the People's Temple. In its early days this largely African American group did commendable community-action work in the Bay Area while rescuing many members from dysfunctional behavior. A combination of Martin Luther King and Huey Long, Jones preached a theology that blended racial justice and wealth sharing. Over time he grew increasingly authoritarian. Public beatings were administered to People's Temple dissenters. Attractive young congregants were pressured into sexual liaisons with their pastor. Fearing investigation by federal authorities, in 1974 Jones moved his entire congregation to three thousand acres of leased land in Guyana's jungle. In what he called "Jonestown," Jones made followers work six days a week on a farm patrolled by armed guards. Captured runaways were imprisoned in small wooden boxes. Creative forms of discipline included lowering children into wells where "devils" (adult congregants) grabbed at their legs. Jonestown residents were expected to call their leader "Dad." Over time **Jonestown** became an analogy for cultlike experiences. To depict her fanatic devotion to her marriage, a character in Nick Hornby's novel *How to Be Good* says, "I am experiencing my own personal Jonestown."

Four years after Jim Jones moved to Guyana, American officials began to take an interest in him. Jones warned followers that it might be necessary to commit suicide en masse. When Congressman Leo Ryan (D-Calif.), some of whose constituents had relatives in Jonestown, traveled to Guyana to investigate, the People's Temple founder prepared his group for Armageddon. Jones first had a male follower kill Ryan and members of his investigating team. He then ordered congregants to drink paper cups of a grape drink laced with Valium and cyanide dipped from two metal tubs. Of 1,110 Jonestown residents, 913 did just that, including 276 children (some of whom had the drink squirted down their throats). Seeing pictures of so many bodies of men, women, and children littering Guyanan ground horrified Americans. Their horror was compounded by the realization that these deaths came from drinking a sugary beverage associated with childhood innocence. If Kool-Aid could kill you, what couldn't? In fact it wasn't Kool-Aid that Jones's followers drank but a knockoff called Flavor Aid. Nonetheless, **drinking Kool-Aid** eventually became synonymous with blind allegiance. This catchphrase took time to come into widespread use, not becoming ubiquitous until early 2000s. After that it has been heard constantly, in different forms, including **Kool-Aid drinker** to refer to mindless followers of another person or ideology. Struck by the uniformity of statements Apple computer employees made to him, a *Time* reporter concluded, "Not only have they all drunk the Kool-Aid; they all have the same favorite flavor."

# 7. Law and Order

On July 21, 1692, my ancestor Mary Lacey appeared before a panel of inquisitors in Salem, Massachusetts. Eighteen at the time, Mary was suspected of practicing witchcraft. The allegations were true, Mary admitted. She had indeed practiced witchcraft. At times she traveled above treetops on a pole. A fellow witch named Richard Carrier sometimes joined her on this pole. They were carried by the devil himself, a black man in a high-crowned hat. Not only that, her mother and grandmother practiced witchcraft as well.

Mary Lacey's confession did not take place in a vacuum. Two years earlier a Boston clergyman named Cotton Mather had published a book in which he sounded the alarm about "Damnable *Witchcraft*" and "prodigious *Witch-meetings*." This popular tome created a climate of suspicion about *witches in our midst* that led to the interrogation of suspects in Salem. Mather took an active part in these so-called trials, intervening at times to make sure that those convicted didn't get off easy. Although he later regretted his role in this episode, the name **Cotton Mather** still evokes an image of puritanical persecution.

Because she was so candid about her witchy ways, the Salem tribunal went easy on Mary Lacey. She was only incarcerated for a year and subjected now and again to what future inquisitors would call "enhanced interrogation." Others were not so fortunate. Mary's mother died in prison after several sessions of enhanced interrogation. Richard Carrier's mother, Martha, was hanged, due in part to testimony against her by her son. Eighteen other men and women were also hanged in Salem for practicing witchcraft, and one man was pressed to death under rocks. Alluding to the vigorous pursuit of witches in Massachusetts and elsewhere, the term **witch hunt** lives on as a reference to persecution in the guise of prosecution. (See discussion of Joseph McCarthy in chapter 5.)

## Trials

Long before Cotton Mather got on their case, witches had been hunted in Europe and England. During the Middle Ages it was common to "try" witches and heretics of all kinds by subjecting them to a physical ordeal. God would protect the innocent, it was assumed, allowing only the guilty to suffer (thus confirming their guilt). That was the theory, anyway. **Trial by fire** was a popular technique, one in which defendants were subjected to extreme heat, such as a long path of hot coals they were forced to traverse barefoot. We hark back to that test whenever we say someone has been **hauled** or **raked over the coals**— subjected to a harrowing, if not literally hot, ordeal. Another way of referring to this type of experience is having one's feet **held to the fire**.

From the late 1400s until the mid-1600s, some English noblemen were tried in special proceedings at Westminster Palace. Recalcitrant defendants were whipped, put in the pillory, had their ears cropped, or were encouraged in other ways to be more forthcoming. The proceedings themselves dispensed with witnesses or juries. Decisions could not be appealed. Since stars were painted on the ceiling of the room in which these "trials" took place, they came to be known as **star chamber proceedings**. This name endured to characterize any secret, extralegal, arbitrary tribunal. America's improvised hearings for accused terrorists after 9/11 have sometimes been called star chamber proceedings.

King George I was an obnoxious German-born monarch who saw no reason to learn English while ruling England from 1714 to 1727. Needless to say this did not endear him to his subjects. Nor did the fact that he divorced and imprisoned his wife while putting mistresses on the royal payroll. After a group protesting the king's high-handedness grew unruly, George demanded that Parliament pass a so-called Riot Act in 1714. One provision of this law "for preventing tumults and riotous assemblies" could be read to any group of twelve or more deemed to be unruly. "Our Sovereign Lord the King chargeth and commandeth all persons being assembled immediately to disperse themselves," they were warned, "and peaceably depart to their habitations, or to their lawful business." Those who did not depart within an hour were subject to long prison terms. From this practice derives the modern term **read the riot act,** or sternly warn a person or group about the consequences of their behavior.

During the American revolution against George III's rule, a western Virginia planter and militia colonel named Charles Lynch headed an informal tribunal that punished alleged criminals and loyalists. Even though it sometimes seized defendants' property or ordered them flogged, Colonel Lynch's court is known to have executed only one defendant, a slave named Hampton who was hanged and quartered for allegedly poisoning his owner's wife. Lynch's methods were well known in Virginia during and after the war. He himself used the term "Lynch Law" for his extrajudicial proceedings. The tens of thousands of Virginians who later migrated west and south took this notion with them. When dispensing vigilante justice, they were fond of saying malefactors had been hauled before "Judge Lynch." This was considered a playful way of alluding to the whipping or worse that lay in store for those suspected of misbehavior. After a Vicksburg, Mississippi, mob hanged five gamblers in 1835, references to *Judge Lynch* and *Lynch's Law* grew common in newspapers. This spawned a new verb: to *lynch*. After the Civil War, **lynching** most often referred to the frequent hanging of African-Americans throughout the United States, especially below the Mason-Dixon Line. The groups that engaged in this practice were called **lynch mobs.** Their punishment-first, trial-never form of jurisprudence was called **lynch law.** We still use this term to characterize extralegal executions, usually by hanging, typically by a frenzied mob. Clarence Thomas called Senate hearings on his appointment as a Supreme Court justice "a high-tech lynching" when questions were raised about his personal conduct. Thomas's future colleague, Justice Antonin Scalia, subsequently defended a proposed military tribunal for suspected terrorists by saying it would not be a "necktie party." This alluded to nineteenth-century frontier slang for a hanging that followed a summary proceeding: **a necktie party**.

## Punishment

The punishments meted out to someone arbitrarily convicted of a misdeed could be as imaginative as the proceedings themselves. One inducement to change his ways consisted of covering the naked body of an accused miscreant with molten tar, throwing feathers on the tar, then escorting him out of town on a rail. One of Abraham Lincoln's favorite stories featured a tarred and feathered man being carried out of town this way. When asked how he was enjoying this experience, the man responded that if it weren't for the honor he'd just as soon walk. In use since the Middle Ages, tarring and feathering was an especially popular way to deal with loyalists during the Revolution and with abolitionists who ventured south before the Civil War. Today we say that someone has been **tarred and feathered** when that person is besmirched in any way. As a reader wrote *USA Today*, when Army General Eric Shinseki accurately predicted that hundreds of thousands of troops would be needed to secure Iraq, "he was tarred and feathered."

A century ago, many American prisoners were made to march with their right hand resting on the right shoulder of the man before them. With heads bowed, no talking allowed, they could only shuffle awkwardly in what was called a *lock-step shuffle*. An 1899 documentary filmed at Newcastle,

Delaware's county jail that portrayed convicts marching this way was titled *The Lock Step*. This vivid term jumped the prison walls and now refers to any group acting in a rigidly uniform way. They are in **lockstep**. According to the *Wall Street Journal*, Republican congressional leaders enforce "lockstep party discipline."

## Cops and Robbers

In 1963 Ernesto Arturo Miranda was arrested in Phoenix for stealing $8. After being interrogated by police, the slight, bespectacled thief signed a statement confessing not only to stealing $8 but to raping an eighteen-year-old woman. However, because his interrogators neglected to warn Miranda that he had a right to remain silent, not make self-incriminating statements, and have an attorney present when being questioned, the U.S. Supreme Court acquitted Miranda in 1966. Ever since then American police officers have been legally bound to warn suspects of these rights in what became known as a **Miranda warning**, one that recognized suspects' **Miranda rights**. Over time this allusion came to characterize punctilious concern for human rights of all kinds. In a *New York Times* column, Thomas Friedman wrote that some Middle Eastern nations crushed Islamic uprisings "without mercy or Miranda rights." As so often happens, this phrase became not only a noun but a verb: to **Mirandize**, or advise those accused of breaking a law about their rights. Of the movie *Mulholland Falls*, in which he played a freewheeling 1950s Los Angeles cop, actor Nick Nolte said, "This is a world pre-Mirandized."

Pre- and post-Miranda, a classic interrogation technique involved having one police officer bully a suspect, another befriend him. "If you won't talk we can't guarantee your safety," the first could say ominously. "But I can understand why you're finding it hard to confess," the second might chime in. Theoretically, anxiety generated by the menacing interrogator was followed by the relief of dealing with an empathetic "good cop." A confession followed. The **good cop–bad cop** concept has broadened to apply to any situation in which tough approaches alternate with lenient ones. According to business writer Jeanette Gilsdorf, trade negotiators in China are experts at this type of " 'good cop/bad cop' strategy."

Another interrogation technique involved shining bright lights in the face of a suspect as questions were shouted at him and he got pushed around. This so-called *third degree* apparently borrowed its name from the "third degree" of initiation rites administered to Lodge of Freemasons members who wanted to become Master Masons. Even though this activity is not especially strenuous, the secretiveness of Mason rituals excited rumors that their **third degree** rite was a harrowing ordeal. In recent years that phrase has been applied to demanding experiences of many kinds. An *Ancestry* magazine article on conducting oral histories is titled "The Third Degree: Tips for a Successful Interview."

## PINKERTONS AND PRIVATE EYES

In 1848 a Scottish immigrant in Chicago named Allan Pinkerton founded one of the nation's first private investigation firms. His agency was the first to take **mug shots** ("mug" being slang for criminals) and to create a **rogues' gallery** from these photographs. The logo of the Pinkerton National Detective Agency was a

large open eye, its motto "We never sleep." Criminals soon began to refer to Pinkerton's firm as "the Eye." In time the term **private eye** became slang for private detective. Pinkerton himself called detectives **dicks**. (In his era *dicked* was slang for "being watched.") During the late nineteenth century a popular series of dime novels featured a character based on Allan Pinkerton called "Old Sleuth," *sleuth* being a Scottish term for the trail left behind by a quarry. **Sleuths** subsequently became a synonym for private investigators, as did **Pinkertons**. After their namesake died, the *Pinkertons* concentrated on foiling union organizers and breaking up strikes, giving that term unsavory connotations.

Another nickname for an investigator is *gumshoe*. This term has been in use since the development of footwear with gum rubber soles late in the nineteenth century. Such shoes were worn by those who needed to skulk about quietly. As a result stealthy operatives of many kinds came to be called **gumshoes**. After 9/11, *Los Angeles Times* reporter Scott Reckard noted that office-bound FBI agents were now leaving their offices to do *gumshoe work*.

## Cons

During the late nineteenth century a bearded man wearing Indian-style buckskins traversed the Oklahoma Territory in a wagon telling fascinated crowds how he'd been kidnapped by Comanches as a one-year-old, then traded to the Sioux for nine blankets, nine horses, and two girls. This man called himself Arizona Bill, "the Great Benefactor of Mankind." After describing his childhood travails in dramatic detail, Arizona Bill told listeners that one of the Comanches' medicine men had showed him how to extract oil from a rattlesnake. It was their great good fortune that for a modest sum he could sell them a bottle of rattlesnake oil, guaranteed to remedy a wide range of ailments.

Snake oil was the renegade ancestor of omega-3 fish oil. A century ago there was no shortage of customers for this liniment, or producers like Arizona Bill willing to supply it. Clark Stanley was another. A onetime cowboy from Abilene, Texas, Stanley wore outfits made of snake skin. He called himself "the Rattlesnake King." By his own account Stanley had spent more than two years with the Moki Indians of Arizona, learning from their medicine man how to produce snake oil. At the World's Columbian Exposition in Chicago in 1893 he astonished onlookers by boiling oil from hundreds of rattlesnakes he'd killed before their very eyes. Stanley then gave them the opportunity to buy a bottle of his Snake Oil Liniment for 50¢. This liniment promised immediate relief from "rheumatism, neuralgia, sciatica, lame back, lumbago,

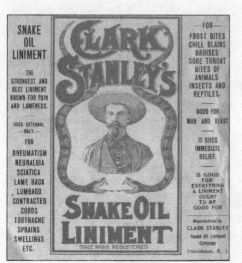

contracted muscles, toothache, sprains, swellings, etc." as well as "frost bites, chill blains, bruises, sore throat, bites of animals, insects and reptiles." Clark Stanley had no trouble selling his Snake Oil Liniment at the exposition, by direct mail, and to druggists around the nation.

When federal authorities tested a shipment of Snake Oil Liniment in 1917, it proved to consist primarily of mineral oil along with 1 percent oil of undetermined origin (possibly from cows), red pepper, and perhaps a dash of turpentine and camphor. Stanley and others who sold concoctions like this left little behind in the way of useful therapies, but did leave us the terms **snake oil** to signify quack remedies, and **snake oil salesman** for disreputable characters of all kinds. "Supercure or Snake Oil?" reads a headline in London's *Daily Mail.* "What's the Truth About Echinacea?" An American Council on Science and Health spokesman warned that the Internet had become a "new medium for the snake oil salesman."

Snake oil wasn't the only dubious product being sold by con men and women a century ago. The Brooklyn Bridge was another. In 1901 a New Jersey confidence man named William McCloundy (aka "IOU O'Brien") was convicted of grand larceny for "selling" this bridge to a gullible dupe. The 1937 movie *Every Day's a Holiday* featured Mae West as an early-twentieth-century hustler named Peaches O'Day who sells the Brooklyn Bridge to a recent immigrant for $200 (scribbling him a receipt for "One bridge in good condition"). Throughout the twentieth century, **selling the Brooklyn Bridge** was synonymous with exploiting gullibility. The catchphrase **I've got a bridge to sell you** grew out of that notion. Eventually it was rivaled by "I've got some oceanfront property in Arizona I'd like to sell you."

Shortly after World War I, an Italian immigrant named Charles Ponzi offered Boston-area investors a 50 percent return on their money within ninety days. Ponzi told them he could do this by exploiting the favorable exchange rate in postal reply coupons (coupons sold in one country for purchase of stamps in another). Some thirty thousand Americans entrusted Ponzi's Securities Exchange Company with nearly $15 million before it became clear that its founder was compensating early investors with money paid by later ones. In time this came to be known as a **Ponzi scheme** or, more generically, a **pyramid scheme.** After pleading guilty to mail fraud Charles Ponzi spent several years in prison.

## The Ladies' Auxiliary of Crime

In late summer, 1892, a plain Fall River, Massachusetts, woman named Elizabeth "Lizzie" Borden was accused of killing her father and stepmother with an axe. Mr. Borden had taken ten blows to the head, his wife nineteen. After a sensational 1893 murder trial, the thirty-three-year-old spinster was acquitted.

Many thought she got away with murder. Borden was later immortalized in a popular jump rope rhyme:

> *Lizzie Borden took an axe*
> *Gave her mother forty whacks*
> *When she saw what she had done*
> *Gave her father forty-one*

Borden's case inspired the term **axe murderer**, a term we use so routinely that one might imagine hatchet-wielding killers are prowling every Wal-Mart parking lot. (With the notable exception of whoever killed Mr. and Mrs. Borden, this clumsy weapon is actually quite unpopular among murderers.) To a lesser degree the name **Lizzie Borden** is still associated with grisly murders, sensational trials, and lingering doubts. Borden's home in Fall River has been converted into a popular bed-and-breakfast whose gift shop sells earrings with dangling hatchet charms and a Lizzie Borden bobblehead doll.

The notoriety of another woman, whose crimes are indisputable, is due mostly to the actress who played her on screen and a popular picture of this actress with one foot on the bumper of a Depression-era car, a gun against her hip, and a cigar clenched in her teeth. That would be Faye Dunaway portraying Bonnie Parker in the 1967 movie *Bonnie and Clyde*. Dunaway was better looking than the real Parker, just as movie mate Warren Beatty was more dashing than her partner, Clyde Barrow. The actual duo were twenty-something Texas lowlifes who held up multiple banks and killed twelve people during a four-year crime spree in the early 1930s. Their life of crime ended when both were shot dead by Texas Rangers in 1934. The movie that glamorized their lives left **Bonnie and Clyde** behind as an allusion to coed criminal teams. A female Tennessee prison guard who married an inmate, then killed another guard while trying to help her husband escape, titled the thirty-four-page journal in which she described their escapades "A Modern Day Bonnie and Clyde."

Another woman who became famous for all the wrong reasons was Long Island's **Amy Fisher**. In early 1991, the sixteen-year-old Fisher took her car for repairs to a mechanic named Joey Buttafuoco. They soon became lovers. The thirty-five-year-old married father of two subsequently found work for his teenage paramour as a prostitute with an escort service. A year after she met him, Amy Fisher rang the doorbell of Buttafuoco's home, then shot his wife in the head after she opened the door. Although Mary Jo Buttafuoco survived, the right side of her face was permanently paralyzed. Reporters dubbed Amy Fisher "the Long Island Lolita." Her saga inspired three TV movies, including one that starred Drew Barrymore. After serving seven years in prison, Fisher coauthored a book and became a *Long Island Press* columnist. On the fifth anniversary of the 2001 attack on the World Trade Center, *Daily Show* host Jon Stewart asked, "So why shouldn't 9/11 get the same respect that the Amy Fisher story gets?"

Two years after Amy Fisher shot Mary Jo Buttafuoco, Lorena Bobbitt amputated the penis of her abusive husband with a butcher knife. This episode sent such a collective shiver down male spines that **Lorena Bobbitt** remains synonymous with the ultimate in female vengeance. For a time, some women wore LORENA BOBBITT FOR SURGEON GENERAL T-shirts. *Eunice aphroditois*, a worm found in deep seas that apparently devours the sexual organ of its mate after coupling, has been dubbed "the Bobbitt worm."

## Disappearing Acts

On August 6, 1930, forty-one-year-old New York Supreme Court Justice Joseph Crater enjoyed a relaxed dinner with two friends in Manhattan. Afterward Crater said he was going to see the Broadway play *Dancing Partner*. He then hailed a cab, got in, and was never seen again. Subsequent investigation revealed that the married judge had gangster pals and showgirl girlfriends, including one of his dinner partners, Sally Lou Ritz. On the day he vanished Judge Crater spent several hours clearing papers out of his office, then asked his secretary to cash two large checks. Crater also emptied his safe-deposit box. Four months after he disappeared, Sally Lou Ritz also turned up missing. Crater's case excited feverish speculation. Was he murdered? Did he have a secret life? Did he seek refuge in Montreal? Or Marrakesh? Was Sally Lou with him? Musing about questions such as these became a popular pastime. Anyone who ever had a passing fantasy of cashing out and taking off found Judge Crater's disappearance a spur to the imagination. For decades after he figuratively fell off the planet, **pulling a Crater** referred to any unexplained disappearance. The very term **Judge Crater** evoked, and still evokes, an inexplicably missing person. For a time, travelers could sometimes hear over train station loudspeakers, "Judge Crater, please report to the information desk."

Nearly half a century after Crater disappeared, *Time*'s Michael Duffy commented on *Meet the Press* that even though John McCain looked hopelessly behind in early Republican presidential primaries, "This field is weak enough that perhaps even Judge Crater could come back again." (Duffy was prescient.)

Four decades after Judge Crater went missing, a well-dressed middle-aged man named Dan Cooper boarded a Northwest Orient flight in Portland, Oregon. After the plane took off for Seattle, Cooper handed a note to a stewardess saying he had a bomb. The note demanded $200,000 and four parachutes. After other passengers and crew got off in Seattle, Cooper was given the amount he'd asked for in $20 bills, along with four parachutes. He then instructed the pilot to fly south. As they approached Oregon, Cooper lowered the plane's rear stairway, walked down those stairs, and jumped from the plane into the realm of mythology. Neither Dan Cooper, his remains, nor the money he was given on November 24, 1971, have ever been found ($5,800 in $20 bills that were discovered near the Washington-Oregon border several years later may have been part of his loot). For a time after this caper, several Cooper copycats made similar attempts to extort money from airlines. In response, Boeing added a latch that kept stairways on its 727 airplanes locked in place during flights. This latch was called a "Cooper Vane." Because a police officer mistakenly recorded Dan Cooper's name as **D. B. Cooper** and reporters identified him this way, that name still suggests an unsolved mystery involving a vanished criminal.

## GENOVESE SYNDROME

Just before 3 a.m. on March 13, 1964, twenty-eight-year-old Catherine "Kitty" Genovese returned to her apartment in Kew Gardens, Queens. Outside this building a mugger confronted the bar manager. Even though several neighbors apparently heard her pleas for help, for half an hour no one intervened or called the police. Policemen were finally summoned and arrived at 4:05 a.m. They found Genovese's badly slashed body in the vestibule of her apartment building. A twenty-nine-year-old office clerk named Winston Moseley was convicted of this random murder and sent to prison for life. Spurred by a *New York Times* feature about the killing headlined "Thirty-seven Who Saw Murder Didn't Call the Police," this crime became a parable of urban indifference. Subsequent investigation determined that not as many neighbors as was first thought had heard Genovese's screams, and at least one did call police, who were slow to respond. Nonetheless, the name **Kitty Genovese** and the notion of a **Kitty Genovese syndrome** still allude to gruesome crimes that go unreported by onlookers.

## Serial Killers

In late 1888, the mutilated bodies of five prostitutes were discovered in London's East End. All of their throats had been slashed, and the internal organs of some had been removed. After these bodies were found, a man who called himself "Jack the Ripper" wrote a letter to the Central News Agency taking credit for the murders. More murders followed. No one was ever charged. How many women Jack the Ripper may have killed and who he actually was have been the source of intense interest ever since. Some 140 books have been written speculating about the identity of this criminal. His *nom de crime*, **Jack the Ripper**, is still used generically for mass murderers, or for the perpetrators of unusually vicious crimes. When British prostitutes began turning up dead in late 2006, one London reporter called the perpetrator "a Ripper-style killer."

An American counterpart to Jack the Ripper assaulted and strangled thirteen women in their Boston-area homes during the early 1960s. Although a meter reader named Albert DeSalvo eventually confessed to these crimes and died in prison, controversy persists about whether he was the actual killer. (DNA evidence tested in 2001 failed to connect him to one of the victims.) The name reporters gave to whoever was the killer, **the Boston Strangler**, was and is second only to *Jack the Ripper* as an analogue for murderers of all kinds.

Unlike DeSalvo, Theodore "Ted" Bundy was connected by overwhelming evidence to dozens of murders committed between 1974 and 1978. Bundy was the first mass murderer to be called a "serial killer." Although not the only serial killer plying his trade at this time, Bundy was the best looking and most charming. He could easily have been a news anchor. This made Ted Bundy the creepiest of mass murderers: one who looked attractively normal. It was hard to imagine someone so bright and well-spoken killing at least thirty young women (the number to which he confessed; the actual number could be higher). While he was raping, strangling, and mutilating women in his spare time, Bundy also volunteered at a Seattle suicide hotline and campaigned for Republicans. As he awaited trial, the handsome sociopath got hundreds of fan letters from females. Before and after the forty-two-year-old killer was electrocuted, his case inspired several TV movies and a number of books. The contrast between his Ivy League demeanor and Jack the Ripper behavior tattooed the name **Ted Bundy** on our collective psyche. ("He seemed like a nice guy, but so did Ted Bundy.")

## Organized Crime

Little of the colorful gangster argot that entered our discourse after World War I came from criminals themselves. Where did it come from? Imaginative journalists, novelists, and screenwriters, primarily. **Mob,** a term originally applied to unruly groups of people, was first used by reporters to characterize organized criminals in the early 1800s. A century later journalists referred to members of such groups as **mobsters. Gangster** itself became press slang for those who belonged to criminal gangs during the late nineteenth century. At the turn of the century **underworld** began to appear in print as a way of characterizing organized crime. (Before that this term referred to Hades-like subterranean worlds.) Prohibition-era mobster Al Capone picked up the term **syndicate** from news stories written about him, ones that said Capone's "crime syndicate" was based in Chicago's Four Deuces saloon. Capone's alleged observation **"You can get more done with a smile and a gun that with a smile alone"** originated in the 1987 movie *The Untouchables,* whose script was written by David Mamet.

**Go to the mattresses** appeared in Mario Puzo's 1969 novel *The Godfather,* and was popularized in the 1972 movie based on that novel. (According to the Phrase Finder website, this is based on folk memories of Italian families who during times of strife fled their homes for apartments in safe areas, where they were protected by bodyguards who slept in shifts on the floor.) Another Puzo contribution was **make your bones**, for an initial mob killing, after which the killer became a **made man**. Anyone who has proven him- or herself in a wide variety of pursuits is now said to have *made his/her bones*. In defense of the controversial appointment of *Today Show* host Katie Couric as CBS's evening news anchor, a former CBS News executive said, "She made her bones as a reporter."

Other slang for killing people—**hit, rub out, put a contract on, take for a ride**—became popular in post–World War II crime coverage. **Hit man, hit job**, and **hit list** went from crime reporting and pulp fiction to the broader depiction of anyone who undertakes to lay someone else low, literally or figuratively. Today those *taken for a ride* are more likely to be duped than killed. Politicians and others in hyper-competitive fields like to say that they figuratively *go to the mattresses* and *put contracts out* on each other.

Postscript: In 1986, neo-newscaster Geraldo Rivera traveled to Chicago to take the audacious gamble of opening on live television a vault once owned by Al Capone. After much fevered speculation about what might be inside, Rivera lost his gamble. The vault contained nothing but dust. Since then **Al Capone's vault** has sometimes been used as shorthand for a treasure-type hunt that discovers nothing. When Senator Chuck Hagel (R-Neb.) called a press conference amid speculation that he would announce his intention to run for president, then said only that he was reviewing his options, *Washington Post* writer Dana Milbank called Hagel's event "the political equivalent of Geraldo opening Al Capone's vault."

## GOING POSTAL

On a hot day in late August 1986, mailman Patrick Henry Sherrill put on his best blue U.S. Postal Service uniform, threw two loaded .45 semiautomatic pistols and a .22 in his mailbag, then drove to the Edmond, Oklahoma, post office where he worked. There the former Marine fired some fifty shots at colleagues, killing fourteen and wounding six. He then shot himself. This carnage shocked the nation. Until then post offices had seemed like safe, subdued environments staffed by placid civil servants. Following the Oklahoma incident, shootings in several other post offices around the country took more than forty lives. Even though that workplace was no more likely than any other to become a killing field, the phrase **go postal** became and remains a way to characterize violent outbursts. But *going postal* needn't involve actual violence. That phrase just as often is used synonymously with the less lethal *go ballistic*. A character in Linda Barnes's novel *Cold Case* says about a man who flies off the handle after a woman surreptitiously reads his journals, "Wow, talk about ballistic! Talk about postal!"

# 8. Good Sports

t's hard to follow American discourse, among men especially, without·at least a rudimentary knowledge of sports allusions. Some cross boundaries. They include *playbook, play by play, cheap shot, the ball's in your court, drop the ball, blow the whistle, make the cut, first string, second string, benchwarmer, on the bench, come off the bench, benched, free agent, know the score, run up the score, on your game, off your game, game plan, game face, game changer, home-field advantage,* and *level playing field.* Others are sport-specific.

## Boxing

In 1974, boxer Muhammad Ali fought twenty-four-year-old George Foreman in Kinshasa, Zaire. Before he became a jovial old guy with a shaved head, Foreman was a sullen young man with a big Afro. Foreman was bigger, stronger, and eight years younger than Ali. He also was considerably less astute. After weeks of taunting—telling his opponent he was going to fight at close quarters, go head-to-head, toe-to-toe—Ali spent their match lounging against the ropes dodging punches until Foreman grew weary. Near the end of the eighth round Ali sent him to the canvas with a left hook followed by a right cross. Foreman didn't get up. Ali called this tactic **rope-a-dope**. Ever since then, that phrase has characterized a defensive strategy in which someone is snookered into wearing himself out. In his novel *True Story*, Bill Maher wrote that one character "rope-a-doped himself out."

Six years after Ali dispatched Foreman, Panamanian middleweight Roberto Durán fought Sugar Ray Leonard. Durán had a reputation as a ferocious puncher. Fears were expressed for the well-being of the more skillful but less rugged Leonard. To the surprise of everyone—especially his opponent—Leonard confronted Durán with a relentless barrage of fists. After eight rounds of punishment, the Panamanian threw up his arms. **"No más,"** he said, **"no más.** No more box." Even among those who don't speak Spanish, *"No más, no más"* has since become synonymous with abject capitulation. After a shaky debate performance by Barack Obama during the 2008 primaries, columnist Mike Littwin wrote, "The best thing you can say about Obama's performance is at least he never said, 'No mas.' " When the Illinois senator begged off further debates, a blogger's headline read, "After bad debate Obama says 'No mas.' "

No sport has fertilized the English language more than boxing. A remarkable number of enduring catchphrases have leaped the ropes of its rings and ended up in general discourse. This has been true since the birth of prizefighting at fairs in eighteenth-century England. Early boxing matches tended to be **rough-and-tumble, knock-down, drag-out** affairs that went on until one contestant was knocked unconscious and dragged out of the ring. There were no limits on the types of punches that could be thrown by **bare-knuckle** prizefighters (so called because they fought for prizes at fairs and such). These contests were **free-for-alls**.

Most early-day fighters kept their distance from each other and threw long punches. In the late eighteenth century, a new type of pugilism emerged, one that involved getting close to an opponent and throwing short punches in hopes of wearing him down. This new style was called **infighting** (a term that soon referred to intergroup conflict of all kinds). In such matches boxers fought **head-to-head** or **toe-to-toe**, phrases now used for close confrontations of many varieties.

Order gradually began to tame the anarchy of boxing. By the mid-nineteenth century boxers were expected to meet at the center of the ring with fists cocked before starting to swing away. Just as opponents of all kinds do today, they were said to **square off**. Some matches commenced **at the drop of a hat**, or when an official dropped his hat to the ground.

In 1865, an Englishman named John Graham Chambers composed a set of rules to impose a measure of civility on this savage sport. Because he was a commoner, Chambers agreed to have his rules introduced by the Marquess of Queensberry (John Sholto Douglas), co-founder of Britain's Amateur Athletic Club. The rules named after him made boxing gloves mandatory, required a count of ten for a knockout, and established that rounds would last for three minutes with a minute's pause between them. Queensberry's rules also forbade "hitting below the belt" (inspiring the remarkably high-waisted shorts prize-fighters wear to this day). In time **below the belt** or **low blows** became synony-mous with foul play in and out of the ring. Eventually Queensberry's standards of fair play in the ring took on metaphorical significance. That is why we some-times say **by Queensberry Rules** or **not according to the Marquess of Queensberry** when discussing appropriate deportment in all sorts of pursuits.

The **knockout punch** that puts an opponent **down for the count** of ten is sometimes abbreviated to **KO** or **kayo**, which in turn can be verbed as **KOed** or **kayoed** and applied to activity-ending events of all kinds. A defeated boxer is **down and out**, as is anyone in straitened circumstances. Calling an inconse-quential event **no skin off my nose** references the way boxers described a punch too weak to scrape skin off an opponent's nose. Boxers being overpow-ered are **knocked back on their heels**. Ones thoroughly overwhelmed are **knocked for a loop**, much like a boxer said to have been punched into the shape of a pretzel. On the other hand, gullible parties came to be known as **pushovers**, like easily floored boxers. They are **stumblebums**.

Inept boxers also were called *palookas*. That term originally referred to a brawny fighter of modest skills and less intellect. Today **palooka** suggests a sorry, ineffectual figure in any walk of life. (A theater critic called one character in the stage adaptation of *Twelve Angry Men* "a loudmouthed palooka.") This reference is less insulting than it used to be, however, due to the 1930–84 comic strip **Joe Palooka**. Cartoonist Ham Fisher said the inspiration for his protago-nist was a good-natured heavyweight boxer he once met who wasn't too bright. Like that fighter, Fisher's amiable Joe Palooka was a lovable big lug. Due to this funny pages fixture, *palooka* became more ambiguous in meaning, as when a Bloomberg.com reviewer called Richard Ford's novel *The Lay of the Land* "a big, friendly palooka of a book." **Palookaville**, on the other hand, remains the place where losers go. A *USA Today* financial columnist cautioned antsy own-ers of a laggard mutual fund to do some homework before they "shuffle the fund off to Palookaville."

Managers of prizefighting palookas routinely had to **throw in the towel**, the traditional way a boxer's handlers conceded defeat: literally tossing a towel into the ring. (In England this practice was called **throwing in the sponge**, referring to the sponge used to wipe down a boxer's face and body.) These handlers stood in the boxer's designated corner of the ring, which is why we say that backers of all kinds are **in your corner**. A century ago, woozy fighters began to be called *punch drunk*, then simply **punchy**, a term that by World War II described anyone whose wits weren't about him. In the same era, a shifty person risked being perceived as someone who **pulled his punches**, a phrase originally used to describe boxers who restrained themselves to deliberately lose a fight. Boxers who **lead with their chin** literally **stick their chin out**, as do those who are bold in any pursuit. **Take it on the chin** refers to suffering a severe blow, in and out of the ring. A boxer who can't withstand punches is said to have a **glass jaw**, a term also applied to those who can't take the heat. Defending himself against charges that he might wither under pressure, onetime Arkansas governor Mike Huckabee said, "I don't have a glass jaw."

Nimble boxers keep their weight on their toes for quick movement. By extension, being **on your toes** refers to being agile and alert in general. Fighters who shift their weight to the back of their feet so they can throw a stronger punch are said to **swing from the heels**. If his punches land smack on an opponent's face, that boxer is said to be **right on the nose**. The staggered recipient of too many blows may end up **on the ropes**, a phrase we apply more broadly to anyone on the verge of defeat. (With luck he might be **saved by the bell**, signaling the end of a round.) A boxer on the defensive might also attempt to protect his face with his gloves, or **cover up**, camouflaging his intentions in the process. *Cover-up* later referred to an attempt to hide misdeeds, as Richard Nixon did during the Watergate scandal.

## Baseball

From 1915 until 1925 Wally Pipp was the New York Yankees' starting first baseman. A solid hitter, Pipp led the American League in home runs in 1916 and 1917. Midway through the 1925 season, however, he was mired in a batting slump. On June 2, 1925, a rookie named Lou Gehrig took Pipp's place. Gehrig proceeded to play 2,130 consecutive games over the next fourteen years. Although his entry into the Yankees' lineup was part of a deliberate team shake-up, by legend Pipp had removed himself due to a headache. Gehrig biographer Jonathan Eig (*Luckiest Man*) calls this "a quintessentially American parable that squares with the nation's Protestant work ethic. Take a day off and you'll suffer for it. The boss will find someone better to do your job. Wally Pipp reminds us that we're all easily replaced." To this day athletes thought to be malingering are routinely called **Wally Pipp** by teammates. Nearly eight decades

WALLY PIPP

after Lou Gehrig replaced him at first base, simply dropping Pipp's name can be enough to get shirkers back to work, in and out of sports. Naturally, this name has become a verb: **Pipped.** Or, as West Virginia's *Charleston Daily Mail* observed about a high school athlete playing through pain, "Let the record show, that Michael Hill would not be Wally Pipp-ed."

French-born historian Jacques Barzun concluded that "whoever wants to know the heart and mind of America had better learn baseball." Because it is such a quintessentially American game, moves at such a leisurely pace, and involves lots of deferred gratification and chesslike strategy, this sport enjoys pride of place among intellectuals such as Barzun. To them, baseball is to football as chess is to checkers. That is part of the reason why, even though we use a lot of baseball terminology in everyday speech (*touch base, cover all the bases, way off base, step up to the plate, throw a curve, hit a homer, strike out, keep your eye on the ball,* etc., etc.) this sport's legends and literature are its primary source of retroterminology.

The quintessential baseball story is, of course, "Casey at the Bat." That epic poem, written by newspaperman Ernest Thayer in 1888, depicts a baseball team in a town called Mudville. Mudville's team is about to lose an important game. If its star—Casey—can get up to bat, however, Mudville is confident it will win. He does go to the plate, takes two strikes, then—a third. As the poem's famous last stanza recounts:

> *Oh, somewhere in this favored land*
> *The sun is shining bright;*
> *The band is playing somewhere*
> *And somewhere hearts are light;*
> *And somewhere men are laughing*
> *And somewhere children shout;*
> *But there is no joy in Mudville;*
> *Mighty Casey has struck out.*

In various versions **"Casey at the Bat"** enjoyed so much popularity that it quickly became an American icon, its ending especially. Condensed to **no joy in Mudville**, Casey's sad fate can refer to any dispiriting event. To characterize her unhappiness with two TV appearances she made in 2008, a blogger told readers, "There is no joy in Mudville."

James Thurber's 1942 story in the *New Yorker* called "The Catbird Seat" features a corporate busybody named Mrs. Ulgine Barrows who likes to ask co-workers, "Are you sitting in the catbird seat?" An office clerk explains to others that Mrs. Barrows must have picked up this expression from Brooklyn Dodgers announcer Red Barber. Barber himself first heard it used by a fellow poker player in Cincinnati who said he knew he was "sitting in the catbird seat" when he had an ace down and one up. This old southernism reflects the fact that the catbird is thought to be an unusually canny bird who directs the action with meowlike chirps from a lofty perch in trees. **In the catbird seat** has endured to depict those who are doing well enough to direct the action. A Cox News financial reporter once noted that when it came to dealing with suppliers, "Home Depot is in the catbird seat."

No baseball allusion has proved more durable than one developed by comedians Bud Abbott and Lou Costello for a classic mid-1940s radio routine. In this routine, baseball manager Abbott tries to tell peanut vendor Costello about a player named Who who plays first base. "Who's on first?" Costello keeps asking, only to be told "Right" or "Yes" or "Who is on first." The longer Abbott and Costello talk this way the more frustrated each gets. Costello finally ends their exchange by exclaiming, "I don't give a damn!" "Oh, that's our shortstop!" responds Abbott. This model of inspired nonsense left **Who's on first?** behind as a way to depict all manner of dysfunction. According to New York University organizational studies professor Paul Light, the federal government's image suggests that it "doesn't know who's on first."

During Abbott and Costello's heyday, fans at Yankee Stadium in the Bronx were famous for responding to a poor play or bad call by pursing their lips and sputtering to make a sound resembling an extended fart. This came to be known as a **Bronx cheer**. (Another term for the same emission is a *raspberry*, probably because in England *raspberry tart* is slang for flatulence.) When New York Mayor Michael Bloomberg proposed a user tax for drivers in congested parts of Manhattan, one blogger commented, "Most likely, quite a few New Yorkers will give the idea a Bronx cheer."

Some concepts from baseball's early days are still heard outside the baseball diamond. Early in the twentieth century, minor league teams that played in scruffy locales were said to be part of a **bush league**. Players on such teams were called **bush leaguers**. Nowadays that term, or **bushers**, refers to anyone thought to be engaged in low-level activity. More broadly speaking, **bush** refers to subpar performance or unprofessional behavior. ("The way he campaigns is really bush.")

When baseball executive Branch Rickey developed a highly organized minor league system to cultivate young players, these players were said to play on **farm teams**. Those relegated from major league teams to ones in the minor leagues were **farmed out**. That concept was soon being used for development programs of all kinds. After Random House invested in an online book-publishing venture, the venerable firm denied that it planned to use this venture as "a farm team" for new authors.

## Football

As his Notre Dame team was about to play Army in 1928, football coach Knute Rockne invoked the name of former player George Gipp. Gipp's deathbed request eight years earlier supposedly had been to use his memory to motivate the Fighting Irish for a big game. " 'Rock,' " the coach said Gipp told him, " 'some day when things look real tough for Notre Dame, ask the boys to go out there and win one for me.' Well, I've never used Gipp's request until now. This is the time." Notre Dame won. Two years later Rockne embellished the legend when he wrote in a magazine article that Gipp told him, " 'Some time, Rock, when the team's up against it, when things are wrong and the breaks are beating the boys—tell them to go in there with all they've got and win just one for the Gipper.' " In 1940, an adaptation of these words provided the denouement of a movie in which Ronald Reagan played George Gipp. That movie, and Reagan's lifelong identification with this role, made **Win one for the Gipper** a permanent part of America's athletic-political lore, and gave Reagan a lasting nickname (*Gipper*) that quite pleased him.

Gippers aside, football talk has made very few contributions to the American lexicon. Nonetheless, a number of words and phrases can be traced back to early days on the *gridiron* (so called because football's field of play looked like the grid made of iron on which decrepit ships are placed for salvage, themselves called *gridirons* after the cooking utensil they resemble).

Even though football has nothing like the literary tradition of baseball, one classic American credo can be found in the last two lines of a 1941 poem by revered sportswriter Grantland Rice titled "Alumnus Football."

> *For when the One Great Scorer comes to mark against your name,*
> *He writes—not that you won or lost—but how you played the game.*

Growing out of Rice's poem, "It matters not whether you won or lost, but **how you played the game**" remains a classic testament of sportsmanship, sometimes referred to sarcastically by those who think *winning is the only thing.* The latter concept, of course, comes from the most familiar of American quotations, one usually attributed to prominent football coach Vince Lombardi: "Winning isn't everything, it's the only thing." The actual author of this motto was Red Sanders, UCLA's football coach in the 1950s. Unlike the sardonic Sanders, Lombardi took the *winning-is-the-only-thing* sentiment quite seriously. So did millions of American men who made this credo their mantra. As a result, the very name **Vince Lombardi** evokes a win-at-all-costs sensibility.

Before it was legal to pass footballs forward, a routine tactic of runners holding the ball in one arm was to stick their other arm straight out like a battering ram, then use it to knock down opponents who tried to tackle them. Known as **stiff-arming**, this concept is now applied to all sorts of activity in which one party rudely pushes others aside. Early in the second term of the Bush-Cheney administration, reporters were said to be reacting angrily to "five years of being stiff-armed by this administration."

---

### BY GEORGE

During his first few years as a professional wrestler before World War II, George Wagner had a meager following. To reverse that course, beginning in 1943 Wagner grew his hair long, bleached it, flaunted gold-plated bobby pins, donned glossy robes, and began entering the ring beneath a purple spotlight to the thunderous chords of "Pomp and Circumstance" while a valet sprayed the air before him

with an industrial-strength perfume he called Chanel Number 10. As *Gorgeous George*, Wagner captivated not only the crowds who packed arenas to watch him wrestle but postwar television audiences who made his new moniker a household name. Entertainers from Liberace to Madonna, adopted the template for flamboyant self-promotion created by Gorgeous George. Soul singer James Brown said his own cavorting on stage was inspired in part ·by the wrestler's antics. So did a young boxer named Cassius Clay, who observed Gorgeous George's shtick with great interest. As Muhammad Ali, Clay said his "I am the greatest" routine was modeled on the bragging flamboyance that filled so many seats when Gorgeous George wrestled. More than four decades since his death in 1963, the name **Gorgeous George** still evokes images of over-the-top grandiosity. *Arizona Highways* magazine once called flamboyant Frank Lloyd Wright "the Gorgeous George of architecture."

## Dance

On antebellum southern plantations, balls typically included a grand march. Back in their quarters, slaves mocked this mannered event by strutting, bowing, arching their backs, and kicking their legs high in the air. After the Civil War, contests were held among freed slaves to determine who could do the fanciest version of this high-stepping "dance." Winners were given a cake. They would **take the cake**. That's why this prancing activity—performed by couples marching side by side, hand in arm, sometimes dressed in tails and white gowns—came to be known as *cakewalking*. By the end of the century that dance was all the rage among blacks and whites alike. During the First World War, American soldiers called any easy task a **cakewalk**, which is how we use that term today. In 2002, as the United States was poised to invade Iraq, former Assistant Secretary of Defense Ken Adelman famously wrote in the *Washington*

*Post*, "I believe demolishing [Saddam] Hussein's military power and liberating Iraq would be a cakewalk."

Cakewalking eventually was eclipsed by so-called "animal dancing," doing the Turkey Trot, Chicken Scratch, Bunny Hug, or Kangaroo Dip. These, in turn, gave way to the sultry, suggestive *tango*. Unlike the animal dances, this import from Argentina required a partner. In ballrooms, hotel lobbies, and nightclubs, couples could be seen attempting the tango's intricate steps, which ended with the man nearly prone over his reclining partner. This dance's erotic flavor inspired Pearl Bailey's popular 1952 song "It Takes Two to Tango." That title quickly wended from the jukebox into popular discourse, especially when someone accused of sexual pecadillos wants to establish that this activity requires the cooperation of a second person. The fact that **it takes two to tango** is also noted routinely as parties in conflict try to resolve differences. When Albanians accepted a proposal to end fighting in Kosovo already spurned by Serbs, a Russian diplomat observed, "It takes two to tango."

Well into the twentieth century women at dances often carried a small piece of cardboard or heavy-gauge paper, or hung a bound booklet from a cord on their wrist. When a man approached, they would languidly hold this out so he could scribble his name on one line of their *dance card*. The use of such scheduling devices largely disappeared by World War II. Nonetheless, the expression "Sorry, but **my dance card's full**" still explains why one can't do something.

## Horse Racing

At early English racetracks the starting line consisted of a scratch on the ground. All horses had to **start from scratch**, a term that now refers most often to cooking with discrete ingredients—"scratch cooking"—or to creating just about anything without existing materials. ("To design our website we had to start from scratch."). Horses **caught flat-footed** kept their hooves on the ground as a race began. Better they should leap **out of the gate.** Impatient harness racers sometimes were warned to **hold your horses,** a phrase used to counsel restraint in general since the mid-nineteenth century. A jockey so sure of victory that he let his hands drop was said to win **hands down.** Maneuvering riders **jockey for position.** Although some believe that **track record** comes from track and field, others say this phrase originally referred to a horse's won-loss record at a given racetrack. At those tracks the odds on horses finishing first, second, or third were written on a blackboard. Those who wagered on all three possibilities for a single horse—win, place, or show—were said to bet **across the board.** Today this expression means simply to consider all possibilities.

Two horses running next to each other without one taking the lead were **neck and neck,** a phrase we also use for any type of contestants who are virtually tied. ("Polls show both candidates are neck and neck going into the election.") **Dead heat** is another term we use for close finishes, an old racetrack expression based on the fact that horse races were originally run in *heats.* When judges couldn't determine which horse won a heat it was declared *dead* and had to be re-run. Once photographs could be taken to determine who won such a close race, it was called a **photo finish.** A horse that won a race unexpectedly was called a **dark horse,** presumably because its owner kept others in the dark about his steed's capabilities. This phrase now is applied more often to politicians who win elections they were expected to lose. Among racetrack touts, a fixed race has long been known as a *shoo-in* (often misspelled "shoe-in"), derived from the command *shoo!* used when herding animals. By now, of course, any sure thing is liable to be called a **shoo-in.**

# 9. Getting Around

For the past half century we've traveled primarily by car, bus, and airplane. The ways we used to get about made an indelible impression on our forms of speech, however, and none more so than trains.

## Trains

Train travel involves a sense of adventure and romance unmatched by any other form of transportation this side of a space shuttle. In a time when important trips took place on trains, our imaginations were filled with lonesome whistles, billowing steam, the click-clack of steel wheels on iron rails, conductors shouting "All aboard!," tearful goodbyes at the station, stolen kisses in passageways, romantic liaisons in sleeping lofts, and the relentless forward thrust of a locomotive's huge wheels. "You know what the most exciting sound in the world is, Uncle Billy?" says James Stewart's character in the movie *It's a Wonderful Life*. "That's it—a train whistle!"

Baby boomers grew up reading *The Little Engine That Could*, hearing about Casey Jones the engineer, and singing "I've Been Working on the Railroad." Postwar teenagers jitterbugged to "The Chattanooga Choo-Choo" and swooned to "The Atchison, Topeka, and the Santa Fe." What do posttrain kids have that could possibly compare? Today's parents don't read to their kids about *The Little Bus That Could*, or sing to them about Casey Jones the airline pilot, or croon about a lonesome horn honking.

Despite the fact that few of us do ride trains any longer, not just our culture but our vocabulary still reflects a time when tracks crisscrossed the American terrain. These tracks were laid at a dizzying pace. After 40 miles of them were first installed in 1830, some 150,000 miles followed in the succeeding half century. This called for bridging rivers, blasting tunnels, pushing through woods, and condemning private property for rights of way. Whatever it took. The very term **railroad** still suggests pursuing one's goal with little regard for its impact on others. It also means to convict unjustly ("He was railroaded").

As a rolling party of workers laid transcontinental railroad tracks after the Civil War, another group followed: gamblers, liquor peddlers, prostitutes and sundry desperados. This unruly group came to be known as **hell on wheels**, a term subsequently applied to anyone of rowdy disposition. Some of America's train tracks were laid on mountains so steep that some locomotives couldn't make it to the top. They weren't able to **make the grade**. Early trains in particular were prone to **derail**, or **jump the tracks**, a concept that now refers to any wayward activity. (Alexander Master's biography *Stuart: A Life Backwards* is touted by its publisher as being about "a boy whose life left the rails early and just kept going.") In general one would rather be **on the right track** than **on the wrong track**, or simply **on track**, and not get **sidetracked** like a train shunted off to a short set of rails leading nowhere. Because railroad tracks often bisected towns, class distinctions came to be made about who lived on which side. Obviously it was better to reside on the more prosperous **right side of the tracks** than the seedier **wrong side of the tracks**. An advance notice said Mike Edison's forthcoming memoir *I Have Fun Everywhere I Go* would recount its author's "raucous, 20-year wrong-side-of-the-tracks career."

Communities so woebegone that trains stopped there only when they needed to take on, or "jerk," water (by reaching up to pull a cable hanging down from a water tank) became known dismissively as **jerkwater** towns. Some small settlements didn't even warrant a regular stop. Passengers who wanted to get off there pulled a cord, getting two toots of the whistle in response from the engineer. These were the **whistle-stop** towns that Harry Truman visited while **whistle-stopping** his way through the 1948 presidential campaign. (See chapter 5.)

Because Italy's Fascist dictator Benito Mussolini **made the trains run on time**, that expression still refers to leaders who sacrifice liberty for efficiency. (According to a liberal blogger, "Republicans are good at certain things—making trains run on time for one.") In or out of government, someone receiving unearned income is said to be on the **gravy train**, railroader slang for lucrative easy runs. The consequences of two trains being accidentally switched to the same tracks and colliding with each other were so catastrophic that being **asleep at the switch** became synonymous with negligence of all kinds. A 1932 cartoon in *Ballyhoo* magazine portrayed a signalman nonchalantly watching two locomotives about to collide in front of his signal box. "Tch, tch," he says to himself, "—what a way to run a railway!" In subsequent years, **what a way to run a railroad** became a popular allusion to badly run enterprises of all kinds.

Until Rudolf Diesel's engines took over, trains were powered by steam engines. In cahoots with steamboats, steamrollers, and steam shovels, this form of locomotion left behind a robust verbal residue: *pick up steam, full steam ahead, full head of steam, burst of steam, steam along, lose steam, run out of steam, blow off steam, full throttle,* and *all fired up* (referring to a steam engine working at peak capacity). Even the term **steamed** refers figuratively to one who is so distraught that it's as if **steam is coming out of his ears**. Such a person might **blow his stack**, alluding to the tall smokestacks that adorned steamboats, and were prone to explode.

## Nautical

When anchors were connected to ships by ropes, sailors on vessels that needed to flee harbor quickly simply severed their anchor's rope and set sail. This was called "cut and run away" or "cut and run off." By the early eighteenth century that had been shortened to **cut and run**. Over time this concept began to refer to human as well as nautical exits. In *Great Expectations* (1861) Charles Dickens wrote of some unwelcome guests, "I'd give a shilling if they had cut and run." During the early twenty-first century Republicans continually charged that this was what Democrats wanted to do in Iraq. A similar nautical expression was *slipping the cable* or detaching one's anchor for a quick, discreet getaway. We use a descendant of this expression every time we talk about sneaking away from someone undetected, giving them **the slip**.

A striking number of terms in common use have nautical origins. Some are self-explanatory: *aboveboard, jump ship, smooth sailing, clear the decks*. Others are phrases whose watery origins are less obvious. For example, an iron ball attached to a stick that was used to heat pitch for insertion into deck seams called a *loggerhead* sometimes doubled as a weapon, inspiring a term we still use for heated confrontation: **at loggerheads.** When sailors prepared for bad weather by caulking the *battens* (pieces of wood that secured cargo hatches) they **battened down the hatches**, as we all do metaphorically when getting ready to face adversity. Since orders were sometimes transmitted by special notes blown on a boatswain's whistle, or *pipe*, sailors making too much noise were told to **pipe down**, as are noisy kids everywhere.

On nineteenth-century British ships, a wooden cask, or *butt*, held drinking water. Its lid had a dipping hole called a *scuttle*. The two pieces combined were called a *scuttlebutt*. As would later be true of office workers sipping water from water coolers, sailors commonly shared gossip beside these containers while quenching their thirst. In time **scuttlebutt** itself became synonymous with gossip, rumors, or inside information. Other barrels aboard sailing ships held salted meat. Fat left over after that meat was cooked was called *slush*. Sometimes this fat was sold to landlubbers on shore. The proceeds went into a **slush fund** to benefit crew members. Eventually that phrase came to characterize secret funds used for illicit purposes. Richard Nixon's Checkers speech was made in response to allegations that a *slush fund* had been established on his behalf by industrialist Howard Hughes. (See chapter 5.)

The shape of *jib* sails fore and aft on seventeenth-century ships could identify their nationality or suggest seaworthiness. By analogy, the appearance of a human being provides similar information to onlookers: "I like the **cut of his jib.**" Sailors preparing a ship to exploit prevailing winds were said to *trim* its sails. That is why we talk of **trimming sails** to opportunistically take advantage of a situation. A ship whose sails were "square" with prevailing winds, or set at right angles to the deck, was **squared away**—ready for action. One whose sails were suddenly turned around by the wind was **taken aback**, a phrase that now means being startled by an unexpected event. ("I was really taken aback when she said she was leaving me.") Sailors who lost track of a ship's position were said to **lose their bearings**. More broadly that now means losing track of where one stands in general. A ship stranded above the waterline so long that its hull dried out was **high and dry**, as is someone drained of resources, tapped out. A ship so beached that it can't be freed is **hard and fast** or, broadly, immovable (e.g., a hard-and-fast rule).

Many seagoing phrases that we've adopted hark back to a time when rope-related terminology was the sailors' lingua franca. Sailors familiar with the hundreds of ropes and cords on a big sailing ship were said to **know the ropes**, as are those familiar with any endeavor today. They've **learned the ropes**. A captain in charge of an orderly vessel with all ropes tight was said to **run a tight ship**, the same thing we now say of one who oversees any enterprise in a well-organized way. Splicing together the frayed ends of a broken rope rather than replacing it was a matter of **making ends meet**, just as the cash-strapped today **make ends meet**. In stark contrast are those who make money **hand over fist**, a term originally used for rapidly climbing a ship's rigging, open hand over clenched fist.

To test the water's depth a weighted, marked line was thrown overboard. Since six fathoms was a common measurement, sailors began to say that whenever they threw something or someone overboard they'd *deep six* it. This nautical term became everyday slang in the 1920s and was the title of a 1958 movie about submariners. After John Dean was advised to **deep-six** incriminating papers during the Watergate cover-up (see chapter 5), that phrase became a way to refer to getting something out of sight, or eliminating it altogether. "DEAR VANCOUVER," an advice columnist advised a whiny supplicant, "Deep-six that negative attitude."

## Horses

On the American frontier, saddles were tightened by beltlike underbelly girths, or *cinches*, made of leather, canvas, or braided horsehair. Then as now, a well-secured cinch kept a saddle firmly in place. Dependable activity in general therefore came to be called **a cinch**. More than a century ago, *lead pipes* were added to the expression to create a **lead-pipe cinch**, or an absolute certainty. This expression could be a verbal amalgam combining saddle cinches and lead pipes used by turn-of-the-century criminals to dependably dispatch their victims. Another explanation may lie with plumbers who found lead pipes a better solution for tricky jobs than ones made of more rigid metal. An easy connector of pipes can be fashioned from a small sheet of lead once known as a "lead pipe cinch." Even though we can't say for sure when, where, or why this catchphrase was born, we do know that in his 1907 story "The Sphinx Apple," O. Henry wrote, "An engagement ain't always a lead pipe cinch."

An impressive number of contemporary references date back to an era when we spent a lot of time around, behind, and on top of horses. The fact that the capacity of car engines is still rated by **horsepower** is one echo of our equestrian past. Another is **spurred on**, being urged to give greater effort in the same way that horses are encouraged to gallop faster by the application to their side of *spurs*, small pieces of metal attached to boots. Medieval knights awarded golden spurs were said to **win their spurs**, an expression we now use for recognition of many kinds. High-status knights and noblemen rode unusually tall horses. This put them above commoners on smaller steeds, and gave these riders an air of being above it all. Like anyone today who puts on airs, they were **on a high horse**.

In order to mount a horse one has to swing one leg over the saddle, or **get a leg up**, a phrase we now apply to getting started in any activity. Skittish horses were often outfitted with *blinkers* or *blinders*, shades placed beside both eyes to restrict their peripheral vision. By extension human beings without much range are said to be **blinkered** or **have blinders on**. A tethered horse who'd eaten all of the grass in his vicinity was **at the end of his rope**, as is a desperate human being who is out of resources.

The best way to gauge a horse's age was by checking its teeth, which push forward more prominently every year as the horse grows **long in the tooth**. That practice left behind **look a gift horse in the mouth** as a reference to distrusting the donor of a present, and **straight from the horse's mouth** for an assertion heard first-hand.

Some hunters crept behind their horse, using its body to hide them from prey. That steed was called a **stalking horse**. Today this phrase is applied to stand-ins, usually a less prominent political candidate paving the way for one who is more prominent. British parliamentarian John Bright observed that trying to revive interest in an 1867 Reform Bill was like "flogging the dead horse." Since then **flog or beat a dead horse** has been standard parlance for engaging in futile activity.

Other commonly used terms that originated in our equestrian past include *horse sense, horse around, hold your horses, get back on the horse, change horses in midstream, put the horse before the cart*, and *work yourself into a lather*, much like an excited, overexerted horse who is dripping white foam. Also: *crack the whip, whip hand, rein in, free rein, take the bit in your teeth, champ at the bit*, and *hobbled*. Minuscule communities were, and still are, called **one-horse towns**.

Not just horses themselves but vehicles they pulled have left behind a rich nomenclature. The decades before cars appeared are sometimes called **horse-and-buggy** days, the connotation being *hopelessly out of date*. A blogger titled his commentary about America's antiquated health care system "Horse-and-Buggy Health Coverage." Not just buggies (four-wheeled people-conveying carriages usually pulled by a single horse), but the whips used by those who drove them, allude to obsolete devices. As an *Oxford English Dictionary* editor commented about an ostentatious piece of slang, "Wouldn't it be nice if it went the way of the buggy whip?" The straps connecting a horse to a buggy were, and are, called *traces*. A steed that could maneuver one leg outside these straps was more likely to kick than run. By analogy, any human being able to slip free of social controls is said to **kick over the traces**.

During horse-and-buggy days in England, **"Home, James, and don't spare the horses"** was a command aristocrats commonly gave their coachmen (or so we imagine). As a slangy catchphrase this admonition endured well into the automobile age. A *New York Times* article on chauffeured nursery schoolers was headlined "Once Around the Block, James, and Pick Me Up After Nap Time." In Los Angeles, a designated driver service calls itself Home James.

Horse-drawn wagons called *stagecoaches* plied American roads until the early twentieth century. Because these vehicles often carried valuables as well as passengers and traveled for long stretches in unpopulated areas, they were magnets for criminals. Indians were also a source of danger on some stage-coach routes. Therefore many companies employed a security guard who sat next to the driver on an elevated perch outside the wagon, shotgun at the ready. Known in his time as *the shotgun*, this guard left behind the term **ride shotgun**, meaning to sit next to the driver of any vehicle, cars especially. Among kids especially a car's front passenger seat is still called the **shotgun seat** or simply **shotgun** ("I've got shotgun!").

## Car Talk

While stopped at a red light, *Dayton Daily News* columnist D. L. Stewart tried to warn the driver of an adjacent car that one of her brake lights was out. To get her attention he honked his horn, then twirled his hand counterclockwise. The young woman glanced at him but didn't respond. Only after both cars took off did Stewart realize what had just transpired. Having grown up in an era of automatic windows, the other driver probably had no idea what his twirling hand referred to (*"Roll down your window"*). This combo of retroterm and retrogesture illustrates the communication gap between those who grew up with different generations of cars.

When most cars had manual transmissions and brakes cost more to repair than clutches, drivers routinely slowed their vehicle's momentum by *downshifting*, or putting its transmission into a lower gear. Today, **downshifting** more often refers to easing the tempo of one's life, particularly since a smell-the-flowers book by that title was published in 1991. The genesis of this term means little to generations of drivers who have never had to **shift gears** or **change gears**, concepts that also refer more to lifestyles than to automobiles nowadays. Other transmission-related retroterms include **get out of first gear** (or **stuck in first gear** or **stuck in neutral**), get **back in gear**, get **into high gear**, and **idle in neutral**.

A car with a manual transmission whose engine won't turn over can be started by placing its gearshift in first gear, depressing its clutch, having someone push the car by hand, then letting up on the clutch once it gains momentum. Since so few American cars have manual transmissions anymore, and so many drivers belong to the American Automobile Association, starting a car this way is rare. The term **jump start** lives on, however, referring to any stalled activity that's given a boost. An analogous phrase—**kick start**—has more to do with engaging a motorcycle's engine by stepping on a pedal, but is used synonymously with *jump start*. A **self-starter** originally referred to the feature of an automobile that made it unnecessary to crank an engine by hand to turn it over. Now this more often refers to a person who can get his or her work done without supervision.

In more frugal times, it was common to renew worn tires with fresh rubber through a vulcanizing process known as *retreading* or *recapping*. So many new treads didn't adhere, however, that American highways became littered with the remains of badly *recapped* tires. Over time this process became associated with shoddy do-overs, and gave way to the routine purchase of new tires. The term **retread** endured, however, referring to any rejuvenated person or activity. World War I veterans who fought in World War II were called *retreads*. That term has also been applied to remakes of classic movies. Other tire-based terms in our language include *not much tread left, spin your wheels, peel rubber*, and *burn rubber*. **Where the rubber meets the road** signifies the point at which an activity begins in earnest. Then there are **tire kickers**, browsers whom sales-people don't consider serious customers.

At one time a *stock car* retrofitted with features to make it faster and more unique was **souped-up**, probably because this often involved *supercharging* an engine with a pump that forced extra air into an engine's valves. Today that term refers to anything made more elaborate. (A *Los Angeles Times* article refers to one home's "souped-up kitchen with restaurant-size appliances.") Drivers of *souped-up* cars called **hot rods** sometimes engaged in games of *chicken*, or races toward walls or cliffs or each other. The driver who swerved first was considered a cowardly "chicken." A dramatic scene in the 1954 movie *Rebel Without a Cause* that features James Dean racing another teenager toward the edge of a cliff exemplifies **playing chicken** or simply **a game of chicken**. According to ABC News, gift buyers who wait for last-minute sales before Christmas are "playing a game of chicken with retailers."

The names of some early cars left retroterms behind. One was Ford's *Model T*. After being introduced in 1908, this no-frills automobile inspired the phrase "**the Model T of . . . ,**" or the most stripped-down version of any product. Until very recently *the Cadillac of* referred to top-of-the-line anything, but that concept has faded along with the luster of General Motors' high-end model. (Today one is just as likely to hear "the Mercedes of" or "the Rolls-Royce of.") When it comes to prestige, however, no car has ever matched the luxurious, custom-built Duesenbergs sold from 1920 to 1937. Duesenbergs were affectionately nicknamed "Duesies." Some believe that this is why we call anything first-rate **a real doozie**. Spoilsport etymologist Michael Quinion notes that this

 phrase antedates the car, however, and may have evolved from the eighteenth-century English slang *a real daisy*. The superlative **doozy** is well over a century old.

In the realm of auto sales, *sticker shock* is a concept that has crossed over into general discourse (referring to surprise at the high price on the sticker attached to a new car's window). Terms and concepts from many professions have made that journey: *knee-jerk reaction* from medicine, *square the circle* from mathematics, *curb appeal* from real estate. Some of these expressions linger in our discourse long after their original users have developed new in-terms. No professions have provided more retroterms than journalism and filmmaking.

# 10. Yes, Virginia, There Is a Casting Couch

**B**ecause they've been at the helm of our means of communication for so long, journalists and filmmakers have given us a wealth of terminology based on their customs and practices. Even though newspapers are ceding ground to websites, and films to video, long after this process is completed we will continue to use retroterms that these media left behind.

### Journalism

In early fall 1897, the *New York Sun*'s editorial-page editor handed staff writer Francis Pharcella Church a letter scrawled in a child's hand. It read:

> *Dear Editor:*
>
> *I am eight years old.*
> *Some of my little friends say there is no Santa Claus.*
> *Papa says, "If you see it in the Sun, it's so."*
> *Please tell me the truth, is there a Santa Claus?*
>
> *Virginia O'Hanlon*

The crusty Church scowled and tried to beg off his assignment to answer this letter. His editor insisted. Finally Church relented and trudged off, letter in hand. He soon returned with several paragraphs of copy. That copy ran in the *New York Sun* on September 21, 1897. Its conclusion was

*Yes, Virginia, there is a Santa Claus. He exists as certainly as
love and generosity and devotion exist, and you know that they
abound and give to your life its highest beauty and joy. Alas!
How dreary would be the world if there were no Santa
Claus!*

Church's piece of sentimental sophistry caught the public's fancy and became one of the most reprinted stories ever to appear in an American newspaper. It is recalled every time someone says, **"Yes, Virginia . . ."** when introducing an observation made with feigned world-weariness. "Yes, Virginia," *New York Times* columnist Paul Krugman once wrote, "polluters do write the regulations these days."

The *Sun* was probably the birthplace of another press retroexpression, one attributed to city editor John Bogart. "If a dog bites a man, that's not news," Bogart is said to have told a cub reporter who asked for his definition of news. "If a man bites a dog, that's news." This is such a bedrock conviction among journalists that they assume everyone realizes **man-bites-dog** refers to a situation so out of the ordinary as to merit press coverage. In general discourse it has become shorthand for any extraordinary event at all. An *Indianapolis Star* article called counterintuitive research findings that show workplace stress is in decline "a man bites dog kind of story."

In pre-computer days, newspaper reporters typed stories on copy paper, then handed the results to harried editors. On the desks of most editors sat what looked like a thin knitting needle attached to a pedestal. Stories unlikely to be published were punched onto this *spindle* (as in: "Do not fold, spindle, or mutilate"), what journalists called a **spike**. There the dead story sat, like a pig on a spit. It had been **spiked**, put on indefinite hold. *Time* magazine once charged that the ABC network, owned by Walt Disney Studios, "spikes story critical of Disney." (Adding confusion to

this retroterm is the fact that *spike* can also refer to an upward trajectory in some graphed activity such as heart rates or electricity usage or, by extension, TV ratings, murder rates, or book sales. They *spike*.)

Journalists have sometimes borrowed terms from other fields, then loaned them out. One is *deadline*. This term originated in American prisons where a *dead-line* was demarcated. Any prisoner crossing that line was liable to be shot. American reporters appropriated this concept for the date on which their copy was due—the **deadline**—and the rest of us now use it for due dates of all kinds.

After the Civil War, reporters borrowed **scoop** from merchants who, since mid-century, had used that verb to mean going one up on competitors. Members of the press still use *scoop* to mean being first out with a news story, and so do the rest of us for any pursuit in which we beat the competition. In the process it has shape-shifted once again to mean "exclusive" or "inside information": **the scoop**. ("Get the scoop on outlet pricing.")

Reporters who actually leave their desk to cover stories like to say they practice **shoe-leather journalism**. In a time of Google, Wikipedia, e-mail, and cell phones, this kind of reporting feels less and less necessary. That is why—combined with the fact that so few soles are made of leather anymore—this phrase sounds rather musty. Nonetheless it has been borrowed by those who do investigative work in other fields: *shoe-leather epidemiology, shoe-leather sleuthing,* etc.

Among journalists, pride of place is given to front-page news stories that appear *above the fold*, or over the folded line of a broadsheet newspaper, where they are seen at first glance. Since such articles are thought to be of paramount importance, **above the fold** has become synonymous with anything thought to merit unusual attention. An e-marketing consultant advises clients to pay attention to what prospective customers see "above the fold," or at the beginning of their e-mails. On the other hand, a blogger once accused CNN of burying a televised story "below the fold."

This concept applies only to traditional broadsheet newspapers with horizontal folds, of course. In the late nineteenth century a new type of format appeared, one with smaller pages that were folded vertically, like those of a magazine. At first readers didn't know what to call this compact type of newspaper. By analogy it resembled a kind of compressed medical pill introduced in 1884 by Burroughs, Wellcome. That pharmaceutical company called its new product line Tabloid. It didn't take long for this term to be applied to any compressed item, including the vertical-fold newspaper format pioneered by London's *Daily Mail* and New York's *Daily News*. Because *tabloid newspapers* tended to emphasize sensational news coverage, their name itself came to signify that style of reporting. Thus: **tabloid journalism** or the **tabloid press**. Over time such newspapers were nicknamed **tabs**.

William Randolph Hearst's *New York Journal* and Joseph Pulitzer's *New York World* may not have been tabloid newspapers in format, but they certainly were in spirit. During the late nineteenth century both vied to outdo each other with sensational news coverage and garish publicity stunts. Capitalizing on that era's bicycle mania, while trying to develop a competitor to Pulitzer's popular Yellow Kid cartoon with one called Yellow Fellow, Hearst mounted a coast-to-coast bike race called the "Yellow Fellow Transcontinental Relay." On August 25, 1896, a bicyclist dressed in yellow left the building of Hearst's *San Francisco Examiner*. For the next two weeks, relays of yellow-clad cyclists braved snow, rain, mud, and tumbling tumbleweeds as they sped across the continent. Daily coverage in Hearst's papers gave breathless accounts of the race beneath screaming headlines. A huge map outside the *Journal* offices in New York recorded the racers' progress for crowds of onlookers. On September 8, the last rider delivered a letter from San Francisco's postmaster to his New York counterpart, who was among a group of dignitaries on a decorated reviewing stand. The charge that the perpetrators of such hoopla practiced *yellow journalism* subsequently became ubiquitous, especially as Hearst and Pulitzer helped provoke the Spanish-American War in 1898 by competing for readers with lurid, often contrived coverage of events in Cuba. Throughout the twentieth century the label **yellow journalism** was applied to sensational, embellished news coverage by the **yellow press**. Author Robert Satloff (*Among the Righteous*) has accused TV network Al Jazeera of engaging in "yellow sensationalism."

Another type of journalism focused on investigative reporting about rampant abuse of economic power by the monopolists known as *robber barons* at the turn of the century. No one knew what to call this group of reporters until the day in 1906 when President Theodore Roosevelt charged that some were "raking the muck" (drawing on John Bunyan's reference to "the Man with the Muck Rake" in *Pilgrim's Progress*). A century later investigative journalists— and snoopers of all kinds—are still called **muckrakers**.

In quite another vein was the work of journalist and short-story writer Damon Runyon. Runyon was the bard of New York street life between the World Wars. His columns and stories were filled with colorful, slang-spouting street figures who sported names such as Dave the Dude, Harry the Horse, and Izzy Cheesecake. (The musical *Guys and Dolls* was inspired by Runyon's work.) Six decades after his 1946 death, that type of figure is still known as a "Damon Runyon character." Runyon's passion for gambling inspired the most famous of his many quotable remarks: "All of life is seven to five against." Runyon also said, "The race is not always to the swift, nor the battle to the strong, but that's the way to bet." This type of cynical, streetwise comment is still known as **Runyonesque**.

Runyon's contemporary Max Miller also made a big contribution to our lexicon, in his case the title of a book. In 1932 Miller stitched together vignettes he'd written during years of covering San Diego's harbor area for that city's *Sun* newspaper. He called his book *I Cover the Waterfront*. In an admirably piquant tone, this book portrayed a world of sailors, smugglers, hustlers, and fish cleaners—including a young Italian man who worked fishing tuna until he was knocked cold by a squid that flew out of the water and hit him in the nose. Miller's surprise bestseller inspired a haunting song by the same title that became one of Billie Holiday's signature tunes. To this day **cover the waterfront** refers to taking a comprehensive look at pretty much anything. After his publishing history was described in detail by an NPR interviewer, author Stephen King commented, "You've got the waterfront covered there."

Hunter Thompson was like a deranged descendant of Max Miller and Damon Runyon. After reading a hallucinatory, stream-of-consciousness magazine article that Thompson wrote about the 1970 Kentucky Derby, his friend Bill Cardoso said, "That is pure gonzo!" Cardoso, a *Boston Globe* reporter, explained that in South Boston, *gonzo* referred to the last man standing after a long bout of drinking. (He thought it derived from the French Canadian term *gonzeaux*, or "shining path.") Thompson's body of work came to be known as

**gonzo journalism**. Today, *gonzo* is applied to any work that is considered off the wall, if not over the top. *Publishers Weekly* once called a novel "gonzo post-apocalyptic fantasy."

Hunter Thompson was one of several journalists featured in Timothy Crouse's 1973 book *Boys on the Bus*. Crouse portrayed reporters who covered the 1972 presidential campaign as a bunch of preening follow-the-leaders who seldom dug beneath the surface and showed little imagination in their news coverage (Thompson being a notable exception). Following the publication of Crouse's pathbreaking book, **boys on the bus** became shorthand for pack journalism. After bloggers became part of that pack, an NPR correspondent reported, "joining the boys on the bus are colleagues reporting online for the Internet." The Huffington Post website calls its iconoclastic political coverage by thousands of non-journalists "Off the Bus."

## Filmmaking

In classic Hollywood Westerns, a static scene quickly grew active when a group of good guys riding horses threw up furious clouds of dust while chasing a group of mounted bad guys. This was called *cutting to the chase*. That concept dates back to the early days of moviemaking. (A 1929 novel by sometime screenwriter J. P. McEvoy included a movie script that repeatedly directed, "Cut to chase.") In subsequent decades **cut to the chase** wandered off screen sets and became synonymous with "Get to the point." **Cut them off at the pass** has also lingered as a catchphrase borrowed from early Westerns. Galloping good guys in those films were often able to capture fleeing bad guys by taking a shortcut. ("Let's cut 'em off at the pass!") An advice columnist suggested that a wife concerned about how much time her husband was spending with a young woman at his golf club take up that game herself and join him on the links. "This maneuver is called 'cutting her off at the pass,'" the columnist explained.

In the early days of Western moviemaking heroes typically wore white hats. That's how you knew they were good guys. Bad guys with whom they tangled generally wore black hats. From this visual device emerged the phrases **white hats** and **black hats**. Of the morally ambiguous reality show *Survivor*, an early contestant observed, "Hopefully in the end you wore a white hat more of the time than you wore a black hat."

Enough pioneers in Westerns wheeled their covered wagons into a circle to defend themselves against attacking Indians that we assume this was a common defensive maneuver. They **circled the wagons**. In fact, as Bill Bryson points out in *Made in America*, that time-consuming strategy was actually a figment of screenwriters' imaginations. Covered-wagon circling happened so often on-screen that **circling the wagons** or **wagon circling** came to refer broadly to any group huddled in a tight defensive posture. When under heavy criticism, defensive White House occupants are typically depicted as *circling the wagons.*

An impressive number of everyday catchphrases were born amid the ranch houses and tumbling tumbleweeds of Western movies. They include: **bite the dust** (signifying someone who is shot off his horse and lands face down on the ground), **cavalry to the rescue** (referring to blue-clad cavalrymen with banners held high who so often rescued victims of Indian attacks at the last minute), **meanwhile, back at the ranch** (a segue line from silent movies and radio serials), **pack iron** (what hired guns did, as well as sheriffs and the like), **notch on your gun** (for every person killed), as well as **trigger happy**, having an **itchy trigger finger** (being overly eager to start shooting, or mix it up in general), **slap leather** (pull a gun from its holster), **shoot from the hip** (the way a quick-draw gunfighter fired his pistol, after yanking it from its holster), and **slow on the draw** (slow to get one's gun out of its holster). According to former Federal Reserve Board Vice-Chairman Alan Blinder, a disastrous housing bubble resulted because the Fed was "slow on the draw" when it came to raising interest rates.

**Dying with your boots on**, or while still active, was thought to be a badge of honor in the Old West, or at least on the old Western screen. Since so many who died this way presumably were gunned down, Western movies and TV shows popularized (and probably coined) the term **boot hill** for the graveyard where such victims were buried. Enough of these productions concluded with the hero galloping toward the setting sun that **riding off into the sunset** became a cliché for endings of many kinds.

Rivaling Westerns for popularity among early moviegoers were weekly serials. Those who filmed these multiepisode thrillers quickly figured out that if they left their hero or heroine in dire distress at the end of one segment—tied to railroad tracks with a locomotive approaching, sinking in quicksand, or hanging from a cliff as the camera dissolved (followed by the words "To Be

Continued")—moviegoers were likely to return for the next one. From this comes the term **cliffhanger** to characterize any dramatic, unresolved situation. Popular serial star Pearl White was known as "the Queen of the Cliffhangers." (See chapter 11.)

Slapstick comedies were another early fan favorite, especially those produced by Hollywood's Keystone Film Company. Some featured a group of hapless policemen who careened about wildly, going the wrong way, waving their nightsticks, falling out of overloaded cars. Even though this zany group appeared in only nine films between 1912 and 1917, they became such an icon of laughable ineptness that **Keystone Kops** still suggests ineffectual manic activity. (Their name was actually spelled Keystone Cops.) Following the devastation inflicted by Hurricane Katrina, hapless federal relief officials were commonly compared to the Keystone Cops. A variant is **Keystonesque.** Alternatively, as Tony Hillerman wrote in his novel *Seldom Disappointed*, "I watched this **Keystone Copish** squandering of our tax dollars."

From moviemakers' earliest days in Queens, New York, studios, their terminology has had a huge impact on our culture and our language. Moviemaking parlance quickly drifted into the vernacular: *close-up, dissolve, outtake, pan, pan in, pan out, fade in, fade out, that's a wrap, wrapped, bit part, slow motion.* In an update on *Potemkin villages*, too-good-to-be-true settings were referred to as looking **like a Hollywood set.** Too-good-to-be-true resolutions came to be known as **Hollywood endings,** the kind that characterized so many American movies.

Although we now use the terms generically, in the era of *double features* or *double bills*, **A-movies** and **B-movies** had very specific characteristics. An A-movie (or *main feature*) was shot with about 135,000 feet of film, included big-name stars on elaborate sets, and took a year or more to complete. A B-movie (or *second feature*) used half that amount of film, featured less-noted actors on rudimentary sets, and enjoyed only a few months of production time to become the second feature at theaters. Until he got **top billing**, Humphrey Bogart made lots of **B-pictures.** *Time* magazine referred to the "B-movie cast of characters" who were plaintiffs in a trial of hapless would-be terrorists.

Before it was done digitally, editing raw film involved literally slicing and splicing pieces of film in the *cutting room*. As a result, any scene that was filmed but not included in the final version was said to have been **left on the cutting-room floor**. Now this expression refers to any element of a product that doesn't become part of the final version. A completed movie was said to be *in the can* (referring to circular canisters in which reels of film are stored), ready for shipment to theaters. This now refers to just about anything that's done, completed, finished. It's **in the can**.

A certain genre of postwar movie was chockablock with sultry women and sinister men in fedoras who smoked cigarettes as they peered through parted Venetian blinds. These movies relied on muted lighting to create a dark, ominous atmosphere. In 1946 a French critic dubbed this genre *film noir*, literally "black film." That concept led to the adjective *noirish*. In her book *Word Watch*, Anne Soukhanov defined **noirish** as "projecting an aura suffused with disillusionment, pessimism, despair, mystery, and often a dark sexuality." Although applied most often to movies, this term has found other uses, as when a *Harrisburg Patriot-News* review of a graphic novel was headlined, "Noirish Story Is Expertly Drawn."

## CASTING

In 1926 a central casting office was created to screen lesser-known actors. Since this venture focused on *types* ("We can send you a Gary Cooper type"), actors as well as people in general who seemed to fit a stereotype came to be known as **straight out of central casting**. A review of John Le Carré's novel *Single & Single* concluded, "Too many characters are straight from central casting." Another way of saying the same thing is that such actors, and stereotypical people in general, are **typecast**. Casting directors willing to break the mold are said to **cast against type**. Actors who take roles outside their usual range **play against type**. The *Wall Street Journal* once reported that the usually restrictive Food and Drug Administration "played against type and gave approval for Avastin as a treatment for metastatic breast cancer." Secondary actors are said to be in the **supporting cast**, a phrase now applied to second-tier participants in other activities as well. At the bottom of the billing, just above non-speaking *extras*, are **bit players**. Author Daniel Yergin called German carmaker Daimler-Benz a "bit player" in the huge U.S. auto market.

Casting directors, producers, directors, and others who demand sexual favors in return for parts are said to have a *casting couch*. Because he was notorious for bartering movie roles for sex, producer Darryl Zanuck was said to have this figurative piece of furniture in his office. When Zanuck's son Richard joined his production company, the producer introduced him to others as "head of the casting couch." **Casting couch** is now applied more broadly to any transaction in which sexual favors are part of the quid pro quo. Needless to say there is also a movie called . . . *Casting Couch*.

## 11. Movie Metaphors

When mounting a program called "Film and Faith," the Museum of Modern Art asked some scholars to nominate movies with religious themes. To the curators' surprise, one film mentioned repeatedly was the comedy *Groundhog Day*. After it was released in 1993, critics and moviegoers were underwhelmed by this depiction of a self-centered TV weatherman played by Bill Murray who is forced to relive a single day until he finally learns from his mistakes. As MOMA's curators discovered, however, over the course of a decade *Groundhog Day* had built a substantial, diverse following. Psychotherapists use *Groundhog Day* to make the point that in order to grow emotionally patients must stop doing the same thing over and over hoping for a better result. Philosophers suggest that it illustrates Nietzsche's concept of eternal return. Some rabbis believe *Groundhog Day* exemplifies the Jewish emphasis on good works over salvation, and some ministers think this movie illustrates a Christian emphasis on salvation over good works. Buddhists have embraced *Groundhog Day* with particular passion, seeing in Bill Murray's time-stuck character the personification of continual rebirth. It is among moviegoers in general, however, that *Groundhog Day* has had its most lasting impact. I'd hazard a guess that no movie is referenced more often. This film struck such a resonant chord that simply saying **Groundhog Day** is sufficient to evoke an image of events repeating themselves in an endless loop. After spending three months in North Korea, an American relief worker reported that life in that austere country had an unvaried "*Groundhog Day* quality."

Psychiatrist Philip McCullough once noted how routinely his patients used cinematic analogies to describe their lives. As the most universal experience

Americans have shared long-term, movies provide a vocabulary for national discourse. Certain films left behind lots of detritus: phrases, buzzwords, names of characters, their titles. Many such allusions outlived the popularity of the movie that spawned them. Ones that evoked primal emotions—lust, fear, and, especially, *dread*—proved especially well suited to this task.

This is why, nearly a century after it was produced, **Perils of Pauline** remains part of our vocabulary. That 1914 serial featured Pearl White, "Queen of the Cliffhangers." (See chapter 10.) In its twenty episodes, the Missouri-born actress played an heiress named Pauline. First she floated aimlessly in a runaway hot-air balloon that crashed at the top of a cliff, sending her hurtling over its side. Pauline later had to dash down a mountain one step ahead of a rolling boulder. This was before bad guys left her tied up inside a burning building, and blew up the yacht on which the heiress was a passenger— moments after she jumped overboard (as moviego-ers discovered in the subsequent episode). Few

remember the name Pearl White, but we continually refer to her most famous role. NASA's onetime director compared the agency's repeated problems with its Galileo space mission to "a *Perils of Pauline* episode."

Cheesy movies are every bit as likely to generate retroterms as better ones, if not more so—especially if they excite the most primitive, emotion-laden parts of our reptilian brains. One memorably horrifying 1954 movie starred a huge, scaly, drooling humanoid that emerged from the dark waters of an Amazon River lagoon. Originally released in 3-D, **The Creature from the Black Lagoon** made an especially big impression on young viewers, who continued to use its title figuratively as they aged. In his novel *The Night Listener*, Armistead Maupin writes of a character wearing a leather jacket and bike helmet, "he looked like the Creature from the Black Lagoon." Four decades after that movie's release, a paleontologist named a fossil of an amphibian she discovered *Eucritta melanolimnetes*, Greek for "the creature from the black lagoon."

*The Birds* is another scary movie whose title became a verbal touchstone. Not considered one of Alfred Hitchcock's better efforts, that 1963 film im-printed moviegoers with a nightmarish vision of actress Tippi Hedren being attacked by battalions of screeching crows. Anyone who has ever looked up at a flock of cackling birds and wondered what would happen if they dive-bombed our eyeballs can relate to **The Birds.** According to *Newsweek*, when Hillary Clinton was first lady, members of her protective staff were "afflicted by Tippi Hedren syndrome—they often look as if they are about to be attacked by birds."

The fact that Hedren sought refuge in a glass-walled phone booth while under avian siege may have hastened the demise of that retrostructure. Hitchcock had a genius for imbuing mundane settings with horror. Nowhere did he do this more effectively than in *Psycho.* That movie's classic murder-in-the-**shower scene** at the Bates Motel is one of the most memorable in film history, partly because it was so well staged, but even more because it acknowledged how vulnerable we all feel while naked behind a translucent curtain that obscures our vision as pounding water muffles outside sounds. Taking a shower in a stall away from home enhances the sense of dread. Movie critic Pauline Kael once said that whenever showering in a motel she flashed on *Psycho*'s murder scene. "Doesn't everybody?" asked Kael.

An Englishwoman once wondered how many other visitors to the United States like her thought about **the Bates Motel** when checking into a modest American hostelry. Tony Perkins's brilliant portrayal of its proprietor—**Norman Bates**—imprinted us with an image of a creepy character who appears normal, sort of, but clearly has *issues* bubbling beneath the surface. In an inspired piece of marketing strategy, theater owners were not allowed to seat customers during *Psycho*'s denouement, to keep them from realizing that Bates is actually a homicidal maniac who shares a home with his dead mother's corpse. The motel owner went on to become a poster child of derangement. According to Jack Maple, the author of *Crimefighter*, under America's loose gun-purchase regulations, "Norman Bates would have no trouble buying a gun."

## Mind Control

Particularly after U.S. soldiers proved so susceptible to brainwashing in Korea, Americans grew increasingly anxious about their own brains being laundered. If the minds of disciplined military men could be controlled that way, whose couldn't? Smart moviemakers tuned into this anxiety with a series of memorable films that still reverberate in our collective psyche. None did so more effectively than **Invasion of the Body Snatchers.** This 1956 adaptation of Jack Finney's novel *The Body Snatchers* features ordinary suburbanites who have been replaced by replica aliens gestated in pods. These beings look exactly like the humans they've replaced but lack feelings of any kind. Their demeanor is cold, robotic. Some saw them as the perfect allegory for mind-controlling Communists. Others thought *pod people* represented lockstep McCarthyites. Jack Finney denied that his novel had any such agenda. Director Don Siegel would say only that the world is full of zombielike pod people, many of whom could be found in Hollywood. Remakes of Siegel's movie took up new cudgels. In the 1978 version, pod people are allegorical for cultists, in 1996 for terrorists. **Pod people**, or simply **pods**, proved to be one of those versatile concepts that could be applied to whomever one wished to belittle. In his novel *Sacred*, Dennis Lehane referred to a group of mindless lowlifes as "Pods." Susan Faludi called members of a conservative women's group "pod feminists." Since there is never any shortage of those eager to do other people's thinking for them and followers eager to comply, *Invasion of the Body Snatchers* itself has proved to be a lasting allusion with shifting targets. The authors of *Suburban Nation* charged that like "an architectural version of *Invasion of the Body Snatchers*, our main streets and neighborhoods have been replaced by alien substitutes, similar but not the same." In her *New York Times* review of Tom Perrotta's novel *Little Children*, Janet Maslin said its suburban mom protagonist "feels that she has been body-snatched out of a stimulating city life."

*The Stepford Wives* provided an even more potent allegory for suburban anomie, one that added a nifty sexual subtext to the body-snatcher notion. Based on Ira Levin's novel by the same title, this 1975 film portrays voluptuous, genetically altered housewives who love to wash dishes and sweep floors when not satisfying their husband's carnal needs. (A 2004 remake that changed the subject to gender ambiguity richly deserved its rapid demise.) These robotic women prove to be lookalike androids whom husbands use to replace wives they've murdered. The substitute spouses gave new meaning to the term "dutiful." Like *pod people*, **Stepford wives** came to symbolize cultlike conformity. A writer for the *Guardian* concluded that a movement of eco-activist women "looks a bit Stepford wives from the outside." In the singular, **Stepford wife** is also a handy synonym for vacuous homemakers who live only to please their husbands. **Stepford** alone is one of our favorite labels to hang on anyone or any group we perceive as too lockstepped. Innumerable examples I've seen include Stepford judges, Stepford novels, Stepford fans, Stepford Democrats, Stepford moms, and Stepford husbands.

With its bleak portrayal of a future Los Angeles populated by pod people and pop buildings, *Blade Runner* set a new standard for ominous times to come. This sci-fi film portrays L.A. as a dark, smoky city filled with "replicants," genetically engineered humanoids who are pursued by cops on Rollerblades. The city it depicts anticipated the ethnic bouillabaisse Los Angeles would become, one deeply divided economically and suffering from the effects of climate change. Though indifferently received when it was released in 1982, **Blade Runner** gradually came to be seen as a prescient forecast of urban horror. In the process Ridley Scott's movie became a verbal touchstone. *USA Today* once referred to the *"Blade Runner*-esque" world of futuristic websites. *New Yorker* architecture critic Paul Goldberger characterized the skyline of Shanghai as one with a " 'Blade Runner' aesthetic."

## Tracking Headlines

At the peak of our anxiety about nuclear holocausts, the 1964 movie *Dr. Strangelove: Or, How I Stopped Worrying and Learned to Love the Bomb* put that fear on film, and invited us to laugh about it. This black comedy was memorable for a few scenes in particular: Peter Sellers as a fanatical German scientist working for the Americans who struggles to keep his black-gloved hand from snapping skyward in a Nazi salute, Sterling Hayden as a paranoid U.S. Army general named Jack D. Ripper who is concerned about Communists tampering with our "precious bodily fluids" by fluoridating American water, and George C. Scott as Air Force General Buck Turgidson casually estimating how many acceptable millions of deaths a nuclear war would entail ("Mr. President, I'm not saying we wouldn't get our hair mussed, but I do say not more than ten to twenty million killed tops, depending on the breaks"). In the movie's denouement, Major T. J. "King" Kong, played by Slim Pickens, rides a nuclear bomb to earth, yee-hawing and waving his cowboy hat the whole way down. This movie made such a lasting impression that **Dr. Strangelove** remains a common way to characterize mad scientists and doomsday theoreticians who might subject the rest of us to mass destruction. Another way of referring to that type of person is **Strangelovian**, an appellation sometimes applied to former Secretary of State Henry Kissinger. After Americans negotiated a deal that allowed India to retain its nuclear weapons, the *Economist*'s cover pictured George W. Bush in full cowboy regalia astride a falling bomb. Its headline read

"George W. Bush in Dr. Strangedeal, Or, How I Learned to Stop Worrying and Love My Friend's Bomb."

Four years before starring in *Dr. Strangelove,* Peter Sellers appeared in **The Mouse That Roared**. Based on a novel by Leonard Wibberley, this 1959 movie portrayed a tiny country called the Duchy of Grand Fenwick that declares war on the United States in hopes of losing and becoming eligible for lots of aid, like Germany and Japan after World War II. Inadvertently, however, Grand Fenwick acquires a potent nuclear "Q-bomb" and defeats the United States. The duchy subsequently forces the great powers to junk all nuclear weapons by threatening to detonate its Q-bomb. This movie's title is still invoked when small powers try to manipulate big ones. After Norway's tiny consumer protection agency complained about Apple's exclusive iPod-iTunes deal, *Business Week* reported that "the mouse that roared is picking up supporters."

## From Violence to Vigilantes

A pioneering low-budget indie film called *Easy Rider* featured Jack Nicholson's breakout role as an alcoholic lawyer picked up by two Los Angeles drug dealers (Peter Fonda and Dennis Hopper) who are riding motorcycles to New Orleans for Mardi Gras. Much of this 1969 movie takes place in rural Louisiana, where the three are harassed by locals and cops. *Easy Rider* captured the sense of mobility, drug-induced mood swings, and paranoia that was rampant as the sixties became the seventies. The film's final line—"We blew it"—uttered by Peter Fonda foresaw the crash of sixties euphoria. All three protagonists are ultimately slaughtered by rednecks wielding shotguns. **Easy Rider**—originally African-American slang for a smooth lover—is still shorthand for bigoted southerners and the settings they inhabit ("*Easy Rider* country"). For want of a fresher term, a contributor to *Newsweek*'s "My Turn" column once referred to "'Easy Rider' type bigots."

Three years after *Easy Rider* came out, *Deliverance* upped the stereotyping ante. Based on James Dickey's novel of the same title, this 1972 movie featured four Atlanta canoers who confront two slovenly, gun-toting crackers in Georgia's backwoods. The film's dramatic opening moments—in which a mute, squinty-eyed young banjo player who has bad teeth conducts a fast-paced musical duel with a visiting guitarist—made enough of an impression that three decades after its release computer columnist "Dr. Bombay" complained about tech supporters who "treated me like the kid from *Deliverance.*" In that movie's most memorable scene, Ned Beatty's character is splayed on the ground by a snarling backwoodsman and told to "squeal like a pig" before being sodomized. That riveting episode provided male moviegoers with the rare experience of having this primordial fear acted out before their very eyes. (For years thereafter Beatty had to endure men shouting "Squeal like a pig!" whenever he was out in public.) The pair of predatory, semi-toothless woodsmen who stalked the Atlantans are often used as an analogy. ("Two men appeared out of the woods, looking like something out of the movie *Deliverance.*" —*People* "He looked like a character from *Deliverance.*" —*Esquire*)

Like *Easy Rider*, *Deliverance* played on northern fear of southern rednecks at a time when this fear was burning brightly. For urban northerners who don't have much contact with rural southerners but do have lots of paranoid notions about what they're like, such movies serve a valuable function: they give form to fantasies and leave behind a useful grammar. According to comedian Bill Maher, an effective heckler-squelcher is "Are you retarded or just auditioning for the dinner-theater company of *Deliverance?*"

*Deliverance* concluded with the canoers pursuing and killing their tormentors. This was a common theme at that time. Against a backdrop of war, crime, and civil disorder, the 1970s were hospitable to movies whose protagonists *take matters into their own hands*. Leading this parade was Harry "Dirty Harry" Callaghan—the San Francisco cop who makes up his own rules while pursuing loathsome crooks in *Dirty Harry* (1971) and several sequels. This freewheeling approach to law enforcement inspired what's still called "Dirty Harry fantasies" among macho moviegoers. Another way of saying the same thing is "*Death Wish* fantasies." That's a tip of the hat to the 1974 movie *Death Wish*, based on Brian Garfield's novel by this title, in which Charles Bronson played pacifistic architect Paul Kersey, who becomes a gun-toting vigilante after his wife is killed and their daughter is raped by savage criminals. That movie and its sequels provided an enduring metaphor. As a college professor wrote to "Miss Manners" (Judith Martin) about facing down some youths who tried to force him off the sidewalk: "My wife thinks . . . I'm merely a Charles Bronson *Death Wish* vigilante."

**Travis Bickle** is a different type of vigilante altogether. Bickle, played by Robert De Niro in Martin Scorsese's 1976 movie *Taxi Driver*, is a deranged cabbie who sees himself as an avenging angel for a young prostitute played by Jodie Foster. The fact that would-be assassin John Hinckley was inspired by the cabdriver's example to stalk Foster herself, then to shoot Ronald Reagan, helped make Bickle's name iconic. When sentencing a man who murdered his brother to six years in prison, a San Francisco judge said, "You became Travis Bickle." In addition to his name, Bickle's soliloquy as he practices threat behavior before a mirror remains iconic. "You talkin' to me?" he asks. "You talkin' to *me?* Then who the hell else are you talkin' to? You talkin' to me? Well I'm the only one here." When someone says in a mock threatening way, **"You talkin' to me?"** Travis Bickle is usually on his mind.

John Rambo was a global counterpart to Travis Bickle, Dirty Harry, and Paul Kersey. Sylvester Stallone enjoyed so much success portraying this buff, bandannaed ex–Green Beret who shoots his way across Southeast Asia in several movies that **Rambo** has become the standard eponym for muscle-flexing males who are ready for action. During the 1991 Gulf War, reckless soldiers were nicknamed "Rambo," their headscarves "Rambo rags." In one episode of NBC's *West Wing* a pugnacious character is referred to as "all Ramboed up." In another a campaign aide talks of being "in some state of deep Ramboesque mission."

With its depiction of an apparently innocent fling turned murderously obsessive relationship, *Fatal Attraction* (1987)—in which Glenn Close's character first beds, then stalks a man played by Michael Douglas before his wife takes her out vigilante-style—became synonymous with risky courtship in general. Reporters called a 1991 case involving a onetime New York schoolteacher who was accused of killing her former lover's wife "the 'Fatal Attraction' murder."

Cinema's vigilante era culminated in a 1991 movie in which Susan Sarandon and Geena Davis portray two friends off on an innocent-seeming road trip. Along the way they kill a man who tries to assault them, then shoot up the vehicle of a harassing trucker, making it explode. This, of course, was *Thelma and Louise.* Their names live on as synonymous with take-no-prisoners women. (Announcing a "Shooting for Women" workshop, New Hampshire's *Portsmouth Herald News* warned, "Don't go all 'Thelma and Louise' after this.") In the movie's conclusion the pair avoid capture by driving themselves off a cliff while holding hands. This scene made a particularly big impression, as when a Los Angeles TV producer noted that a car chase his station was broadcasting live might culminate in "a Thelma-and-Louise off a cliff."

## Classics

As we've seen, movies that leave retroterms behind aren't necessarily considered classics. Those that are thought to be classic seldom produce lasting verbiage. There are some exceptions, however, and *Citizen Kane* is one. Charles Foster Kane, the protagonist of Orson Welles's 1941 roman à clef about publisher William Randolph Hearst, remains a lasting icon. Press tycoons such as Rupert Murdoch and *Rolling Stone*'s Jann Wenner are sometimes compared to Kane. More often the term *rosebud* is referenced. This is the word murmured by a dying Kane as the movie opens. It provides *Citizen Kane*'s spine as a reporter struggles to discover what *rosebud* refers to. In the movie's closing scene that word is shown to be the name of a sled the publisher was riding as a child the day his mother left him. **Rosebud** has since come to stand for elements of a life that provide a key to someone's character. According to book critic Louis Menand, biographers are susceptible to "the Rosebud assumption that the real truth about a person involves the thing that is least known to others."

In her memoir *Washington*, journalist Meg Greenfield referred to onetime boy wonders in that city as "political Norma Desmonds." Greenfield was referring to the faded actress Gloria Swanson played in *Sunset Boulevard* (1950). Swanson's riveting portrayal of this delusional character left **Norma Desmond** behind as shorthand for has-beens. When a man in *Sunset Boulevard* says, "You used to be big," the fiery Desmond responds with one of the most famous lines in cinema history: **"I am big! It's the pictures that got small."** Suggesting that it wasn't voters as much as political elites who had grown narrow and partisan, *New York Times* columnist John Tierney wrote, "As Norma Desmond might put it, We're still big. It's the parties that got smaller."

In the case of *High Noon* it's not a specific character or line but the movie overall that became allegorical. Considered by some to be the best Western ever made, *High Noon* features Gary Cooper as small town sheriff Will Kane, who is abandoned by townspeople as he's about to confront four criminals bent on killing him. Throughout this 1952 movie, close-ups linger on Cooper's expression of restrained anguish (the actor actually was in constant pain from a recent hernia operation). When not studying Cooper's face, the camera sometimes shifts to a clock whose hands are approaching noon. That is when the bad guys are due. Because *High Noon* was released during a period of anti-Communist hysteria and its screenplay was secretly written by Carl Foreman, a blacklisted victim of that hysteria, some considered this movie an allegory for victims like him who were deserted by friends. Over time, however, **High Noon** simply alluded to showdowns of any kind. During a standoff between warring factions in Najaf, Iraq, *Newsweek* reported that "a spooky 'High Noon' atmosphere hung over the whole town."

Like *High Noon, On the Waterfront* is considered one of the best movies ever made. That's not the main reason we remember this 1954 film, however. What we remember best is a single scene in which Marlon Brando's character, washed-up boxer Terry Malloy, castigates his brother-manager Charley (Rod Steiger). Years before, Charley had Terry throw a fight that could have led to a championship bout. "I coulda had class!" Malloy tells his brother. "I coulda been a contender. I coulda been somebody, instead of a bum, which is what I am." Enough of us can relate to this feeling that **I coulda been a contender** is a recurring part of everyday discourse, even among those who have never seen *On the Waterfront*. A blogger once argued that if it hadn't been overshadowed by more-hyped video games, one called *Katamari Damacy* "coulda been a contender" for game of the year.

"Plastics" is another comment made famous by a classic movie: *The Graduate*. In Mike Nichols's 1967 adaptation of Charles Webb's novel, as young Benjamin Braddock, Dustin Hoffman is on the receiving end of an exchange with a friend of his parents who says he has just one word of advice for him: *"Plastics."* Long after "plastics" became a lasting buzzword, and emblematic of *The Graduate* as a whole, director Mike Nichols confessed that he'd initially wondered whether that word belonged in the movie at all. He and scriptwriter Buck Henry considered alternative terms to portray a stultifying conversation-stopper. Luckily for posterity, they could not improve on **plastics.** Although hardly original, after *The Graduate* became a hit, the term **plastic** took on new life as a synonym for tacky, superficial, and disposable. ("He's so plastic." "We live in a plastic world.")

In another *Graduate* scene, the mother of Hoffman's girlfriend strips to bra and panties, then runs her fingers suggestively down one calf for the benefit of a goggle-eyed Ben Braddock. Teenage boys in the audience could barely contain themselves as they watched that scene. This seductive mother, played by Anne Bancroft, is the immortal **Mrs. Robinson.** "You're trying to seduce me, aren't you, Mrs. Robinson!" Braddock exclaims. It is a tribute to Bancroft's acting ability that at the age of thirty-six—just six years older than

Hoffman—she could create a template for older women hitting on younger men. *Washington Times* writer Emily Wilkinson once referred to an alleged affair between Branwell Bronte and "a Mrs. Robinson, [the] mother of a boy he tutored." Helping cement this name into our collective memory was Simon and Garfunkel's song "Mrs. Robinson" with its memorable stanza "Coo, coo, ca-choo, Mrs. Robinson / Jesus loves you more than you will know (Woo, woo, woo)." For reasons her children can't fathom, one ravishing middle-aged woman is known to friends as *Coo Coo Ca-Choo.*

In another memorable 1967 movie, Spencer Tracy and Katharine Hepburn play an enlightened San Francisco couple who are nonplussed when their daughter (Katharine Houghton) brings home a black boyfriend played by Sidney Poitier. This plotline was a rare attempt to deal with the issue of interracial dating. It was so rare, in fact, that for years thereafter this movie's title— **Guess Who's Coming to Dinner?**—alluded to racial mingling in general. On *Meet the Press*, Eugene Robinson of the *Washington Post* said that if Hillary Clinton were to eat as well as speak at a black church, "it could be a kind of reverse *Guess Who's Coming to Dinner?*"

It's hard to know where to begin considering leftover allusions from Francis Ford Coppola's adaptation of Mario Puzo's novel *The Godfather*. Referencing its crime family head Vito "Don" Corleone, *Newsweek* once called Osama bin Laden "the **Don Corleone** of terror." In his book *Big Blues*, Paul Carroll said that some employees considered CEO Steve Ballmer "the **Luca Brasi** of Microsoft," referring to one of Corleone's more brutal henchmen. In the same book Carroll observed that some software executives who tried to deal with Microsoft head Bill Gates ended up "hoping that Gates might soon find a bloody **horse's head** lying under his sheets one night." This alluded to the classic *Godfather* scene in which a movie executive wakes up with the severed head of his prize horse beside him in bed as a warning that he'd better cast a friend of Don Corleone in his next movie. Before it became clear that White House operatives had deliberately outted Valerie Plame as a CIA operative, bloggers debated whether this act reflected a "horse's head theory"—that it was intended to intimidate anyone who had the temerity to dissent from administration policy on Iraq—or a "Keystone Kops theory," in which clueless Bushies didn't realize Plame was covert when they leaked her name to the press.

According to *Time* reporter Matthew Cooper, White House aide Karl Rove told him about Valerie Plame on "double super-secret background." The reporter later explained that this expression came from *National Lampoon's Animal House*, in which the Delta House fraternity is placed on *double secret probation* (Cooper himself added "super"). One might think that the boorish behavior engaged in by Bluto Blutarsky (John Belushi) and his Delta House brothers would put a nail in the coffin of Greek life. In fact it was the other way around. After **Animal House** came out in 1978, fraternity pledging shot up, and the type of toga party it portrayed became de rigueur on college campuses. At the very least this movie bequeathed us its title as useful shorthand for frat-boyish behavior. While Jimmy Carter was in the White House, his staffers were said to engage in "*Animal House* partying." Bill Clinton was later accused of "*Animal House* lewdness," and George W. Bush was commonly said to engage in *Animal House* antics, including constant fart jokes. *Food fights* certainly antedated that movie's signature scene, in which students toss plates of food around the college cafeteria, but *Animal House*'s exuberant portrayal of hamburgers and salad greens flying through the air was so memorable that after its release, **food fight** became a common allusion to mayhem of all kinds. TV shoutfests were called "verbal food fights," as were debates in Congress.

Some movies capture the mood of an era so effectively that their titles become allegorical. Such was the case with *The Big Chill*, Lawrence Kasdan's 1983 movie about seven University of Michigan graduates from the sixties who reunite at the funeral of a friend who has committed suicide (Kevin Costner, seen briefly as a corpse). While together, members of this group reflect on the vagaries of life after college. Despite enjoying lucrative, high-status careers, they agree that post-collegiate life can't compare with their heady days at Michigan. A lawyer played by Mary Kay Place, who has come to assess her male classmates as possible sperm donors, laments that her "biological clock is ticking" (apparently the public debut of this now-common concept). *Big Chill* still refers to those who struggle to grow up, baby boomers in particular. Boomers as a group are sometimes referred to as **the Big Chill generation**. When *Dreamgirls* was released in 2006, writer Ashley Kahn said this movie's Motownish sound track contained "feel-good songs for the Big Chill generation."

Long before *When Harry Met Sally* was released, many men had—let's call it a *hunch*—that the throes of ecstasy they excited in women weren't always what they seemed to be. This 1989 movie confirmed their hunch so vividly that its title has become our go-to reference for feigned orgasm. That's because in this so-so movie's most famous scene, while eating lunch with Billy Crystal in Katz's Deli, Meg Ryan demonstrates an "orgasm" that builds in intensity until she's shouting loudly and pounding the table while exclaiming "Yes! Yes! Yes!" This scene made such a big impression that **When Harry Met Sally** is now just as likely to refer to feigned orgasm as to the film itself. It was a woman who suggested the deli scene, of course, screenwriter-director Nora Ephron. But Billy Crystal came up with its most memorable line: **"I'll have what she's having."** This is the response of an older woman at the table next to Meg Ryan's, when she is asked for her order. After excerpting an overripe sex scene in a novel, *New Yorker* reviewer Louis Menand felt no need to elaborate when he commented, "I'll have what she's having."

## Titles

If there's such a thing as a retrographic, the picture of Marilyn Monroe standing on a subway grate trying to push down her dress as it billows around her thighs certainly qualifies. This still photo from *The Seven Year Itch* is that movie's best-remembered visual. We also like to recall Monroe—playing a ditzy blonde who is tempting married man Tom Ewell—saying that on hot summer days she stays cool by wearing panties she's put in the freezer. But what we remember best from that 1955 movie is its title. *The Seven Year Itch* alludes to the wandering eye that husbands in particular supposedly develop after seven years of marriage. According to George Axelrod, who wrote the 1952 Broadway play on which the movie was based, this phrase referred to a microbe-based skin condition that typically lasts for seven years. Axelrod picked it up from a comedian he heard say, "I know she's over twenty-one because she's had the seven-year itch four times!" William Safire traced this concept back to the mid-nineteenth century, when "the seven years' itch" was such a common allusion that Henry David Thoreau used it in *Walden* without further explanation. Axelrod's character originally had been married for ten years, but the playwright liked the sound of *seven-year itch* so well that he revised his script to match this amount. Even though his play's co-producer hated the title so much that he wanted to take an ad in *Variety* disowning it, **seven-year itch** quickly entered the vernacular as a catchphrase and has never left. In recent years, American voters' tendency to vote for members of the opposition party in the middle of a president's second term has been called a *six-year itch*.

Unlike *The Seven Year Itch*, which was a superb movie, many films that left their titles behind were anything but. Regardless of a film's quality, we seem especially partial to titles that lend themselves to blank-filling. For example, *If It's Tuesday, This Must Be Belgium* is a widely forgotten 1969 movie about a group of American tourists who visit so many countries on a whirlwind European tour that they determine where they are by the day of the week. Enough of us have felt this way that *If it's* _____ *it must be* _____ has lasted far longer as a catchphrase than did the movie it came from, as when MSNBC's Chris Matthews said on the day of Iowa's primary, "If it's Thursday, it must be Iowa."

Despite a bravura performance by Madonna, *Desperately Seeking Susan*— about a bored New Jersey housewife who is determined to locate an East Villager whose personal ads she's read in a New York newspaper—registered in our memory only because of its evocative title. We continually recycle the first two words of that 1985 movie. Daniel Farber and Suzanna Sherry called a 2002 book *Desperately Seeking Certainty: The Misguided Quest for Constitutional Foundations*. A flyer for Trader Joe's later asked that store's customers, "Desperately seeking a truly LARGE gift basket?" A Google search of thirty days' news articles turned up more than a hundred variations on "desperately seeking."

Steven Soderbergh's maiden effort, *sex, lies, and videotape* has held up somewhat better as a film, but that movie too is remembered primarily for a title that lends itself to fill-in-the-blank adaptation: **"sex, lies, and** _____**."** In the years since it was released in 1989, countless headlines, book titles, TV episode titles, and other headings have made use of Soderbergh's creation. *Time* headlined a murder case account "Sex, Lies, and a Porcupine."

## Memorable Characters

A completely different order of cinematic allusion comes in the form of characters such as Jefferson Smith, played by Jimmy Stewart in *Mr. Smith Goes to Washington*. That classic 1939 movie portrays a naive Mr. Everyman who is picked by a political machine to complete an unexpired Senate term. Expected to be compliant, Smith takes on entrenched interests, culminating in a passionate, sweaty, mussed-hair filibuster that lasts all night. Stewarts's character has become so iconic that **Mr. Smith** is routinely invoked when any nonpolitician is elected to office. A 2006 movie about a young congressional aspirant in Missouri was titled *Can Mr. Smith Get to Washington Anymore?*

Nearly as iconic is Holly Golightly, the character played by Audrey Hepburn in *Breakfast at Tiffany's*. In this 1961 movie, based on a Truman Capote novella, Golightly is an uptown gadabout with more charm than brains who eventually trades her feckless ways for domestic bliss. Hepburn's brandishing of a long cigarette holder became the visual icon of *Breakfast at Tiffany's*. The name **Holly Golightly** still symbolizes an attractive woman of little substance. According to biographer Sydney Ladensohn Stern, during the early 1960s, feminist Gloria Steinem wanted to be seen as "Holly Golightly with brains."

If Holly Golightly represented uptown insouciance, Rico "Ratso" Rizzo stood for downtown sleaziness. In *Midnight Cowboy*, the 1969 movie based on James Leo Herlihy's novel with the same name, this short, limping, shabbily dressed lowlife was not particularly memorable. What Dustin Hoffman's character did have was an unforgettable name, and one captivating scene. While crossing a midtown Manhattan street beside Western-clad Texan Joe Buck (Jon Voight), Rizzo pounds the hood of a car with his fist, angrily proclaiming his right to his space. Who couldn't relate to that? *Midnight Cowboy* also caught moviegoers' attention with its hint of homosexual love between Rizzo and Buck. **Ratso Rizzo** has proved to be a durable retroallusion. According to conservative commentator Jonah Goldberg, in its self-appointed role as arbiter of good versus bad whistleblowing, "the truth of the matter is that the press is simply not a reliable arbiter of who is Thomas More and who is Ratso Rizzo."

One reason Rizzo's name has stuck around, of course, is that offputting characters tend to carve a deeper groove in our memory than appealing ones. Think: **Nurse Ratched**. The American Film Institute named Mildred Ratched fifth among its top fifty movie villains (right after the Wicked Witch of the West and Darth Vader). Even though Jack Nicholson and Louise Fletcher both won Oscars for their performances in *One Flew Over the Cuckoo's Nest* (1975), it is Fletcher's insidious character whose name has stuck around. How many remember the name of Nicholson's more sympathetic character? That would be Randall Patrick "Mac" McMurphy, the zany insane asylum inmate who stars in the movie based on Ken Kesey's novel of the same name (inspiring Maureen Dowd's reference to Vice President Dick Cheney's "one-flew-over daftness"). As Kesey intended, men especially see in Nurse Ratched any controlling female who has ever tried to restrain their exuberance by whatever means prove necessary. Nurse Ratched is not so much a castrating female as a lobotomizing one, less interested in cutting off men's testicles than in reducing the size of their brain. The movie actually softened this character a bit from Kesey's original portrayal of "Big Nurse" as a severe nurse-warden whose taut frame and tight lips are at odds with her mammoth bosom. Though more svelte, with her cool smile and passive-aggressive manner, Louise Fletcher's version is no less menacing. George W. Bush's tall, formidable spokeswoman Karen Hughes was nicknamed Nurse Ratched by reporters. When Bush's diminutive counsel Alberto Gonzales withheld information from statuesque national security adviser Condoleezza Rice, then–Secretary of State Colin Powell noted admiringly how Rice dressed down Gonzales "in full Nurse Ratched mode."

## Mouths of Babes

In *Being There*, the 1979 movie based on Jerzy Kosinski's same-titled novel, Peter Sellers played a dim-bulb gardener named Chance who works for a wealthy Washingtonian. Television is Chance's only source of information about the outside world. After his employer dies, Chance dons one of this man's tailored suits and ventures into D.C. society, where he is taken to be an upper-crust executive named Chauncey Gardiner (because he introduces himself as "Chance . . . the gardener"). Due to his elegant dress, appearance of self-possession, and deliberate manner of speech, Chance is assumed to be a man of means and breeding. His inane observations are confused with genuine profundity, especially "All is well—and all will be well—in the garden." Because these homilies involve very few words, Chance proves an ideal television guest and adviser to those—including the president—who prefer to do the talking themselves. Eventually this simple ex-gardener is touted as a candidate for president himself, a harbinger, some thought, of Ronald Reagan's candidacy the following year. **Chauncey Gardiner** is still a common way to refer to pseudo-profound figures of limited intellect. In an interview, *New York Times* columnist Frank Rich commented that George W. Bush had "a slight, almost Chauncey Gardiner quality."

A Chauncey Gardiner analogue who is referenced even more often is Leonard Zelig. In *Zelig* (1983), director Woody Allen played this chameleonlike figure who has a knack for mirroring the demeanor of those around him and insinuating himself into historic events. Zelig shows up alongside prominent prewar figures such as Calvin Coolidge, Charles Lindbergh, Babe Ruth, and Adolf Hitler. Among other things he plays baseball for the New York Yankees and attends a Nazi rally in Munich. *Zelig* was a filmmaking tour de force in which Allen was able to insert himself into actual newsreel footage without the aid of modern digitizing. This fact and his movie's memorable protagonist made such a big impression that the term **Zelig-like** or, less often, **Zeligesque** is routinely used to characterize those who are not who they seem to be. When Ronald Reagan falsely said he had helped liberate the Buchenwald concentration camp, the president was called a *Zelig*. Edmund Morris was too, after giving himself a role as an imaginary Reagan pal in *Dutch*, his biography of the fortieth president.

Yet another simple-profound character is Forrest Gump, played by Tom Hanks in the 1994 movie based on Winston Groom's novel by that title. Like Zelig, Gump finds himself in the midst of historic events: fighting in Vietnam, scoring a touchdown for the University of Alabama, and teaching Elvis Presley how to dance, in addition to meeting Kennedy, Johnson, and Nixon at the White House. Like those of Chauncey Gardiner, the utterances of this low-IQ figure are thought to contain considerable wisdom. They include "Stupid is as stupid does" and "Life is like a box of chocolates. You never know what you're going to get." Those thoughts and the name **Forrest Gump** itself were left behind by this overrated movie, alluding to a good-hearted person whose limited intellect gives him insights denied the rest of us. After former president Gerald Ford died, commentators routinely compared this unadorned midwesterner to Forrest Gump.

Even though he was not presented as a fount of wisdom, the autistic character played by Dustin Hoffman in *Rain Man* (1988) made such a vivid impression with his eerie powers of recall that this movie's title came to represent mentally challenged figures of all kinds, and/or anyone with an impressive memory. Republican operative Ken Mehlman had such a prodigious ability to keep track of campaign minutiae that his colleagues called him **Rain Man**.

# 12. Home & Hearth

So many settlers' hogs wandered in the forests and swamps of early America that owners routinely nicked their ears in unique patterns to show who owned them. This was a centuries-old way to identify livestock. According to a late-eighteenth-century Wareham, Massachusetts, registry, Joshua Briggs's pigs had "a Seware Crop in ye under side of ye Right ear," Thomas Whittens's "a mackerels tales in Both Ears." Metaphorically, **earmarking** refers to singling out something or someone for special treatment. Special projects that legislators sneak into appropriations bills are called **earmarks**.

This is just one of a multitude of ways we verbally recall household life in the past, when pigs were a prominent presence.

## Pork

On the eve of the Civil War, pork was second only to wheat as Americans' most popular foodstuff. Southerners were especially partial to this meat: freshly slaughtered or as salt pork, fatback, cracklings, chitterlings (chitlins), pickled pig's feet, headcheese, bacon, or ham. Such delectables were liable to be served three times a day. Noting the many forms in which Americans ate the flesh of hogs (large pigs), an antebellum doctor in Georgia thought our country should change its name to the Great Hog-Eating Confederacy, or perhaps the Republic of Porkdom.

Pork was typically stored in a barrel. The fuller the barrel, the richer its owner. Poor folks sometimes had to **scrape the bottom of the barrel**. That type of pig-based terminology is still heard routinely when politicians distribute money. **Pork**—or **bringing home the bacon**—signifies largesse. **Pork barrel politics** is based on accumulating and distributing public resources among backers and constituents. When it comes to hogs themselves, we still refer to being *hog-tied* and going *hog wild* or *whole hog*. We also continue to call dubious statements *hogwash*.

Before shortening took its place, the rendered fat of pigs—*lard*—was Americans' grease of choice. Lard was used much as butter or margarine is used today: for frying, baking, or even as a bread spread. (Some pie bakers still contend that a crust made with lard can't be matched for flakiness.) This saturated fat did not survive modern-day concerns about cholesterol and the like, but its name did. We **lard it up**, or embellish. Something bloated with ephemera is **larded up**. Similar commentary is made about human anatomy. Among a wide variety of lard-based terms in American English, **lard-ass** has survived for fat people, especially ones with ample behinds. To disparage such a person we might call him on her a **big tub of lard**.

Those who grew up in homes where poultry was slaughtered had direct evidence that the bodies of chickens whose head had just been chopped off ran around frantically for a few seconds before keeling over. The rest of us had to take their word for it. That didn't keep us from using **running around like a chicken with its head cut off** as an allusion to anyone scrambling about blindly, aimlessly, or **no spring chicken** for human beings of a certain age (because that was what wary customers called winter-ravaged birds whom poultry dealers tried to pass off as ones born in the spring). We also took the word of our country cousins that soaking chickens with water made them very angry whenever we called someone **mad as a wet hen**. Similarly, **wet behind the ears** harks back to an assumption that the small of the ear in newly born livestock was the last place to dry. Today this phrase refers to anyone considered childishly naive. ("When Jack started working here he was really wet behind the ears.")

## Comestibles

Early public gatherings of all kinds—fairs, carnivals, church socials—crackled with the sizzle and pop of cornmeal batter being fried in hot lard or bear grease. Because the results tasted best when hot, these fritters were called **hotcakes**. This repast was so popular that those cooking hotcakes could usually sell them as fast as they could cook them. Although pancakes have taken the place of hotcakes, based on our cultural memory we still say fast-moving products **sell like hotcakes**.

Cornmeal, boiled in water or milk, was called *porridge* or *mush*. This breakfast dish, which could also be made from oats or other grains, is seldom seen these days, but its name has lingered in our language. Alice Roosevelt Longworth is famous for having called her cousin Franklin Roosevelt, whose wife, Eleanor, was also her cousin, a combination of mush and Eleanor. Longworth denied ever saying this. Fastidious about her language, Theodore Roosevelt's irascible daughter said she'd never use a pedestrian word like *mush*. "There's no ring to 'mush.'" One begs to disagree. *Mush* is fun to say and evokes images of *mushers* driving their huskies. ("Mush!") *Mushy* adapts that term. If anything, **mushy** is heard more often than its root, when referring to something that is soft in texture, vague, or over-the-top sentimental. *Mushy* is what kids call movies with too much hugging and kissing.

A mushlike cereal was formulated in 1930 by three Canadian pediatricians from various grains with some bone meal thrown in. The name they gave this easily digested, almost tasteless goo can still be heard whenever we call something as bland as **Pablum** (whose name derives from *pabulum*, Latin for "food"). A blogger once charged that the television series *Grey's Anatomy* of having plots that were "insipid Pablum."

Domestic oats—now used primarily as the basis for oatmeal, oatmeal cookies, and oat bread—once were a staple in America's kitchens. A cousin to this grain is *Avena fatua*, more commonly known as the *wild oat*. Like honeysuckle and kudzu, the wild oat is an invasive weed that has long bedeviled farmers. Since this plant is basically useless, for centuries the phrase *to sow one's wild oats* has characterized rowdy behavior that leads to nothing constructive. Although that phrase has generally been applied to young men who are getting carousing out of their system, young women also have been known to **sow wild oats**. That can happen only in youth, though. Men and women of any age can **feel their oats**. This references the grain fed to horses that enhances their energy level. Human beings who are **feeling their oats** conduct themselves in an unusually frisky manner.

So do those who **cut the mustard**. There are many theories about where this catchphrase comes from, and why it has sexual connotations. Since at least the mid-seventeenth century English speakers have used "mustard" as a superlative (e.g., "keen as mustard"). When late-nineteenth-century Americans said "the real mustard," they meant the same thing as "the real soufflé" today, or "the real deal." In time, "cut" was added to that concept. Eventually the new phrase's meaning came to focus on virility, and was usually expressed in the negative. ("He's too old to cut the mustard anymore.") This suggests that the earlier concept of "just can't cut it" was simply coupled with "mustard" to create **can't cut the mustard**.

No condiment is more significant in our culinary and linguistic heritage than salt. Although important enough to warrant a social history of the subject (*Salt*, by Mark Kurlansky), this flavor enhancer is not nearly as central to our lives as it once was, especially since doctors warned us that sodium can raise blood pressure. At one time, however, the utility of salt combined with its scarcity made it an unusually valuable commodity. The fact that Roman soldiers were paid in salt-equivalents inspired our word *salary*, based on the Latin word *sal*. Due to its value we still use expressions such as **worth one's salt** and **salt of the earth** ("Ye are the salt of the earth," Mat. 5:13). For most of human existence one of the best ways to preserve fresh food, meat especially, was by treating it with salt, as we still do when curing country ham. To this practice we owe the phrase **salt away**, or set aside for future use.

### On the Farm

Dried grass used to feed livestock was, and is, called *hay*. Creating this *fodder* inspired innumerable catchphrases, some of which we still use. They include **make hay** (do well, an abridgement of *make hay while the sun shines*), **hit the hay** (go to bed), and **roll in the hay** (make love). Pre–World War II America was filled with sex jokes set in *haylofts*, many of which involved traveling salesmen and farmers' daughters. Hay-based terms include **hayseed** for a country bumpkin, someone likely to have a piece of hay clenched in his teeth, and the powerful punch boxers call a **haymaker** (perhaps because it generates enough wind to dry grass).

Bales of hay were secured with a type of cheap wire called *hay wire*. Once cut apart, pieces of this wire were used for makeshift repairs around the farm: tying up a loose stovepipe, say, or securing a broken fence. Hay wire was the duct tape of its time. Fastidious farmers regarded repairs made with this wire as temporary. Sloppy farmers never got around to doing them over. Their spreads were filled with gear held together by rusting strands of hay wire. In the vernacular of the time they'd *gone haywire*. Poorly run organizations of many kinds were called *haywire outfits*. Today **haywire** has come to mean berserk, chaotic. Those in that state **go haywire**.

Wheat is a close cousin to hay. Once this grass was harvested, its grain had to be threshed, or *winnowed* from its casing and bits of leftover stalk called *chaff*. We still use the term **winnowing** to refer more broadly to sorting things out. ("We had to winnow all those résumés.") **Separating the wheat from the chaff** alludes to weeding out the significant from the insignificant. It's been said that newspaper editors separate the wheat from the chaff, then print the chaff.

Dried stalks left over once grain was threshed were, and are, called *straw*. Straw served many purposes, especially as bedding for livestock and human beings of lesser means. In more straw-centric times it was common to choose someone for a task by holding several stalks of different lengths of straw behind one's hand with only their evenly lined-up tops visible. Those involved then had to **draw straws**, much as we would flip a coin today. Whoever drew the short straw usually was designated to undertake some task, seldom an appealing one. That phrase has endured to signify bad luck and losers of all kinds. They **drew the short straw**. **Straw men** are ones of no more significance than a scarecrow made of straw, and **straw bosses** have an impressive title but no authority. Those who buy products for others—guns especially—are called **straw purchasers**.

In an ancient Arab tale, a camel loaded with straw is unable to move after one straw too many is placed on his back. This is the proverbial **straw that broke the camel's back**. It also is why we call seemingly inconsequential events that, when added to others, make continued activity impossible **the last straw**.

In his 1865 novel *Our Mutual Friend*, Dickens said that a character had overreached "by grasping at Mr. Venus's mere straws of hints." To this day **grasping at straws** signifies looking for hopeful signs where few exist. **Straw votes** or **straw polls** are ones in which an informal vote is taken before one that counts. The name of that type of tally presumably draws on the old-time practice of throwing pieces of straw in the air to determine which way the wind is blowing. From this custom comes the broader notion of **straws in the wind**, or indicators of which way things are headed.

And what of the grain threshed from straw? After being milled, much of it was made into bread, of course. Baking that bread could be problematic, particularly in the uneven heat of wood-fired ovens. From the Middle Ages on it was considered appropriate to offer only the tender upper crust of a baked loaf to those of elevated social rank, noblemen and the like. Whether one was fed that part of a loaf, the middle section, or the tough bottom crust was a pretty good gauge of one's social standing. That probably is why **upper crust** became a lasting synonym for those of high status.

## Housewares

In 1805, a twenty-one-year-old Bostonian named Frederic Tudor was challenged by his brother to make a profit from something as mundane as frozen water. Taking up the challenge, Tudor cut large blocks of ice from frozen bodies of water outside Boston (including Walden Pond) and shipped them south—as far away as the sweltering Caribbean. Although most of his early cargo arrived too shrunken to turn a profit, within a decade Tudor figured out how to insulate ice blocks with enough sawdust and straw inside double-walled compartments to allow them to arrive at their destination a mere 10 percent smaller than when they left Boston. By midcentury Tudor was filling orders throughout the country and world. His remarkable enterprise made it possible to enjoy cold drinks on the hottest days of summer. Some thought that the availability of ice water, iced tea, and a cool lemonade might reduce consumption of alcoholic beverages. (They were mistaken.) Terms left over from our long romance with blocks of frozen water include **breaking the ice**, **cut no ice**, and **iced**.

But it wasn't iced tea and lemonade that became the most important end point of commercial ice. Stored in well-insulated **icehouses**, blocks of ice soon found their most important use in preserving food. It was **put on ice** (an

allusion similar to *put on hold*). This was accomplished inside enamel-lined **iceboxes** that chilled food. After being introduced in the 1830s, that appliance enjoyed a century's popularity. Even when gas and electric refrigerators became viable after World War I, many preferred the familiarity and silence of an icebox. In a classic example of using old names for new products, refrigerating units that became the preferred method for cooling food in the late 1930s were still called *iceboxes* for years, even decades. That's what my mother called our refrigerator, and if I'm not careful I sometimes do myself.

Blocks of ice for iceboxes were delivered on a weekly basis by hefty *icemen* wielding large tongs and **ice picks** with which they would chip off pieces of frozen water for excited kids. This long, sharp tool is now more likely to show up sticking out of a victim's eye socket in pulp fiction than actually chipping ice. As for the man wielding it, we may talk about children resembling the mailman, and our parents might have joked about them looking like the milk-man, but our grandparents speculated that some kids bore a definite resem-blance to the **iceman**. This breed was immortalized in the title of Eugene O'Neill's 1940 play *The Iceman Cometh*.

Kitchens with iceboxes and early refrigerators had a soundscape far differ-ent from our own. Ours feature the ping of microwaves and hum of toaster ovens, but the kitchen of our parents and grandparents was filled with rum-bling, hissing, and the bubbling that accompanied coffee being made. Long be-fore coffee was dripped, pressed, or brewed in other exotic ways it was usually prepared in a *percolator*. This called for scooping coffee grounds into a covered metal basket perched on a rod inside a *coffee pot*. That container was then filled with water, which was boiled until it saturated the elevated grounds and pro-duced an acrid dark liquid. Those who spent years brewing coffee this way can still be heard calling any coffee-making implement a **percolator**. And we all talk of letting unresolved matters **percolate**, much like coffee being slowly brewed in that device.

Accompanying the bubble of percolators in many kitchens was the hissing of *pressure cookers*. These ominous appliances always seemed on the verge of exploding from the force of their barely contained energy. Some cooks still use this implement, and it has even enjoyed a modest revival. In general, though, we use its name more often than the appliance itself, whenever we talk of being in a **pressure-cooker** situation.

Another once-common convenience that is rarely seen in contemporary kitchens is the **breadbox**. In its time this rectangular box with a firmly closed lid helped keep bread fresh. Today that smallish container is less likely to be used for its intended purpose than as a unit of measurement. "About the size of a breadbox" can still be heard, or "no bigger than a breadbox." That's because

"Is it **bigger than a breadbox**?" was a running gag on the TV show *What's My Line?* from the time host Steve Allen first asked this question in 1953, when trying to determine what product a contestant worked with, until the show expired in 1967. (It lived on as a common query in the word game Twenty Questions.) Four decades later, when asked about the size of proposed economy-stimulating tax rebates, Treasury Secretary Henry Paulson said, "I

don't want to play 'bigger than a breadbox.'" Shortly before that, NPR's Charlene Scott described an early camera as "the size of a breadbox." For the information of those who have grown up in breadbox-free times, a typical breadbox was about as big as a medium-sized microwave oven.

## Furniture

Mattresses on old-time bed frames were supported with crisscrossed ropes. Over time these ropes would loosen, causing the mattress to sag. When this happened, forked sticks were used to tighten the ropes. As they demonstrate ropy beds in restored old homes, tour guides on both sides of the Atlantic explain that this is why we say "sleep tight." Some historians concur. According to the *Oxford English Dictionary*, however, this expression merely reflects the fact that at one time the adverb "tightly" meant "soundly," and that **sleep tight** therefore means little more than "sleep soundly." A century ago *tight asleep* meant the same thing as *sound asleep* today.

Beds with high vertical posts at the corners were known as *four-posters*. Curtains hung from these posts were thought to offer protection from drafts and, more important, from inquisitive eyes. Since the early nineteenth century, the expression **between you, me, and the bedpost** has suggested a discreet situation.

From 1880 to 1906 the A. H. Davenport Company of Boston designed, manufactured, and sold a Davenport Sofa Bed that could be used for sitting and—when folded out—sleeping. For a time **davenport** drifted into the vernacular as a generic term for sofas of all kinds. Those who still use that term date themselves as surely as if they said "hubba hubba" or "23 skidoo!"

Davenports could usually be found in what was called a *parlor* (today's *living room*). Until recently this was such common terminology that a number of retroterms include *parlor* as their root: **parlor games** for diversions ranging from charades to Parcheesi, or **parlor pinks** for those whose Communist sympathies were expressed only in the safety of their homes. Early last century, American men who liked to pet in parlors with women they never took on actual dates were called *parlor snakes* or *lounge lizards*. In time **lounge lizard** came to refer to dubious characters of many kinds who hang around hotel lobbies and such, on the lookout for wealthy women to exploit.

---

### MATTRESS TAGS

In a less regulated time, American mattress makers were free to stuff their product with any bug-infested ticking they had at hand. Customers too often discovered what their new bedding harbored when they woke up itching. In the early twentieth century, however, states began to require mattress makers to list the contents of their product on a label. This label warned in the most dire terms that tearing it off was illegal ("Do not remove under penalty of law"). Although most such tags went on to say that customers themselves could remove them, alarmed new mattress owners didn't always read that far. For many, the thought of heedlessly ripping off a **mattress tag** led to an image of cops breaking down their bedroom door in the middle of the night, yanking them off their untagged mattress, slapping on the cuffs, and taking them to jail. This fantasy became so widespread that surreptitiously removing a mattress tag became virtually synonymous with the prospect of becoming a middle-class desperado. As an *Orlando Sentinel* headline once read, "GO NUTS: DRIVE IN CAR-POOL LANE, RIP OFF MATTRESS TAG." In a 1998 cartoon, plump little Ziggy stands abjectly before a policeman saying, "I can't stand it anymore! I want to turn myself in! I pulled the tag off a mattress back in 1977."

## Rugs

During the pre–vacuum cleaner era, rugs were hung over a clothesline once or twice a year, then beaten hard amid clouds of dust. The rest of the time they could only be swept. Resulting piles of dirt were best swept into a dustpan and thrown out. But a housekeeper in a hurry, or one who simply couldn't be bothered, might simply sweep that dirt under the rug. When referring to hiding a problem rather than solving it we still say that we **sweep it under the rug**.

Couples who wanted to dance in a room with a rug first had to expose bare floor by rolling up that rug and pushing it off to one side. As a result, **roll up the rug** became synonymous with partying in general. In the 1920s revelers were said to **cut a rug**, perhaps because wearing out a section of carpeting is sometimes called *cutting a rug*. In its current use this expression suggests that some unusually vigorous dancing is going on.

Elegant carpets are associated with those in a position of authority. Because employees summoned to the boss's office so often stood on one, they came to call this experience being **called on the carpet**. Today we use that idiom more broadly, for any occasion of reprimand. ("My adviser really had me on the carpet.") A better experience is enjoyed by dignitaries provided with a scarlet rug to walk on when visiting another country, or Hollywood stars arriving at the Academy Awards ceremony. They get **red carpet treatment**.

## Laundry

When Richard Nixon's attorney general John Mitchell warned *Washington Post* reporter Carl Bernstein that "Katie Graham is going to get her tit caught in a big fat wringer," Americans of a certain age had no problem visualizing what fate Mitchell had in mind for the *Post*'s publisher. Those who grew up in homes with automatic washer-dryers were more puzzled. They didn't realize that Mitchell envisioned Ms. Graham standing before an early washing machine, leaning in too far, and getting one of her breasts flattened between the rubber rollers that squeezed water out of wet laundry in such machines. Few of these *wringer-washers* are still in use, blessedly (untold numbers of fingers and other body parts were consumed by their merciless rollers). Nonetheless, **caught in a wringer**, or in England **caught in a mangle**, still alludes to getting mired in a tricky situation from which it's hard to escape. Those who have endured arduous experiences, ones that figuratively squeezed them dry, sometimes say they were **put through the wringer**.

Before there were wringer-washers there were washboards. Well into the twentieth century these wooden frames with rippled galvanized steel were the tool most often used for scrubbing soiled laundry. Nowadays washboards are more likely to be used for making music than cleaning clothes. The constant bumps on **washboard roads** are thought to resemble the ripples of that implement. For a similar reason **washboard abs** refers to the rippled abdominal muscles of an unusually buff body, usually male.

Some could afford to take their dirty clothes to commercial laundries, of course. After turning these over to the proprietor they were given a list of what articles of clothing they'd brought. This **laundry list** now refers to the systematic recording of just about anything. A group of Wikipedia participants who call themselves "Wikiproject Laundromat" try to discourage entries on this online encyclopedia that consist disproportionately of *laundry lists* of bulleted items.

It was not so long ago that those washing their own clothes, or their employers', relied on water gushing from hand-levered pumps. These pumps could be cranky. No matter how vigorously one pushed the handle up and down, water did not always emerge from its spout. Often that was because pockets of air blocked passage. In such cases it became necessary to **prime the pump** by adding a bit of water in order to expel that air and get the mechanism working. Few of us pump water by hand anymore, but many still talk of **priming the pump** or **pump priming** to get stalled activity under way. Creation of public works to stimulate a moribund economy is typically referred to as *pump priming*.

With water from working pumps, early American clothes were washed out of doors in cauldrons over fires. The risk here was not only of getting scorched by flames but of having passersby note what was being laundered—undergarments especially. As a result, **wash your dirty linen** (or **underwear**) **in public** lingers as a figure of speech for putting one's private life on public display. **Air your dirty laundry** is another way of saying the same thing. This alludes to the fact that until quite recently laundered clothes were usually hung on *clotheslines* with *clothespins*. This practice is so infrequent in the age of washer-dryers—and indeed is forbidden by many homeowners' associations—that these terms are now most often used figuratively. Football players **clothesline** an onrushing opponent when they stretch out an arm held in front of him. **Clothespins** are figuratively put on noses in the presence of foul smells, literal or figurative. (William Safire once referred to a *clothespin vote* cast for a candidate so off-putting that one could vote for him or her only with pinched nostrils.) Another clothes-drying expression evokes an image of a hapless person clipped to a clothesline with clothespins. This is what we often say is the fate of scapegoats. They are **hung out to dry**.

## Undergarments

During the Victorian era it became fashionable for women of means to present the world with a behind far larger than the one nature gave them. To do so they put what was called a **bustle** beneath their full skirts, a prosthesis made of horsehair, whalebone, or steel mesh. This short-lived fashion craze made certain adaptations necessary, such as chairs with cutouts in the back to accommodate bustle-wearing women. It is commemorated today in the admonition to **put a hustle in your bustle**.

Women who sported bustles below generally wore corsets above. By judicious tightening of its laces this undergarment shifted flesh from places where it wasn't welcome—in the waist primarily—to parts of the anatomy where it was less obvious. **Straitlaced** wearers tied their corsets very tight. (*Strait* is an archaic term for a narrow space, such as the Straits of Magellan.) This evoked an image of a rather prim and proper person—*uptight*, if you will— which is the way we use that phrase today. Although she wasn't, really, Queen Victoria is considered the epitome of a straitlaced woman.

Updates of corsets called *girdles* relied less on laces and more on whalebone, rubber, and steel stays to accomplish the same flesh-shifting purpose. Those who wore them exchanged comfort for a better silhouette. The classic sotto voce lament of women wearing this undergarment—**"My girdle's killing me"**—became part of Playtex ads in the 1960s. It subsequently showed up in many comedians' routines. A *Village Voice* article about comic Eddie Izzard noted that "no 'my girdle's killing me' jokes have slipped into his act."

## Shirts and Pants

For centuries men have had to choose between a belt and suspenders (called *braces* in England) to hold up their trousers. Anyone who wore both was thought to be unusually cautious. By extension **belt and suspenders** or **belt and braces** is used to depict any situation involving fastidious redundancy. Word sleuth Nigel Rees considers the fact that two microphones are always provided for a British sovereign's Christmas address a classic *belt-and-braces* approach. After Robert Rubin became a banking executive, the onetime treasury secretary said that when it came to legal limitations on his freedom to lobby the government, "We'll be belt and suspenders with respect to those."

Men's trousers were originally called *breeches*. The head of a household, a man of course, was said to *wear the breeches*. As breeches became *trousers*, then *pants* (in the United States), this expression evolved into **wear the pants**. That phrase rings hollow in a time when both sexes wear pants, but it echoes a time when men alone wore that garment and—in theory, anyway—ruled roosts.

During breech-wearing times, men who could afford them wore shirts with billowing sleeves (think: Henry VIII). A man who wanted to conceal amusement might bury his head in such a sleeve to stifle a grin or a laugh. This became known as *laughing up one's sleeve*. Even though shirtsleeves are too snug to permit this subterfuge today, we still talk of **laughing up your sleeve** to conceal amusement. Something else men did with the generous sleeves of old was to hide useful objects (a knife, say, or a winning card) within their folds. They had **something up their sleeve**. So does any deceptive person today, metaphorically.

Before World War I it was common for men to wear removable shirt cuffs made of stiff celluloid. Merchants, saloonkeepers especially, were prone to scribble amounts owed them by customers on this cuff, then erase that figure once a customer settled up. From this practice grew the phrase **on the cuff**, meaning to purchase something on credit. **Off the cuff**, by contrast, refers to speaking extemporaneously, presumably because one has no need for prompts written on that surface.

## Shoes and Socks .

Centuries ago, loose-fitting *slipshoes* were worn·inside British homes. Some enjoyed the comfort of these early-day slippers so much that they wore them outside as well. This was not considered good form. In fact, during the sixteenth century anyone so gauche as to wear slipshoes in public risked being derided as **slipshod**. That term was subsequently applied to those of sloppy appearance, then to anything at all—work performance especially—judged second-rate. ("He did a really slipshod job of fixing my car.")

Well into the twentieth century, Yale University students considered *shoe* a good thing to be: suave, well dressed, upper-crust. Not just individuals but groups could be judged *shoe* or not. There were gradations, however. To be *black shoe* was to be a grind, in college for an education. *Brown shoe* was applied to middling sorts, basically okay but rather dull. Top honors were awarded those judged *white shoe*. This alluded to the white buck shoes that were de rigueur among postwar swells. It brought old money to mind, seersucker suits, bow ties, and *white bucks* worn by those playing croquet. A descendant of this concept is the **white shoe law firm**, or one with unusual social cachet. According to a *New York Times* account, early in his career a Brooklyn lawyer "was rebuffed by a white shoe law firm because he was Jewish."

Footwear with rubber soles and canvas tops was introduced after the Civil War. At first these shoes were called "croquet sandals." Five years later they were dubbed *sneakers* (for the same reason that *gumshoe* referred to skulking about: rubber-soled shoes facilitated sneaking about). A version of this shoe developed for tennis players was called a **tennis shoe**. This soon became generic for all rubber-soled canvas footwear. In 1961, California Attorney General Stanley Mosk referred to "an old lady in tennis shoes." Perhaps playing off the "little old lady from Pasadena" whom comedians used to joke about at that time (and whom Jan and Dean later sang about), this morphed into *a little old lady in tennis shoes*. That brought to mind a certain type of wizened woman who was sober, intent, and opinionated. Liberal detractors liked to debunk conservative zealots, especially Barry Goldwater's backers in the run-up to his 1964 presidential nomination, as out-there extremists exemplified by **little old ladies in tennis shoes**. When Ronald Reagan subsequently ran for governor of California he sometimes opened speeches to right-wing backers by saying "Gentlemen—and little ladies in tennis shoes."

Postwar high school girls liked to wear tennis shoes or saddle shoes with rolled cotton socks called *bobby socks*. Where "bobby" came from is anyone's guess, though it may owe something to the *bobby pins* many wore in their hair. Compared to tattoos, tongue studs, and thong underwear, bobby socks were a pretty mild style statement. During gray-flannel times, however, they were considered rather audacious. In their *Encyclopedia of Popular Culture*, Jane and Michael Stern call bobby socks "one of the earliest ways modern teenagers set themselves apart from traditional adult society."

Those who wore this in-your-face fashion came to be known as *bobby-soxers*. **Bobby-soxers** were giddy, trend-conscious adolescents, the type who might be found swooning at a Frank Sinatra concert or spinning some Johnnie Ray platters in their bedroom. Long after bobby socks had gone the way of crinolines and 45s, Bill Clinton's friend Vernon Jordan tried to dismiss Monica Lewinsky's infatuation with the president as a "bobby-soxer" crush.

Like footwear, hosiery has long been a source of social stratification. The silk stockings upper-class Englishmen wore beneath knee britches in the eighteenth century gave others unmistakable evidence of their wealth and status. At one time *silk stocking* was used sarcastically for ostentatious wealth display. Thomas Jefferson himself referred derisively to the "silk stocking gentry." Today it refers more often to an affluent or **silk stocking** geographic area. The commercial venue from midtown to Ninety-sixth Street on Manhattan's tony east side has long been known as the *silk stocking district*. This term is also applied to a Manhattan congressional district with lots of wealthy voters.

*Bluestocking*, on the other hand, refers to a woman more interested in ostentatious learning than showy wealth. The origins of that term can be found in a group of well-educated fifteenth-century Venetians who wore blue stockings as a symbol of their erudition. This fashion statement made its way to Paris, where an intellectual group called itself Bluestockings. It then moved on to London, where—in the mid-eighteenth century—Lady Elizabeth Montagu founded the Bluestocking Society for women who wanted to discuss matters literary and intellectual. Following the Meiji restoration, a feminist magazine in Japan called itself *Bluestocking* (*Seito*). With this varied and extensive pedigree, it was almost unavoidable that a certain type of overbearing woman came to be called a **bluestocking**. Historian Arthur Schlesinger Jr. said he found Hillary Clinton's demeanor one of "bluestocking severity."

## Hats and Gloves

Until fairly recently a well-chosen hat was an essential part of respectable male wardrobes. The fact that John Kennedy gave his 1960 inaugural address with wind whipping through his hair heralded the collapse of the men's hat industry. (Jackie Kennedy kept the women's version alive a bit longer with her trendsetting pillbox hats.) Certainly lots of American men wear baseball caps these days—indoors as well as outdoors—but no well-bred person would consider them proper head covering.

Where hats do still appear routinely is in our lexicon. Based on centuries of routine head covering, a hat-based vocabulary remains part of daily discourse. From the old-timey practice of gents respectfully removing their hat indoors or when meeting a woman we still say **hats off** as a reference to showing respect. Because lesser beings were expected to remove their hat in the presence of their betters and hold it humbly, **hat in hand** suggests abject subservience. Briefly lifting one's hat or simply touching it with a forefinger in acknowledgment of another person left behind **tip of the hat** (as when bloggers acknowledge someone else's contribution to their Web log with a *hat-tip*). In hat-wearing days **I'll eat my hat** became an allusion to extreme confidence. ("If Dewey doesn't win, I'll eat my hat.") Other hat-based phraseology includes *talk through your hat* (pretend to know more than you actually do), *keep it under your hat* (keep it a secret), *hang your hat on* (rely upon), and *old hat* (antiquated).

Like hats, gloves were once considered essential out-of-house wear, for women especially. Because white was the preferred color for those worn by well-equipped women (note how often Jackie Kennedy wore white gloves), **white-glove treatment** suggests getting the best possible service. **Kid-glove treatment** is a variation on this theme, alluding to the expensive handwear made from kid leather (goatskin). **Hand in glove** suggests a close relationship, as close figuratively as a hand in a glove. ("Vision and Hearing May Diminish

Hand in Glove in Older Age" warns a medical website.) The fact that the closable container on most cars' dashboards is called a **glove box** or **glove compartment** reflects a time when drivers' ubiquitous gloves were stowed there. This was also a time when the names of various products and commercial practices entered our discourse and stuck around.

## 13. Sizzling Widgets

I n *Beggar on Horseback*, a 1924 play by George S. Kaufman and Marc Connelly, a young composer has a disturbing dream in which he's about to join his future father-in-law's business. The young man asks his fiancée's father what business he's in. "Widgets," the older man responds. "We're in the widget business."

"The widget business?" says his prospective son in law.

"Yes, sir!" replies the older man. "I suppose I'm the biggest manufacturer in the world of overhead and underground A-erial widgets."

*Widget* caught on quickly in the American business vernacular. In addition to being fun to say, this made-up word proved very useful as a generic term for hypothetical products. Unlike a *doohickey*, say, a *doodad, whatsit, thingamabob, thingamajig, thingie, or gizmo*, a **widget** sounds like it might actually do something. Although unimaginative enterprises such as Guinness and Apple expropriated the term *widget* for actual product or software applications, in general we still use it generically. As business columnist James Surowiecki observed in the *New Yorker*, "the more widgets you produce, the cheaper each widget becomes."

A decade after Kaufman and Connelly called our attention to *widgets*, marketing wizard Elmer Wheeler urged all merchants to follow the lead of smart steakhouse owners who greet customers with the mouthwatering sound of beefsteak hissing, sputtering, and popping on the grill. "It is the sizzle that sells the steak and not the cow," observed Wheeler, "although the cow is, of course, mighty important." Wheeler elaborated on this theme in *The Sizzle Book*

(1938) and *Sizzlemanship* (1940). More than seventy years since Wheeler coined his *Principle Number 1 of Salesmanship*, "**Sell the sizzle**, not the steak" remains such a bedrock admonition to market perception over product that it's still cited routinely by those who have never even heard of Elmer Wheeler. A single word from this adage is usually enough to evoke the general idea, as in *USA Today*'s headline, "AOL CHIEF WANTS 'SIZZLE' BACK IN SERVICE."

## Great Moments in American Commerce

With great fanfare, in 1957 the Ford Motor Company launched an all-new designed from scratch automobile. This futuristic vehicle featured a push-button transmission and a speedometer whose glow grew brighter after the car exceeded a preset speed. What to call it? The company's board settled on Edsel, the name of founder Henry Ford's late son. Ford's head of marketing research thought that name had "a certain ring to it. An air of gaiety and zest." This suggested that everything about their new car hadn't been carefully thought through. The company put lots of money into advertising its new vehicle. Ford chairman Ernest Breech cosigned an ad that announced, "Everyone who has seen it knows—with us—that the Edsel is a success." Breech was wrong. Despite the massive amounts of resources that went into designing and promoting this car, few customers bought one. They didn't care for the Edsel's toilet-seat-like front grille, its underpowered engine, and its indifferent handling. As complaints mounted about this car's appearance, performance, and lack of support from Detroit, company head Henry Ford II addressed dealers by closed-circuit television. "The Edsel," he told them, "is here to stay." Two years later Ford stopped producing Edsels. Ever since this car crashed in a forlorn heap after being introduced with so much fanfare, **Edsel** has alluded to catastrophic failure. The problem-plagued B-1B bomber has been called "the Edsel of national defense."

Two decades after its Edsel fiasco, Ford enjoyed the dubious distinction of having a second product become a synonym for automotive malfeasance: the Pinto. Not only was the Pinto a mediocre car (to which the author can attest, having owned one), but its exposed gas tank was prone to explode in rear-end collisions. Adding an $11 shield would have solved this problem. In 1978, seven years after its 1971 introduction, pressure from the press, public, and government forced the company to recall 1.5 million Pintos for fuel-tank retrofitting. Two years later this brand disappeared from the marketplace, but not from the national conversation. In the 1994 movie *Speed*, when asked if she can drive a bomb-laden bus, Sandra Bullock's character responds, "Sure, it's just like driving a really big Pinto." **Pinto** is still used as a metaphor for faulty design and corporate indifference to the welfare of customers. When fiasco followed fiasco in the use of electronic voting machines, Representative John Conyers (D-Mich.) charged that voters were being forced to cast ballots on "the Ford Pinto of voting technology."

Ford got company in the annals of corporate calamity after the 1985 introduction of New Coke. Introduced in part because market testing showed customers preferred its sweeter, more Pepsi-like taste, this product outraged loyal Coke drinkers. They were not shy about expressing their outrage. Coca-Cola head Roberto Goizueta got years of one-liners from reactions to his New Coke fiasco, such as the irate letter he received from a traditional Coke lover that began, "Dear Chairman Dodo." Coca-Cola quickly reinstated its original formula as "Classic Coke." Eventually New Coke disappeared, "Classic" was deleted from the name of its alternative, and all was well in the world of Coca-Cola devotees. Where **New Coke** lives on is in America's collective memory as an allusion to non-starters of many kinds. Commentator George Will once said that, like New Coke, the Republican Party had become a brand nobody wanted to buy.

---

## THE HARDIEST PET

In 1974, freelance copywriter Gary Dahl grew weary of listening to a woman sitting next to him at the Grog & Sirloin in Los Gatos, California, fret about what to do with her pets while on vacation. Dahl said he had no such problem with his pet. Why not? she asked. Because, he explained, his was a rock. No fuss, no muss, no need to get a sitter. Then the lightbulb went on. Why not sell rocks as pets? Dahl gathered over a million fist-sized rocks on a beach in Baja California, then sold these Pet Rocks for $3.95 apiece. Packaged in a vented box that resembled a miniature pet crate, each came with a manual showing how to train the rock to sit, stay, play dead, and roll over (with a little help from the owner).

During the Christmas season of 1975 more than a million Americans bought **Pet Rocks.** Even though their commercial life lasted a mere three months, for decades thereafter the saga of this product became a marketing parable. "Another pet rock" or "this year's pet rock" can still be heard when new products are discussed. This allusion is ambivalent. Since the Pet Rock essentially made something out of nothing, it took on broad metaphorical significance, especially after H. Ross Perot compared his fellow General Motors board members to *pet rocks*. *Time* magazine disparaged a slim management tome by calling it a "literary pet rock," then echoed Perot when characterizing compliant corporate directors as belonging to "pet-rock boards."

## Stores

Before there were dollar stores, there were dime stores, aka five-and-ten-cent stores, or five-and-dimes. Five-and-dimes were the Wal-Marts of their era, only more inviting. This was where you went to buy a tube of lipstick, a box of Milk Duds, or a package of fish hooks. Kids were welcome there, lured in part by parakeets chirping in cages and goldfish swimming in tanks. Sounds of the latest hit by Eddie Fisher or Patti Page being played in the record department made five-and-dimes a teen magnet. Songs such as "Love at the Five and Dime" and plays such as *Come Back to the Five and Dime, Jimmy Dean, Jimmy Dean* celebrate that fond setting-memory. Nowadays, **dime-store** refers to low-end merchandise of many kinds. When my wife's middle-aged ophthalmologist suggested that she buy herself some "dime-store glasses," Muriel went right to Dollar General and bought a pair of inexpensive reading spectacles. The use of that concept extends well beyond merchandise, however. In his memoir *Dreams from My Father,* Barack Obama referred to absentee fathers like his own who communicate with "once-a-year letters full of dime-store advice."

Unlike dime stores, drugstores still flourish, but with nothing like the social cachet of earlier counterparts. Those versions typically hosted a *soda fountain* where one could buy ice-cream sodas, floats, milkshakes, malted milks, and phosphates, all served up on a marble counter by a *soda jerk* wearing a white paper cap. The sound of carbonated water being squirted into a glass with a loud hiss is a nostalgic retrosound for many. Most important, though, were the swiveling counter stools and intimate booths that made drugstores a place to see and be seen. After World War I, young men who hung around soda fountains looking for action were called **drugstore cowboys**. A 1989 movie starring Matt Dillon was titled *Drugstore Cowboy*.

Advances in glassmaking technology during the late nineteenth century allowed drugstores, dime stores, and, especially, *department stores* to sport huge plate glass windows, which they filled with elaborate displays. These were known as **window dressing**. We still use this term to refer to anything that's more show than substance. Airline efforts to mollify stranded passengers with hotel vouchers and free pizza have been called "window dressing."

In department stores, five-and-dimes, and any other high-volume retail enterprise, money flew in and out of *cash registers*. When their drawer was opened a bell rang, inspiring the phrase **ring it up** for making a purchase. That unnecessary chime was engineered into cash registers (originally called Ritty's Incorruptible Cashiers after inventor James Ritty) so employers would know when employees were handling money. Referring back to a time when retailers' cash was kept in a container known as a *till*, cash registers presumably discouraged sales clerks from **sticking their hand in the till**. According to social historian Bill Bryson, the reason product prices were so often uneven (49¢, $1.29, etc.) was to force these clerks to open their cash registers and make change—triggering the telltale chime and making it less likely that they'd simply pocket the customers' cash. To American consumers, cash register bells became like those that made Pavlov's dogs drool. (See chapter 20.) They signified *money*. Their sounds made such a big impression that in 1992 the Rally's hamburger chain created a short-lived TV ad featuring a rival fast-food clerk played by actor Seth Green who shouts *"Cha-ching!"* every time an item is added to a customer's burgeoning bill. (This ad can be seen on YouTube.) Even though that sound had already been replaced by the beep of electronic cash registers, it tapped our collective memory and caught the public's fancy. The term **"cha-ching"**—sometimes spelled **"ca-ching,"** **"ch-ching,"** or **"ka-ching!"**—long outlived the commercial that spawned it, and became slang for money itself. Newscaster Katie Couric once asked if the reason airlines were squeezing so many passengers into planes was "because cha-ching?"

## Money

In 1257 a gold piece worth 20 shillings was issued in England. Like America's Susan B. Anthony dollar, this coin did not catch on. Few were minted. When one did show up, it was considered a rarity and possibly a good-luck charm. The expression **a pretty penny** referred to that attractive coin, and many another form of value considered *worth a pretty penny*. In stark contrast is the *bad penny*. Pushy individuals who keep coming back, and back, and back unbidden **turn up like a bad penny**.

There is much talk of eliminating the penny as an obsolete coin in inflationary times. But if we deep-six this coin, what will happen to all of the great penny-based phrases that are part of our language? A short list includes *penny ante, penny pincher, a penny for your thoughts,* and *a penny saved is a penny earned.*

Many fairs and carnivals featured a **penny arcade**. This precursor to today's video arcade featured mechanical games that were activated by putting a penny in a slot. It usually took a while for this coin to wend its way through the gears and levers. That left behind **until the penny drops** as an expression meaning to wait for something to happen. **The penny dropped** suggests a belated moment of recognition. Author Tim Flannery (*The Weather Makers*) said that in order to grasp the enormity of global warming he first had to read a lot about climate change and interview experts on this topic before "all of a sudden, the penny dropped."

Although nickels lack the verbal cachet of pennies, they do enjoy a modest presence in our retrotalk. **Not worth a plugged nickel** refers to the practice of removing a valuable piece of metal from the center of gold or silver coins and filling this hole with a *plug* of cheaper metal. A related catchphrase, **don't take any wooden nickels**, harks back to an alleged practice of passing off counterfeit coins made of wood to unsuspecting rubes. As lexicographer Stuart Berg Flexner pointed out, however, in early-nineteenth-century America, jokes based on fake merchandise made of wood—nutmeg, cucumber seeds, even hams—were an American staple, and may well have inspired the one that stuck around: the *wooden nickel*.

Calls made from early-twentieth-century pay phones cost 5¢. "It's your nickel—so talk!" was a common statement in the heyday of these phones. When that price doubled, the expression inflated to "It's your dime." **On your nickel** or **on your dime** still refers to conversing with someone who is paying. Congressmen who accept gratuities from lobbyists are said to be *on their dime*. **Drop a dime, dime out**, or simply **dime** (as a verb) all refer to reporting misdeeds, an artifact of the time when this was commonly done by public telephone. Whistleblowers are sometimes called **dime droppers**. According to author George Packer (*The Assassins' Gate: America in Iraq*), U.S. soldiers were struck by how routinely Iraqis would "dime each other out."

Another group of dime-related expressions has less to do with this coin's value than with its modest size: **turn on a dime**, for example, or **stop on a dime**. To **get off the dime**—meaning to get moving—originated in the 1920s as an admonition to slow-moving marathon dancers. Why is unclear. Why not get off the nickel, or the quarter? Linguist Robert Hendrickson speculates that this expression might have originated in Depression-era *dime-a-dance* halls as an exhortation for dancers to get a move on.

At one time a Spanish peso, or dollar coin, could literally be cut into pieces: halves, quarters, or even eight pieces shaped like pizza slices. These pieces were called *reales* in Spanish, *bits* in English (from the Old English *bite*, which was reduced to *bit* as common parlance for any small amount of money). Each was worth 12½¢. Since the Spanish dollar and its subdivisions were common currency in colonial and post-revolutionary America, Americans adopted some of their nomenclature, too. Calling a quarter (a quarter of a dollar, of course) **two bits** harks back to this time. Today that term survives mainly as a reference to something cheap or small-time, "a two-bit politician," say, or a "two-bit hustler."

In the first few decades of United States history, dollar coins were rare. When someone with a stack of them used one from the top, he paid **top dollar**. When that person exhausted his stack, there was little more where these coins came from. He'd reached his **bottom dollar**.

## Products

Like many of her prewar generation, my mother-in-law calls any and all electric mixers **Mixmasters**. Well into the 1990s, she called her Whirlpool refrigerator a **Frigidaire**, after the early success story in this field that was introduced by General Motors in 1918. A friend tells me that his relatives in rural Kentucky still call their refrigerators Frigidaires. More often this implement was and is called a **fridge**, a contraction of either refrigerator, Frigidaire, or both.

In Britain, where "hoover" is still interchangeable with "vacuum cleaner," the act of using one is called *hoovering*. This is the top branding achievement: when one's name becomes a verb. By its own intention, that's what happened with Simoniz, a paste wax first introduced by inventor George Simons in 1910. This carnauba-based product set a standard for polishing automobile bodies. In the golden age of radio after World War I, its slogan—"Motorists wise, Simoniz"—was repeated ad nauseam over the air. Although Simoniz is still the brand name of a wide range of car care products, George Simons's original paste wax product proved a bit taxing for weary American elbows and has largely given way to ones that offer faster gratification. The term **simonize**—defined by my dictionary as "to polish with wax"—lives on in song lyrics, as a website name, and as slang for wild ranting by podcasters (referencing one of their breed named Simon).

It is not an uncommon fate for the name of products that overwhelm the competition to become generic. Typically, the first one to market gets naming rights. Kleenex, Jacuzzi, Dustbuster, Weed Whacker. This can be a mixed blessing. Onetime trademarks that lost their legal protection due to common usage include elevator, escalator, thermos, yo-yo, dry ice, raisin bran, granola, trampoline, ping-pong, and loafer. So did cellophane. That crackly transparent wrap made from cellulose was introduced in 1912 as Cellophane (an alloy of the French terms *cellulose* and *diaphane*, or "transparent"). To this day one can hear old-timers calling see-through food wrapping of any kind **cellophane**. Some made the switch to **wax paper** when this product became popular. In 1953 Dow converted a polymer-based product used to waterproof airplane hulls into a transparent, unusually flexible food wrapping they called Saran Wrap. Although a number of successors have stolen market share from the original, all tend to be called **Saran Wrap** by baby boomers whose mothers wrapped their peanut butter and jelly sandwiches in that product.

## MOXIE

When Vice President Calvin Coolidge heard that President Warren Harding had died in late summer 1923, his response was "Guess we'd better have a drink." That's exactly what Coolidge, his wife, father, and some colleagues did—acknowledge the occasion by chugging down bottles of Moxie. This bitter brew, concocted from ingredients such as sassafras, gentian root, wintergreen, and juice from Maine's moxie berries, was a popular beverage in Silent Cal's era. Originally called Moxie Nerve Food, it was said to promote "pep and vigor." This may have had something to do with the fact that—like Coca-Cola—when it was introduced in 1876, Moxie apparently included cocaine

among its ingredients. Back then this ingredient was considered a benign pepper-upper. Even though the Pure Food and Drug Act of 1909 put an end to Moxie's medicinal claims, it remained popular as a soft drink. In its time Moxie was as ubiquitous as Coke and Pepsi are today. The jingle "Just Make It Moxie for Mine" was on many American lips before World War I. "The Moxie Trot" enjoyed a vogue among vigorous dancers after the war. "Moxiemobiles"—cars whose cab was filled by a wooden horse with a steering wheel protruding through its neck that was used by a man in the saddle—promoted this soft drink all around the country. Moxie was a fixture at fairs, resorts, dance halls, and any other setting associated with pep and vigor.

When Coca-Cola took over the pep and vigor market after World War II, Moxie retreated to its roots as a regional product that is still popular among New Englanders and cultists around the world. Its historic association with vitality and gumption gave Moxie a lasting verbal cachet. Since early Depression days, the generic term **moxie** has referred to brash self-confidence, comparable to the Yiddish *chutzpah.* ("He's got a lot of moxie!")

## Slogans and Jingles

Before and after World War II, the backs of countless comic books featured a full-page ad for an unusually buff figure named Charles Atlas. These ads were in comic-book form themselves. The most famous featured a scrawny young man named Mac who sits next to a woman at the beach. A burly older man runs by, kicking sand in his face. When Mac protests, this bully sneers and threatens to smash Mac's face. The humiliated young man resolves to stop being a "puny 97-pound 'runt.'" He sends for Charles Atlas's bodybuilding course. After a brief period of building his body under Atlas's tutelage, our former weakling returns to the beach and pummels the bully who kicked sand in his face. In the last panel, titled "HERO OF THE BEACH," his girlfriend says, "Oh, Mac! You are a real man after all."

One of Charles Atlas's great discoveries was how many comic book readers dreamed of looking like him. ("You too can have a body like mine," his ads promised.) Actually, this discovery came from advertising man Charles Roman, who met Angelo Siciliano in 1928 when he was a down-and-out thirty-five-year-old bodybuilder. Roman renamed Siciliano "Charles Atlas" and built him into a mail-order behemoth by creating the ubiquitous ads that ran for decades in male-oriented publications. The beach version in particular made such an indelible impression that nearly three decades since Atlas's death, **98-pound weakling**—one pound got added along the way—remains shorthand for wimpiness. "Does your browser perform like a 98-pound weakling?" asked *PC World*. (An article in *Business Week* got the weight right when observing, "There's a lot of talk about America becoming a 97-pound weakling.") **Kicking sand in someone's face** represents any act of extreme provocation. At a time when McDonald's and its franchisees were feuding, one of the latter said this dispute took place in a spirit of "I'm going to kick sand on you, and you're going to kick sand on me."

The Charles Atlas ads were a rarity: ones in print that left retroterms behind. Another that did so pitched a home piano-playing course in the late 1920s. It was headlined "THEY LAUGHED WHEN I SAT DOWN AT THE PIANO. BUT WHEN I STARTED TO PLAY!" Hundreds of words followed about how a onetime musical dunce became a piano virtuoso after sending for the U.S. School of Music correspondence course. In the process he grew far more popular. "As the last notes of the Moonlight Sonata died away," this man reported, "the room resounded with a sudden roar of applause. . . . Men shook my hand—wildly congratulated me—pounded me on the back in their enthusiasm!" For decades after this ad began running in American publications, **"They laughed when I . . ."** was the set-up for many a mock comment. Arthur Asa Berger began the preface to his book *Li'l Abner* with "They laughed when I sat down at the typewriter!" Over time our memories added the word "all" to this expression. Several book titles, including Ira Flatow's *They All Laughed . . .* , echo this classic ad, as does the George Gershwin song "They All Laughed."

Another classic ad campaign featured the dreaded "5 o'clock shadow" that Gem Razors promised to help eliminate. From the mid-1930s until the late 1950s Gem warned men with heavy beards that if they didn't use their blades in the morning, they risked having dark jowls by dinnertime. "Avoid '5 o'clock shadow' " was the slogan of these ads. That concept came into political play after Richard Nixon squared off against John Kennedy in the first televised presidential debate in 1960. Nixon's glowering presence was accentuated by a whisper of dark beard stubble (he'd refused makeup). For decades afterward it was said that Nixon's pronounced **5 o'clock shadow** during this debate may have cost him the presidency. *Washington Post* political cartoonist Herbert Block ("Herblock"), who always drew Nixon with dark jowls, said the real problem was his subject's "moral 5 o'clock shadow."

## It Slices! It Dices!

In the early 1980s copywriter Cliff Freeman dreamed up a TV spot that compared Wendy's square, beefy burgers with those of a fanciful rival called the Big

Bun. This ad starred a wizened eighty-something retired manicurist with a bullfrog voice named Clara Peller. Peller and two elderly sidekicks examine a hamburger they've just been given at the Big Bun. The bun itself dwarfs the burger. "It certainly is a big bun," says one of the women. "It's a very big bun," agrees another. "A big, fluffy bun," reiterates the first. At that point Peller starts croaking loudly, "Where's the beef? Where's the beef? Hey, where's the beef?" This question quickly became a national catchphrase. Cliff Freeman thought it captured a widespread sense of frustration about . . . lots of things. While prepping Walter Mondale for a 1984 presidential primary debate, his campaign manager suggested he pose Clara Peller's question to Democratic rival Gary Hart. Although Mondale said he'd never heard it, the onetime vice president rehearsed Wendy's slogan a few times, then popped the question before a national audience while pressing his fellow Democrat about the substance of his "new ideas." It's the best-remembered line of an unmemorable campaign. **"Where's the beef?"** is still heard routinely as a way of asking "Where's the content?" A British blogger attributed the rise of a vapid, good-looking London politician to the fact that no one was asking him "Where's the beef?" In time **beef** alone became synonymous with *substance* in political discourse. According to NPR commentator E. J. Dionne, when it came to George W. Bush's plans for victory in Iraq, "there wasn't much beef there." In the comic strip *Doonesbury*, Bush himself tells a news conference, "Take my new proposals for Head Start. If *that's* not beef, I don't know what is."

American discourse would be crippled without catchphrases left over from long-forgotten ad campaigns. Some enjoy a season or two. ("Thanks! I needed that." "You've come a long way, baby.") Others endure far longer. They include: **"It's not nice to fool mother nature!"** (Chiffon margarine), **"We make money the old-fashioned way. We earn it!"** (Smith Barney), and **"Is it live, or is it Memorex?"** *Time* magazine alluded to this famous 1970s ad campaign for cassette tapes when it said that author Jonathan Schwartz had a "Memorex ear for dialogue." Margaret Carlson later wrote in *Time* that delegates to a Democratic convention had "given up trying to figure out what's real and what's Memorex."

Another way I've seen this slogan cited is in reference to " 'Is it live or is it Memorex?' moments." That could be considered a twofer, referencing two series of ads at once—three, actually. In the late 1980s, the antacid Maalox introduced an advertising campaign built around heartburn-inducing *Maalox Moments.* A few years later *Kodak Moment* ads were even more successful in leaving the "moment" concept behind (in their case referring to heartwarming occasions that lent themselves to being photographed). "What a **Kodak moment!**" can still be heard, sardonically. In conjunction with other words, "moment" could be the single most enduring word-concept from a long-dormant ad campaign (e.g., "senior moment," referring to age-associated forgetfulness, or the "Muskie moment" discussed in chapter 5).

In other cases it's not a catchphrase but a character in an ad that captures the American imagination. None did so more effectively than the one Dick Wilson played in twenty-five years' worth of televised commercials for Charmin that first appeared in 1964. These ads featured Mr. Whipple, an officious merchant with a bristly mustache who reprimanded grocery customers for squeezing rolls of Charmin toilet tissue to confirm their softness. A 1979 poll found that **Mr. Whipple** trailed only Billy Graham and Richard Nixon as America's best-known human being. Today his name is shorthand for any prissy, fussy man. A retired Oakwood, Ohio, police detective once told a reporter how surprised he was when a serial killer he'd interrogated turned out to be a "Mr. Whipple kind of guy."

Another memorable ad from the late Mr. Whipple era featured an elderly woman lying on the floor of her home. "I've fallen, and I can't get up!" was the operative slogan of this late-night commercial for Life Alert Emergency Response Inc. That slogan quickly became a pop culture catchphrase. After Jay Leno had a motorcycle accident, he returned to *The Tonight Show*, crutches in hand, "I've fallen and I can't get up" on his lips. **"I've fallen, and I can't get up!"** remains one of the best remembered of all televised catchphrases. It inspired a popular T-shirt slogan: i've fallen and i can't reach my beer.

Yet another late-night commercial, this one for a pre-Cuisinart kitchen utensil called **Veg-o-Matic**, loudly proclaimed its ability to **slice and dice**. Even though viewers loved to hate that ad, they did apply its key three poetic words to a wide variety of unrelated activities. Soon after George W. Bush took office, Ken Herman of Cox News wondered why the president was "running a Veg-o-Matic legislative strategy aimed at slicing and dicing his way to victories." The demographic segmentation engaged in by marketers and politicians alike is routinely called *slicing and dicing* by press commentators.

But wait! There's more!

# 14. On the Job

**W**orking conditions in early coal mines were appalling. Miners who weren't killed or maimed by collapsing timbers, falling debris, or unsafe equipment regularly succumbed to toxic fumes. Because it was odorless, carbon monoxide was particularly lethal. In the late nineteenth century, English physiologist John Scott Haldane proposed a simple but elegant solution to this problem: miners should take a caged bird with them below ground. Since they are ultra-sensitive to carbon monoxide fumes, canaries proved to be the perfect poison detector. At a concentration as small as 0.29 percent of carbon monoxide in the atmosphere these small yellow birds get woozy and fall off their perch in about two and a half minutes. Whenever miners noticed their caged canary beginning to teeter, they skedaddled fast. Over time the notion of canaries as organic oracles became metaphorical. The **canary in the mine, the miner's canary,** or simply **the canary** is a common way to refer to heralds of ominous events on the horizon. As awareness of global warming has grown, reference to this bird has become increasingly common, and ever more urgent. When polar bears began to succumb to the shrinking of their icy habitat, Canada's *National Post* called them "the 650-kilogram canary in the climate change coal mine." More broadly, any organism whose decline can be attributed to global warming has been called a *climate canary.*

Logging rivaled mining as a hazardous occupation. More than a few loggers' limbs were lost to the saws and axes they used. Since handles didn't always fit snugly, an axe's head sometimes flew off in the midst of tree chopping. This alarming event gave rise to the expression **fly off the handle.** Just as aggravating were the long two-man *whipsaws* loggers used to cut large tree trunks into boards before the Civil War. "Misery whips" they called these cumbersome, dangerous tools. Their use involved digging a deep pit, then dragging the trunk over that pit, where one man stood below to saw in tandem with another man on top. Today we use the term **whipsaw** to mean being pulled in two directions at once. ("I felt whipsawed between my wife and my mother.") Based on the fact that loggers' saws were commonly "gummed up" by tree sap, **gum up the works** still refers to obstructing activity.

In a time when roads were primitive, and impassable in bad weather, massive numbers of cut logs were floated to their destination on rivers. At times this floating armada became so congested that it couldn't move. A *logjam* resulted. Today, **logjam** refers to any stalled situation in which movement is impossible, a crowded customs inspection, say, or a long line of airplanes waiting to take off in bad weather.

To break up logjams, loggers climbed onto the stalled logs and used their feet to get them moving. This risky operation sometimes called for two men to work together at either end of a jammed log, kicking their feet in opposite directions. Such *logrolling* became a popular event in logging contests, determining which pair of contestants could keep one spinning the longest. Only by synchronizing their motion could both stay afloat. The norm was to fall

off, however, which is why we say **easy as falling off a log.** "Logrolling" also referred to semi-social occasions in which neighbors of American settlers gathered to help roll aside tree trunks felled while clearing land. Either use of the term "logrolling" suggests mutual aid. Since the early nineteenth century **logrolling** has alluded to any situation in which two or more people swap favors. *Spy* magazine had a regular feature called "Logrolling in Our Time" that featured authors promoting each other's work.

Many loggers' tools were made by blacksmiths. These brawny men were a common sight, pounding away at glowing pieces of iron they pulled from their fires. Smiths had to work quickly, before the iron cooled and lost its malleability. That's why we say **strike while the iron is hot** when discussing an activity that must proceed briskly for maximum effect. A blacksmith who put too many pieces of iron in his fire risked not being able to keep them all sufficiently hot. "Many irons in the fire," advised a Scottish proverb, "some must cool." Alternatively, when too many pieces of iron lay in a fire too long, some might actually ignite. In the words of a Danish saying, "He who has many irons in the fire will let some of them burn." Thus **too many irons in the fire** alludes to the perils of trying to do too many things at once.

Although cabinetmakers are somewhat more common today than blacksmiths, the terms we've borrowed from them go well back in time. One has to do with the trapezoidal male and female joints cabinetmakers cut to connect pieces of wood. When executed neatly this *dovetail* joint is a thing of beauty. Outside of carpentry we use that term as a verb. People or activities that mesh smoothly are said to **dovetail**. We also call activities or people that are as they ought to be **on the level** or **on the square**. This refers to the bubble levels and T squares carpenters have used for  centuries to make sure that their work is even all around. Those who wouldn't know a T square from a tea party or a bubble level from a bubble bath still say, "His stories just didn't square" or "She didn't seem on the level."

Well below carpenters on the status ladder were *tinkers*, itinerant utensil repairers who plied their trade in England before the Industrial Revolution. Tinkers were not known for having a civil tongue. In fact, their penchant for profanity was so notorious that *not worth a tinker's cuss* was once a common catchphrase. That morphed into **not worth a tinker's damn**. This phrase posed problems for tender ears, however, so in Victorian times an alternative etymology emerged to explain that this expression had to do with the mound of dough that tinkers built around a flawed utensil segment they then flooded with solder. Since this dam could be used only once, something of no lasting value might be thought of as **not worth a tinker's dam**. From the Victorian era on this was the genteel form of that expression.

Another group of itinerant workers traveled about with pedal-driven grindstones to sharpen knives. This work required careful concentration. To make sure it was being done properly a knife sharpener had to watch closely as blades were honed by a whirling stone. He **kept his nose to the grindstone**. For nearly five centuries that expression has been used figuratively to describe someone paying careful attention. Nowadays "nose to the grindstone" refers more broadly to working hard and intently. A related expression is **put your shoulder to the wheel**, as one might when trying to free a wagon wheel stuck in mud.

In another vocational sphere, beginning in the Middle Ages newly woven wool was first scrubbed clean, then stretched tightly on wooden frames called *tenters*. The wet fabric was attached to L-shaped hooks inserted along the tenter's perimeter to keep it from shrinking. By the sixteenth century *on tenters* had become slang for being in a strained state. Two centuries later this phrase gave way to **on tenterhooks**, an expression we still use to mean being in a state of tense suspense. When discussing a vote in Congress that sharply divided Republicans and Democrats, NPR's Ken Rudin said, "Both parties are on tenterhooks about what to do."

During the early nineteenth century, textile manufacturers in central England began to use mechanized weaving looms. These labor-saving devices allowed them to get rid of some employees and reduce the wages of others. Prohibited by law from unionizing, textile workers organized protests under the aegis of a mythical leader named General Ludd. During some of these protests mechanized looms were smashed. As a result the term **Luddite** has come to refer generically to anyone who blindly resists technological progress. ("My boss is such a Luddite that if he had his way I'd be using an abacus instead of a computer.")

In the mid-nineteenth century, surveyors began to demarcate locations

by placing markers in the ground, typically small metal plaques. They called these *benchmarks*. Within a few decades **benchmark** had come to refer to any point of reference from which measurements or comparisons could be made. The practices of leading companies are sometimes used by others for *benchmarking*, or serving as a standard of comparison.

## HEAVY EQUIPMENT

After the Civil War, southern vigilantes used bullwhips to beat former slaves who did not do their bidding, especially those who had the temerity to run for office. Such a savage, sometimes fatal lashing was called a *bull-dose*, or a beating sufficient to subdue a bull. This term came to be spelled *bulldoze*. Those who administered them were called *bulldozers*. Eventually "bulldoze" was applied more broadly to getting one's way by intimidating others. **Bulldoze** still signifies action that heedlessly pushes obstacles out of the way. When a diesel-powered earthmoving machine was introduced in 1930, it quickly became known as a **bulldozer**.

A related piece of heavy equipment inspired the verb *steamroll* for a similar notion: getting one's way without regard to others, rolling right over them in essence. Even though it's been a long time since any piece of heavy equipment has been powered by steam, we still refer generically to **steamrollers** and **steam shovels**, perhaps because so many of today's adults read *Mike Mulligan and His Steam Shovel* as children. To the *New Yorker*'s Elizabeth Kolbert, a gigantic earthmover resembled a "huge, Mike Mulligan–csque shovel."

## Office Supplies

When correspondence was mailed through real space rather than cyberspace, envelopes played a much more prominent role in our lives. Certain envelopes became renowned for what was supposedly written on their backs. According to one popular legend that's where Abraham Lincoln composed his Gettysburg Address. (He actually wrote it on White House stationery.) As a result, *back of an envelope* still alludes to just about anything scribbled on scraps of paper. Spontaneous notes scribbled on available paper are commonly called **back-of-the-envelope** ideas. More broadly this refers to roughly developed concepts. In his book *The Myths of Innovation*, Scott Berkun writes, "As a back-of-the-envelope sketch of innovation difficulty, let's assume there is a 50% chance of succeeding at each challenge."

The most common instruments used to write on envelopes were pencils and pens. For centuries pens were made of sharpened goose quills that had to be constantly dipped in an ink-filled container called an *inkwell*. (A prominent Manhattan literary agency calls itself Inkwell Management.) Whenever it needed sharpening, this quill's nib would typically be trimmed by a small **penknife**. *Fountain pens* made this laborious task unnecessary. They housed a reservoir of ink in rubber bladders. Those who used fountain pens suffered constant low-grade anxiety. Suppose it leaks? But leaking wasn't the only way ink stained clothing and skin. This could also happen by contact with freshly written documents. An ever-present danger was the unsightly **ink blot**. (Former Secretary of State Colin Powell told Barbara Walters that his speech to the United Nations incorrectly arguing that Iraq had weapons of mass destruction

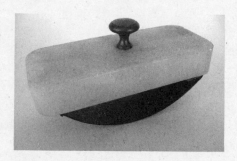

constituted a **blot** on his record.) To minimize this problem, those writing with fountain pens pressed absorbent pieces of paper called **blotters** on their freshly written words. Although that term can still be heard, as fewer and fewer fountain pens are used, its secondary meaning—as a guest book for the recently arrested (**police blotter**)—is more prevalent. ABCNews.go.com includes a section devoted to investigative news called "The Blotter."

Editors historically commented on authors' manuscripts with a pencil that had blue lead. Today their pencils are just as likely to have lead that is red, orange, or even graphite gray. Nonetheless, **blue-pencil** as a verb still refers to making written suggestions for revision of a manuscript. Regardless of its lead's color, accountants who cast a skeptical eye on financial sheets were said to wield a **sharp pencil**. This essentially meaningless phrase conjures an image of a tight-lipped auditor with garters on his sleeves and a green eyeshade on his forehead making tiny notations on papers filled with numbers. Why a green eyeshade? Because green effectively filters glare from overhead lights. Although few employees other than casino dealers wear them any longer, **green eyeshades** still brings to mind a parsimonious person carefully checking figures. As the economic impact of immigrants became more evident, suggested poll-ster Kelly Ann Conway, Americans were "starting to look at immigration through green eyeshades."

Centuries ago, British and American bureaucrats tied up official documents with a type of red ribbon called *tape*. In order to access those documents, these bureaucrats had to untie that ribbon, then retie it afterward. Needless to say, this was not a welcome task. To avoid doing so, bureaucrats routinely came up with excuses for not retrieving tied-up documents at all. As a result, since at least the mid-nineteenth century **red tape** has referred figuratively to bureaucratic foot-dragging. In the mid-nineteenth century Thomas Carlyle referred continually to the fact that human affairs were strangled by what he called the "world-wide jungle of red-tape." **Cutting through red tape** implied simply snipping this ribbon with scissors, much as Alexander the Great used his sword to sever the Gordian knot. (See chapter 3.)

Moving down the color palette, even though actual slips of pink paper informing employees that they've been laid off can't be found, the likelihood that they once existed is indicated by our regular use of the term **pink slip** to depict such an event. (Well over a century ago problematic messages such as insurance policy rate increases were typed on slips of pink paper.) Presumably these slips showed up in pay packets of discharged workers to curtly inform them of their fate. According to an ABC News account, "400 Radio Shack employees got their pink slips electronically." "Pink slip" is such a common synonym for termination of services that it's even become a verb. A Fox Sports announcer once reported that a released baseball player had been "pink-slipped."

## Modern Office Gear

In the early 1950s, small, stout bottles of ink capped with felt tips began to appear in offices and schools. With them one could write on almost any surface. Their inventor, Sidney Rosenthal, called his product a Magic Marker. This was the first incarnation of felt-tip pens. To promote fast drying, Rosenthal's version used a spirit-based ink whose acrid smell helped imprint its brand name in the collective cortex of baby boomers. By 1980 competition from skinnier, odor-free, water-soluble felt pens had forced the original Magic Marker company into bankruptcy. (Binney & Smith later bought this brand name and put reformulated Magic Markers back on the market.) Where this product remains front and center is in the memory of those who grew up using it. Boomers in particular date themselves and confuse their offspring by referring to any and all felt pens as **Magic Markers**. In his novel *An Unfinished Life*, Mark Spragg wrote of a schoolgirl's backpack that had "zippered pockets for her pencils, pens, and Magic Markers." The *New Yorker* subsequently referred to a "Magic Markered announcement," then ran a cartoon by Roz Chast that featured older protesters holding blank picket signs that was captioned "Rebels without a Magic Marker."

About the same time that Magic Markers made their debut, a twenty-seven-year-old Dallas bank secretary named Bette Nesmith grew fed up with trying to correct mistakes made by the carbon film ribbon on her electric typewriter. While helping paint some bank windows in her second job as a commercial artist, Nesmith noticed the way experienced colleagues corrected lettering miscues by simply painting over them. Making a technology transfer, she mixed up a white tempera liquid in her kitchen blender, then used this brew to paint over typing mistakes. In 1956 Nesmith started a company to sell small bottles of what she called "Liquid Paper." That fragrant, spirit-based product quickly became one of those "how did we ever live without it?" inventions. Competitors called **Wite-Out** and **Ko-Rec-Type** have had more success as metaphors, however. Bill Moyers once said, " 'Mitigating circumstances' are the Ko-Rec-Type of politics." According to a sportswriter, Cincinnati Reds outfielder Ken Griffey Jr. was "white-outed" from his team's lineup just before a game got under way.

### RUBBER STAMPS

At an office supplies rummage sale, I once bought a box full of old rubber stamps complete with an antique revolving wheel that gripped several in metal pincers. I used them to stamp letters to friends with messages such as GOLD DRAFT, DISCOUNT ALLOWED and HIS WIFE AS TENANTS BY THE ENTIRETIES. (Don't ask me. I just wielded the stamp.)

There was a time when bureaucrats' lives were consumed with stamping such messages on documents. This began in the Civil War

era, when stamps made of vulcanized rubber proved far better suited to this task than ones made of metal or wood. Those impressing them on multiple pieces of paper used a repetitive up-and-down elbow movement. That act gave birth to the verb **rubber-stamp**, meaning to authorize reflexively. Those who follow someone else's lead mindlessly are said to be *rubber stamps*. As early as 1919, biographer William Thayer speculated that William Howard Taft, who at one time was considered a mouthpiece for Theodore Roosevelt, might well have been advised: "Be your own President; don't be anybody's man or rubber stamp." Today this allusion is most often used to depict cowed legislators who approve decisions made by authoritarian executives. They constitute a "rubber-stamp parliament" or a "rubber-stamp legislature."

## Means of Reproduction

Since the days when medieval monks laboriously wrote out copies of the Bible by hand, human beings have pined for a better way to reproduce documents. In offices, making copies of outgoing correspondence was a particular problem. The main job of pen-wielding copy clerks, or *scriveners*, was to recopy letters. Bob Cratchit in Dickens's *A Christmas Carol* held such a position. So did the eponymous protagonist of Melville's classic story "Bartleby the Scrivener."

After the Civil War, a revolutionary method of document reproduction was devised. This involved coating filmy paper with a combination of lampblack and wax. When sandwiched between two sheets of paper, that coated stock allowed an original on top to be copied on the one below. The subsequent development of typewriters made this "carbonic paper" or "carbonated paper" the preferred way to copy outgoing correspondence. As many as ten copies of a document could be made by a secretary employing nine pieces of what came to be known as **carbon paper**. Smudged fingers and clothing linger in the sour memory of onetime office workers who had to make **carbon copies**. To their great relief, this process did not survive the invention of copying machines (except in some invoices, credit card receipts, and parking tickets). Nonetheless, we still use the term **carbon copy** to refer to exact replicas. According to a reporter for the Trinity College *Tripod*, "In today's age of carbon-copy pop stars and pseudo-rock bands, classical music is underrated."

Carbon copies could only be made of letter-sized documents, of course. For the large, graphics-heavy documents used by architects and engineers another reproduction process had to be invented. This process involved pressing a drawing next to paper treated with photosensitive chemicals, then placing the two under glass in a frame beneath a bright light (sunshine, ideally). That mid-nineteenth century invention was called the *blue process* because its copies—known as *blueprints*—consisted of white lines on a blue background. Although they have largely been replaced by other copying methods, we still allude to these large, detailed documents whenever we call something a **blueprint**. Countless proposals for resolving the Israeli-Palestinian conflict have been called "blueprints" for Middle East peace.

## Can Purple Ink Get You High?

My first job out of high school involved wrapping sheets of waxy green paper with typed indentations around a metal drum, priming them with a bit of gooey ink, turning the drum manually while pushing through a piece of copy paper to test the results, then pushing a button to continue this process automatically. The machine I used to do this was a *Gestetner*, named after David Gestetner. In the late nineteenth century this Hungarian-born kite maker noticed how the inks used to decorate kite paper seeped through to other pieces of paper in perfect patterns. This gave him the idea for creating *stencils* that would systematically do the same thing. For a time the machines his company sold to do this were so ubiquitous that the term "Gestetner" became a verb synonymous with "copy" in some offices. Gestetner's rival, the A. B. Dick Company, called its own stencil machine a *Mimeograph*. That quickly inspired the verb *mimeographing*. **Mimeo** became generic for any means of reproducing documents that involved "cutting" stencils. This term was apt, as all methods involved embossing letter-shaped impressions on stencil paper. Typewriters with their ribbon removed were ideal for this task. The phrase **cut a copy** may hark back to the heyday of stencils. (It may also have to do with cutting copies of metal keys.) Similarly, the expression "I'll cut you a check" reflects a time when checks were embossed by a special machine, one still used by banks to make certified checks.

A close cousin of mimeograph machines was called a *spirit duplicator*. Invented after World War I, this inexpensive copying process involved typing, writing, or drawing graphics on treated paper. That created thick lines of purple ink on a backing sheet or "master." The master was then placed on a roller which gradually absorbed an alcohol-based solvent that softened the ink just enough to make copies on paper fed through rollers cranked by hand. Because the best-known manufacturer of spirit duplicators was the Ditto Corporation, this process became known as *dittoing*, its output *dittos*. Such documents were easily identified by their smelly purple ink. That fragrance looms large in the smell memory of those who spent years taking dittoed quizzes in school. During the 1960s rumors ran rampant that sniffing purple ink could get you high. (It couldn't.) In one classroom after another, students could be seen surreptitiously pressing pop quizzes to their noses. I don't think this is why devout Rush Limbaugh fans call themselves *dittoheads*, but it's fun to think it might be. Though long out of fashion as a copying process, **ditto** is still used generically for all manner of reproduction.

To the everlasting gratitude of ink-stained office workers, new and improved means of copying documents became widespread after World War II. One camera-based device was sold by the Photostat Corporation. The results were generically called **photostats**, a term old-timers still use to refer to copies of all kinds. As recently as 1999, Carpentersville, Illinois, parents were advised that in order to sign their children up for little league baseball, they had to "provide the league with a Photostat [of their birth certificate]." Thermo-Fax was a chemical-based copying method. Still used by tattoo artists to make templates, *Thermo-faxing* copied originals onto chemically treated paper with heat and light. Copies that emerged from the Thermo-Fax felt as warm as biscuits fresh from the oven. Whenever we use the phrase **burn a copy** we recall this primitive form of photocopying in which documents were literally branded onto paper.

## WATER COOLER COUNTRY

Like sailors huddled around *scuttlebutts*, post–World War II office workers flocked to water coolers not only to wet their whistles but to quench their thirst for human contact. These were magnets for employees who slowly sipped at Dixie cups while they discussed Ed Sullivan, Sputnik, and whether Jonas Salk's new vaccine might conquer polio. In time other gathering points rivaled water coolers: coffee makers, microwave ovens, photocopiers. Companies such as Google and Microsoft had hipper amenities to offer employees than generic water in flimsy cups. Bottled spring water grew popular. Not far from my home, a huge stack of decommissioned water coolers rusts like cars in a junkyard. Even though this amenity can still be found in

some offices, water coolers are associated with gray flannel suits and bouffant hairdos. Nonetheless, the term **water cooler talk** persists in our language to depict casual conversation about issues of the day. The Internet has been called "the water cooler of the planet." TV critic David Bianculli called *Twin Peaks* "a true water cooler show, with everybody talking about it the next day."

## 15. Over the Wires and in the Groove

ike Bill Gates several decades later, Samuel Morse combined an ability to put existing pieces of technological puzzles together, dogged persistence, and a flair for self-promotion with keen awareness that hardware was useless without software. Others had come up with ways to communicate via electric pulses before this onetime portrait painter did so in 1844, over wires strung between Baltimore and Washington. Morse, however, was the first one to devise a plausible language to do this. In his language, letters and numbers were represented by short or long pulses of electric current—*dots* and *dashes*—tapped out on telegraphers' keys. To develop this means of communication, Morse and an assistant counted how many letters were in each box of printer's type, then assigned symbols accordingly. The frequently used *e* got one dot, or a brief pulse, *t* got a single dash, or a long pulse, while the rarely used *z* was given two dashes followed by two dots. What at first was called "the Morse alphabet" eventually became known as "Morse code." Even though few use that language anymore, **Morse code** remains synonymous with hard-to-decipher communication. Comic strip parents *Hi and Lois* once stood outside the door of their son's bedroom as he furiously text-messaged friends. "It's like a teenage Morse code," said Lois. "And we can't crack it," lamented Hi.

Contrary to a widespread assumption, the most famous Morse-coded message of all—*SOS*—does not stand for "Save our ship." *SOS* is actually a meaningless acronym chosen in 1906 for its ease of transmission (three dots—three dashes—three dots) to say "Emergency! Help!" The 1912 sinking of the *Titanic*, whose telegraph operator kept signaling "SOS! SOS!", seared that acronym in the public's mind. Although a global satellite communication system replaced this message on large ships in 1999, we still sometimes say SOS! to convey a sense of urgency and emergency.

## Telegraphy

The social impact of telegraphy was similar to that of the Internet today. (Tom Standage's history of this medium is called *The Victorian Internet*.) Almost overnight, information that used to take days or weeks to convey could be transmitted in minutes. By the eve of the Civil War telegraph lines strung from coast to coast allowed California's chief justice to wire newly elected president Abraham Lincoln, "STAND BY THE UNION . . . ON THIS, ITS DAY OF TRIAL." After the mid-nineteenth century such messages were called **telegrams** (a term coined in 1852 by one E. P. Smith of Rochester, New York). Those sent on cables strung beneath the waters of the Atlantic were called **cables**. Other terms left behind by this means of communication include **wire** and **telegraph your message** or **telegraph your punch**, meaning make your intentions clear in advance.

Well into the twentieth century telegraphers were an elite band, their era's geeks. The image of them conversing with lightning-fast keystrokes stirred our imagination. The sound of keys tapping out dots and dashes itself became iconic, and was a common sound effect. Walter Winchell's edgy daily radio commentary used this sound as a backdrop, provided by Winchell himself tapping a dummy telegraphy key. The end of phrases in telegram messages was denoted by the word STOP, the end of a telegram itself by FULL STOP. Today we use **full stop** as a form of verbal punctuation, for emphasis, as when then–White House Press Secretary Dana Perino warned those who visit pariah countries such as Syria, "We discourage it. Full stop." Because telegram senders paid by the word, a form of terse communication evolved, similar to that used for text messaging. GM was "Good morning," SFD "Stop for dinner." This led to a culture, even a humor, based on telegraphese. In one famous yarn, actor Cary Grant intercepted a telegram sent to his studio which inquired, "HOW OLD CARY GRANT?" Grant himself responded, "OLD CARY GRANT FINE. HOW YOU?"

Until fairly recently telegrams were the preferred method of conveying urgent information. From them we learned of births, safe arrivals, and death— including casualties during both world wars. ("WE REGRET TO INFORM

YOU . . .") One of my own most prized pos- sessions is a yellowed piece of paper about four inches by six inches. A few words in capital letters are printed in purple ink on strips of tape pasted onto that paper. They read: "IT'S A BOY. CHET IN FINE SHAPE. LOVE = SCOTT." Scott was my father. Chet was my mother. This is an announcement of my birth that was sent by telegram to Chet's mother. It is stamped with a date:

1945 JAN 13. Big bold letterhead at the top announces WESTERN UNION.

This, of course, was the company that sent and received American tele- grams. In 1929 Western Union dispatched twenty million of them. By 2005 that figure had dropped to twenty thousand. The following year this company sent its last telegram ever. **Western Union** was often used figuratively, and sometimes still is. "If you have a message, send it by Western Union," is the hoariest cliché in Hollywood. In the sitcom *Wonder Years*, a teenage boy tells a girl he is trying unsuccessfully to keep from sitting next to him in the school cafeteria, "What do I have to do here, call Western Union?"

## Telephone

Western Union actually turned down an opportunity to take an interest in Alexander Graham Bell's 1876 invention of a way to transmit voices over wires. As board member J. P. Morgan explained, the telegraph company considered Bell's device little more than "an interesting novelty" that would never rival telegram sending. Bell himself thought his invention was primarily an upgrade of telegraphy. He called this device a "speaking telegraph" or a "harmonic tele- graph." At his wife's suggestion Bell eventually gave it the name *telephone*, an existing term that combined the Greek words *tele* for "distant" and *phone* for "sound."

Bell initially relied on telegraphic clicks to let telephone users know some- one was trying to reach them. However, his assistant Thomas Watson (the one whom Bell summoned by saying "Mr. Watson, come here, I want you" in his first electronic voice transmission) suggested that a ringing bell might be eas- ier to hear. So bell ring it was. We have yet to reach the point where sundry songs, stanzas, statements, jokes, and speech excerpts have replaced telephone rings altogether, but we're headed in that direction. For want of a better term, we call such sounds *ringtones*. **Ring** itself remains in play when we say "I'll ring you" or "Give me a ring." And, harking back to early telephones with separate earpieces that hung in a U-shaped hook on the side, we still say an inoperative phone is **off the hook**, talk of busy phones **ringing off the hook**, and **hang up** after completing a call.

During the telephone's first few decades, calls were placed by operators who used the once familiar salutation "Number, please," followed by "I'll connect you now." At first most of those who connected callers to the party with whom they wished to speak were male. These young men proved too rambunctious, however, and eventually gave way to more reliable young women. Within a decade after Boston's Telephone Despatch Company hired Emma Nutt as America's first woman operator, most were female. For even the fastest operators, all that pulling and pushing of plugs took time. This tried customers' patience. What's worse, operators knew who called whom. That led to a certain amount of paranoia. The ubiquitous Bell Telephone Company—a monopoly until 1968—was nicknamed **Ma Bell**. Lily Tomlin's most popular televised comic character was Ernestine, the obnoxious operator who once squelched an irate customer by saying, "I don't see why you're kicking up such a ruckus when, according to our files, your present bank account, plus stocks, securities, and other holdings amounts to exactly three—Pardon? Privileged information? Oh, Mr. Veedle, that's so cute! No, no, no, you're dealing with the telephone company. For instance, as I look through your income tax return for 19—"

In the late nineteenth century, a cranky Kansas City undertaker named Almon Strowger concluded that telephone operators were deliberately giving his customers busy signals and wrong numbers. The fact that one local operator was married to a competitor did nothing to allay the funeral director's suspicions. So Strowger began fiddling with a round collar box and straight pins in hopes of inventing an exchange system that could bypass operators altogether. To the consternation of Bell Telephone's researchers, the bearded Kansas City undertaker succeeded where they'd failed. In 1891 he patented what came to be known as the "Strowger System" for automatically making telephone connections. After this system's 1892 debut in LaPorte, Indiana, the *New York Tribune* predicted that it would "do away with the sometimes impudent and lazy girls at the central station." Strowger's dialing device—which called for repeated pressing of three levers (one for single digits, another for double digits, the third for those over 99)—eventually led to the development of rotary dial phones, which Bell Telephone offered customers from 1921 on.

Rotary dials may seem primitive today, but at the time they were a revolutionary breakthrough. Imagine the sense of independence this mechanism conveyed. Like a child who ran away from home, we no longer were at the mercy of parentlike telephone companies and their nosy Ernestines. The ability to place our own calls permeated our lives, our awareness, and our vocabulary. Even though it's been a few years since rotary phones were common, we still use the term **dial** in a multitude of ways. Political fundraisers *dial for dollars*. The sound we hear when picking up a phone's receiver is called the **dial tone**. **Dialing direct** alludes to contacting someone without intermediaries, as long-distance phone-callers could do once area codes were introduced after World War II. The most paradoxical example of the persistence of "dial" in our vocabulary is the so-called *dial-up* services that many computer owners use to access the Internet, ones requiring a push-button telephone.

Some operators survived the introduction of automatic telephone systems. Until quite recently one called an **information** operator to get a phone number. In her novel *The Pilot's Wife*, Anita Shreve wrote about a character who "reached for the telephone on the wall and called information." That name for this service couldn't last. Too many callers considered it an open invitation to ask how the Red Sox were doing, or whether an upside-down cake could be baked right-side-up. That is why the phone company changed this service's name to **directory assistance**, itself an endangered phrase in the era of Switchboard.com.

## Groovy

On a brisk fall day in 1877, Thomas Edison visited the editors of *Scientific American*. In his hands he held a modest-sized contraption that consisted of a cylinder on an axle with a crank and an attached megaphone-like cone. Edison placed his gizmo on a desk and began to turn its crank. According to one editor's account this "strange device" then "inquired as to our health, asked how we liked the phonograph, informed us that *it* was very well, and bid us a cordial good night."

The editors were astounded. One said it was impossible to listen to recorded

speech like this without feeling that his senses
were deceiving him. *Scientific American*'s editors saw great prospects for recording spoken
words: those of witnesses in court, say, or
someone reciting a last will and testament. Edison himself looked forward to a golden age of
recorded letters, books, speeches, and school
lessons. That was why he called his device a
**phonograph**, combining the Greek words
*phone* ("sound") and *graphein* ("to write"). When others began recording mu-
sic on his wax cylinders—by John Philip Sousa's Marine Band and the great
tenor Enrico Caruso—Edison was taken aback. That was *not* what he had in
mind. In any event, the inventor had little doubt that recording music commer-
cially was merely a fad.

If we'd stuck with his format, Edison might have been right. Cylinders were
a bit of a nuisance. Among other things, the wax base on which their grooves
were etched was easily dinged. The cumbersome cylinders were also hard to
store. Nor were they easy to duplicate in volume. Nonetheless, Edison
insisted—accurately—that cylinders had better fidelity than rival formats. So,
like Sony with its Betamax videotape several decades later, even when cylinders
gradually gave way to platters in the late nineteenth century, Edison stubbornly
backed his own system.

Platters were the brainchild of a onetime Washington, D.C., store clerk
named Emile Berliner. Berliner viewed them as an ideal medium for home entertainment. By the turn of the century his United States Gramophone Company was selling single-sided "plates" made of hard rubber for 50 ¢ apiece, or
$5 a dozen. These featured songs such as "Old Folks at Home" or "Marching
Through Georgia." Eventually Berliner's offspring came to be known as *discs*.
The subsequent appellation **disc jockey**—soon shortened to **dj** or **deejay**—is
an artifact of that era.

A remarkable amount of data was etched into the grooves of early discs
(some of which was only discovered after the development of sophisticated
tracking equipment). Unaccustomed to this new technology, early adopters
had to be told to make sure that the needle of their phonograph stayed **in the
groove** of platters being played. It didn't take long for this expression to take on
broader significance, meaning *on track* in general, especially after the 1932

song "In the Groove" became a jazz classic. For the better part of a century, needles tracking grooves in platters (actually one long continuous groove per side) remained the primary way to reproduce sound. This is why we still call individual segments of recorded collections **tracks**. Other concepts that owe their existence to a phonograph needle doing its job include **find your groove, get your groove back, groove**, and, of course, **groovy**.

At times needles got stuck, of course, causing one sound to repeat endlessly. As a result, anyone or anything that can't break free from a repetitive course of action was, and is, **stuck in a groove**. Because cracks in discs were so often what kept needles from moving forward, those who repeat themselves are said to sound **like a broken record**.

Early in the twentieth century it became possible to record on both sides of discs. The side not being played was the **flip side**. From this we derived the saying "catch you on the flip side," or somewhere else. More broadly "flip side" alludes to a hidden dimension at odds with one that's visible. A news commentator called Gerald Ford's lack of pizzazz "the flip side of an inner confidence." Typically a recorded song with strong commercial prospects was called the **A-side**, while a song simply thrown in became the **B-side**. To the dismay of record makers and the delight of everyone else, B-sides sometimes proved more popular than A-sides: "Rock Around the Clock" by Bill Haley and the Comets, for example, "Unchained Melody" by the Righteous Brothers, and "Maggie May" by Rod Stewart. A website devoted to independent films is called *B-Side*.

Early platters that spun at 78 revolutions per minute ("78s") were made of easily cracked shellac. After World War II a durable, lightweight plastic called *vinylite* replaced that brittle medium. This material—and the discs recorded on it—were, and are, known as **vinyl**. The *long-playing* twelve-inch records perfected in 1948 that spun at a snaillike 33⅓ revolutions per minute quickly became known as **LPs**. (*Newsweek* once compared Steve Martin's manic stand-up comedy routines to "an LP turned up to 78 rpm.") A year after LPs made their debut, a competitor appeared: seven-inch records played at 45 rpm. In an early example of demographic market segmentation, **45s** and their stubby record players became the sound system of choice for teenagers. These compact, highly portable, easily stacked discs were ideal for listening to three-minute sets by Elvis, the Supremes, or the Beach Boys. LPs, also known as **33s**, were their parents' medium, better suited to extended symphony movements. According to an ad for the American College of Physicians, "IF YOU KNOW WHAT COMES BETWEEN 33⅓ AND 78, IT'S TIME TO CALL AN INTERNIST."

And what to call the devices that played discs? Emile Berliner called the one he developed a *gramophone*. This term became standard in England, and inspired the recording industry's annual award of *Grammys*. Edison's original term *phonograph* held sway in the United States until it was challenged by **Victrola**, the brand name of a popular record player introduced in 1906 by the Victor Talking Machine Company. (In his novel *Manila Time*, Jack Trolley said a character "sounded like an old Victrola. Worn record, scratchy needle, and he wanted rewinding.") During the Depression **record player** became generic for any playback device. This term lasted until component-based *high-fidelity* gear became de rigueur in the 1950s. After that, calling one's sound system a **hi-fi** suggested that you were a hip sort of person in the *Playboy* sense, spinning some platters on your hi-fi while mixing up a dry martini as a sultry young lady lounged at your feet. As so often happens, however, what identified you as with it in one era flagged you as out of it in another. When recorded signals were split and sent to pairs of speakers in the 1960s, **stereo** became the preferred term for any sound system worth mentioning. Even in the era of multi-track home theater amplifiers, we're still prone to call any and all sound systems *stereos*.

# 16. Kid Stuff

When most homes were heated with burning logs, woodsheds were a common sight outside. These drafty, spider-infested shacks had one big asset: most were far enough from houses themselves that what happened inside was hard to see, smell, or hear. That made woodsheds an ideal location for smoking corn silk and touching one's privates, or someone else's. It also was where parents beat their children. A 1907 article in *St. Nicholas* magazine alluded to "unpleasant reckonings in various and sundry woodsheds." Long after oil and natural gas were used to heat most homes, a **trip to the woodshed** still alluded to being disciplined. After Zimbabwe's president Robert Mugabe was reprimanded by fellow African leaders for his despotic ways, the U.S. ambassador to Zimbabwe said, "My understanding is that they took him to the woodshed." When a Justice Department official thought a U.S. attorney should be rebuked, he suggested to the attorney general that she be "woodshedded."

Back in woodshed times, American boys itching for a fight sometimes announced this fact by placing a chip on their shoulder, then daring anyone to knock it off. Although fastidious contemporary ears like to think this was a sliver of wood, the chip in question was more likely to be dried cow dung. Hard as it is to picture any boy putting a piece of excrement on the shoulder of his Abercrombie & Fitch shirt, **having a chip on your shoulder** still suggests touchy belligerence. An obstreperous prisoner was described in the *Chicago Reader* as having "a chip on his shoulder as big as his mouth."

## Games and Toys

Many expressions we use as adults originated in the playgrounds, classrooms, and empty lots of our childhood. "Say uncle," "connect the dots," "stay within the lines," and "stuck-up" are just a few. The term *hoodwink* is left over from another children's game, *blindman's buff* (not "bluff"). In this traditional English game, the *it* person was blindfolded, slapped on the behind, or "buffed," then made to stumble about trying to grab other players. Blindfolded participants were said to be *hoodwinked*. Originally, that term referred to having one's eyes covered. Over time **hoodwink** came to mean "trick someone."

Many such expressions are rooted in the type of hands-on game that has given way to PlayStation and Xbox. One of the oldest involved small round spheres made of clay, glass, ceramic, or stone. These, of course, are marbles. Marbles could be used in an infinite variety of games, but—in America, anyway—the most popular in-

volved trying to knock each other's marbles out of a circle drawn in the dirt. Those playing this game, usually called *Ringer*, had to *knuckle down*, or squat on one knee with a knuckle on the ground, then propel a *shooter* into the ring from this hand. As adults, we say we're ready to **knuckle down**, or get serious, as we once did when marbles were on the line. To **knuckle under**, on the other hand, is to succumb, much like a marble player yielding to an opponent's demand that he shoot with knuckles inverted. Players in some games **played for keeps**, or "keepsies." Winners of those games kept every marble they could knock out of the ring. Another way of saying the same thing was **going for all the marbles**. In Ringer as in life this meant aspiring to all or nothing. **Losing your marbles** was infuriating of course, and is probably why we apply that phrase to out-of-control adults who have *lost it.*

Although marbles was a game played primarily by boys, *pick-up sticks* could be coed. Players gripped these multicolored giant-size toothpicks in a tight stack, let them drop, then tried to pick the sticks up one by one without disturbing any of the others. This game descended from versions played in ancient Asia and Europe, as well as one played by North American Indians using reeds. Although still on the market, **pick-up sticks** are now most likely to be talked about metaphorically. The splintery debris left behind by hurricanes, tornadoes, and earthquakes are commonly compared to this once-popular toy. A Biloxi, Mississippi, resident said that after Hurricane Katrina demolished his hometown, the terrain "looked like pick-up sticks, with snapped trees and power poles all over the place."

Another news account reported that the remains of demolished buildings brought **Lincoln Logs** to mind. Invented during World War I by John Lloyd Wright (son of architect Frank Lloyd Wright), these interlocking small replicas of actual milled logs were used to build miniature log cabins and other buildings. Even though Lincoln Logs clutter few floors anymore, they remain a prominent point of reference among adults who once played with them. In an interesting switch, although Lincoln Logs were devised to create replica log homes, such dwellings themselves are now compared to ones made with Lincoln Logs. According to the sales director for a company that builds homes from milled tree trunks, their components are "stacked like Lincoln Logs."

Modular homes, on the other hand, are said to "go up in seconds, like an Erector Set." That's how the *New York Times* characterized this process, alluding to that onetime geek's delight. **Erector Sets** included small strips of metal lattice that could be connected with little nuts and bolts to create bridges, buildings, houses, and the like. More advanced versions added pulleys, wheels, and even a small engine with which young engineers-in-the-making could assemble trucks, steam shovels, airplanes, and Ferris wheels. They were the perfect kid's complement to an exuberant industrial era. Although a flimsier version can still be purchased, Erector Sets made before 1963 are prized by collectors who remember playing with them as children. Enough boys did, and enough dads helped them, that *like an Erector Set* remains a popular simile.

## Fairs, Carnivals, and Circuses

While crusading in the Middle East, European invaders were impressed by the skill of local equestrians. What particularly caught their eye was a contest in which galloping riders with lowered lances speared metal rings hung from tree limbs or between two posts. In their own jousts the Europeans used each other as targets. They called this *tilting*. (Don Quixote later *tilted at windmills*.) Knights on the Continent went at each other **full tilt**. Unfortunately too many good knights were lost this way. Early in the seventeenth century, Europeans added a spear-the-ring contest to their own competitions. The French subsequently came up with a contraption to help prepare novice knights for tournaments called *carrousels* (from an Italian and Spanish term meaning "little war") that didn't wear out so many horses. This consisted of four wooden horses suspended from a raised wheel that was turned by steeds or servants. Boys astride these faux horses attempted to spear rings hung on the roundabout's circumference. That game came to be known as "catch the brass ring."

A carnival ride based on that game incorporated a bigger wheel with many more carved animals. When steam engines were added to this ride in the 1870s, the golden age of *carousels*—what Americans called *merry-go-rounds*—ensued. To simulate the earlier jousting game, many of these carousels installed a hollow arm filled with metal rings that lowered slowly as the ride started up, just out of reach of those astride horses on the outer row. Bold riders strained to grab a ring as they passed by. One lucky customer per ride got a brass ring to keep as a souvenir, or exchanged it for a free ride. Due to liability concerns, few merry-go-rounds offer a grab-the-ring feature any longer. In its time, however, this was such an exciting challenge that **go for the brass ring** or **reach for the brass ring** still alludes to striving for something that's hard to attain. After auditioning to be the new Maytag repairman on TV commercials, Tulsa journalist David Jones reported that his fellow contestants were clearly hoping that "however unlikely the possibility, the brass ring will wind up in their palm."

Carousels were a staple of fairs and carnivals. Like other rides, and most games of chance, they were grouped along a *midway*. *Carnies*—those who worked there—called such games *hanky-pank*. This was a contraction of **hanky-panky**, a fun phrase in use since the mid-nineteenth century that referred to the type of **hocus-pocus** magicians hid behind handkerchiefs, and eventually to surreptitious activity of many kinds (including sexual). In one midway game, men sledgehammered a lever that shot a puck upward toward a bell at the top. With much fanfare, anyone who succeeded in ringing this bell was awarded a prize such as a cheap cigar. **"Give that man a cigar!"** was a resulting catchphrase. The many men who swung their hammer hard, but not hard enough to ring the bell, were likely to be told, **"Close, but no cigar!"** Although that exclamation is no longer heard in today's smoke-free fairs and theme parks, as a catchphrase it is still commonly used to acknowledge a good try.

Women who won midway games of chance such as the Wheel of Fortune were more likely to be offered a chubby, rosy-cheeked, wide-eyed doll with wings and a topknot. This doll was created by commercial artist Rose O'Neill on the eve of World War I. Because she thought it resembled an impish Cupid, O'Neill called her creation a *Kewpie Doll*. In its time the Kewpie Doll was as popular as the teddy bear. Some girlishly cute women are still referred to as having a **kewpie doll** look. On the Monsters and Critics website, actress Alex Borstein was characterized as "a kewpie doll–faced vocal chameleon." Her colleague Molly Ringwald was described as having "kewpie-doll wide eyes" by a *Salt Lake Tribune* writer.

Carnivals and circuses alike featured secondary events off to one side, usually in tents. At these *sideshows* one might find patent medicine being hawked, or bearded ladies to gawk at, or—most exciting of all—*cooch dancers*, undulating women in filmy harem outfits whom we acknowledge when using the term **hoochie coochie** for a wide range of risqué activity. Although what went on at sideshows was sometimes more exciting than what took place at the main event, today **sideshow** suggests an activity of lesser magnitude. As America's primaries have become the *main event* in nominating political candidates, conventions are said to be merely a *sideshow*.

Because the main events at some circuses took place in three rings simultaneously, **three-ring circus** came to suggest a big deal of any kind. Smaller circuses were disparaged as **dog and pony shows**, ones that could afford only modest animals (no tigers or elephants). This phrase is still used to characterize events with more show than substance. *National Review* commentator Bridget Johnson called Iran's conference on Holocaust denial a "dog-and-pony show." At the bottom of the heap were circuses whose ponies could do only one stunt. They were **one-trick ponies**. Daredevil Evel Knievel, who made a career out of doing dangerous stunts on a motorcycle, was a *one-trick pony*.

Mounting circuses called for lots of wagons: equipment wagons, animal wagons, candy wagons, and many more. Of them all, none was more prominent than the *band wagon*. This ornately decorated vehicle not only transported the band's instruments, but was pressed into service as part of a parade wending its way through towns where circus participants were about to perform. Musicians sat atop the band wagon blasting their instruments to stir up excitement. During the late nineteenth century politicians began to employ "band wagons" of their own that featured blaring musicians and shouted announcements of rallies. Young boys ran after these vehicles trying to jump aboard. By the turn of the century, politicians said that those eager to join a campaign as it gained momentum resembled boys **hopping** or **jumping on the bandwagon**. In an 1899 letter, Theodore Roosevelt belittled the many opportunists who "tumbled over each other to get aboard the band wagon" of his nominee for a state commission. By extension, those who attract a following with stampeding tactics are said to create a **bandwagon effect**. Economists say this effect underlies purchasing decisions based on perceived peer pressure. Political scientists apply *bandwagon effect* to fickle voters easily swayed by the crowd. The opposite syndrome, of course, is **jumping off the bandwagon**. As support for the war in Iraq waned, political scientist John Mueller noted that once people "drop off the bandwagon, it's unlikely they'll say, 'I'm for it again.' Once they're off, they're off."

Not long after showman P. T. Barnum put the first band wagon on parade in the 1840s, another type of wagon—the *water wagon*—began spraying unpaved roads to keep down dust. Reformed drinkers were said to "be on the water wagon," so committed to abstinence that they'd mount such a wagon for a drink of water before they'd take another sip of alcohol. In time this phrase began to refer to renunciation of many kinds. In his 1938 book *Honesty*, Dr. Richard Cabot wrote that after deceiving patients as a young doctor, "I swore off and have been on the water wagon of medical honesty ever since." Such a commitment gradually became shortened to **on the wagon**, and, of course, **off the wagon** for those who *backslide* (a religious term meaning return to heathenish ways).

## PUPPET SHOWS

During the Renaissance, a pugnacious new puppet named Pulcinella appeared at fairs all over Europe. When he arrived in England, this character's name was shortened to "Punch." Punch and his wife, Judy, made their New York debut at the Park Theater in 1828. *Punch and Judy* tickled Americans' funny bones. They loved the way Punch used a stave to batter anyone who crossed him. They howled when he beat his crying baby with this stick. After Punch tossed that howling baby out a window audience members rolled in the aisles. When Judy objected to this treatment of their child he whacked her dead with his stick, leaving onlookers in stitches. They cheered when Punch then turned his ire and his pole on a doctor, a policeman, a lawyer, and a defenseless Negro. "That's the way to do it!" said the beak-nosed Punch after each whacking. Until movies, radio, and television eclipsed puppet shows, *Punch and Judy* was a staple of children's entertainment. So much of its action derived from Punch's slapping one and all with his stick that **slapstick**—referring to an implement long used in

European farcical comedies—became synonymous with broad, physical comedy. **Pleased as Punch** refers to anyone who seems happy with his own actions. A chaotic event of any kind is called **a real Punch and Judy show**. Political scientist Ross K. Baker characterized modern candidate debates as "*Punch and Judy* shows for grown-ups."

The popularity of puppet shows for so many centuries left behind many variations on the term **puppet** to signify someone or something controlled by someone else (e.g., a **puppet state**). Since marionettes were manipulated by strings attached to their limbs, **pulling the strings** came to refer to manipulation of another person. **No strings attached** suggests unfettered activity. ("I'll donate some money to your group, no strings attached.")

## Readin', 'Ritin'

Americans of a certain age know that the **three R's** are "readin', 'ritin', and 'rithmetic." In less-complicated times this was all that teachers—many of them barely better educated than their students—attempted to teach. At best they were equipped with a *McGuffey Reader* or two as well as a **blackboard** (or **chalkboard**) on the wall and a few smaller framed boards called **slates**, on which students could write letters and *do their sums* with a piece of chalk. Some students became **blackboard monitors**. These lackeys erased blackboards, then clapped the felt erasers together, creating clouds of chalk dust aimed at classmates they didn't like. The fact that most early blackboards were made of slate led to a related nomenclature: **blank slate**, **clean slate**, and **wipe the slate clean** (to name just a few). Presumably because their names were once written with chalk on blackboards, teams of candidates for office are still called a **political slate**.

Another vocabulary grew up around the use of chalk: **chalk it up to experience**, **chalk up points**, and **not by a long chalk.** *Chalk talk* was an artistic genre in which a chalk-wielding artist would quickly sketch images on a blackboard to illustrate a point. Even though this genre was roughed up by Magic Markers, then kayoed by PowerPoint, **chalk talk** is still a generic term for illustrated presentations. According to the Laconia, New Hampshire, *Citizen*, members of an arts workshop in that town enjoyed "an interactive chalk talk."

Blackboards themselves gradually gave way to whiteboards. Why? Dust. The tiny white granules given off by erased chalk penetrate computers, making crashes more likely. Another reason we prefer whiteboards is that the sound of fingernails scraping their smooth, shiny surface does not arouse the same frisson of horror that nails scratching a blackboard do. Even though few have ever scraped their fingernails across a blackboard, or heard someone else do this, the very thought makes us shudder. Shudder-inducing events are commonly compared to **fingernails scraping a blackboard**. NPR's Juan Williams once observed that when Republicans refer to the "Democrat Party," members of that party find it "like fingernails on the blackboard."

In less-commercialized times students sometimes gave their teacher an apple as a Christmas gift. The more conscientious ones first rubbed their present shiny. This gave rise to the term **apple-polisher**, one we now apply to anyone who tries to please superiors. When circumspect Robert Gates was nominated as secretary of defense, a commentator questioned whether the veteran bureaucrat was an ideologue who kept his views to himself, or simply "a skilled apple-polisher who curries favor with those above him."

After school attendance became compulsory, some students did not comply. They were said to *play hookey*, a piece of slang that apparently originated with the Dutch name for hide-and-seek: *hoekje spelen*. John Sinnema, a Professor of German at Baldwin-Wallace College, determined that in the New World this became *play hoeky*. When compulsory attendance laws outlawed being *truant*, the culprits themselves called skipping school and eluding truant officers *playing hookey*. In *Tom Sawyer* (1876), Mark Twain wrote that class-cutting Tom "moped to school gloomy and sad, and took his flogging, along with Joe Harper, for playing hookey the day before." Today anyone who skips work or any other type of required activity is said to **play hookey**. When he was a U.S. senator, Harry Truman wrote his wife, Bess, "I played hookey from the Appropriations Committee this morning."

## Kid Lit

An early novel for children featured a poor orphan named Margery Meanwell who owns only one shoe. When given a match, Margery is so excited that she goes about exclaiming, "Two shoes! Two shoes!" The title of this 1765 novel is *The History of Little Goody Two-Shoes*. Its protagonist is an unusually well-behaved little girl who grows up to be a wealthy doyen. The book is dedicated "To all young gentlemen and ladies who are good, or intend to be good." Goody Two-Shoes was held out as a role model for generations of long-suffering children who were urged to follow this little girl's example. Nowadays a **Goody Two-Shoes** is thought to be an insufferably right-minded person. When questions were raised about his financial dealings, Senator Harry Reid (D-Nev.) conceded, "I'm not Goody Two-Shoes."

Goody's male counterpart—Little Lord Fauntleroy—first appeared in an 1886 book that compiled magazine stories about a seven-year-old American boy named Cedric "Ceddie" Erroll. Ceddie turns out to be the heir to a title in Britain. There, as Lord Fauntleroy, Ceddie learns the ways of an aristocrat, and teaches those instructing him how to be nicer. "He had a beautiful face and a fine, strong, graceful figure," wrote author Frances Hodgson Burnett; "he had a bright smile and a sweet, gay voice; he was brave and generous, and had the

kindest heart in the world, and seemed to have the power to make every one love him." As much as the text itself, detailed drawings of Little Lord Fauntleroy in a dark velvet suit with a scalloped white collar created an indelible image of this idealized child. They inspired a type of formal (some would say prissy) boys' wear. The humiliation felt by children of upwardly mobile parents who were forced to wear this type of outfit, including my father, helped make **Little Lord Fauntleroy** a sneer of an icon. According to *Time* essayist Lance Morrow, by slowly enunciating the name "George Herbert Walker Bush," Democratic orators created a "piled-on, Connecticut preppie–Little Lord Fauntleroy effect."

At the other end of the class ladder were *Ragged Dick, Tattered Tom*, and other urchins featured in scores of books written by Horatio Alger Jr. Drawing on his post–Civil War experience as the chaplain of the Newsboy's Lodging House in Manhattan, from 1867 until he died in 1899 Alger wrote scores of *rags-to-riches* novels about poor boys who get ahead through hard work and pluck. A typical Alger hero was described by the author as "a broad-shouldered, sturdy boy, with a frank, open face, resolute, though good-natured." His novels generally featured a wealthy older man who mentors deserving boys like them. Eyebrows had always been mildly raised about this continually recycled plot. Might there be more to it than appeared on Alger's pages? Probably so. It turns out that Horatio Alger had a record of showing more than altruistic interest in young boys. During a brief stint as a Unitarian minister immediately after the Civil War, Alger had been defrocked for "contemptible contact" with young male parishioners. Although largely lacking in literary merit, Alger's uplifting stories were wildly popular bestsellers that made him famous if not wealthy (since he gave away most of his money). More than a century since their author's death, **a Horatio Alger story** or a **Horatio Alger hero** still refers to someone who rises from humble beginnings through grit and gumption.

This was not the sort of boy Alger's contemporary George Wilbur Peck wrote about in his *Peck's Bad Boy* series. These stories and books featured an incorrigible prankster. In one, Henry Peck lines his father's hat with smelly Limburger cheese. In another he substitutes rubber tubes for his mother's cooked noodles. Yet a third has Henry placing playing cards and a rum-soaked handkerchief in his father's pocket just before he goes to church. During the late nineteenth century *Peck's Bad Boy* was so popular that Mark Twain was accused of jumping on its bandwagon by writing *Huckleberry Finn.* **Peck's Bad Boy** remained part of the vernacular for decades after its creator's death. Onetime NFL player Bill Romanowski was known to some as "the Peck's Bad Boy of football."

The anti-Peck was a wealthy Yale student named Frank Merriwell. His creator, Gilbert Patten, said this character's name was "symbolic of the chief characteristics I desired my hero to have: Frank for frankness, merry for a happy disposition, well for health." Merriwell neither drank nor smoked. He did play football and basketball, ran track, and rowed for the Eli crew. Merriwell also was very deft at solving the many mysteries that crossed his path. Patten's creation first appeared in an 1896 magazine serial, then in a series of dime novels in which he bested antagonists such as Fred Fearnot and Diamond Dick. **Frank Merriwell** came to stand for clean living and a can-do spirit. "Straight out of Frank Merriwell"

referred to dramatic events involving all-American types. By contrast, the checkered life of football star and World War II hero Tom Harmon was once compared to "a Frank Merriwell story gone bad."

## Allow Six to Eight Weeks for Delivery

During his 1933–51 heyday, *Jack Armstrong, the All-American Boy* was widely admired by an estimated nine million radio listeners. His name still brings to mind a high-minded young man in the Frank Merriwell spirit. A three-letter athlete at Hudson High School, **Jack Armstrong** flew airplanes, operated submarines, and spoke Zulu as he foiled evildoers around the globe. During one episode Armstrong and two pals used a Hike-o-Meter to navigate a South American jungle, where they rescued their kidnapped friend Betty. At the end of this show Jack announced that for two Wheaties boxtops and 10¢ listeners could order their own Hike-o-Meter. Well over a million did.

For nearly three decades in the mid-twentieth century a wide variety of pedometers, pins, rings, ray guns, badges, buttons, and spy scopes were the reward for any kid who sent the required number of boxtops with a few cents for postage and handling to an exotic locale such as Battle Creek, Michigan. "Allow six to eight weeks for delivery," they were advised. Rings were the most popular premium, especially ones that had secret compartments for miniature maps and bits of microfilm. "Secret" features were a major attraction in all manner of premiums: secret seals, secret messages, secret codes.

My brother Gene still remembers ordering a Captain Midnight Key-O-Matic Code-O-Graph badge and manual complete with charts, codes, and confidential information so he could join the crusading pilot's Secret Squadron and help him fight the villainous Ivan Shark. After weeks of antsy anticipation Gene was crestfallen to finally receive a flimsy piece of plastic with two revolving wheels. One had numbers, the other letters. This was a **decoder**. Built into badges and the like, "decoders" allowed young radio listeners to decipher "secret" messages broadcast at the end of a program by matching up numbers and letters. "Today's message, boys and girls," they'd be told at the end of a program, "is 1 12 45 M" or " 'E Z W T." Wow! Off to the decoder to decipher the secret message! This usually turned out to be something inane ("Watch out for spies") or insipid ("All men are created equal").

Even though most decoders took the form of badges, cards, or plastic gewgaws, and few ever graced rings, it is the latter version that registered most vividly in baby boomers' addled memories. *Secret decoder rings* have been referenced by so many older cereal eaters, including Woody Allen in his movie *Radio Days*, that we assume countless boomers' fingers sported one and now use them as a figure of speech. Before reporting some complicated primary results, NBC news anchor Brian Williams said, "Take out your decoder ring." There is also a rock group known as Decoder Ring, and a leading form of encryption for computer language is called—what else?—Secret Decoder Ring.

What was the actual most popular ring ordered by young cereal eaters? Why, the Lone Ranger's Atom Bomb ring with an adornment in the very same shape of the bombs that obliterated Hiroshima and Nagasaki.

# 17. Stay Tuned!

A fiery horse with the speed of light, a cloud of dust, and a hearty Hi Yo Silver! The Lone Ranger! With his faithful Indian companion Tonto, the daring and resourceful masked rider of the plains led the fight for law and order in the early western United States. Nowhere in the pages of history can one find a greater champion of justice! Return with us now to those thrilling days of yesteryear. . . . The Lone Ranger rides again. Hi-Yo Silver and awayyyy!

This stirring show opening—accompanied by pounding hooves and the *William Tell Overture*—could be recited verbatim by radio listeners of all ages. After making its debut on Detroit's WXYZ radio in 1933 *The Lone Ranger* ran for 2,956 thrice-weekly episodes through 1954. Its millions of fans were reminded regularly that, as John Reid, this show's hero was the sole survivor of a group of Texas Rangers who were ambushed in Bryant Gap by members of the brutal Butch Cavendish Gang. Gravely wounded himself, Reid was discovered and nursed back to health by an Indian named Tonto. When Reid asked what happened to his companions, Tonto replied, "Other Texas Rangers all dead. You only Ranger left. You *lone* Ranger now."

After settling down on a ranch with a silver mine, Reid was frequently summoned to fight forces of evil. Before doing so he would don the black mask and Western garb of the Lone Ranger. "Do you have a plan, kemo sabe?" Tonto would ask him. "Yes, I do," was the usual reply. These plans would often involved elaborate strategies, story lines that thrilled young boys in particular. Their masked-cowboy hero represented a classic American man: mysterious, inscrutable, a loner. The name **Lone Ranger** burrowed deeply in the American psyche and is trotted out regularly to refer to a type of freelancer common in American lore: explorers, trappers, entrepreneurs. Although he denies saying any such thing, Henry Kissinger is notorious for having called himself a Lone Ranger. It fit.

Molded from ore excavated at his silver mine, the Lone Ranger's bullets always hit their target. Like the silver stakes needed to kill a vampire, these bullets were more lethal than ones made of lead. Today the term *silver bullet* is applied to any sharply targeted weapon of great potency. As the population ages there is increasing talk of finding pharmaceutical **silver bullets** to remedy sundry ailments.

After completing his mission, the masked man would rear high on his white horse Silver, then gallop furiously toward the horizon, leaving behind a single silver bullet. (A character in Richard Price's novel *Samaritan* says of her tendency to flee sticky situations, "For me it's like Hi-Yo Silver and go.") "Who *was* that masked man, anyway?" a puzzled onlooker would ask as Silver's hoofbeats faded in the distance. "Why, don't you know?" another would respond. "That was the Lone Ranger!" **Who was that masked man?** is yet another Lone Ranger legacy, a question posed ironically when someone's identity is unclear. Samantha Power, author of *Chasing the Flame: Sergio Vieira de Mello and the Fight to Save the World*, told NPR listeners that when first meeting the charismatic United Nations official whom she later wrote about, her response was "Wow, who is this masked man?"

Tonto's origins were a bit of a mystery. Scriptwriters were advised that he was the son of a Pottawatomie chief from Michigan's Great Lakes region. The father-in-law of WXYZ's creative director, James Jewell, owned a boy's camp in this region called "Kamp Kee-Mo Sah-Bee." According to Jewell, a rambunctious Indian who sometimes visited that camp was called "Tonto" by tribesmen. (In Spanish *tonto* means "fool.") For lack of anything better Jewell used this nickname for the Lone Ranger's sidekick and the name of his father-in-law's camp for Tonto's favorite expression—*kemo sabe*—supposedly meaning "faithful friend" (on the radio) or "trusty scout" (on television). After extensive research, anthropologist Martha Kendall found phrases resembling *kemo sabe* in a number of dialects spoken by a variety of tribes. A *Far Side* cartoon by Gary Larson depicted the Lone Ranger looking up *kemo sabe* in an Indian dictionary and discovering that it's Apache for "a horse's rear end." Eventually **kemo sabe** settled into national discourse as semisarcastic conversational punctuation. "In addition to her Brooklyn accent and attitude," reported the *Atlanta Journal-Constitution*, "[Judge Judy] Sheindlin also retained her faithful bailiff Petri Hawkins-Byrd, the reticent Tonto to her chatty Kemo-sabe." **Tonto** itself—a name that once symbolized a devoted aide, an American Sancho Panza—has become a derisive term for compliant Indians. On the other hand, a popular joke in the 1960s featured the Lone Ranger and Tonto surrounded by a band of savage Indians. "I guess we've had it this time, old friend," says the Lone Ranger. "What do you mean *we*, white man?" responds Tonto.

## On the Air

A striking number of terms that we use in everyday discourse originated in early radio studios. They include: *on the air, airtime, mike, commercial, static, serials, soap opera, quiz show, station break, announcer, newscaster, network,* and *payola*. Radio also added **broadcasting** to the lexicon, a term borrowed from the farm implement that scatters seeds in all directions. Borrowing an earlier catchphrase, program directors who signaled that broadcasters were on schedule by touching their snout indicated they were *on the nose*. Other lingering radio catchphrases are generic: "Stay tuned," "Don't touch that dial!" "Same time, same station," and "Keep those cards and letters coming." Others were associated with specific shows or genres of shows ("Calling all cars!" "The hit parade," "Crime doesn't pay"). **"Write if you get work"** was Ray Goulding's sign-off line on the *Bob and Ray* show. **"I'll bet you say that to all the girls"** was something comedienne Gracie Allen said repeatedly to her partner and husband, George Allen. Radio gossip Walter Winchell made a deliberate, and sometimes successful, effort to inject catchphrases into the national conversation. Two of the most lasting were **making whoopee** for sex and **blessed event** for childbirth.

When it came to generating lasting terms and phrases, radio proved far more fertile than television. Unlike TV, which could employ sight gags, radio had to rely on memorable words. The slang and catchphrases of this first coast-to-coast medium became part of our everyday discourse. Radio also engaged the imagination in a way that television could not and cannot. One not only listened to but *visualized* what was being broadcast. This active process imprinted what we heard on our synapses: words, phrases, jokes, jingles. An elite handful stuck.

*Gang Busters* is one. Billed as "the only national program that brings you authentic police case histories," this fast-paced cops 'n' robbers show opened with earsplitting sounds of glass breaking, whistles blowing, guns blasting, and sirens wailing. These sounds got listeners' attention. The exciting story lines that followed held it. Within a few years of its 1935 debut, **like gangbusters** had become part of the vernacular. The catchphrase *come on like gangbusters* long outlived the 1957 demise of the show that spawned it, eventually doubling as a modifier (e.g., "that concert was gangbusters").

The popularity of a radio program was no guarantee that it would leave verbal remnants behind. Successful shows such as *Sergeant Preston of the Yukon, The Jack Benny Program,* and even the wildly popular *Amos 'n' Andy* generated no lasting expressions. The signature line of bombastic Senator Beauregard Claghorn on *Allen's Alley*—"That's a joke, son!"—was adopted by Fred Allen's listeners but few of their offspring. Claghorn himself lasted longer as an icon of political windiness. During the 2000 presidential campaign, *Time*'s Margaret Carlson reported that Al Gore tried to avoid " 'Senator Claghorn' oratory."

Beloved sitcom couple *Fibber McGee and Molly* created a national vogue that outlived their show. This had to do with Fibber's cluttered closet, whose contents spilled out with a tumultuous clatter whenever he opened its door. "Gotta straighten out the closet one of these days," was his usual response. Since few listeners didn't have cluttered spaces of their own, **Fibber McGee's closet** became lasting shorthand for any space in need of straightening. Jam-packed computer hard drives have been compared to *Fibber McGee's closet.*

Unlike popular radio shows that left little retroterminology behind, some that did were not especially successful. For one reason or another some element of such shows struck our fancy and lingered in the language. For example, references to **$25 words** (or $40, or $50, or $10) hark back to a forgettable Depression-era radio show called *Paul Wing's Spelling Bee*, in which the words that contestants had to spell were given a dollar value depending on their difficulty. During the 1940s on radio and 1950s on TV, *Quiz Kids* featured brainy children answering tough questions. As a generic term, **Quiz Kid** still refers to that type of child. During John Kennedy's presidency, a group of smart young executives brought to the Pentagon by Defense Secretary Robert McNamara were called "Whiz Kids."

## Game and Quiz Shows

When *Queen for a Day* was on the air, we kids knew better than to disturb our mother's rapt attention. From 1945 until 1955, this popular radio show (that later appeared on television) featured four guests who vied to tell the most heart-rending stories about themselves. By their level of clapping (registered on an "applause meter"), audience members determined which contestant would be crowned "Queen for a Day." The winner was draped in a red velvet robe, adorned with a crown, and seated on a throne while the studio orchestra played "Pomp and Circumstance." She might win a washing machine, new car, or year's supply of deodorant. *Queen for a Day* combined elements of game shows and makeover shows. Each segment was introduced with the stirring words "Do you want to be . . . QUEEN . . . FOR . . . A . . . DAY?" As we watched

our mother glumly dust shelves, sweep floors, and put tuna casserole in the oven, my siblings and I had little doubt that her answer would be "Yes!" Certainly enough listeners felt this way that the title of the show became figurative for anyone who enjoys short-lived triumph. In his novel *Election*, Tom Perrotta

wrote of a high school boy whose election as senior class president is quickly negated due to vote fraud, "I guess that's like Queen for a Day or something."

In another hokey show and national guilty-listening secret, contestants were paid $15 for trying to answer virtually unanswerable questions, or for doing something silly such as putting a diaper on a piglet or spraying shaving cream down their pants. In one of the funnier stunts, a soldier called his girlfriend while a female member of the audience sat in his lap purring, "Watch out, honey. You're ruining my hair." This 1940–57 radio show (which later ran on television) was called **Truth or Consequences**. Psychologist Paul Ekman once called a jury's efforts to assess the honesty of witnesses a courtroom version of *Truth or Consequences*.

Contestants on the 1940s radio quiz show *Take It or Leave It* were asked questions whose difficulty and value kept doubling—from $1 all the way up to $64! The suspenseful last question put to them was called **the $64 question**.

Eventually the show itself adopted that phrase as its name. This concept inspired a routine way to describe perplexing issues. ("That's the $64 question.") On television the program was reborn as ***The $64,000 Question***. Talkers today date themselves by whether they consider stumpers to be "$64 questions" or "$64,000 questions."

*Major Bowes and His Original Amateur Hour* was a talent show that ran on radio from 1934 until its host died in 1946. Tens of thousands of show business wannabes vied to appear on this former-day *American Idol*. During one month in 1935, 1,200 of them needed aid after being marooned in New York, where they'd come in hopes of making the cut. A successor, *Ted Mack's Amateur Hour*, ran on television from 1949 until 1960. Both contributed **amateur hour** to the lexicon as a way to depict any slipshod operation. ("That seminar was a real amateur hour.")

## Gonged

Fifteen years after *Ted Mack's Amateur Hour* ended its run, a diminutive television producer named Chuck Barris discussed ideas with a friend. Barris wanted to revive the talent show concept, but didn't think there was enough good talent around to make it fly. Most of those who auditioned were awful. So go with awful suggested his friend. Stock the show with mediocre performers, then have their acts judged by a celebrity panel. When performers are particularly bad, make a big commotion, then usher them offstage.

From this brainstorming session emerged a brand-new type of program. Debuting in 1976, *The Gong Show* featured laughable amateur acts that were routinely banished with a loud strike of a padded mallet on a huge brass cymbal. For five years a bizarre collection of off-key singers, overweight dancers, belch musicians, unfunny comedians, maestros of the kazoo, elderly ballet dancers, and two young women who sucked Popsicles suggestively were combined with a few legitimate performers, then judged by a rotating jury of B-list celebrities under Chuck Barris's hyperkinetic oversight. Like a carny Caligula, Barris whipped his audiences into a frenzy. "Gong 'em!" they would shout. When this happened, as it did several times a show, the cut-short performer was led offstage by a stolid onetime Miss Sweden named Sivi Aberg.

*The Gong Show* was one of the most ludicrous programs ever broadcast on television. At best it was a people's theater of the absurd. At worst it exploited naive contestants too clueless to realize they were being humiliated. Needless to say, *The Gong Show* was a big hit. Within its first season Americans did not just discuss the latest *Gong Show* outrages around water coolers, they made its key concept part of their lexicon. Any kind of tryout situation was liable to be called **the Gong Show of** _____. This concept then broadened to incorporate a wide range of outrageous occasions. ("That party was a real gong show.") Inadvertently, Barris had stumbled on a concept, a word even, that seduced us with its very pronunciation: *Gong!* You bet. Americans began to talk of **gonging** elements of their lives that they'd like to get rid of, or of being **gonged** themselves. As *Sacramento Bee* columnist Vince Vosti noted, in the best of all worlds "we could gong lawyers for grandstanding. We could gong cashiers for chitchatting while a long line of customers wait. We could gong salespeople when they are caught in lies. We could even gong the words of long-winded columnists."

## Catchphrases

A benign distant cousin to *The Gong Show*, **Candid Camera** (1948–67) was one of television's longest-running programs. It was based on a simple concept: set up situations that force unsuspecting dupes to behave ridiculously, record the results, then let them in on the joke by saying **"Smile. You're on Candid Camera!"** (One of the show's most ingenious premises involved sealing both ends of filmy plastic bags at a supermarket produce section, then recording the exasperated struggle of customers to open these bags.) This catchphrase enjoyed a particular vogue during the 1960s and still shows up on occasion, as when a topless Israeli actress was photographed with stickers on her nipples that read, "Smile, you're on *Candid Camera*." One character in Richard Ford's novel *The Sportswriter* tells a woman companion that his weakness is waiting for exciting and unusual things to happen. The woman responds, "You have to know, though, when what you're waiting for says, 'Smile, you're on candid camera,' then you got to be ready to smile."

*Gunsmoke* was another long-running show. On this "adult Western," big James Arness played Dodge City, Kansas, sheriff Matt Dillon from 1955 to 1975. The actual Dodge City was notorious for its bourbon-and-bordello lawlessness during the late nineteenth century. Dillon accomplished what no actual Dodge sheriff could: getting this rowdy town under control. One way he did so was by ordering bad guys to *get out of Dodge*. This catchphrase has been in common use since at least the mid-1960s. During his swaggering days after the United States invaded Iraq in 2003, George W. Bush was often depicted as ordering dictator Saddam Hussein to **get out of Dodge**. When the situation in Iraq deteriorated, that catchphrase reversed course. Now Marine General John Sheehan characterized the pragmatist's position on Iraq as "how the hell do we get out of Dodge and survive?"

The inspired nonsense of the 1969–74 sketch show *Monty Python's Flying Circus* is recalled whenever we use the term **Monty Pythonesque** or simply **Pythonesque** to describe ridiculous situations. A couple of their catchphrases also stuck around: **And now for something completely different**, and **Nudge, nudge, wink, wink**. This show's famed "Ministry of Silly Walks" made such an impression that three decades after its last episode aired, an ornithologist referred to the plover bird's "Monty Python silly walk." And, of course, it was a Monty Python routine in which Vikings in a restaurant make it impossible for anyone else to talk by chanting "Spam, Spam, Spam, Spam, lovely Spam, lovely Spam." This routine inspired early cyber-chatters to call masses of data that interfered with online discourse *Spam*.

During its heyday in the late 1970s and early 1980s, *Saturday Night Live* was like a fish farm of catchphrases—most of which enjoyed the lifespan of minnows. Among them were: "You ignorant slut!" "Excuuuuse me!" "But noooooo!" "Never mind," "Isn't that special!" "Schwing!" and "Not!" Mocking a short-lived variety show hosted by Howard Cosell that featured the Prime Time Players, *Saturday Night Live* called its cast the "Not Ready for Prime Time Players." To this day anyone who isn't considered quite up to speed is liable to be called **not ready for prime time**.

Like those born on *Saturday Night Live*, most of the catchphrases thrust into general conversation by television disappeared quickly. (Can anyone say "Sock it to me!"?) The handful that did last weren't always remembered accurately. As Sergeant Joe Friday, *Dragnet*'s star Jack Webb did sometimes say, "All we want are the facts, ma'am," but our memories edited his words to **"Just the facts, ma'am."** Unlike the hypercaffeinated cops of shows such as *Gang Busters*, Friday was a low-key, dogged investigator who used real police jargon, such as *bunco squad, APB* ("all points bulletin") and *MO* ("modus operandi"). Such terminology helped give *Dragnet* viewers a sense that they were getting the real soufflé, police procedure–wise. The show's assurance that its stories were true and **"only the names have been changed to protect the innocent"** became part of our national conversation. But it's the name of *Dragnet*'s hero himself that has lasted longest as a retroreference. All manner of laconic investigators are still compared to **Sergeant Joe Friday**. The *New York Times* noted the "Joe Friday manner" of U.S. Attorney Patrick Fitzgerald, one that conveyed a "just-the-facts appeal" to jurors.

Another misremembered catchphrase from the golden age of television is "Lucy, **you got some splainin' to do**." This comment is heard often when public figures are caught engaging in hanky-panky. After George W. Bush was shown to have authorized warrantless wiretapping, Representative Dennis Kucinich (D-Ohio) said, "Lucy, you got a lotta splainin' to do." That remark was never actually made by Lucy Ricardo's Cuban-born husband, Ricky, on *I Love Lucy*. (He did once ask his wife to "splain" herself.) In a memoir titled *The Red Devil*, Katherine Russell Rich compared her ex-husband to Ricky Ricardo in a bad mood. Such references are a tribute to the lasting impact of TV's first hit sitcom. In its most famous scene, Lucy and neighbor Ethel Mertz take jobs on a candy-making assembly line. As the conveyer belt before them is speeded up, Lucy and Ethel begin stuffing chocolates into their mouths and uniforms in a futile attempt to keep pace. Nearly half a century later this classic episode is continually referenced to depict out-of-control situations. A Rhode Island doctor said the rising demands of his work made him feel like Lucy at the conveyor belt, "and before you know it you're stuffing chocolates in your pockets."

## All-Americans

During 1944–66 run of *The Adventures of Ozzie and Harriet* on radio and television, audience members could only compare their own sulky, argumentative, even abusive family lives with that of the sunny Nelsons and wonder where they went wrong. Cardigan-clad Ozzie had lots of time for his wife and two sons. Apron-wearing Harriet bustled in and out of the kitchen carrying plates of cookies. Although Harriet did once observe that "sometimes this modern psychology puzzles me a little," the Nelsons' world was unsullied by contemporary concerns. In their happy, placid, middle-class guise the televised Nelsons became one of the most durable of American icons. As society grew more candid and more diverse, however, **Ozzie and Harriet** went from being an envious allusion to one of disdain. When *Philadelphia Daily News* columnist Sandy Grady wanted to disparage Al and Tipper Gore, he called them "as bland as Ozzie and Harriet."

Like *The Adventures of Ozzie and Harriet*, **Leave It to Beaver** was so ubiquitous in the lives of baby boomers that, with no need to elaborate, actor Ed Harris could say that he grew up in a "very *Leave It to Beaver* kind of neighborhood." Reference to the residents of 211 Pine Street, Mayfield, USA—Ward, June, Wally, and Theodore "Beaver" Cleaver—still evokes worlds, as when someone says "**the Cleavers** we are not." Another way to characterize that type of family is **Cleaveresque**. Beaver Cleaver represented a certain type of mischievous but basically wholesome boy we still call **Beaveresque**. His mother remains in a bake-off with Harriet Nelson for best fifties-mom icon. Her name is iconic enough that in the heyday of minivans, an auto industry figure referred to them as "the **June Cleaver** of vehicles." As for Beaver's well-behaved older brother, to convey how she sees herself, MSNBC show host Rachel Maddow once said "I'm a bit of a Wally Cleaver." The Cleavers' neighbor—smarmy, know-it-all **Eddie Haskell**—remained a familiar point of reference long after *Leave It to Beaver* went off the air in 1963. "Some call it the Eddie Haskell effect," a *New York Times* reporter wrote of Al Gore's pedantic manner.

If the Nelsons and the Cleavers spoke to our yearning for *family*, *The Andy Griffith Show* addressed our hunger for *community*. This heartwarming portrayal of the North Carolina village of Mayberry suggested what life might be like in an idyllic setting where fathers fished with sons, and neighbors baked each other pies. (Very few nonwhite faces could be seen on Mayberry's leafy streets, but who's counting?) Aside from the fact that this 1960–68 sitcom was well conceived, well written, and well acted, Americans' craving for human connection is what launched Mayberry and its residents into our lasting iconography. We acknowledge *The Andy Griffith Show* every time we use the term **Mayberry** interchangeably with "small town." To explain why she liked the village of Rosendale, New York, a resident said, "I get this really good Mayberry feeling here." In her novel *The Kindness of Strangers*, Katrina Kittle referred to the "Mayberry-ish sense of security" enjoyed by those living in an affluent town outside Dayton. Although the show's main character, Sheriff Andy Taylor, seldom shows up as a retroterm, his laughably ineffectual deputy **Barney Fife** certainly does. An online forum participant in Flint, Michigan, called that city's mayor a "Barney Fife wannabe."

## Characters

Robinson J. Peepers, the bespectacled junior high school science teacher played by Wally Cox from 1952 to 1955, left his name behind as shorthand for timid, spectacles-wearing men like him: **Mr. Peepers**. When the irascible John Bolton was nominated as U.S. ambassador to the United Nations, Senator George Allen (R-Va.) observed, "We're not electing Mr. Peepers to go there and just be really happy, and drinking tea with their pinkies up."

As played by portly Raymond Burr from 1957 to 1966, **Perry Mason** was a resourceful lawyer who generally pulled his client's chestnuts out of the fire at the last minute with some deftly posed question or just-discovered piece of evidence. The many times this happened inspired common references to a **Perry Mason moment**, a dramatic denouement during legal proceedings when everything becomes clear. As Senate hearings were being held on John Roberts's nomination to be chief justice of the Supreme Court, NPR correspondent Dahlia Lithwick reported, "There is going to be no Perry Mason aha! moment in these hearings."

Lieutenant Columbo (first name unknown), the rumpled, Peugeot-driving police detective played by Peter Falk from 1971 to 1978 and intermittently from 1989 to 2003 was known for his signature stained trench coat and pregnant pauses before springing one last question that caught suspects by surprise. This left **Columbo** behind for that kind of deceptively casual interrogation technique. Low-key reporter Bob Woodward has been called "the Detective Columbo of journalism." British physicians call the tendency of male patients to say what's really bothering them only as an examination is about to end *the Columbo Effect*.

**Donna Reed** played a peppy, perpetually smiling suburban mom to such perfection on *The Donna Reed Show* (1958–66) that her name alone evokes this sort of woman in that sort of place. Reed achieved the ultimate in iconhood when, in her memoir *Cherry*, Mary Karr used the actress's name as a verb: "I had always thought that what I lacked in my family was some attentive, brownie-baking female to keep my hair curled and generally Donna-Reed over me."

After years of playing the pluperfect male parent in *Father Knows Best*, Robert Young portrayed everyone's fantasy figure of a warm family doctor: Marcus Welby, M.D. It's a sad irony that the actor who played these two heartwarming characters was himself clinically depressed for most of his adult life and relied on copious amounts of alcohol to get through shooting schedules. Ever since that show's nine-year run, the name **Marcus Welby** has been synonymous with idealized family physicians, as when the director of the University of Pennsylvania's Center for Health Policy characterized this fast-disappearing breed as "the Marcus Welby type of doctor."

## Titles

Before and after World War II a mustachioed Rhode Island show cowboy named Victor De Costa went by the stage name *Paladin*. After performing, the black-clad De Costa handed out cards that read, "Have Gun, Will Travel. Paladin / San Francisco." A subsequent TV series called *Have Gun Will Travel* (1957–63) featured mustachioed Richard Boone as a gun for hire named Paladin who dressed in black and handed out cards that read *Have Gun Will Travel / Wire Paladin / San Francisco*. In 1974, CBS lost a lawsuit filed by Victor De Costa for plagiarizing his concept. Not that anyone noticed. The title of Richard Boone's adult Western lives on as a fill-in-the-blank. Nearly half a century after that show galloped into the sunset, one still hears "**Have** _____, **will travel.**" *Newsweek* once referred to "have-laptop-will-travel workers who straddle time zones in today's borderless economy."

On Rod Serling's ***The Twilight Zone*** (1959–64) anything could happen, and did. In one episode, altruistic-seeming aliens arrive on Earth carrying a manual called *To Serve Man* that turns out to be a cookbook. In another, a passenger in an airplane's window seat spies an odd-looking creature tearing off parts of a wing, though no other passenger sees the same thing. "I felt like I was in the twilight zone" is a common way to depict being in a situation that makes no sense. Maureen Dowd invoked the name of that show's creator to characterize the "Rod Serling–type feeling" she experienced while driving through Riyadh, Saudi Arabia, and seeing no women on the streets.

Even though *The Jetsons* ran only from 1962 to 1963 and in a 1984–87 revival, this animated show gave viewers such a vivid template of ultra-automated twenty-first-century life that **Jetson-like** or **Jetsonian** remains common shorthand for futuristic settings and devices. *New York Times* reporter Amy Harmon predicted that the Segway people transporter "will not usher in a Jetsonian era of space ports in every garage." The *Times*'s Thomas

Friedman subsequently invoked the Jetsons' stone age antithesis when he wrote that traveling from Zurich's ultramodern airport to New York's shabby counterpart LaGuardia was "like flying from the Jetsons to the Flintstones."

## IT'S HOWDY DOODY TIME!

From 1947 to 1960 *The Howdy Doody Show* featured a freckled, redheaded, blinking marionette with a goofy smile. **Howdy Doody** was fun to say, and a bit risqué to young fans. His name and demeanor became so familiar that no further explanation is assumed to be necessary when it's used figuratively (as when social critic Camille Paglia compared Bill Clinton to "Nero crossed with Howdy Doody"). Up to fifty kids sat on bleacher seats in *the peanut gallery* during each *Howdy Doody Show*. This inspired the most lasting catchphrase that program left behind, one exclaimed often by host Bob "Buffalo Bob" Smith: "No comments from the peanut gallery." Since then **No comments from the peanut gallery** has suggested dismissal of views no more worth considering than ones offered by a child. Sometimes that phrase is used as a form of mock modesty, as when columnist Leonard Pitts introduced an opinion by writing, "The view from this row of the peanut gallery . . ." *Peanuts* itself has long signified insignificance. *Gallery* refers to a theater's upper balcony, where historically those of limited means, and, by implication, vulgar taste, were relegated (which is why *play to the gallery* suggests pandering to the lowest common denominator of public opinion). Those seated in nineteenth-century English galleries were not hesitant to pelt performers with shells from their favorite snack. Thus: the **peanut gallery**, a phrase in common use since the early twentieth century.

## 18. Seen in the Funny Papers

When she was secretary of state, Madeleine Albright baffled China's ambassador to the United States by asking him to treat her nicely because it was Sadie Hawkins Day. Any American of a certain age knew what Albright was referring to: an annual race run in Dogpatch, USA, where the comic strip *Li'l Abner* was set. Worried that his homely daughter Sadie might never get married, Dogpatch resident Hezebiah Hawkins organized an event to make sure this didn't happen. On October 16, 1937, the mayor of Dogpatch proclaimed, "Whereas there be inside our town a passel of gals what ain't married but craves something awful to be . . . we hereby proclaims and decrees . . . Saturday, November 4th Sadie Hawkins Day, whereon a foot race will be held, the unmarried gals to chase the unmarried men and if they ketch them, the men by law must marry the gals and no two ways about it." This race, which became a recurring episode in *Li'l Abner*, inspired decades of **Sadie Hawkins Day** events in American schools, including dances to which girls invited boys.

At the peak of *Li'l Abner*'s popularity, the antics of buff, amiable, dimwitted *Abner Yokum* and his hillbilly pals in **Dogpatch** fascinated some sixty million readers of nearly nine hundred newspapers. From 1934 to 1977, the words and phrases Dogpatch residents liked to toss around—*natcherly, druthers,* and *as any fool can plainly see*—were picked up by readers. Nobel laureate John Steinbeck, who considered Capp himself worthy of a Nobel, said *Li'l Abner*'s creator "not only invented a language but . . . planted it in us so deeply that we can talk it ourselves."

Capp's real contribution to retrotalk was characters and settings so vivid that three decades since his death in 1979 we still refer to them. Stephen King characterized the hardscrabble Maine town where he grew up as "Dogpatch with no sense of humor." Critic Rex Reed compared King himself to "an over-weight Li'l Abner." On NBC's *West Wing*, U.S. president Jed Bartlett called his elderly secretary "Mammy Yokum." This referred to Abner's mother, a wizened little woman with a black bonnet and corncob pipe clamped in her teeth who dominated Pappy Yokum and everyone else in her vicinity. **Mammy Yokum** was the only Dogpatch resident able to thwart the dastardly **Evil Eye Fleegle.** This gnomish, scowling, zoot-suited hoodlum from Brooklyn could flatten any man or woman alive with "nature's most stupefyin' equipment—THE UNLIM-ITLESS POWER OF THE HUMAN EYEBALL!" Fleegle harnessed this power by focusing one eye on his targets while pointing in their direction. That was a **whammy.** Capp then upped the ante by having Fleegle train both eyes on his victims and point at them with two fingers. This was a **double whammy**, pow-erful enough to topple the Empire State Building or melt a locomotive going full steam. In an era when swollen SUVs clog our highways and combo meals are routinely supersized, one seldom hears about single whammies any longer. References to double whammies, on the other hand—two strokes of misfor-tune endured at once—are commonplace. The lethal combination of drought and wildfires in southern California is a classic *double whammy.*

Some Dogpatchers worked at the Skonk Works brewing liquor from dead skunks, old shoes, and other debris. They called this concoction **Kickapoo Joy Juice.** That name remains synonymous with any strong drink, usually cheap, often homemade (and has become an actual brand of soda pop). The name of this drink's brewery inspired Lockheed Martin's research and development de-partment to call itself "the Skunk Works." Working in tents and big packing crates, 120 *skunk workers* needed just forty-three days to build the first World War II–era airplane that could fly faster than five hundred miles an hour. **Skunk works** was subsequently applied to any loosely knit group within a larger organization whose members engage in creative activity.

Not far from Dogpatch was the Valley of the Shmoon, home to a band of smiling creatures shaped like bowling pins who lived to make human beings happy, even when this meant rolling over and dying so their flesh could be con-sumed. Shmoo flesh tasted like whatever the consumer wanted it to taste like: chicken when fried, steak when broiled, oysters on the half shell when eaten raw. Their skin made sturdy lumber when cut thick, or fine leather if cut thin. Shmoo eyes made excellent buttons, their whiskers outstanding toothpicks. During the late 1940s and early 1950s **Shmoos** captivated Americans, even appearing on the cover of *Time* magazine. Decades later *Time* called an Alexander Calder sculpture "shmoo-like."

One of Capp's most endearing—and enduring—creations was a forlorn little man in rags who was followed about by a dark cloud raining down on his head. This cloud signified the misfortune that always accompanied the figure below: Joe Btfsplk. Since we all feel like **Joe Btfsplk** at times, "Btsflpk" remained part of the national conversation long after his creator had the ultimate misfortune of dying. Columnist Bob Ortman once reported that "during a Colorado vacation I discovered that I have that rare Joe Btfsplkian talent to turn on clouds. . . . All I had to do was walk outdoors." Since Joe's last name is hard to pronounce and harder to spell—"Joe Btfsplk," he'd say, "pronounced B-t-f-s-p-l-k"—we sometimes content ourselves with referring to someone who, like him, lives **under a dark cloud** or **a black cloud**. "Union Carbide has been like the cartoon character with a black cloud over its head," reported the *New York Times*.

## The Cartoonists' Contribution

As the case of Al Capp illustrates, cartoonists have been key contributors to the American vernacular. Their panels and strips created far more retroterms than any other medium, including television. One reason is that comic strips last a lot longer than the average TV show, giving them more time to take root in the national psyche. Parents and children can read and discuss comic strips in a way that's seldom possible with sitcoms, say, or movies. Comic strips also are a source of unusual passion. Over time readers become *very* attached to strips and their characters, as newspaper editors invariably discover when trying to cancel one.

Cartoonists have not only given us an actual vocabulary but a visual one as well. *Balloons* were, and are, a key tool. Some incorporate mixed punctuation (*$%*&!*) to suggest cursing. (*Newsweek* once referred to the **"$%*&! moment"** every computer user has experienced.) The balloon of a character speaking coldly has icicles hanging from its bottom border. (In *The Girl's Guide to Hunting and Fishing*, Melissa Bank wrote that if her angry first-person protagonist had been a cartoon character, "there would be icicles hanging from my balloon.") Words a character is thinking but not saying appear in a **thought balloon** with scalloped edges. (According to *Fresh Air* host Terry Gross, when counseling clients, psychologists "try to get inside that thought balloon as opposed to what's on your face.") Someone with closed eyes beneath a log being sawed, or lots of ZZZZZZ's, is asleep (relating to the catchphrase *I'm going to catch some Z's*). And, of course, when a lightbulb flashes above the head of a character, he or she has just had a revelation. **Lightbulb moment** is a common, nearly clichéd expression journalists use to depict sudden insight. Some think a bulb goes *on* at such moments, others *off.* In his novel *A Man in Full*, Tom Wolfe wrote that "a lightbulb went on over Charlie's head." According to Malcolm Gladwell's *Blink*, "Insight is not a lightbulb that goes off inside our heads."

## Strips

Just after World War I, Billy DeBeck created a new comic strip called *Take Barney Google, F'rinstance*. This featured an amiable little loser married to a big battle-axe of a wife. Many a man and boy, including *Peanuts* creator Charles Schulz, was nicknamed "Sparky" after Barney Google's swaybacked racehorse Spark Plug. Little else from this popular strip made its way into the vernacular except for the fun last name of its pint-sized, pop-eyed hero. Billy Rose's hit 1923 song "Barney Google (with the Goo-Goo-Googly Eyes)" referenced De-Beck's strip. "Goo-goo eyes" was already slang for simpering looks, but **googly-eyed** was Barney Google's emendation, usually referring to someone with protruding eyes. In his novel *Little Scarlet*, Walter Mosley called an ex-boxer "googly-eyed."

Another strip popular during the early twentieth century was Frederick Burr Opper's *Happy Hooligan*. For a time that label was hung on unusually cheerful persons. The name of Happy's brother, **Gloomy Gus**, can still be heard depicting an unusually melancholy person. A second Opper creation did even better in the retroterm department. This one featured two bowing and scraping French dandies who treated each other with elaborate deference. "After you, my dear Alphonse," one would say, only to be told, "No, after *you*, my dear Gaston." Although

*Alphonse and Gaston* lasted for only a few years after debuting in 1901, its protagonists made such a big impression that **Alphonse and Gaston** remains
shorthand for two people who elaborately defer to each other. "I doubt that
trade ministers have the political authority to break this 'Alphonse and Gaston'
routine," wrote a *Financial Times* reader about an impasse in World Trade Organization negotiations.

Soon after Alphonse and Gaston made their debut a ten-year-old scamp
with long hair and fancy clothes joined them on the funny pages. This boy
looked like Little Lord Fauntleroy but acted like Peck's Bad Boy. *Buster Brown*
was a towheaded trickster who threw water from high win-
dows on passersby and made a container of pot cheese explode
in the face of a man trying to open it. Brown's pit bull Tige may
have been the first talking pet in American cartooning. Buster
himself became the first cartoon character licensed for commercial products—shoes most notably. Yet **Buster Brown** is
best remembered for his long blond pageboy bob, huge-
brimmed hat, and flowing tie. A character in the movie *No Country for Old
Men* was characterized by NPR film critic Bob Mondello as "a psycho with a
Buster Brown haircut."

Five years after Buster Brown was introduced, cartoonist Bud Fisher began
a comic strip called *Mr. A. Mutt Starts In to Play the Races*. This strip featured a
racetrack tout named Augustus Mutt. Early on, Mr. Mutt—a rangy man with a
mangy mustache—befriended a short, bald fop with a top hat and cane who
thought he was heavyweight boxer Jim Jeffries. Their improbable friendship
catapulted Fisher's strip—retitled *Mutt and Jeff*—to a new level of popularity.
James Joyce even alluded to this pair in *Finnegans Wake*. The most memorable
thing about Mutt and Jeff was the disparity in their heights, and that's what we
remember about them. Even those who have never heard of the comic strip are
likely to call a pair of short and tall human beings **Mutt and Jeff**. Author Carlos Fuentes considered artist-lovers Diego Rivera and Frida Kahlo "almost
comical in their Mutt and Jeff disparity."

Another funny paper feature whose name proved more durable than its
content was inspired by a rickety horse-drawn streetcar that ferried passengers
around Louisville, Kentucky, before the Depression. Fontaine Fox, who took
that trolley to high school in the early part of the century, tapped his memories
of this enjoyable form of transportation to create a daily newspaper cartoon

called *Toonerville Folks.* Fox's creation featured a cast of eccentric characters who careened about their town in the Toonerville Trolley, routinely jumping the tracks, crashing through outhouses, and getting tangled in clotheslines. **Toonerville Trolley** still refers to slapdash enterprises of all kinds. A blogger once characterized the *Chicago Tribune* as having "a Toonerville Trolley of a news operation."

Yet another strip whose title caught on grew out of the real-life experience of sketch artist Arthur "Pop" Momand. When he was twenty-three, Momand and his wife moved to the affluent community of Cedarhurst, Long Island. Despite Momand's decent salary, the young couple couldn't match the lavish lifestyle of wealthier neighbors. After they stopped trying and moved to a modest apartment in New York City, Momand reflected on the absurdity of trying to keep up with those who have so much more money than you do. This musing led him to create a comic strip about the antics of a middle-class family who try but fail to emulate wealthy neighbors. Momand thought about calling this strip *Keeping Up with the Smiths.* That didn't work very well euphonically, however, so the cartoonist renamed it *Keeping Up with the Joneses.* Although his strip was successful enough to run for twenty-eight years after it was introduced in 1913, Momand's creation is little remembered today. Its title, on the other hand, **Keeping Up with the Joneses**, is one of our most durable catchphrases, signifying a frantic, futile effort to match affluent peers through conspicuous consumption. This impulse, of course, is what keeps the American economy vibrant.

## THE SAILOR MAN

In 1929 Elzie Segar introduced a new character to his ten-year-old comic strip *Thimble Theatre.* This character was a brawling, pipe-smoking, one-eyed sailor named *Popeye.* Even though the cartoonist hadn't meant for Popeye to take over *Thimble Theater*, that's exactly what he did. How could readers not fall for a feisty man in a sailor suit who—when asked in his first appearance "Are you a sailor?"—responded, " 'Ja think I'm a cowboy?"

Throughout the 1930s and for decades thereafter the strip retitled

*Popeye* was among America's most popular. In the process Elzie Segar contributed many words, phrases, and concepts to our discourse, including his hero's. Unusually buff figures such as baseball players Mark McGwire and Barry Bonds were said to have "Popeye-like biceps" (though, in a more innocent time, no one suspected the sailor man of pumping up his biceps with anything stronger than spinach). Its hero's self-assured credo—**"I yam what I yam an' tha's all I yam"**—was adopted by many. **"Blow me down!"** was another popular Popeyeism (later updated in popular vernacular to *"Blow me away!"*), as was the proposal of his friend J. Wellington Wimpy: **"Let's you and him fight."** **Wimpy** became not only synonymous with timid cowardice, but the name of a British hamburger chain.

Another *Popeye* character, *Eugene the Jeep*, was a cheerful, preternaturally strong being with a bulb nose who could only say "Jeep, jeep, jeep." This character is credited with inspiring the name **Jeep** for the four-wheel-drive vehicles that helped win World War II. Other words that entered the vernacular via *Popeye* were **goon** (after a repulsive family in this strip named *the Goons,* who lived on Goon Island) and **dufus,** the name of Popeye's dimwitted nephew. Soon after Elzie Segar's successor Forrest Sagendorf introduced this character in 1958, the re-spelled term **doofus** became slang for lamebrained individuals.

## More Strips

In 1924, comic strip artist Harold Gray introduced a curly haired, hollow-eyed orphan named Annie. The spunk that young Annie displayed while fleeing orphanages, riding the rails, and outwitting sinister villains helped lift Americans' spirits in the midst of hard times. *Little Orphan Annie* inspired radio shows, movies, and, of course, the hit Broadway show *Annie.* Annie's moptop visage became iconic enough to inspire references to a **Little Orphan Annie look.** Her signature phrase **"Leapin' lizards!"** was popular for a time. But *Little Orphan Annie*'s most lasting verbal contribution came in the form of Annie's foster father, Oliver "Daddy" Warbucks. As his name suggests, this baldheaded character had accumulated a fortune dealing arms during World War I. Because he vividly personifies a certain type of irascible tycoon, the name **Daddy Warbucks** has outlived that of Annie herself. One newspaper columnist in Michigan warned against treating God as "a divine version of Daddy Warbucks," while another in California pined for a razor blade that would leave his skin "smoother than a shrink-wrapped Daddy Warbucks."

Comic strip characters have always been a primary vehicle for introducing futuristic technology. No one did this better than Anthony "Buck" Rogers. Rogers was a young Army Air Corps lieutenant who passed out in a gas-filled mine in the twentieth century and woke up five centuries later. *Buck Rogers in the 25th Century* gave many Americans their first glimpse of the robots, ray guns, and spaceships that went through a *countdown* ("10, 9, 8 . . .") then shot into space at the command of *Blast off!* Space jockey Buck and gal pal Wilma Deering battled the Tiger Men of Mars as well as pirate Killer Kane and his female accomplice, Ardala Valmar. At a time when so little seemed possible, this strip—introduced just before the stock market crash of 1929—portrayed a future in which little seemed *im*possible. **Buck Rogers** is still shorthand for futuristic technology. ABC's Brian Rooney called a solar energy plant in Portugal "proof that solar power is not off in some Buck Rogers future." Another rocket man, the title character of *Tom Corbett, Space Cadet*, starred in a comic strip, a TV series, books, and comic books that were inspired in part by Robert Heinlein's 1948 novel *Space Cadet*. Tom Corbett is largely forgotten, but **space cadet** lives on to describe a loopy individual, someone who is *out in space*.

In its time, *Tom Corbett* was known for the seductive women who slinked and slithered about its comic strip panels. One reason was that its artist, Ray Bailey, learned his craft from Milton Caniff. Although his two major comic strips, *Terry and the Pirates* (1934–45) and *Steve Canyon* (1947–88), starred manly, heroic men, Caniff's real flair was for drawing strong, sultry, intriguing female characters. None was more memorable than the *Dragon Lady*. This caped renegade of the high seas gave new depth to the term *femme fatale*. The Dragon Lady looked as though she'd as soon strangle as seduce any man who crossed her path. After capturing the hero of *Terry and the Pirates*, the pirate vixen mused about what she might do with him. Perhaps keep Terry chained like a chimpanzee in a dinghy tied to her boat and watch him starve, or else drag him off the side so sharks could nibble her captive to death. Ever since the

Dragon Lady made her debut before World War II, severe women such as hotel impresario Leona Helmsley and Florida politician Katherine Harris have routinely been called **dragon ladies**.

## FROM GOLDBERG TO GEARLOOSE

Cartoonist Reuben Goldberg spent much of his long career lampooning technological progress. Goldberg did this by drawing elaborate contraptions that were rich with pulleys, switches, whistles, bellows, fans, kicking donkeys, melting ice, and dropping balls. His version of an alarm clock consisted of: *"Shot put in cup (a) is counterbalanced by water in cup (b). Water evaporates, tipping shot into ice-covered pail (c) containing piranhas (d). When ice (e) is smashed, piranhas seize bait (f) attached to string (g) which pulls pin (h), releasing 500 lbs. of ball bearings (i), which roll down chute (j) striking bass drum (k) next to the head of sleeper (l)."* Linguistically speaking, a **Rube Goldberg contraption** or **Rube Goldbergian** or **Rube Goldbergesque** still refers to anything that's overly complicated, requiring twenty-five steps to accomplish what could take two. The hybrid primary-caucus system Texas Democrats use to choose candidates is often compared to "a Rube Goldberg contraption." An unusually elaborate video game was characterized as "Rube Goldberg-esque" by a *Newsday* reviewer.

Unlike Goldberg's inventions, those of Gyro Gearloose didn't work. His one-wheeled vehicles, noiseless rocket engines, and device for converting dirt to food were modern-day alchemy. This eccentric comic book character with his pince-nez glasses and maroon hair sometimes wore a "thinking cap" filled with miscellaneous contraptions and chirping birds that helped him concentrate. Along with Mickey Mouse, Donald Duck and Scrooge McDuck, **Gyro Gearloose** is one of the few Disney Studio creations whose name remains common in our discourse. An imaginative character in Richard Ford's novel *Lay of the Land* is said to come up with "Gyro Gearloose brainstorms."

## Lovable Losers

Like Joe Btfsplk, some of our most memorable comic strip characters have been lovable losers. At some level we all can identify with such schlemiels. Buck Rogers or the Dragon Lady may be fantasy fulfillment, but who can't see him- or herself in *Ziggy*? Or *Cathy*? Or *Charlie Brown*?

The template for that type of character can be found in a cartoon created by H. T. Webster. Introduced in 1924, *The Timid Soul* featured a morbidly meek and pathologically unassertive protagonist. Webster called him "the man who speaks softly and gets hit with a big stick." Short, skinny, and jittery, this white-haired character wore both belt and suspenders. In one panel a beefy cigar smoker sitting next to him on a park bench asks, "Whadd'ya think of th' Dodgers' chances this year?" Looking dismayed, the Timid Soul responds, "Uh—er—ah—I'd rather not say, if you don't mind." The name of Webster's retiring character suited him perfectly: *Caspar Milquetoast*. (*Milk toast*— toasted bread soaked in milk—was long an epithet applied to meek and mild men.) Although *The Timid Soul* lasted for only a few years, its protagonist's last name remains a lowercased synonym for pushovers. According to one reviewer, a character in Kate Atkinson's novel *One Good Turn* is "not quite the **milquetoast** he seems."

Of the many soldier-oriented comic strips introduced in World War II, only one left its name behind: *The Sad Sack*. Drawn by George Baker for the military publication *Yank*, this strip featured a forlorn army private with a cucumber nose who can't do anything right. His name remains synonymous with any ineffectual human being, so widely used that it is sometimes seen as a term unto itself: **sad-sack** or even **sadsack**. The depressed loser played by Paul Giamatti in the movie *Sideways* was referred to by one critic as a man with a "sad-sack psyche."

In the mid-1950s, a group of upmarket sad sacks burst on the American scene: beetle-browed, big-nosed, world-weary figures called *nebbishes*. Their creator, Herb Gardner, adapted this name from the Yiddish *nebbich*, meaning "poor soul." A classic nebbish cartoon featured two of these figures with long legs resting on a coffee table, quizzical smiles on their mouths. "Next week we've got to get organized," reads the caption. Well into the 1960s nebbishes enjoyed a commercial vogue as dolls, greeting card illustrations, and cocktail napkin graphics. Unlike nerds, who can be socially inept high achievers, **nebbishes** are softer, less productive, and more appealing. Bill Gates is a nerd. David Sedaris is a nebbish. *New Yorker* writer George Packer characterized an Iraqi psychiatrist as "a small, nebbishy man of forty-three."

A nebbishlike character preceded Gardner's creation, first appearing on the funny pages in 1950. This was Charlie Brown, the squat, roundheaded little putz who starred in Charles Schulz's strip *Peanuts*. **Charlie Brown** cannot hit a baseball, fly a kite, or get other kids to like him. His name still alludes to well-meaning but ineffectual types. A recurring gag involved Charlie Brown's inability to have malicious playmate Lucy Van Pelt hold a football for him to kick without pulling it up at the last second, leaving him flat on his back. By analogy, in a **Charlie-and-Lucy** relationship one party repeatedly dupes the other. During George W. Bush's presidency, a congressional staff member said, "A lot of us feel like we have a Charlie Brown and Lucy relationship with the White House." According to *Newsweek*, before they invaded Iraq, Bushies themselves referred to "the exasperating game of Lucy-and-the-football" that they thought Saddam Hussein was playing with United Nations inspectors.

Charles Schulz's most notable creation retroterm-wise was the small blue bedcovering that Lucy's brother Linus clutches to his cheek while sucking his thumb. This quickly became known as a **security blanket** or *Linus blanket*. Enough of us have used physical objects for solace that the concept of a *security blanket* caught on quickly. Schulz himself once said, "Perhaps the best idea I ever had . . . was Linus and the security blanket. . . . It suddenly made security blankets and thumb-sucking okay all around the world, and if we made parents a little less worried about their kids, then this would have to be one of my biggest thrills with the strip." After *Peanuts* lost its edge and became a licensing machine in its later years, Schultz gave us the saccharine expression *"Happiness Is a Warm Puppy."* This book about Charlie Brown's beagle Snoopy stayed on the *New York Times* bestseller list for forty-five weeks in 1962–63. Its first four words became the introduction for all sorts of items we thought might cheer us up, and was satirized in the Beatles song "Happiness Is a Warm Gun."

## 19. Between Covers

A t a party in 1920, H. L. Mencken and drama critic George Jean Nathan met a pimply redhead from Minnesota whose favorite topic of conversation was himself. The young man said he was writing a novel. After hearing him brag that he was "the best writer in this here gottdamn country," Mencken and Nathan fled the party. "Of all the idiots I've ever laid eyes on," said Mencken after they sought refuge in a tavern, "that fellow is the worst!" Three days later Mencken wrote Nathan, "Grab hold of the bar-rail, steady yourself, and prepare yourself for a terrible shock! I've just read the advance sheets of the book of that Lump we met . . . and, by God, he has done the job! It's a genuinely excellent piece of work. Get it as soon as you can and take a look. I begin to believe that perhaps there isn't a God after all."

The "lump" Mencken referred to was Sinclair Lewis, his book *Main Street*. This novel was set in Gopher Prairie, a thinly disguised send-up of Lewis's home town of Sauk Centre, Minnesota. Its residents were portrayed as ignorant, intolerant, self-satisfied, hypocritical philistines who resist the efforts of a doctor's wife to open their eyes to the beauties of culture. *Main Street* did not make its author popular in Sauk Centre. On the other hand, misfits who had fled provincial locales for ones that were more cosmopolitan could relate. **Gopher Prairie** became shorthand for small towns in general, and **Main Street** for small-minded settings of all kinds. Over time the latter has lost its negative connotations. Today *Main Street* is routinely juxtaposed with *Wall Street* when corporate financial interests are compared with those of the country as a whole. *Main Street Republican* refers to a moderate member of that party.

As *Main Street* rose on the bestseller lists, its author worked on another novel, this one about a small-city booster named G. T. Pumphrey. Lewis characterized him as "the ruler of America, the tired Businessman, the man with toothbrush mustache and harsh voice who talks about motors and prohibition in the smoking compartment of the Pullman car, the man who plays third-rate golf and first-rate poker at a second-rate country club near an energetic American city." Pumphrey was also vice president of his city's Booster Club. Lewis, who was not good at titling (his title for *Main Street* was *The Village Virus*) or at naming characters, was persuaded to call his protagonist George Follansbee Babbitt, probably because a cleaning compound called B. T. Babbitt was widely advertised at the time. Published in 1922 as *Babbitt*, his second novel enjoyed nearly as much success as *Main Street* and ignited a similar firestorm of controversy. Some thought Lewis had placed an accurate mirror before American businessmen. Others thought he'd employed a fun-house mirror. Accurate or distorted, when we use the term **Babbitt** we're usually referring to a mindless conformist in happy lockstep with whoever is leading the latest parade.

A third Sinclair Lewis novel featured an evangelist–con man who preaches the gospel on Sunday and carouses the rest of the week. Elmer Gantry steals money from the donation basket, seduces parishioners, and plagiarizes his sermons. Since this eponymous novel was published in 1927 there has been no shortage of sinners crusading against sin. Whenever such a self-righteous crusader is exposed as a closet sinner, the name **Elmer Gantry** gets resurrected. The case of Representative Mark Foley, who sponsored legislation against online sexual predators while himself sending salacious e-mails to congressional pages, prompted columnist George Will to write that "Elmer Gantry . . . is making yet another appearance."

Another iconic character who debuted in a 1920s American novel is Jay Gatsby. The protagonist of F. Scott Fitzgerald's 1925 classic *The Great Gatsby* is quintessentially American in the worst sense. Born Jay Gatz, Gatsby parlays a phony vita and shady activities (bootlegging, securities fraud) into an opulent lifestyle in his West Egg, Long Island, mansion. As one prominent American after another has been unmasked as a poseur with spurious credentials, the terms **Gatsbyesque**, **Gatsby-like**, and **a Gatsby** have been reinvigorated. Such appellations suggest a self-invented figure with dubious ethics. Sometimes it's Gatsby's home alone that is alluded to, however, as when a *Philadelphia Daily News* website post referred to Daddy Warbucks's mansion in the musical *Annie* as "Gatsbyesque."

Set far from West Egg and Gopher Prairie, literally and figuratively, was Erskine Caldwell's *Tobacco Road*. Caldwell—who grew up in tiny Wrens, Georgia—published this bestselling novel about a backwoods southern family in 1932. The gaunt countenance and stark sexuality of its Jeeters, Ellie Mays, and Sister Bessies in their tattered calico dresses and stained bib overalls excited readers' imaginations. So that's what those folks are like down there! It was hard to tell whether shock at the squalid living conditions *Tobacco Road* portrayed among Georgia sharecroppers was what aroused so much interest, or titillation at its depiction of their sex lives, but I'm going with the latter. Although denounced by many for stereotyping and sensationalizing life in the rural South, the author of this mega bestseller said he was simply portraying accurately the world in which he was raised. Despite yielding ground to *Deliverance* (see chapter 11), **Tobacco Road** remains shorthand for Dixie squalor. As *New Yorker* architecture critic Paul Goldberger wrote about a simple but elegant home, "It's not Tobacco Road, but it's not Greenwich, either."

Even farther from West Egg and Gopher Prairie than Tobacco Road was the futuristic setting of Aldous Huxley's novel *Brave New World*. Huxley took his title from the island that Miranda and her father, Prospero, inhabit in Shakespeare's *The Tempest*. Miranda uses the phrase "O brave new world" in all sincerity, but Aldous Huxley did not. His brave new world (set in 632 AF, or "After [Henry] Ford") was one in which those who start out seeking utopia end up suffocating each other. Families have been outlawed in Huxley's world of tomorrow, babies are created in laboratories, and citizens are kept in a docile haze with drugs and sex on demand. Huxley's 1932 novel tapped into a sneaking suspicion that this was the direction in which society was headed. Nothing has happened since to allay that suspicion. By now **brave new world** is used far more often in the Huxleyan sense than the Shakespearean.

Aldous Huxley had a spiritual ancestor in Franz Kafka. In the few stories and uncompleted novels he wrote before dying of tuberculosis in 1924 at the age of forty, Kafka captured in words a sense of dread that has imbued life since his death. The Prague author had a fertile, darkly distorted view in which some men wake up as cockroaches, and others are hired to do work that is never specified. *The Trial* is what made Kafka's name iconic, even among those who have never read that novel. In Kafka's fable a bank manager named Joseph K. is charged with unspecified crimes. During a year's imprisonment he is interrogated by hidden authority figures, then tried before unseen judges who summon anonymous witnesses. Joseph K. is finally convicted of breaking laws he hasn't been told about, then executed for reasons that have never been revealed to him. In the years after its 1925 publication, *The Trial*'s premise became less and less preposterous. Germany's Nazis felt little need to tell their victims why they'd been apprehended. Nor did Stalin's secret police. During the McCarthy era accused "Communists" could not confront their accusers, and following 9/11 prisoners were held for years in Guantánamo Bay, Cuba, without being told why. As headlines kept pace with Franz Kafka's dark outlook, the term **Kafkaesque** was heard with increasing frequency.

---

### ORWELLSPEAK

George Orwell foresaw a world in which private acts and personal thoughts were kept under constant scrutiny. In Orwell's classic novel *1984*, the tightly controlled universe of Oceania was filled with ways for **Thought Police** to manipulate its citizens' thought processes. These means typically had *think* at the end, **doublethink** in particular. "Doublethink," wrote Orwell, "means the power of holding two contradictory beliefs in one's mind simultaneously, and accepting both of them." This mindset made possible such Oceanic slogans as "Ignorance Is Strength," "Freedom Is Slavery," and, most memorably, "War Is Peace."

In Oceania a dumbed-down language called *Newspeak* permits only the use of politically approved words. Forbidden terms such as "liberty" and "equality" are relics of *oldspeak*. Then there is *duckspeak*, the parroting of approved thoughts. From this product of Orwell's prescient imagination has grown the common use of **speak** as an appendage to all manner of nouns: *adspeak*, *cyberspeak*, *diplospeak*, *Bushspeak*, etc. The Orwellian term that most permeates our discourse is one he transformed from benign to sinister: *big brother*. In *1984*, Big Brother is the dictator of Oceania. His subjects are continually warned that *Big Brother Is Watching You*. This slogan is incorporated into a poster with eyes that seem to follow passersby. In Oceania television screens are not only watched by viewers, but watch viewers.

As technological advances create breathtaking opportunities for electronic surveillance, the concept of a **big brother** watching us seems fathomable indeed. Nearly six decades after Orwell's death in 1950, a London reporter counted thirty-two surveillance cameras positioned within a two-hundred-yard radius of the Islington flat where he wrote *1984*.

Four years before the appearance of *1984*, George Orwell published *Animal Farm*. Although the book itself—in which farm animals revolt against their human owners, only to be betrayed by their pig leaders—remains memorable, as does its title, one piece of *Animal Farm*'s contents in particular lingered in general discourse: the pigs' slogan **"All animals are equal, but some are more equal than others."**

Based primarily on George Orwell's two best-known books, and *1984* in particular, the term **Orwellian** is commonly used for a world in which private lives are controlled by public figures, and respect for truth gives way to manipulation of language.

## Titles

World War II veteran Joseph Heller spent years trying to convey in fiction the insanity of combat. When he finally completed this task, Heller titled the results *Catch-18*. As it was about to be published, the book's editor discovered that an upcoming novel by Leon Uris was called *Mila-18*. He proposed adding four digits to Heller's title. The author consented and in 1961 his book was published as *Catch-22*. Heller's novel included a key exchange between bombardier John Yossarian and medical officer Doc Daneeka in which they discuss a flier named Orr who is buckling under the pressure of multiple missions and may ask to be grounded. The only catch is "Catch-22." According to this concept, concern about one's safety when faced with genuine danger is a sign of sanity. So if Orr asks to be relieved from flying because he's feeling a bit crazed, making that request would indicate he's sane and fit to fly. This is the catch. Yossarian marvels at its sheer simplicity. "That's some catch, that Catch-22," he observes.

"It's the best there is," agrees Doc Daneeka.

Would this concept have lasted so long if Heller's novel had been called *Catch-18*? We'll never know. Certainly the *18* version sounds foreign to ears accustomed to *22*. There are many other ways to depict the same kind of paradox—*a no-win situation; a double bind; damned if you do, damned if you don't*—but **Catch-22** is the one we use most often. It could be the book title most commonly repeated in everyday conversation.

Like *Catch-22*, the titles of some books gain stature over time because they prove so prophetic. Such was the case with Eugene Burdick and William Lederer's *The Ugly American*. Published on the eve of America's involvement in Vietnam, this 1958 collection of stories about Americans in Southeast Asia featured a do-gooding engineer who ineffectually tries to win the hearts and minds of Asians. Even though Burdick and Lederer's title referred to the physical homeliness of its protagonist, under the weight of events the term ugly American took on a completely different significance. It was almost as if Burdick and Lederer wrote with a crystal ball focused on the succeeding decade and a half in Vietnam, Laos, and Cambodia, where Americans wreaked havoc with their pushiness, incompetence, and willful ignorance of local culture. **Ugly American** captured perfectly the bull-in-a-china-shop quality of U.S. adventures abroad, and its country's expats. In a feature story on American tourists, NPR's John Ydstie said, "They're commonly referred to as the 'ugly American.' You know, the businessman who is always complaining about the food, the drink, and the customs of the country he's visiting."

Another type of businessperson is the one who simply can not do his or her job. Why do so many such incompetents end up supervising others? Psychologist Laurence Peter suggested an answer in his 1969 bestseller **The Peter Principle**: "In a hierarchy every employee tends to rise to his level of incompetence." So many of us have had to work with, or for, people who are in over their head that Peter's principle long outlived his book. One might speculate that this principle inspired the comic strip *Dilbert* with its clueless boss, to say nothing of airheaded managers in the movie *Office Space* and NBC's sitcom *The Office*.

As was true of *The Man in the Gray Flannel Suit* and *Psychobabble*, some titles proved more lasting than the books that spawned them. *The Gang That Couldn't Shoot Straight* is a classic example. Jimmy Breslin's 1969 novel about a feckless bunch of New York crooks sold reasonably well but got mixed reviews. The 1971 movie it inspired disappeared quickly, followed by the book itself. Their title was a different story. Decades after Breslin's novel was published,

**The Gang That Couldn't Shoot Straight** still refers to ineffectual groups of many kinds. After a poor World Cup performance, the U.S. national soccer team was called "the gang that couldn't shoot straight" in *USA Today*. A 2006 book about new journalists was titled *The Gang That Wouldn't Write Straight*, and NPR's coverage of a book about a failed Equatorial Guinea coup by mercenaries was headlined "The Gang That Couldn't Coup Straight."

In 1978, Christina Crawford published a memoir that portrayed her late mother, actress Joan Crawford, as an alcoholic shrew. Crawford called this book *Mommie Dearest* because, she said, that is what Joan Crawford demanded her children call her. The most memorable episodes in *Mommie Dearest* featured the movie star's bizarre forms of discipline—tying Christina to her bed, feeding her raw meat, or cutting up her favorite dress, then making her wear the shreds—for infractions as minor as hanging clothes on metal coat hangers. Although some friends rallied to Joan Crawford's defense, with her football-grade shoulder pads, severely sculpted eyebrows, and troweled-on lipstick, this actress was easy to envision as someone who couldn't pass for June Cleaver. (Crawford was the model for Milton Caniff's Dragon Lady.) Massive news coverage riveted **Mommie Dearest** into our collective consciousness. When Britney Spears proved to be an out-of-control mother, airwaves were filled with references to the singer as a *Mommie Dearest*. Another metaphorical use of this term concerns children who write unflattering books about parents. In her book *The Forest for the Trees*, agent-editor Betsy Lerner wrote about this genre, "There is a clear bias in the culture against those who pull a *Mommie Dearest*."

## Allusions

In Arthur Conan Doyle's story "Silver Blaze," a murder mystery is solved by detective Sherlock Holmes's observation of a "curious incident." On the night of the murder, a dog in the stable where the body was later found did *not* bark. This suggested that nothing was amiss until the racehorse this man was trying to maim reared up and killed him. That is the famous case of **the dog that didn't bark**. This concept has since become a popular allusion to all sorts of situations in which a revealing element is something that *did not* happen. *Washington Post* reporter Bob Woodward called the fact that throughout Richard Nixon's Watergate tapes neither he nor any aide ever asked what would be the right thing to do *the dog that didn't bark*.

In notes for his uncompleted novel *The Last Tycoon*, F. Scott Fitzgerald wrote, "There are no second acts in American life." Although this observation is generally taken to mean that, like the author himself, Americans tend to burn out young, another interpretation is that we like to skip second-act complications while leaping from first-act dilemmas to third-act resolutions. Whatever Fitzgerald was getting at, the idea that Americans are at their best when starting out struck a lasting chord and spawned a common catchphrase: **no second acts**.

Some authors make up words or concepts that catch on and enter the lexicon. One is **grok**, a reference to "getting" something on a deep level. Robert Heinlein introduced this invented term (Martian, supposedly) in his 1961 novel *Stranger in a Strange Land*. Two years later novelist Kurt Vonnegut's novel *Cat's Cradle* revolved around the imagined religion of "Bokonism." Bokonists believe that everyone is assigned to a team called a *karass*. Of various terms that Vonnegut coined, **karass** is the one that endured, usually referring to a group of people with a strong spiritual connection. ("The moment we met I knew you were part of my karass.")

## Characters

Other than William Shakespeare, no English author left more characters' names behind than Charles Dickens. Ebenezer **Scrooge** is the most iconic Dick-

ens character, the only one to have his name lowercased and converted into an adjective: **scroogish.** The nickname of *Oliver Twist*'s expert pickpocket, the **Artful Dodger**, has endured to suggest anyone who can slip and slide out of difficult situations. (Bill and Hillary Clinton have both been called Artful Dodgers.) **Miss Havisham** in *Great Expectations*, who was abandoned at the altar as a young woman and spends the rest of her life alone, dressed in her wedding gown and brooding about life's injustice, is now synonymous with backward-looking rigidity (as when the Manhattan Institute's Heather MacDonald accused teacher-training curriculums of being "more unchanging than Miss Havisham"). In *Martin Chuzzlewit*, Seth Pecksniff is a pious fraud whose greedy behavior belies the moral maxims he spouts. Dickens was particularly brilliant in his naming of this character, suggesting a beak-nosed man who pecks the ground, then raises his nose to sniff the air. Since that sort of person is so prevalent in our lives and on our screens, we still call pious hypocrites **Pecksniffs**, their behavior **Pecksniffian**. Similar to Seth Pecksniff is Uriah Heep, the hypocritically "'umble" · clerk in *David Copperfield*. This character is so associated with wicked obsequiousness that "Uriah" has been permanently crossed off naming lists for baby boys (never mind that the biblical Uriah was a gallant officer in King David's army). Comparing someone to **Uriah Heep** suggests that he is a sniveling toady. Heep's clerk, the irrepressible **Mr. Micawber**—ever hopeful that something will "turn up"—has become emblematic of the type of blind optimism that is sometimes called **Micawberesque**.

No one was more Micawberesque than Candide. In Voltaire's eponymous 1759 novel, Candide is a young man whose tutor, Dr. Pangloss, teaches him that in this best of all possible worlds, all is for the best. In the guise of telling a tale, Voltaire was actually challenging the belief of German philosopher Gottfried Wilhelm Leibniz that "all is for the best in this best of all possible worlds." After being flogged, shipwrecked, beset by disease, tumbled by an earthquake, and nearly hanged, **Candide** begins to wonder if all is for the best after all. His name is today associated with innocent optimism. **Pangloss**, and the adjective **Panglossian**, refer to anyone whose outlook on life is more willfully, if no less naively, optimistic. Those who thought that Ronald Reagan's "morning in America" approach to governance was based primarily on wishful thinking considered him Panglossian.

A New World counterpart to Voltaire's characters is, of course, Pollyanna. The freckle-faced heroine of Eleanor Porter's 1913 novel by that title, eleven-year-old orphan Pollyanna Whittier lives in the dark attic of her dour aunt's house. Nonetheless, through the power of irrepressible good will, Pollyanna—whose goal in life is to always find "something to be glad about"—finally melts the frozen heart of her bitter aunt, and lifts the spirits of all she meets. This tale so beguiled the American reading public that *Pollyanna* and its many sequels were phenomenal bestsellers. Over time **Pollyanna** or **Pollyannish** has come to suggest ineffectual naiveté. Calling someone "a Pollyanna" is not a nice thing to do.

Another type of female protagonist is Trilby O'Ferrall, the model and singer who is the protagonist of George du Maurier's popular 1894 novel *Trilby*. Although this novel itself has not held up over time, one of its characters has: Svengali. An unappealing Austrian musician with a mesmerizing personality, Svengali helps Trilby win public acclaim. When Svengali dies, his pupil loses her ability to sing. Allegorically speaking, a **Svengali** is a sinister character who bends others to his will. According to *Time* magazine, actress Liv Ullmann "was no mere Trilby to [director Ingmar] Bergman's Svengali."

Unlike Svengali, there actually was a Captain Bligh, British naval officer William Bligh, who headed an ill-fated 1787 South Seas voyage by the HMS Bounty. As their destination neared, his crew mutinied, setting Bligh and loyal crew members adrift in a dinghy. This true story is memorable enough. But we remember Bligh's name best as a tyrannical character in the 1932 novel *Mutiny on the Bounty* by Charles Nordhoff and James Norman Hall, as well as in several movies based on that novel. Even though historians have been kinder to their protagonist than Nordhoff and Hall were, **Captain Bligh** remains synonymous with cruel, inflexible discipline. So does his flakier American counterpart Captain Queeg. In Herman Wouk's 1951 bestseller *The Caine Mutiny* this erratic, unbalanced minesweeper commander clicks ball bearings in his hand while obsessing about trivial matters (most notably the theft of some strawberries). At one point Queeg is so caught up with reprimanding a sailor about a petty infraction that he allows his ship to sever a towline. Humphrey Bogart's riveting portrayal of **Captain Queeg** in a movie based on Wouk's novel welded his name into our lexicon. Anyone in power who is deranged or simply obsessed with minutiae is liable to be called a **Queeg**. Supreme Court justice Anthony Kennedy once said of serving on the nation's highest court, "Sometimes you don't know if you're Caesar about to cross the Rubicon or Captain Queeg cutting your own towline."

At the other end of the psychic scale—the anti-Queeg, if you will—is Charles Edward Chipping. A classics teacher at an English boarding school,

Chipping is called "Mr. Chips" by his pupils. Hence the title of James Hilton 1935 bestseller about this man, *Goodbye, Mr. Chips*. As he lies dying in this novel's denouement, the elderly schoolmaster overhears a visitor lament that he never had children of his own. "But you're wrong," he exclaims. "I have . . . thousands of them . . . thousands of them . . . and all boys!" Since Hilton's novel enjoyed so much success, then was made into a popular 1939 movie, the protagonist's name became a lasting part of our language. **Mr. Chips** remains our favorite eponym for dedicated teachers beloved by their students.

Hilton's contemporary James Thurber had a flair for portraying meek men and overbearing women. One notable 1939 *New Yorker* story by Thurber, "The Secret Life of Walter Mitty," featured a henpecked husband who enjoys a rich fantasy life of imagined adventure. In that life Mitty flies fighter planes, guns down bad guys, and conducts complicated surgical operations. Since so many of us harbor secret dreams of imagined derring-do, this story struck a nearly universal chord. In fact, it resonated so widely and deeply that decades after he made his debut, **Walter Mitty**—or *Walter Mitty dreams*, or *Walter Mitty fantasies*—still refers to imagined lives of glamour and adventure.

In 1955, Vladimir Nabokov's novel *Lolita* had the good fortune to be banned by France as obscene. When *Lolita* appeared in the United States three years later, this advance publicity helped that book become a number-one bestseller. Nabokov's novel raised unsettling questions that have yet to be resolved. Does it portray a middle-aged man understandably captivated by a twelve-year-old temptress, or a dirty old man who is a borderline pedophile? Regardless of how one feels about this book and the two movies it inspired, **Lolita** firmly established itself as the preferred name for alluring *nymphets* (a term introduced by Nabokov). A reviewer of one woman's sexual memoir said it portrayed vividly the many roles its author had played, "from Lolita, to dutiful wife and mother, to surprised participant in an extra-marital fling." The hazards of not being up on your retroterms were illustrated when Woolworths, in Britain had to stop selling a bed for young girls that it called the *Lolita Midsleeper* after enraged parents called this company's attention to the name's association with preteen sexuality. It turned out that no one involved in marketing their bed knew about Nabokov's character. "We had to look it up on Wikipedia," said a Woolworths spokesman. "But we certainly know who she is now."

In another controversial novel, Philip Roth mined his own adolescence for material with which to flesh out a young Jewish lawyer named Alexander Portnoy. Portnoy is fascinated by Gentile girls and obsessed with memories of his guilt-inducing mother and ineffectual father. After the 1969 publication of *Portnoy's Complaint*, Roth was pilloried by fellow Jews for writing such an unflattering portrait of a *landsman*. Readers of many faiths were revolted by his novel's exuberant sexuality. The part of *Portnoy's Complaint* that most captured readers' imaginations, however, was its unblinking depiction of what later came to be known as *self-pleasure*, an act Roth's protagonist sometimes engages in while grasping a piece of raw liver. After *Portnoy's Complaint* topped the bestseller lists, novelist Jacqueline Susann said that she might like to meet its author, but wouldn't want to shake his hand. **Portnoy** remains an allusion to onanistic men. Nearly four decades after the publication of Roth's opus, TV critic Nancy Franklin wrote in the *New Yorker* about Jon Stewart's "masturbatory" delight in the adulation of his *Daily Show* audience, "as if he were Portnoy and the audience his slab of liver."

## Drama

In the early nineteenth century, a new type of entertainment began to appear on American stages: *minstrel shows* featuring dialect-spouting white performers made up in grotesque blackface. One popular minstrel performer named Thomas Rice was famous for singing these lines:

> *First on de heel tap, den on de toe*
> *Every time I wheel about I jump Jim Crow.*
> *Wheel about and turn about and jump jis so*
> *And every time I wheel about I jump Jim Crow.*

This song was apparently based on a Louisville slave with a pronounced limp who called himself Jim Crow. (Blacks had been called "crows" for at least a century before that, and when dancing were said to "jump Jim Crow.") Rice imitated this slave's limping gait when singing that popular song, to the howling delight of his audience. It didn't take long for *Jim Crow* to become a demeaning term for Negroes in general. Stores that catered to blacks were called "Jim Crow stores," train cars designated for them were "Jim Crow cars." Race-separation laws enacted after the Civil War came to be known as **Jim Crow**

**laws**. The entire system of racial segregation was labeled **Jim Crow**, and 1960s civil rights activists often chanted "Jim Crow must go!"

**Stanley Kowalski**, a character in Tennessee Williams's 1947 play *A Streetcar Named Desire*, became our model for boorish, sexually alluring lowlifes. The object of Kowalski's taunts and advances—his sister-in-law, **Blanche DuBois**— is rivaled by only Scarlett O'Hara in *Gone With the Wind* as a symbol of shattered southern womanhood. After being raped by Stanley, Blanche descends into madness. A courtly asylum official comes to take her to a mental institution. After first resisting, Blanche finally takes this man's arm, telling him with a winsome smile, **"I have always relied on the kindness of strangers."** The more impersonal our lives grow, the easier it becomes to understand Blanche's forlorn line. To depict the existence of six hundred residents left in a Mississippi town devastated by Hurricane Katrina, CBS News correspondent Byron Pitts said, "They rely on each other and the kindness of strangers."

Arthur Miller's 1949 play *Death of a Salesman* revolves around an aging lingerie salesman whose dreams exceed his achievements. *Willy Loman* describes his modus operandi as getting by on **a shoeshine and a smile**. A friend of Willy's tells his son Biff that such behavior is part of traveling salesmanship, that **"it goes with the territory."** As Willy Loman's life disintegrates, his long-suffering wife suspects that he plans to kill himself. In a moving peroration she tells their son, "I don't say he's a great man. Willy Loman never made a lot of money. His name was never in the paper. He's not the finest character that ever lived. But he's a human being, and a terrible thing is happening to him. So attention must be paid. He's not to be allowed to fall into his grave like an old dog. Attention, attention must be finally paid to such a person." The key phrase in that soliloquy—**attention must be paid**—lingered long after the play ended its extended run on Broadway. Willy finally does kill himself in hopes that his life insurance will give his sons a better shot at success than he enjoyed. **Willy Loman** is often invoked allegorically to suggest a forlorn man whose dreams have been shattered. In a *New Yorker* essay, author Robert Stone referred to the "Willy Loman–like submissiveness" of onetime State Department wunderkind Alger Hiss after he served time in prison for perjury.

# 20. Retro U

I n the mid-1960s social psychologist Stanley Milgram asked several hundred Nebraskans to try to convey a document to a Boston stockbroker they didn't know. All were instructed to send their document to the friend whom they thought was most likely to know the intended recipient, asking this person to do the same thing until the envelope reached its destination. Milgram expected dozens if not hundreds of intermediaries to be involved in successful deliveries. As he later reported, however, it took an average of only five to seven handoffs before the documents began to arrive at their destination. Milgram called this a "small-world" phenomenon.

Milgram's study attracted quite a bit of attention and became part of American folklore. "I read somewhere that everybody on this planet is separated by only six other people," says a character in John Guare's 1990 play *Six Degrees of Separation*. In the mid-1990s game "Six Degrees of Kevin Bacon," players tried to connect actors to Bacon through other actors who appeared with him in movies. Malcolm Gladwell's celebration of the **six degrees of separation** phenomenon in his 1996 bestseller *The Tipping Point* reinforced its presence in our psyche. By now the notion that we're all more closely interconnected than we realize is often referred to by the words **six degrees** alone. ("I bumped into my cousin from Vancouver in Times Square the other day. Talk about six degrees!") But is it valid? When University of Alaska psychologist Judith Kleinfeld reviewed Stanley Milgram's papers at Yale, she discovered that his conclusions were based on fewer than twenty successful document deliveries out of nearly a hundred attempts. Similar studies conducted by Milgram produced so few deliveries that he didn't even report them. In other words

Milgram's entire premise—that we're all connected by a few shared acquaintances—was based on a skimpy, ambiguous data set. This led Kleinfeld and others to question whether six degrees is the right amount of human separation. Perhaps the real number is closer to sixteen, or sixty, or six hundred. Who knows? Certainly Stanley Milgram didn't. After trying to replicate Milgram's experiment, with ambiguous results, Columbia University sociologist Duncan Watts concluded in his 2003 book *Six Degrees,* "The claim of the small-world phenomenon is an incredibly difficult one to resolve empirically."

## Sociology

Depression-era researchers at Western Electric's Hawthorne Works outside Chicago set out to determine if making lights brighter in Hawthorne's Relay Assembly Test Room would increase worker output. It did. When the lights were dimmed, however, productivity kept rising. This puzzled the researchers. They ended up concluding that the novelty of being studied had a greater impact on worker behavior than what was supposedly being observed. Subsequent research questioned this assumption, which was based on a small sample of workers and sketchy data. Nonetheless, such debunking has done little to undermine the enduring axiom that just about any alteration of a workplace can have a salutary effect. That is the **Hawthorne effect.** When reduced levels of violence were recorded at a school after students were made to wear uniforms, a *Journal of School Health* contributor wondered if this might simply be due to the Hawthorne effect.

Similar ambiguity surrounds a question meteorologist Edward Lorenz raised in 1970: could the gentle flapping of a butterfly's wings in Brazil cause a tornado in Texas? Lorenz called this hypothetical illustration of chaos theory a **butterfly effect.** It was popularized by James Gleick's 1987 book *Chaos,* and became the title of a 2004 movie. In a Cox News story about the big fashion impact of a small amount of pashmina wool from Himalayan goats, Nedra Rhone commented, "Talk about a butterfly effect."

Yet another interesting-to-talk-about, hard-to-prove syndrome has to do with a 1.5-million-square-mile section of the Atlantic Ocean bordered by Bermuda, Puerto Rico, and Florida. An unusual number of ships and planes are said to have disappeared without explanation within this triangular area. In 1974 Charles Berlitz published a bestselling book called *The Bermuda Triangle* that called attention to this fact. Much fevered speculation followed about what could have caused these vessels to disappear. Some of the more popular possibilities included temporal holes, extraterrestrial abduction, or possibly even inclement weather. Most suggestions were subsequently debunked. According to the Coast Guard, ships and planes are not lost in this part of the Atlantic any more frequently than in any other. Lloyd's of London charges shippers no more for insurance to travel in the so-called Bermuda triangle than anywhere else. Be that as it may, Berlitz's bestseller attracted so much attention that **Bermuda triangle** still alludes to mysterious goings-on, particularly unexplained disappearances. Allegorically it signifies being in a deep, unexplained limbo. To explain why he called adolescence "the Bermuda triangle of human development," Advocates for Youth president James Wagoner said, "We know what goes in, but we have no idea what comes out."

## Sexology

When about to undertake their conjugal duties, English wives of a century ago were supposedly advised to close their eyes and think of England. This advice is so Victorian that it is routinely, and mistakenly, attributed to Queen Victoria. When he was having doubts about his impending marriage to Lady Diana Spencer, Prince Charles was told by his sister Anne to close his eyes and think of England (ironically, one assumes). This counsel is such a bedrock part of Britain's sexual heritage that the phrase **think of England** is sufficient to evoke a frigid wife staring listlessly at the ceiling as her husband has his way, her head filled with thoughts of Trafalgar Square, the Union Jack, Cornish pasties, and a nice hot cup of tea.

Another sexual allusion given birth on the British Isles involved Mrs. Patrick Campbell (Beatrice Stella Tanner)—the first actress to play Eliza Doolittle in Shaw's *Pygmalion*. After being told of a homosexual love affair between two actors on the eve of World War I, Mrs. Campbell famously remarked, "I don't care what people do, as long as they don't do it in the street and frighten the horses." This observation circulated so widely for so long that **don't frighten the horses** is still shorthand for sexual tolerance, or erotic situations in general. When asked if she'd do a nude scene, septuagenarian actress Judi Dench responded, "Well, not unless I want to frighten the horses."

Another actress who left behind an enduring sexual allusion is Mae West. When she was the subject of a kidnapping threat in the mid-1930s, West left Hollywood for a couple of weeks. Upon her return a group of friends greeted the voluptuous movie star as she got off the train. One young L.A. cop carried a bouquet of flowers. "These are from the fellas down at the station," said the policeman as he handed them to her. "Then he leant down and kissed me," West later recalled, "and said, 'And that's from me. It's good to have you back with us, Mae.' And I said, 'Oh yeah, and is that a gun you got in your pocket or are you just glad to see me?' " One suspects this wasn't the first time the queen of double entendres unleashed that quip, or the last. After many retellings it became one of her most famous remarks. **A gun in your pocket** remains a common euphemism for an erect penis.

Couples forced to marry because the woman is pregnant are said to have a *shotgun wedding* or *shotgun marriage*. This alludes to the choice a gun-toting father offers a man who has impregnated his daughter: marry her or I'll shoot you. In classic American mythology that scenario involves a bib-overalled father straight out of *Tobacco Road* training a double-barreled shotgun on his lascivious daughter and some hapless traveling salesman who enjoyed a *roll in the hay*. Today **shotgun wedding** or **marriage** is applied more broadly to any involuntary relationship. When political rivals are forced by circumstances to work together, that partnership is often called a shotgun marriage.

What would a *Tobacco Road* dad have made of the work of Ernest Grafenberg? Grafenberg was the German gynecologist who in 1950 identified a spot deep within women's vaginas that was unusually sensitive sexually. This came to be known as the *Grafenberg spot*, subsequently shortened to *the G-spot*. A 1982 bestseller called *The G-Spot and Other Recent Discoveries About Human Sexuality* excited feverish speculation about where that spot might be located.

Probing consideration of this issue proved inconclusive for many couples. Questions were raised about whether any such spot existed. The very notion of a **G-spot** aroused so much interest, however, that this phrase not only stuck around but became metaphorical, as when *Newsweek*'s Jonathan Alter wrote, "Smart politicians have always known that the G Spot of the American body politic is in the middle."

## Psychology

For most of humankind, the mentally ill were thought to be possessed by demons and treated accordingly. Ravers, howlers, and streetside mutterers were shackled, flogged, and dunked in freezing water. Beginning in the early fifteenth century, however, lunatics were admitted to London's Bethlem Royal hospital as patients rather than penitents. Known to Londoners as *Bedlam*,

this early insane asylum grew notorious for the raucous behavior of patients housed in squalid, overcrowded conditions. Eighteenth-century Londoners were invited to gawk at Bedlam's rambunctious inhabitants. Watching them fondle or fight with each other was considered worth the price of admission (a penny; the first Tuesday of every month was free). Those who wanted to be sure they saw interesting goings-on brought long sticks to poke at Bedlamites and stir them up. That popular pastime went on for well over a century. In time the term **bedlam** came to refer to pandemonium of all kinds. ("It's absolute bedlam here at Yankee Stadium.")

British physician William Battie, who pioneered humane treatment of the insane at London's St. Luke's Hospital in the mid-eighteenth century, may have left his last name behind as slang for crazy: **batty**. Beginning in Dr. Battie's era, struggling patients were sometimes restrained in jackets with long sleeves crisscrossed in front and belted in the back. Originally known as "strait-waistcoats," these eventually were called **straitjackets**. Dotty George III was sometimes constrained in one. Today those who feel hamstrung by circumstances beyond their control are said to be **straitjacketed**.

In classic psychoanalysis, a note-taking analyst sits behind the head of a couch (a chaise, actually) on which a patient reclines. This has led to countless jokes and cartoons involving recumbent patients and goateed psychiatrists who compose grocery lists as they pretend to listen, stifle laughs, or simply nod off. (Sigmund Freud himself admitted to writing letters or dozing off as prone patients prattled on.) Although psychiatric patients are rarely recumbent anymore, **on the couch** remains an allusion to self-revelation. Public figures who resist being questioned about their personal lives routinely say they won't be put *on the couch*. *Newsweek* once referred to comedian Drew Carey as not being "couch-shrunk." This alluded to the fact that after World War II we began to call psychiatrists *headshrinkers*. The allusion here is to Jivaro Indian warriors in Ecuador and Peru who scooped the brains from some of their victims' skulls, then filled the brain cavity with hot sand to shrink this skull for use in rituals. Since that approximated what we thought psychiatrists might do to us, **headshrinkers** was a natural nickname for members of their profession, or **shrinks** for short.

Using such a nickname is one way we have kept therapists at bay. Humor is another. In one classic joke, after describing the sexual content he sees in inkblots and being told he has a problem, a patient heatedly tells an analyst, "Well you're the one with all the dirty pictures." That joke refers to the *Rorschach* or *inkblot* test. Developed by Swiss psychiatrist Hermann Rorschach in 1921, this diagnostic tool involves asking patients to describe what they see in blots of ink on several cards. Their responses—heavy with breasts and vaginas (among men, anyway)—are considered an accurate road map of inner obsessions. Today the term **Rorschach test** has far broader application. Former Secretary of State Madeleine Albright once compared the way government officials interpret intelligence reports to a Rorschach test in which they see whatever they want to see.

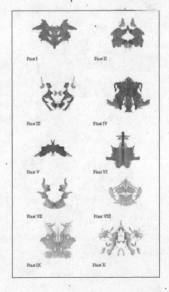

Far from Western Europe's inkblots and analytic couches, Ivan Petrovich Pavlov studied dogs' salivary glands in a St. Petersburg lab. The Russian physiologist noticed that his canine subjects began to drool whenever they expected to be fed, whether food was forthcoming or not. To determine why, in an ingenious set of experiments Pavlov engaged a stimulus—blowing a whistle, striking a tuning fork, ringing a bell—every time his dogs were fed. Eventually the animals began to salivate whenever they heard such a sound. This came to be known as a *conditioned reflex* or a *conditioned response*. Reference to **Pavlov's dogs** evokes images of an automatic response like this, and is often applied to human beings. (Those who reach for their BlackBerry at the sound of any beep have been compared to Pavlov's dogs.) The idea that one's responses to stimuli become automatic over time is called **Pavlovian.** Journalist James Wooten once noted that the loud tire squeal of the president's plane landing evokes a *Pavlovian* response among waiting reporters who dash en masse in its direction.

## Theology

During an annual religious procession in India, a huge representation of the Hindu deity Jagannath is transported on a heavy wagon. Centuries ago, worshipers who got in the way of this wagon risked being crushed. English chroniclers of this event Anglicized the

deity's name to *Juggernaut*. Today we call any force that can roll over opposition a **juggernaut**. To Hindus, embodiments of the divine are **avatars**, a term computer gamers have borrowed for online representations of themselves. Another notion we've borrowed from Hindus has to do with their reverence for cows. Because they consider these animals sacred, members of this faith won't eat their flesh. Non-Hindus acknowledge this fact any time they refer to a **sacred cow,** or something that can't be tampered with, much less eaten. The expression **holy cow!** may also owe a debt to Hindu beliefs.

From the world of Islam we regularly recall the occasion when Muhammad was challenged to prove his credibility. To do so he commanded Mount Safa to move. When it didn't, Muhammad said this proved God's mercy. Had Mount Safa moved it would have collapsed and killed them. Muhammad then led a pilgrimage to the mountain, where thanks were given to God. Growing out of this story is an enduring advisory on the need to accommodate reality: **If the mountain will not come to Muhammad, Muhammad must go to the mountain.**

A group of monks called Hesychats who lived on Greece's Mount Athos in the fourteenth century considered navels the heart of human souls. According to a visitor, these Eastern Orthodox mystics believed that any man who spent extended periods of time in solitary contemplation "gazing towards his navel" would achieve enlightenment. More generically those who **contemplate their navels** are now called **navel gazers,** a mocking label hung on those thought to engage in too much introspection.

Among Zen Buddhists, *koans* are a teaching tool, riddles that challenge dependence on logic alone. The best known koan is attributed to seventeenth-century Zen master Hakuin Ekaku. After demonstrating the sound produced when one hand claps another, Hakuin would ask pupils, "What is the sound of a single hand?" Their struggle to answer this unanswerable question made it the perfect koan. Because Hakuin's riddle is a bit passive for Western ears, we've revised it to **"What is the sound of one hand clapping?"** This version has inspired countless "What is the sound of _____?" variations. After a twelve-hour interruption of BlackBerry service, ABC's John Berman asked, "What is the sound of sixteen million thumbs going silent?"

Medieval Christian theologians were quite interested in angels. Thomas Aquinas wondered how many angels could occupy the same space. Some centuries later Isaac D'Israeli, father of British Prime Minister Benjamin Disraeli, asked ironically how medieval theologians such as Aquinas might have answered this question: "How many angels can dance on the point of a very fine needle, without jostling one another?" In modern translation, **How many angels can dance on the head of a pin**?—for some reason "head" replaced the more logical "point" in this question—has become an allusion to unanswerable questions. Economist Paul Krugman says he considers his colleagues' disagreements about whether an economic slowdown deserves to be called a recession "an angels-on-the-head-of-a-pin debate." Incidentally, employing superstring physics, American physicist Phil Schewe has calculated that 10 to the 25th power angels can fit on the point of a pin.

## Philosophy

Late in the Middle Ages, philosophy that was once God-bound took a decidedly humanistic turn. Far from being under sacred supervision, some philosophers began to see human beings as masters of their own fate. A few even questioned whether one could say there was any human existence at all independent of our perception of that existence. René Descartes, the "Father of Modern Philosophy," authored the signature expression of what came to be known as *Cartesian* logic: *I think, therefore I am.* (*"Je pense, donc je suis."*) If he accomplished nothing else, Descartes inspired a plethora of fill-in-blank variations: "**I** _____, **therefore I am.**" Versions I've seen include "I empathize, therefore I am," "I shop, therefore I am;" and "I itch, therefore I am."

Across the English Channel, George Berkeley had his own take on this theme. "To be is to be perceived" was the essence of Berkeley's belief system (the basic idea being that nothing exists independent of our perception of that object or event). Bishop Berkeley once wrote that a sound unheard by human ears was "merely a vibrative or undulatory motion in the air." Popular distillation of Berkeley's view produced the jokey question: **"If a tree falls in the forest and no one hears it, does it make a sound?"** The winning reader's caption for a *New Yorker* cartoon of a woman addressing a man disguised as a tree was, "But what if you fall when no one is around?"

Thomas Hobbes had a jaundiced view of the human condition so pronounced that gloomy world outlooks are sometimes called **Hobbesian**. In his 1651 opus *Leviathan*, Hobbes disparaged those such as Rousseau who regarded primitive human existence with nostalgia. One long sentence enumerated the many deprivations of premodern existence, then concluded that for most it was "solitary, poor, nasty, brutish, and short." The last three words of this observation were the ones that caught our eye and entered our discourse: **nasty, brutish, and short**. *Newsweek* called the TV show *American Idol* "nasty, brutish and not short." *New York Times* columnist Thomas Friedman called Vice President Dick Cheney "nasty, brutish, and short-tempered."

In keeping with the Yankee can-do spirit, American philosophers such as Ralph Waldo Emerson had a more positive, pragmatic outlook. In 1871 Emerson gave a lecture in Oakland, California, titled "Hospitality and How to Make Homes Happy." One member of his audience, sixteen-year-old Sarah Yule, was struck by an observation he made and jotted it down: "If a man can write a better book, preach a better sermon, or make a better mouse-trap than his neighbor, though he builds his house in the woods, the world will make a beaten path to his door." Eighteen years later Yule included this line in a collection of sayings called *Borrowings*. As so often happens, that thought was edited by memories, mouths, and sundry pens until it ended up as one of America's most familiar quotations: "Build a better mousetrap and the world will beat a path to your door." This quotation became so familiar that allusions to its key element—**a better mousetrap**—are routine. In his book *Small Things Considered*, Henry Petroski wrote, "No inventor or designer is likely ever to lay claim to a 'best mousetrap,' for that would preclude the inventor herself from coming up with a still better mousetrap."

In *Walden*, Emerson's Concord neighbor Henry David Thoreau wrote, "If a man does not keep pace with his companions, perhaps it is because he hears a different drummer." **Different drummer** went on to become shorthand for those who are out of step with those around them and don't wish to get in step. In a feature on flamboyant ice skater Christopher Bowman, ABC sports commentator Jim McKay said Bowman clearly marched to a different drummer.

The most enduring and widespread school of American philosophy is defined more by context than concepts. This is the one espoused around overturned barrels in general stores. Because many of these barrels once held crackers, those who held forth while seated beside them came to be known as **cracker barrel philosophers**. They engaged in **cracker barrel philosophizing**.

## Jurisprudence

In 1735, New York printer-editor-publisher John Peter Zenger was accused of "seditious libels." Since so many political forces were arrayed against him, Zenger's case was considered unwinnable. His defense lawyer, Andrew Hamilton of Philadelphia, proved unusually resourceful, however, and Zenger was acquitted. This suggested that a high quality of legal counsel could be found in the City of Brotherly Love. Philadelphia was the hub of U.S. legal life

back then, and *Philadelphia lawyer* came to suggest a particularly astute barrister. Protesting traffic fines he considered excessive, the writer of a letter to the
Fredericksburg (Va.) *Free Lance-Star* concluded, "It doesn't take a Philadelphia
lawyer to figure out that there's something wrong here." Just as often, however,
a **Philadelphia lawyer** has come to be seen as more tricky than talented, shady
rather than sharp.

**Shouting fire in a crowded theater** is thought to identify the outer limits
of free speech. This concept originated when Supreme Court Justice Oliver
Wendell Holmes Jr. wrote in *Schenck v. United States* (1919), "The most strin-
gent protection of free speech would not protect a man falsely shouting fire in
a theater and causing panic." According to Holmes, that theater didn't even
have to be crowded. In the aftermath of 9/11, a postal inspector compared repeated hoax anthrax scares to "yelling fire in a crowded theater."

Jurists have an informal legal concept they call the *elephant test*. This refers
to something that's easy to spot but hard to describe. The best illustration occurred in Supreme Court Justice Potter Stewart's concurring opinion in *Jaco-
bellis v. Ohio* (1964). According to Justice Stewart, even though hard-core
pornography is difficult to define, "I know it when I see it." The key six words
in this opinion became so associated with its author, and with the difficulty of
defining pornography, that when he retired in 1981, Justice Stewart mused that
it would probably be engraved on his tombstone. **I know it when I see it** is trotted out routinely whenever a hard-to-define situation is under consideration.
Without referring to Potter Stewart himself, an editorial in the Austin (Tex.)
*American-Statesman* observed that "unlike obscenity, the Supreme Court apparently can't recognize partisan redistricting when it sees it."

Two lay legal concepts are rooted in food: Twinkies and ham sandwiches.
The first grows out of the 1978 murder of a San Francisco supervisor and that
city's mayor. At his 1979 trial, lawyers for Dan White, a former San Francisco
supervisor, conceded that their client had killed both men, but claimed there
were mitigating circumstances. White consumed so much sugary junk food,
they argued—soda pop, candy bars, doughnuts, cupcakes—that his brain
chemistry and judgment may have been altered. The press quickly dubbed this
the *Twinkie defense* (referring to the oblong cupcake that goes by this name).
Jurors were unimpressed. White was convicted of voluntary manslaughter and
spent five years in prison. He committed suicide nearly two years after being
paroled in 1984. His legacy is what's still known as the **Twinkie defense**, de-

fined by law.com as "a claim by a criminal defendant that at the time of the crime he/she was of diminished mental capacity due to intake of too much sugar, as from eating 'Twinkies,' sugar-rich snacks."

Another food-based legal concept—the **ham sandwich theory**—gets trotted out every time a high-profile public figure is about to be indicted by a grand jury. According to that theory, any good prosecutor can get a grand jury to indict a ham sandwich. Sol Wachtler, onetime Chief Judge of New York's State Court of Appeals, put this adage on the record in 1985. Wachtler, who is Jewish, later told word sleuth Barry Popik that he wished he had cited pastrami instead of ham. In 1992 Wachtler himself was indicted for harassing a former girlfriend and spent eleven months in prison after being convicted.

## Theater

As far back as Greek plays such as *Antigone*, spear-carrying soldiers stood in the background. Such nonspeaking spear-bearing characters can still be seen in operas today. Metaphorically, a **spear-carrier** is one who takes part in an activity but plays no significant role. A member of Hewlett-Packard's board once said that another member thought only a handful like him should make decisions and everyone else should be a *spear-carrier*.

Early American touring companies sometimes performed in barns. This practice came to be known as *barnstorming*. In time that concept was applied to politicians who made brief stops in many areas, then to athletic teams who traveled about playing games with local teams and to pilots who flew around the country doing aerobatic displays. Nowadays anyone at all who tours extensively while playing, performing, piloting, or politicking is said to be **barnstorming**.

During the 1820s a new type of lamp incorporated a rotating container of incandescent lime which was heated to the point that it gave off intense light. So-called *limelighting* was used by theaters around the world until it was replaced by electric arc lamps late in the nineteenth century. Nonetheless we still say that actors and others being paid a lot of attention are **in the limelight**. Those hungry for this kind of attention **seek the limelight**.

Early in the twentieth century the manager of a New York vaudeville theater improvised a long hook to yank amateur performers off the stage. The ensuing laughter encouraged many comedians to incorporate this sight gag into their act. A 1907 movie was titled *Amateur Night; or, Get the Hook.* Today anyone whose activity is cut short is said to **get the hook.**

Because out-of-sight areas on either side of a stage are known as *the wings,* actors waiting there to go on are said to be **in the wings.** Politicians waiting their turn to be nominated for office are *in the wings,* so to speak as are minor league baseball players hoping to get called up to the majors. Unprepared actors who need prompting from someone offstage were said to **wing it.** Anything done without preparation can also be given that label. ("I didn't have time to study for the test so I had to wing it.")

# 21. Miscellany

quite a few retroterms that we use frequently don't fall into any broad category. This chapter compiles those terms, beginning with ones that originate in the world of animals, vegetables, and minerals.

## Animals

Six-year-old Thorleif Schjelderup-Ebbe was fascinated by a flock of chickens that came with the house his family rented one summer outside Oslo. He subsequently got hens of his own and began taking notes on how they interacted. What at first looked like random milling about proved to be a carefully choreographed dance of dominance. Thorleif took particular note of the way his chickens used their beaks to determine who stood where. Some seemed free to peck any other hen without getting pecked back. Others got pecked a lot but did little pecking of their own. Members of a third group pecked some hens and were pecked by others. Years later, as a university student in zoology, Schjelderup-Ebbe based a classic 1922 paper about the dominance hierarchy among hens on his boyhood observations. **Alpha hens** at the top of this hierarchy, he reported, **ruled the roost**. Beneath them were subservient chickens who existed in a complex status system determined by constant pecking. Schjelderup-Ebbe called this arrangement the *peck order*. In 1929 an American social psychologist wrote of his findings, "When a flock of hens are placed together in a run, 'pecking order' is soon established." Soon this concept was being applied to other animals, and to human beings as well. Early in World War II anthropologist Margaret Mead observed that "fifth- and sixth- and seventh-generation Americans lost the zest which came with climbing to the top of the pecking order in their own town or city." Today **pecking order** is so commonly used to describe human hierarchies that it's easy to overlook the fact that it originated with Norwegian hens.

In mid-eighteenth-century England, **lame duck** referred to a stock trader who hadn't paid his debts. A century later that phrase took on political overtones in the United States, gradually acquiring its contemporary meaning: one whose term in office is coming to an end, making him or her bankrupt politically. Because a duck at rest is so much easier to shoot than one on the wing, we generalize from the experience of hunters when calling an easy human target a **sitting duck**. A *dead duck*, in avian or human form, is a goner. Originally applied to defeated politicians after the Civil War, **dead duck** is now applied to anyone whose prospects are nil. As hunters have said for the past couple of centuries, "Never waste powder on a dead duck."

One of Aesop's lesser fables features an old woman whose goose lays golden eggs. Growing impatient, this woman kills the bird, hoping to put her hands on all its gold at once. To her dismay all she gets for her efforts is a dead goose. Like anyone today who liquidates a reliable source of income in hopes of making a quick killing, the old woman **killed the goose that laid the golden egg**. In another fable of Aesop's, an ox who approaches a manger to eat its straw is driven off by the furious barking and snapping of a dog who was napping there. Finally the ox wanders off, musing that even though the ill-tempered dog does not intend to eat this straw himself, he is determined that no one else should either. That type of person is now known as a **dog in the manger**.

During the late nineteenth century *dog* was slang for pretension. Ostentatiously handing someone your business card was a form of dog. So was making sure that others knew your ancestors fought in the Revolution. In time *dog* fused with *putting on airs* to become **putting on the dog**. Lyman Bagg, an 1869 graduate of Yale, later wrote about student norms at his alma mater, "To put on dog, is to make a flashy display, to cut a swell."

*Old Yeller* notwithstanding, in rural America a yellow dog has never been considered particularly desirable. After the Civil War, unreconstructed Confederates vowed that they would vote for a *yaller dog* before they'd vote for a Republican. This inspired the term **yellow dog Democrat** for one who is blindly loyal to that party. Today those willing to work with Republicans call themselves *blue dog Democrats*.

## Vegetables

A writer friend of mine likes to muse about the humor quotient of plant products. Rutabaga is funny. Potatoes aren't. Kumquats are funny. Apples aren't. Bananas are the funniest fruit of all. In large part that's because vaudeville comedians so often slipped on banana peels during pratfall routines. To old-timers, **banana peel** allusions need no further explanation. Noting the decline of humor in movies about academics, *New Yorker* film critic David Denby wrote "the banana peels have been swept away."

Sensing the humorous potential of this fruit, Frank Silver and Irving Cohn based their 1923 hit song **"Yes, We Have No Bananas"** on a Greek grocer who never gave no for an answer: "We have an old fashioned toMAHto / A Long Island poTAHto, but / Yes! We have no bananas / We have no bananas today!" In New York City at this time, burlesque dancers sometimes gyrated like a quivering bunch of bananas. The troupe's tallest, most noticeable member was called the **top banana**. By extension, any performer of any kind who did not get top billing came to be known as a **second banana**. After World War II that title was applied widely to those in subordinate positions, usually one rung below the top. Vice presidents are *second bananas*. So are supporting actors.

The United Fruit Company—a huge conglomerate specializing in bananas—did not hesitate to exert its political will. From the early-to-mid-twentieth century, this company wielded so much power in some countries south of the border that these countries came to be known as **banana republics**. In time that phrase (first used by author O. Henry in 1904) was applied more broadly to any country ruled by shady leaders who are propped up by commercial interests. Because a trendy clothier founded in 1978 calls itself **Banana Republic**, it's easy to lose sight of how cruel and corrupt the countries were to whom this term was originally applied.

## Minerals

Despite being a flimsy material whose use is in decline, *tin* still permeates our discourse. This highly malleable, corrosion-resistant metal was long used for cans, pans, foil, roofs, whistles, and toy soldiers. **Tin cups**, once a common beverage vessel, are now most likely to be held by beggars, literally or figuratively. (George H. W. Bush's fund-raising trips when soliciting support from other countries for the 1991 Gulf War were called "tin cup exercises" by some.) Cans more likely to be made of aluminum today were plated with tin for so long that these tube-shaped metal containers are still called **tin cans** or, less often, **tins**. Similarly, because the thin metal foil now made of aluminum was originally made from tin, old timers call any metal-based wrapping material **tin foil**. (A blogger dated himself when he wrote that Representative William Jefferson [D-La.] had been "caught with $90,000 wrapped in tin foil in his freezer.") That term is enjoying a revival since reference is so often made to *tin foil hats*, metal foil of any kind fashioned into headgear meant to shield brains from microwaves or alien broadcasts, and to prevent others from monitoring one's thoughts. Since wearing this headgear suggests a certain degree of paranoia, **tin foil hats** has become an allusion to derangement. When computer scientists at Princeton showed how easy it was to hack into electronic voting machines, a defender of theirs said that these cyber-gumshoes might be geeky, "but they don't wear tinfoil hats."

Cheap implements of all kinds are still called **tinny**. So is poorly reproduced sound, like that coming from inexpensive speakers. A century ago, the sound produced by out-of-tune pianos in offices of song sheet publishers was sometimes compared to banging on *tin pans*. That's why the lower Manhattan neighborhood where those publishers were concentrated came to be known as **Tin Pan Alley**. Eventually this phrase became generic for the type of popular music that began there. ("Their song had a Tin Pan Alley quality.")

Anyone with little musical sense, a tone-deaf person, is commonly said to have a **tin ear**. Small-time gamblers are called **tinhorns**, a derisive term coined during California's mid-nineteenth century gold rush for those who played chuck-a-luck, an elementary game involving three dice shaken inside a *horn* made of tin. That term may also reference the cheap *tin horns* played by children. More broadly *tinhorn* is applied to those considered of little consequence, such as *tinhorn politicians*.

Other tin-based terms include **tin soldier**, **tin man**, and **tin god**. (In his poem "Public Waste," Rudyard Kipling wrote about officious bureaucrats, "Wherefore the Little Tin Gods harried their little tin souls.") Ineffectual law enforcement officers were said to wear a **tin star**. (A *New York Times* article on the toothlessness of most "czar" positions was titled "The Tin-Star Title for the Too-Tough Job.") Petty despots who liked to parade about in elaborate military gear, including helmets, came to be known as **tin-pot dictators**, evoking an image of an absurd soldier with an inverted cooking pot on his head. British and American infantrymen in World War I called their steel helmets **tin hats**, a term later applied to feeble officials.

In both world wars **brass hats** was slang for military officers, ones with gilt on their caps. Eventually this was abridged to **brass**, then applied to officials in and out of uniform. ("The home-office brass was out in full force.") This alloy of copper and zinc is used in a number of metaphorical ways. Since at least the late sixteenth century *brass* has been synonymous with "impudence." Obnoxiously direct individuals, women especially, are said to be **brassy**. This could owe something to the harsh, direct tone of brass musical instruments. ("You've got a lot of brass.") *Brassy* also suggests gaudiness. The **brass knuckles** some street fighters used to give their fists heft gave rise to a common allusion to dirty tactics. One liberal blogger said of conservative political figures, "They play politics and exploit America's divisions with back-alley brass knuckles." A Republican state legislator in Florida accused Democrats there of engaging in "brass-knuckled politics at its very worst."

## Colors

Figuratively speaking, red is our most functional color. To be unusually angry is to **see red** (based on a misconception that the scarlet color of a bullfighter's cape enrages bulls, who in fact are color-blind). Because Christian holidays were once noted in red on calendars, **red letter day** came to signify any day that's notable. **Red ink** has less positive connotations, referring to the color with which deficits were recorded in ledgers. Enterprises **in the red** operate at a loss. Saying someone has been **caught red-handed**, or with no doubt of his or her culpability, harks back to poachers who were apprehended with prey's blood on their hands, or murderers whose hands were stained with the blood of their victims.

After World Wars I and II the color red took a serious hit because of its association with radicals who carried banners of that color. They were **reds**. *Red scares or red hunts* became common, along with *red-baiting*, trying to belittle others by implying that they had Communist sympathies. (Those only somewhat so inclined were said to be *pink, pinkos,* or *parlor pinks.*) Things got so bad in the 1950s that the Cincinnati Reds baseball team began calling itself the Cincinnati Redlegs. Plain-spoken Harry Truman thought all this foofaraw was nothing more than a *red herring* meant to keep us from facing legitimate issues. This phrase originated in Elizabethan England, where smoked herring, a pungent comestible of bright red color like that of smoked salmon today, was dragged along the ground by fugitives to throw pursuing dogs off the scent. That inspired the expression *drag a red herring across the trail,* which in turn gave rise to **red herring** as a way of describing diversionary tactics. A proposed landfill was denounced by Clarington, Ontario, residents as a *red herring* intended to scare them into accepting a trash incinerator.

For well over a century Americans have called indecent talk *blue*. Obscenity-laced palaver was said to "make the air blue." Possibly due to the raciness of books published in a low-cost French series called La Bibliotheque Bleu, or because imprisoned English prostitutes were once made to wear blue gowns, erotic movies and literature also came to be called **blue**. Another possibility has to do with **blue laws** some states enacted during the colonial era that until quite recently limited Sunday commerce (among other things). A puritanical type who supported such regulations was said to be a **bluenose**. On a more positive note, because the unusually colorfast dye *Coventry blue* was prized in Elizabethan England, *true as Coventry blue* referred to dependability. Eventually this expression was shortened to **true blue** and applied to those considered steadfast.

At one time Spain's pale-complected nobility referred to themselves as *sangre azul,* or *blue blood* because their visible arteries and veins were bluer than those of people they considered beneath them, Moors and Jews in particular. Over time, members of the upper class in other countries came to be known as **blue bloods**. Members of England's Most Noble Order of the Garter had their knee adorned with strips of gilt-edged blue velvet. In France, a *cordon bleu,* or blue ribbon from which a medal hangs, was first awarded to knights, then to chefs. From the mid-nineteenth century on, blue ribbons were given to ships that set speed records during transatlantic crossings. They are still awarded to best-in-class entries in contests of many kinds. By analogy, any group or venture considered top-of-the line is liable to be called a **blue-ribbon** panel, say, or blue-ribbon commission. Because blue chips are the most valuable ones in card games, top companies or stocks or commodities of many kinds are called **blue chip**.

**Out of the blue** is an abridgement of *bolt out of the blue*, referring to a bolt of lightning that streaks earthward from clear blue skies. The **blue streak** left in its wake came to signify any rapidly moving object and inspired the expression *talk a blue streak*—fast and nonstop. The occasional moon that takes on a bluish tint due to atmospheric conditions is called a *blue moon*, inspiring the phrase **once in a blue moon** for rare events.

*Black* is at the opposite end of the status palette from blue, or white. Sixteenth-century Scottish tenant farmers paid English landlords in what was called *mail*—*white mail* for actual money, *black mail* for payment in kind (livestock, produce, etc.). When outlaws along the English-Scottish border began demanding tribute from farmers for "protection," this demand was called **blackmail**. Eventually that term was applied to extortion in general. This is pretty typical of the way *black* is incorporated into words and phrases. **Black magic** was said to be practiced by witches and others who got their way by using **black arts**. Threatening communications were once known as **black hand** letters. After King Charles II made up a "black list" of those involved in his father's execution, many of whom were executed themselves, any ostracized person was said to be on a **blacklist**. Employees considered troublesome were put on such lists by employers. After World War II alleged Communists or Communist sympathizers in the American movie industry were **blacklisted** and banned from employment. **Blackball** refers to a similar process wherein fraternal organizations rejected candidates for membership who were the target of a black ball placed in a ballot box by an existing group member. To be **blackballed** is comparable to being blacklisted, though not on such a sweeping scale.

A rare exception to black's bad reputation is **in the black**, the antonym to *in the red*, referring to turning a profit. More typical is the fact that a wayward offspring is said to be a **black sheep**, presumably because wool from animals that color could not be dyed, making them less valuable than their lighter counterparts. Because they wore shirts of this color, the thuggish enforcers of Italian dictator Benito Mussolini's Fascist policies were called **blackshirts**, a term still applied to political thugs. One contributor to the Daily Kos blog charged that right-wing talk-show hosts "sound like blackshirts."

The German counterparts to Mussolini's enforcers were brown-uniformed Nazi troopers who supported Hitler's rise to power. These so-called **brownshirts** did not help that color's reputation. Before UPS gave it a certain cachet, brown was the most pedestrian of colors. Those who packed a lunch in paper sacks were said to **brown-bag** it, suggesting a dutiful, penny-pinching employee. At one time prurient material was mailed to purchasers in a **plain brown wrapper**. Those whom Americans would call *pissed* or *ticked off* the English say are **browned off**. To kids especially a **brownnoser** was not something one wanted to be. It suggested a sycophant, one who kept his or her nose deep in the behind of an authority figure.

**Brownie points** were what one earned by good, even obsequious behavior. No one is entirely sure why, but here are some possibilities: In the late nineteenth century, a New York railroad superintendent named Brown initiated a reward-penalty system based on points. The good kind came to be known as "brownie points." Depression-era delivery boys who distributed magazines for the Curtis Publishing Company were rewarded with green and brown vouchers they called "greenies" and "brownies." During World War II, food and other items were rationed to those who had sufficient stamps or tokens known as "points" that were color-coded. Beef could be bought only when one had a sufficient number of *brown points*. Finally, the aspiring Girl Scouts still called Brownies earn rewards that aren't called "points" but might as well be. Whatever the reason, since World War II "brownie points" has been slang for what one earns by good behavior. ("Those flowers I bought my wife got me lots of brownie points.")

Bringing up the rear on the palette-prestige scale is *gray*. Gray is an ambiguous color, as signified by *shades of gray*, referring to moral ambiguity. Especially since *The Man in the Gray Flannel Suit* became a bestseller this color has also suggested nondescriptness. In France, a **gray eminence**, or *eminence grise*, was an obscure clergyman who controlled more prominent ones, and by extension the king they advised. (Vice President Dick Cheney was sometimes said to be George W. Bush's gray eminence.) Purple, on the other hand, historically has had quite a good reputation. Due to the high cost of dye for this color and its subsequent association with royalty, those **born to the purple** either belong to a royal family or might as well. Purple was such a prestigious color in ancient Rome that some Romans sewed scraps of purple cloth onto more ordinary clothing in hopes of looking wealthier. This practice prompted Roman poet Horace to compare overly ornate verse to *purple patches* stitched onto plain garments in hopes of making them seem more grand. That is why we call flowery writing **purple prose**.


## Ethnic Groups

In 1908 a play called *The Melting Pot* popularized this phrase as a figure of speech. It alluded to a vessel in which heated metals and other materials were combined. "America is God's Crucible," wrote playwright Israel Agnail, "the great Melting-Pot where all the races of Europe are melting and re-forming!"

There were limits to the **melting pot** concept, however. Asians need not apply. During the late nineteenth century Americans and Europeans alike were alarmed by the prospect of hordes of Asians diluting their racial purity. This prospect came to be known as the *yellow peril*. Immigrants from China in particular were the target of countless slurs. Because those already in this country were considered unlikely to win a case in court, a **Chinaman's chance** came to mean no chance at all.

Immigrants from China ate so quickly and precisely with chopsticks that **chop chop** became slang for "get a move on." Our interpretation of the Mandarin term for prostrating one's self before superiors started out as *koo-too* and ended up as *kowtow*. Today **kowtow** refers broadly to obsequious behavior. ("He's really been kowtowing to the boss.")

The pidgin English spoken by Chinese immigrants became a popular source of mockery. One century-old expression that still circulates is *no tickee, no washee*. This referred to the small pieces of paper on which Chinese laundrymen recorded items of clothing that customers left for washing. Presumably those who couldn't produce this "ticket" were not given their clean clothes. **No tickee, no washee.** According to proverb scholar Wolfgang Mieder, it is unlikely that this expression was actually used by laundrymen. More likely it was part of dialect humor popular after the Civil War. Ira Gershwin used it as the title for a 1933 show tune. In time this kitschy admonition referred to any activity that couldn't proceed without verification. A blogger once called the unspoken requirement that online gay cruisers post a picture of themselves "the harsh decree of 'no tickee, no washee.'"

Many other musty phrases in our language are based on ethnic stereotypes. Few are flattering. A **Mexican standoff**, for example, suggests two men who pretend they want to fight but actually don't. **Gyp** is short for Gypsy, and is based on that group's perceived tendency to shortchange others in **gyp joints**. Calling police vans **paddy wagons** incorporates the nickname "paddy" commonly used for Irishmen (a contraction of "Patrick"), and alludes either to the fact that so many Irish-Americans worked as policemen, or that so many of them were thought to show up inside police vans. Not surprisingly, the single bit of lasting slang hung on Caucasians is only mildly pejorative: **WASP**. That acronym for White Anglo-Saxon Protestant was coined by sociologist E. Digby Baltzell in his 1964 book *The Protestant Establishment*. A *New York Times* article on the demise of *American Heritage* said that the popular history magazine had published "a fair a mount of WASPy nostalgia."

When Anglo-Saxons competed with Dutchmen for dominance on land and at sea, disparaging references to the Dutch became ubiquitous. Many of these terms migrated to the New World, where they are still part of our vernacular. **Dutch courage**, for example, suggests bravado fueled by alcohol (because it was said that Holland's sailors would fight only under the influence of brandy). Based on the reputation for parsimoniousness of those from Holland, a **Dutch treat** is one in which two parties share the cost. On a male-female date in particular, to **go Dutch** means to split the tab. A **Dutch auction** is one in which bids start high and go low. To be **in Dutch** is to be in trouble. A **Dutch uncle** is a blunt advice-giver. *The Facts on File Encyclopedia of Word and Phrase Origins* includes a list of sixty English expressions unflattering to the Dutch, a list that editor Robert Hendrickson said could easily have been tripled.

## Britannia

In the mid-sixteenth century, Henry VIII's son Edward had a young servant named Barnaby Fitzpatrick. Whenever Edward misbehaved, Barnaby got a whipping. Well before then it was common for young members of many country's royal families to have servant-surrogates who were flogged when they themselves got caught in a misdeed. This practice has long disappeared, but anyone who feels castigated for someone else's transgressions commonly refers to him- or herself as a **whipping boy**.

Following Henry VIII's reign, Matthew Parker became Archbishop of

Canterbury. Because he was known for snooping in other people's affairs, we imagine that the term **Nosey Parker** refers to this busybody clergyman. An alternative explanation is that *nose-poker* originally referred to such a person, and mutated into *Nosey Parker*. My favorite explanation, however, is that workers in London's Hyde Park were once called *parkers*, and those who peeked on lovers in the grass were *Nosey Parkers*. Some still use this nickname for snoopers of all kinds. A muckraking website calls itself Nosey Parker's News.

Hyde Park has a centuries-old tradition of permitting all comers to speak there on any subject they wish. Think of such speakers as in-the-flesh bloggers. During the nineteenth century these orators stood on wooden crates that had been used to ship soap or the like. That is why we say those who vociferously advocate a position are **on a soapbox**. They are **soapboxers**. According to *Time* magazine, Berkshire Hathaway's acerbic vice chairman Charlie Munger has a tendency to "soapbox."

## Places

For centuries England's coal mining was concentrated near the northeastern port city of Newcastle-upon-Tyne. Coal was shipped around the world from that city. As a result, **carrying coals to Newcastle** became a lasting way to characterize something as absurd as shipping ice to Antarctica, say, or bananas to Costa Rica.

Soldiers captured by Oliver Cromwell's army during the mid-seventeenth-century civil war were sent to the antimonarchist stronghold of Coventry, where residents simply ignored them. Since then, **sent to Coventry** has alluded to shunning. In Russia, criminals and troublemakers were exiled to Siberia, that country's frigid five-million-square-mile northern province. To this day being **sent to Siberia** refers to banishment of all kinds, if only from a choice corporate corner suite to a small windowless office by the elevator. Since so many of those actually sent to Siberia were made to mine salt, **back to the salt mines** became a lasting catchphrase for any sort of drudgery.

In his 1925 prospectus for a new magazine to be called *The New Yorker*, editor Harold Ross assured readers that it would not be "edited for the old lady in Dubuque." This magazine's credo flattered its big-city readers and their wannabe provincial cousins. Dubuquians were another matter. To the mortification of the sixty thousand residents of that Iowa city, with the word "little" added to Ross's original version, a **little old lady from Dubuque** became a common allusion to middle American cluelessness, the preferred way to disparage those who don't have sense enough to be big young women from Manhattan. A *Pittsburgh Post-Gazette* book critic called one novel "not a book for the little old lady from Dubuque."

In 1978 Edward Albee titled one of his plays *The Lady from Dubuque*. By then Peoria rivaled Dubuque as the proverbial headquarters of provincial America. That's because "Will it play in Peoria?" was the question members of Richard Nixon's White House routinely asked when wondering if a given policy would pass muster in the hinterlands. This referred to a small city in west central Illinois that was considered a silent-majority stronghold. (Raunchy comedians Richard Pryor and Sam Kinison were from Peoria, as was feminist Betty Friedan, but who's quibbling?) **Play in Peoria** became a shorthand way of saying something would be acceptable to middle Americans. Over time, reference to *Peoria* alone became sufficient to suggest heartland residents in general, and their presumed state of mind. In contrast to so many of his colleagues in Los Angeles, said actor George Wendt (*Cheers*), "I like a little bit of Peoria."

Another way of referring to this type of setting is with fanciful place names such as *Lower Slobbovia* (an Al Cappism from *Li'l Abner*), *South Succotash* (the way Ronald Reagan referred to isolated settings that he thought received more than their share of media attention), and, most often, **Podunk**. Thought to be based on an Indian name for swampy lowlands, there have actually been a number of American communities named Podunk. The last town by this name to merit a post office was in Kansas in 1881. Adaptations include *podunk college* for a mediocre backwater institution of higher education.

## Publishing

During the late eighteenth century, a British physician named John Wolcott wrote satiric verse under the pseudonym Peter Pindar. Wolcott once observed about some doggerel written by a colleague, "I think this piece will help to boil thy pot." *Boil thy pot*—an expression presumably familiar in Pindar's time—is the genesis of the term **potboiler**, referring to popular writing done by authors who need to put food on the table, to "keep the pot boiling."

Stanford University has a collection of eight thousand potboilers, most of them inexpensive, action-packed novels aimed at male readers. This genre got its start in 1860 with Ann S. Stephens's *Malaeska, the Indian Wife of the White Hunter*, the first entry in the Beadle's Dime Novels series. Later entries

featured protagonists such as Buffalo Bill and Calamity Jane. Then and now, **dime novels** came to characterize cheap works of sensationalized fiction, the literary equivalent of tabloid journalism. (A *Publishers Weekly* review of a Bat Masterson biography said its subject bristled at "dime-novel exaggerations" about his gunfighter's life.) A synonymous phrase, referring primarily to crime writing of the 1930s and 1940s that was printed on inferior paper, is **pulp fiction**. This phrase was expropriated by director Quentin Tarantino as the title of an over-rated 1994 movie.

Watchdog groups in some settings tried to ban popular fiction that they found unseemly. One particularly active group called the Watch and Ward Society was able to get many books banned in Boston during the early twentieth century. Since this proved to be a sales booster elsewhere, publishers vied to get their books on Watch and Ward's list. After World War I, **banned in Boston** became a facetious catchphrase signifying mildly risqué writing censored for puritanical reasons.

## Acronyms

Every era has its favorite acronyms. Ours is dense with those used for cyber-chat (*lol, omg, gtg,* etc.). Just as their parents and grandparents may be vague on what these acronyms stand for, young cyberchatters may not always be clear on the concept of ones used by their elders. When company came to dinner and there were more diners than there was food, it was common for one member of the host's family to murmur **FHB** for "family hold back." In prewar Britain FHO stood for "family—hold off!" or "family, hands off!" During dance-card days, a **BMOC**, or big man on campus, was high-status indeed. At Andover, George H. W. Bush—a multiletter athlete who was elected student body president and Best-All-Around Boy—was a BMOC's BMOC. Those of a certain age still apply this post–World War I acronym to *big wheels* of all kinds.

The widespread use of acronyms is a relatively recent phenomenon. One reason is that before World War II initials did not play such a big role in military life. During the Second World War their use exploded, and many acronyms came home with veterans. *SNAFU*, for example. For public consumption, **SNAFU** was bowdlerized to "situation normal, all fouled up." GIs also created *VIP*, or "very important people," to refer to the officers who were fawned over during rare public appearances. They got what is still called **VIP treatment**. *R & R* is another acronym that made the transition from military to civilian life. We understandably think this refers to "rest and relaxation," but among soldiers it actually meant, and means, "rest and rotation." First used in World War II, *R & R* referred to the practice of removing soldiers from combat for a few days. Civilians began to use **R & R** generically for all manner of relaxing occasions. A *USA Today* reviewer who thought director Spike Lee had slacked off when making one of his movies called the result "cinematic R & R."

During World War II, as in previous wars, **AWOL** meant "absent without leave." This military counterpart to hookey-playing was first used by both sides during the Civil War. According to lexicographer Stuart Berg Flexner, Confederate soldiers who took unauthorized R & R were sometimes made to do hard labor while wearing a sign reading "AWOL." World War I soldiers spelled it out as "A-W-O-L," but by World War II the acronym had become a word unto itself pronounced "A-WOL." In civilian life this term refers to anyone who doesn't report for expected duty. An ABC News report on government employees who don't show up for work concluded that "they're AWOL."

## Cards

Early in Harry Truman's presidency one of his friends saw a sign on the desk of an Oklahoma prison warden that read THE BUCK STOPS HERE. This friend gave a replica to the president in October 1945. Truman displayed that sign on

his desk during much of his presidency, and sometimes referred to it in speeches. The sign's message became central to Truman's credo. It plays off an earlier expression, **pass the buck**, which originated among poker players who passed a buck knife among themselves to indicate whose turn it was to deal the cards and, presumably, to defend themselves if another player didn't like the cards he was dealt. Timid souls who preferred not to deal at all *passed the buck*.

Truman, an avid poker player, advocated a **fair deal** for the American people. Truman's predecessor Franklin Roosevelt had called for a **new deal**, echoing his cousin Theodore's promise of a **square deal**. All of these slogans originated with card players. "Hurrah! for a new deal," wrote an 1858 novelist about some men playing cards. In Mark Twain's 1883 memoir *Life on the Mississippi*, a poker player says, "Thought I'd better give him a square deal." A few years later, Teddy Roosevelt told Americans in a 1905 speech, "When I say I believe in a square deal . . . all I mean is that there shall not be any crookedness in the dealing."

Even though card playing isn't nearly as central to American life as it once was, we still use its nomenclature: *ante up, penny ante, raise the stakes, put up or shut up, lay down your marker, in the chips, when the chips are down, ace in the hole, ace up your sleeve, stacked deck, close to the chest, overplay your hand, play your trump card, tip your hand, stand pat, call you, fold, sweeten the pot,* and *hit the jackpot*. In cards and life a **piker** is one who will play only for low stakes. Because in poker a *flush*—five cards of the same suit—is a strong hand but four cards of the same suit is not, those who bet on a so-called *four-flush* are called **four-flushers**. So is anyone who engages in bluff and deception.

## Classic Current Events

On May 4, 1937, a huge airship with swastikas on its tail left Frankfurt, Germany, for the United States. Alarmed by Hitler's rise, the American government had restricted the sale of helium to Germany. As a result, this *zeppelin*— the *Hindenburg*—was filled with the far more flammable hydrogen. Two days after its departure, as it was about to moor outside Lakehurst, New Jersey, the *Hindenburg* exploded. Of thirty-five passengers and sixty-one crew members aboard, thirty-five perished. This horrific catastrophe was immortalized in the recorded words of radio reporter Herbert Morrison ("It burst into flames! . . . Oh, the humanity!"). The crash of the *Hindenburg* was recalled when, during a speech to White House correspondents seven decades later, comedian Stephen

Colbert said of George W. Bush's White House, "This administration is not sinking. This administration is soaring. If anything, they are rearranging the deck chairs on the *Hindenburg*!"

In the late 1970s and early 1980s Americans were transfixed by news of a boy in Houston whose immune system was so compromised that he was confined to a sterile plastic bubble. In 1984 this twelve-year-old died after an unsuccessful bone marrow transplant. His encapsulated existence became a lasting metaphor for extreme isolation. *New York Times* columnist David Brooks once referred to "the freakish, **boy-in-the-bubble** life that is the modern presidency."

Although Robert Bork was considered an able, albeit extremely conservative, jurist, his name is best known not for anything he did but for something done to him. After Ronald Reagan nominated the appeals court judge to fill a vacancy on the Supreme Court in 1987, Bork's nomination was defeated by a Senate vote of 58–42. Bork's imperious manner at his confirmation hearings sealed his fate as much as his views did. That's not how his supporters looked at it, however. They thought he got the political shaft. This is why Robert Bork has joined an elite group whose names have become verbs. To **bork** means to scuttle someone's candidacy for partisan reasons. Those who are **borked** have this done to them. After the *New York Times* trashed a book by conservative linguist Charles McWhorter, columnist Mona Charen observed, "The 'borking' of McWhorter has already begun." It helps that Robert Bork's last name is monosyllabic, and sounds a bit like *boff*. If he had been named Breyer, say, or Roberts, or Alito, or Ginsburg, or Rehnquist, it's doubtful that *bork* would have entered the vernacular. *Breyered? Robertsed? Alitoed? Ginsburged? Rehnquisted?* I don't think so.

Four years after Bork bit the dust, the Tailhook Association held its thirty-fifth annual convention in Las Vegas. This fraternal organization brings together active and retired naval personnel who share an interest in aircraft carriers. ("Tailhook" refers to the metal hook that protrudes beneath the tail of airplanes and catches a cable to stop its forward motion when landing on such carriers.) Their 1991 Las Vegas convention attracted some four thousand participants. Ninety later said they were sexually harassed while there: eighty-three women and seven men. In the worst cases, servicewomen were made to walk gauntlets of drunken gropers in hotel corridors who tugged at their clothing and grabbed their privates. This scandal deep-sixed the careers of more than three hundred officers, and the Navy Secretary as well. The Tailhook bacchanal focused attention on the sexual perils faced by a growing number of women in military service. **Tailhook** remains an allusion to such perils. Fifteen years after their notorious convention, *Atlantic* magazine's Josh Green referred to military retirees who have a "Tailhook attitude toward gender differences."

## Going Nuclear

After the United States dropped atomic bombs on Japan, and Russia developed its own nuclear weapons, the prospect of being incinerated in nuclear conflict concentrated our minds. This prospect was especially intense during the 1950s, when terms such as *mushroom cloud, radioactive, fallout,* and *fallout shelter* became ubiquitous. Generations of schoolchildren were taught how to survive a nuclear attack ("Get under your desk!"). In the mid-1950s, atomic motifs— heavy with the sticks, balls, and crisscrossed hoops of nuclear chemistry—were a popular design motif. Modernistic homes from that era are still called *Atomic Ranch.* For a time *atomic* was a popular way to suggest potency in products of many kinds, including Atomic Fire Ball Candy. **Go nuclear** followed as an allusion to getting really, really mad.

A few months after Hiroshima and Nagasaki were destroyed, the point directly beneath an atomic bomb's explosion was dubbed *ground zero.* According to a legend popular among Pentagon workers, when Soviet satellite photographs showed how many of them congregated in a central courtyard snack bar at midday, the Kremlin aimed a couple of missiles right at their tables. With mordant military humor this snack bar came to be called the Ground Zero Café. Over time **ground zero** referred to any setting of intense devastation, in particular the charred remains of the World Trade Towers after 9/11.

Nuclear terminology didn't just refer to bombs, of course. As the cold war eased, these terms referred more often to nuclear energy and its associated terrors. A 1970 article in *Esquire* noted that fast-breeder reactors needed constant cooling to "prevent the 'China syndrome'—a constant worry to technicians, for once she starts melting she'll melt her way all the way down to China." In a fortuitous piece of timing, publicity-wise, the movie *The China Syndrome* was released just two weeks before the core of the Three Mile Island nuclear reactor outside Harrisburg, Pennsylvania, partially melted down. After it became clear that there was a problem at Three Mile Island, a spokesman for this nuclear power plant assured the public that "we are not in a *China Syndrome* type of situation." For years afterward **China Syndrome** was synonymous with all manner of nuclear-power disaster, core meltdown especially. **Three Mile Island** itself, or *TMI*, became metaphorical for any nuclear-reactor failure, the kinds nuclear power experts had spent decades reassuring the public were inconceivable. Seven years later, the Soviet reactor at Chernobyl in Ukraine exploded, spewing radioactive fallout all over northern Europe—four hundred times the amount released by the atomic bomb dropped on Hiroshima. Even more than its American predecessor at TMI, the accident at **Chernobyl** left the name of that town behind as a synonym for nuclear catastrophe. According to a sportswriter, the collapse of one baseball team's pitching staff during a game made for a "Chernobyl meltdown night." **Meltdown** itself became a way of referring to any sort of calamity. Those in distress are commonly said to be *melting down* emotionally. During a more innocent time before World War II, *meltdown* referred to nothing more ominous than having ice cream drip all over one's cone.

Who could have foreseen the more lethal connotations of that term? Anticipating how the words we currently use will evolve over time is dicey. Be that as it may, let's conclude by trying to foresee which terms we use today will become tomorrow's retroterms.

# 22. The Future of Retrotalk

**W**ords have always been a key tool for marking boundaries. Such verbal borders have historically been ethnic and geographic. According to an East Indian proverb, "language changes every twenty miles." Now the words we use differentiate generations. One might say "language changes every twenty years," although in our turbocharged times that could be a bit pokey.

Fashions, ads, music genres, TV shows, and blogs now appear and disappear at warp speed. Words, allusions, and catchphrases follow in their wake. Most blow through our national conversation like a summer storm. ("Wassup?" "Wardrobe malfunction." "No soup for you!") As the pace at which new words come and go accelerates, those who use them are vulnerable to seeming retro sooner than ever. Nowadays retrotalk can distinguish not only parents from children but younger siblings from older ones. As recently as 1999 those who compile Beloit College's Mindset List said incoming students were familiar with Max Headroom, Star Search, and cassette singles. Such references would need explaining to eighteen-year-olds today.

During a transitional period old terms are often applied to new products. "Horseless carriage" is the best example, for the means of transportation that would eventually be called an *automobile*, or *car*. These self-propelled vehicles incorporated *dashboards*, a term borrowed from the angled board used to protect buggy users from the muddy backsplash of horses' hooves. A century later, even though few of us record television programs on videotape any longer, we still talk of *taping* shows on our TiVo or DVD recorders.

The need for terminology in the brave new world of technology has led to much repurposing of old terms. For a long time the Enter key on computer keyboards was called a Return key because that's how it was labeled on electric typewriters (since pushing this key made the carriage return). For lack of a better word, even those who rarely read books *bookmark* their favorite sites on the Internet. When highlighting and moving blocks of text on a computer screen they *cut and paste*. After *Newsweek*'s Steven Levy told some young Google employees that he used to literally cut text from one page of copy and paste it onto another with Elmer's glue, one exclaimed, "So *that's* where 'cut and paste' came from!"

Some terms lie dormant for a time, then spring to life when needed. Think of these as *cicada terms* (after the insect that sleeps for seventeen years before making an appearance). *Cut to the chase*, for example, was part of moviemaking nomenclature early in the twentieth century, disappeared along with clichéd Westerns, then was revived in the late 1970s as a way of saying *get to the point*. Similarly, it took decades after Andy Warhol wrote, "In the future everybody will be world famous for fifteen minutes" in 1968 for us to refer routinely to "fifteen minutes of fame." *Kumbaya* only became synonymous with "sappy" long after protesters sang that song in the sixties, and *drink the Kool-Aid* didn't grow common until well after the 1978 Jonestown massacre to which it alluded. More than a decade after a pipe-wielding thug employed by figure skater Tonya Harding severely injured the knee of her 1994 Winter Olympics rival Nancy Kerrigan, "do a Tonya Harding" showed up as an allusion to badly hurting another person. After alleging that Barack Obama was being too restrained when being attacked, Maureen Dowd said on *Meet the Press*, "He doesn't have to be Tonya Harding to fight back."

Words and phrases continually shape-shift: appearing, changing form, disappearing, reappearing again. That's why predicting what terms in use today will become retroterms of the future is so risky. Let's do so anyway.

## Predictions

If it ever stops going, and going, the **Energizer Bunny** will undoubtedly outlive its ad campaign as an allusion to persistence. *The Perfect Storm* is referenced more than any other recent book title, and will certainly enter retroterm country when memory of Sebastian Junger's bestselling 1997 book itself begins to fade. So will the term **tipping point**, the concept Malcolm Gladwell borrowed from social science as the title of his 1996 bestseller. Once *A Prairie Home Companion* finally signs off on radio, the term **Lake Wobegon effect** will become retrotalk for settings like Garrison Keillor's fictional town where all the children are above average. Among psychologists this notion already refers to an optimistic assessment of capabilities that is exemplified by inflated grades. More broadly, a group of corporate heads interviewed by *USA Today* acknowledged that "CEOs live in a Lake Wobegon world where every dinner or lunch partner is above average in their deference." *Lake Wobegon* itself will eventually rival *Mayberry* as an emblematic village. In a *New York Times* op-ed essay, Orlando Patterson called Gerald Ford "a fine-looking man in a Lake Wobegon sort of way."

*Subprime* is a bit trickier to assess. This reference to the type of below-market mortgage rates that led to so many defaults and foreclosures was chosen as 2007's "Word of the Year" by the American Dialect Society. And sure enough it has not taken long for this term to transition from the business page to the style section. ("I subprimed that test.") *Time* film critic Richard Schickel described a movie character as leading a "sub-prime sort of life." Whether **subprime** will outlast the crisis that made it a household word remains to be seen.

In the realm of icons, since his 2004 death comedian *Rodney Dangerfield* has become iconic based on his signature line "I get no respect!" Thus "**the Rodney Dangerfield of** ____." (Detroit has been called "the Rodney Dangerfield of American metropolises.") As memories of that comedian fade, this allusion will become a retroterm. So will **Jack Kevorkian**, the physician who spent 1999–2007 in prison for assisting so many suicides. Even before then his last name had caught on as an allusion to those who help put others out of their misery, as when *Car Talk*'s Ray Magliozzi suggested that the owner of a dying automobile might want to "make an appointment at Kevorkian Motors." Although she died in 2007, **Tammy Faye Bakker** will continue to be an icon for those wearing over-the-top makeup—extended false eyelashes in particular—like that worn by this garish televangelist. Noting how much makeup was slathered on Katie Couric for her debut as CBS's news anchor, *New Yorker* TV critic Tad Friend worried that "our little girl had grown up and become Tammy Faye Bakker."

*Rolodex* is a term I've no doubt will eventually transition from current to retro. At the moment this address organizer is widely used both in fact and as an analogy. As a *Newsweek* writer observed, Hillary Clinton benefited from "her husband's Rolodex." Even though that card-holding device is giving way to electronic address books, its usefulness as a verbal analogy will endure long after **Rolodex** cards themselves have become landfill.

Another leading retroterm candidate is **Xerox** used as a verb. It's been a while since Xerox machines dominated the photocopying market, but those who remember when they did still use that brand name as a verb meaning "to copy." Will future generations get the allusion? As a number of commentators pointed out, when Hillary Clinton accused Barack Obama of using a *Xerox* to copy passages from a speech given by the governor of Massachusetts, she laid down a generational marker. Better Hillary should have said Barack *scanned* those lines or *cut and pasted* them.

Timekeeping is an area rich with retrotalk potential. **Clockwise**, for example, is not yet a retroterm, but if digital timepieces with numeric readouts supplant ones with hands and dials, it certainly could become one. The notion of **winding a watch** is already a retro concept to those who have never had to do this. *Matchboxes* are in a similar category (the small containers holding matches, not toy cars named after them). *The Harvard Medical School Guide to Healing Your Sinuses* characterized sinus cavities directly behind the nose as "about the shape and size of a matchbox." I've seen matchboxes used as a measuring device elsewhere. In an era of disposable lighters, however, **the size of a matchbox** is on the verge of becoming a retroterm, if it hasn't already. So is **packed like sardines**. Since so few Gen-whatevers eat canned sardines—ones packed fin by tail in rectangular tins—this expression is about to go retro. Would a contemporary teenager know what essayist Nancy Peacock meant when she wrote in *A Broom of One's Own* about some teddy bears being "sardined" in a basket?

## Commerce

Comedian Pat Hazell calls his nostalgic one-man show "The Wonder Bread Years." Boomers like Hazell grew up eating soft, white Wonder Bread and watching Buffalo Bob pitch this product on *Howdy Doody* ("Builds strong bodies eight ways!"). A decade after it was introduced in 1921, Wonder Bread pioneered pre-sliced loaves, helping inspire the catchphrase *best thing since sliced bread*. In our crunchy whole-grain era, **Wonder Bread** has fallen on hard times (its parent company went bankrupt in 2004) but is still sold and lives on as a metaphor for anything that is soft, tasteless, and virtually devoid of nutrition. A reviewer compared reading the bland memoir of Representative Charles Rangel (D-N.Y.) to "eating a supermarket aisle's worth of Wonder Bread."

In 1931 the company that developed Wonder Bread, Continental Bakery, introduced a new product altogether: smallish crème-filled oblongs of pound cake they called *Twinkies* (because Continental's manager was inspired by a billboard for Twinkle Toe Shoes). Like Kool-Aid, Twinkies is a still-sold product whose name has been besmirched by unflattering and unfair connotations. Similar products are sold by other companies, most notably Tastykakes, but there is something about the name "Twinkie" that invites derision. In addition to the so-called *Twinkie defense* (see chapter 20), within the television industry less-than-profound news anchors are called **Twinkies**. So is anyone considered not up to speed intellectually, especially if that person is young, female, and blonde.

Another food-based retroterm-in-the-making is *secret sauce*. This concept seems a bit jejune in the age of cookery-as-theater, but is one that had great resonance in the early days of Big Macs. In part that's because so many urban legends surrounded the dubious ingredients thought to be part of any foodstuff whose contents are kept a secret (HIV-infected semen was a particular favorite). This also illustrates the power of the word *secret,* as illustrated by the retroterm *secret decoder ring.* (See chapter 16.) There is no such thing as *secret sauce,* however, and never has been. There is, however, *special sauce*—the enhanced thousand-island dressing that McDonald's squirted on Big Macs from day one. Because McDonald's was so proprietary about the contents of this sauce, it came to be known as a **secret sauce**. This term proved to have lasting metaphorical significance. According to a technology blogger, entrepreneurs are searching for "the secret sauce of success."

When Jeffrey Immelt bested other contenders to become chief executive of General Electric, *Time* magazine said he'd "won GE's CEO bake-off." This alluded to Pillsbury's "bake-offs" in which contestants vie to win a prize for recipes they're created using that company's products. (In 1949 Theodora Smafield won the first bake-off with her "No-Knead Water-Rising Twists"; this was followed by Lily Wuebel's "Orange Kiss-Me Cake" in 1950.) **Bake-off** eventually began to be used generically for contests of all kinds and will undoubtedly outlive the contest itself as a retroterm.

## Current Current Events

After Iraq invaded Kuwait in 1991, George H. W. Bush diligently lined up support from other countries to oust Saddam Hussein's occupying forces. At one point his most stalwart ally—British Prime Minister Margaret Thatcher—fretted that the president might be losing his nerve. "This is no time to go wobbly, George," she warned him. The evocative phrase **go wobbly** still refers to losing one's nerve. A *Seattle Times* editorial addressed to Washington state legislators is headlined "Don't Go Wobbly on Education Reform."

**The mother of all** _____ has already survived what Iraqi dictator Saddam Hussein called the *mother of all battles* he planned to fight against the United States during the ensuing Gulf War. A euphemism that American soldiers in that war used for bombing casualties—**toast**—became a lasting reference to casualties in many walks of life. (GIs picked it up from the 1983 movie *Ghostbusters* in which Dan Aykroyd's character says, "I'm gonna turn this guy into toast!") Other terms that outlived the Gulf War and will probably stick around include *line in the sand, mission creep, exit strategy,* and *stealth.* A comparable list from the second Iraq war includes *regime change, embed* (as both a verb and a noun), *WMD, surge,* and *high-value target.* **Shock and awe** is a special case, a phrase that originated in the Nazis' blitzkrieg playbook. (Seven years after the 2000 presidential primaries, a political consultant said that when Bush raised $29 million at that time, his competitors responded with "shock and awe.") I have little doubt that Bush's claim of **mission accomplished** soon after the invasion of Iraq will also live on as an ironic allusion to any task that seems to be completed but isn't. Recently I've been hearing the term *Gitmoed,* or dealt with harshly, alluding to America's severe prison for enemy combatants at Guantánamo Bay, Cuba (whose nickname is Gitmo). *Waterboard* is another term that will undoubtedly go retro. The comic strip character *Dilbert* once compared being assigned onerous tasks to "getting waterboarded on your birthday."

During John Kerry's 2004 campaign for president, a group of Vietnam veterans—only one of whom had actually served with him in that war—challenged the Democrat's account of his service on a *swift boat* (a small aluminum boat used by American sailors to patrol Vietnamese rivers). Even though these charges were subsequently debunked, they proved so damaging that **swiftboat** became a verb, meaning to torpedo someone's political campaign with dubious but devastating allegations. Long after we have trouble remembering what Democrat ran for president in 2004 that term is likely to remain in play when negative political tactics are being discussed.

During George W. Bush's second term in office, Senator George Allen (R-Va.) was videotaped calling an East Indian-American "Macaca." This turned out to be a North African term of derision derived from a genus of monkey. Allen's 2006 campaign for re-election never recovered from constant reruns of him hurling this epithet, on YouTube, other websites, and television. **Macaca moment** became a common allusion not only to Senator Allen's gaffe but to a recorded, game-changing blunder of anyone in the public eye, one that will probably remain in play after the name George Allen elicits only a scratch of the head.


## Cinema

The most memorable line in *Field of Dreams* (1989) is "If you build it, he will come" (uttered from on high by Ray Liotta, playing Kevin Costner's dead father, urging his son to build a baseball field in the midst of Iowa's cornfields)— caught on quickly and stuck around as a catchphrase. Real estate developers are especially fond of **build it and they will come** rationales for dubious developments. Erecting new buildings on the theory that they will find customers is sometimes called a "Field of Dreams rationale."

The title of *Fargo*, the Coen brothers' vivid 1996 portrayal of a pregnant Minnesota sheriff who wears a trapper hat, has become shorthand for the heartland in general, as when *Time* writer Lev Grossman called the midwestern accent of a blogger "straight-out-of-Fargo." Earlier, *People* magazine had reported that a sitcom character wore "a *Fargo*-esque hat." "Fargo-esque" was later applied to Sarah Palin's accent, when it wasn't simply called "Fargo."

Another relatively recent movie that generated a retroterm candidate is *Wag the Dog*. Based on Larry Beinhart's novel *American Hero*, this 1997 movie featured a U.S. president who hires a political consultant to help him cope with a budding sex scandal. That consultant fakes an impending war with Albania, complete with phony newscasts. Because this movie was released less than a month before Bill Clinton became embroiled in the Monica Lewinsky affair, any subsequent military action authorized by Clinton was derided by detractors as a *wag-the-dog* strategy. More broadly **wag the dog** has come to suggest diversionary tactics of many kinds, as when information about an out-of-wedlock child fathered by Jesse Jackson was leaked to the *National Enquirer* on the eve of a rally he organized to protest election irregularities. In the sense of smaller events controlling larger ones, this catchphrase has been around for centuries. Some believe it originated in an old joke: "Why does a dog wag its tail? Because a dog is smarter than its tail. If the tail was smarter, the tail would wag the dog."

A year after *Wag the Dog* ran in theaters, another movie followed that I'm confident will produce a cicada retroterm. That movie is *The Truman Show*. Starring Jim Carrey as a sunny suburbanite who has unknowingly lived his entire life in an elaborate TV set before millions of viewers, *The Truman Show* was evocative enough when released in 1998. Several years of reality shows, surveillance cameras, and YouTube postings later, this movie has grown in relevance. As that trend continues and grows, **The Truman Show** will increasingly become a knowing allusion to the always-on-display world we're creating, even by those who haven't seen this underappreciated movie. Montreal psychiatrists Joel and Ian Gold (who are brothers) call the conviction that one's life is being broadcast on television *Truman Show Delusion*.

## Future Sources

Today, movies and television shows are our leading supplier of future retroterms. As such media fragment, and references to their components grow less universal, we will turn to other media as our primary source—computers in particular. We already use the programmers' term **de-bug** for correcting mistakes in general. Political figures talk of **re-booting** stalled campaigns.

Cyber acronyms on the verge of becoming retroterms include **GIGO** ("garbage in, garbage out"—another way of saying that computers can generate nothing better than the data and programming entered into them) and **WYSIWYG** ("what you see is what you get," an eighties-era acronym meaning that what shows up on a computer's monitor is an accurate rendition of what will be printed out—not always the case with early computers, where what you saw was seldom what you got). Though few of us realize it, **in the loop** and **out of the loop** date back to the cyber-concept of a *feedback loop*, in which data already generated influence data being generated in a continuous cycle.

Of the many video games now consigned to computer museums, the name of only one is likely to persist as a retroterm: **Pac Man**. It's not the appeal of this game that will ensure its recognition so much as the image of a big mouth munching everything in its path. That wonderfully evocative graphic is too metaphorically useful to die. A study of rats found that a blow to their head could cause ongoing brain damage because a "Pac-Man-like" enzyme kept gobbling up surrounding brain proteins.

Unlike *Pac Man*, the venerable *Whac-a-Mole* game is still popular among players, and even more popular among those who use its name figuratively. In this arcade game, hitting a mole whose head sticks up from one hole causes other moles to emerge from other holes. **Whac-a-Mole** has outpaced *Pac Man* in metaphorical significance, especially among soldiers fighting Iraqi insurgents who disappear in one area only to reappear in another.

Today's Internet undoubtedly will be a primary source of retroterms for tomorrow's talkers. So will other sources we have yet to imagine. What won't change is the pervasiveness of retroterms themselves. We enjoy using them too much. Each era contributes its own retroterminology to the national discourse. We have. Our kids will, and their grandchildren. It's part of the fun of talking.

# Acknowledgments

For invaluable ongoing help with this project I would like to thank in particular my brother Gene for his meticulous and helpful reading of the manuscript. My brother Steve also gave me helpful consultation and encouragement, as did Sol Steinmetz.

Librarians at the Olive Kettering Library—Sue Weldon, Richard Kerns, and Scott Sanders—were their usual helpful selves on this project, as were the librarians of the Greene County Library.

For their help on specific aspects of this book I would like to thank Wendy Hart Beckman, Louisa Bradtmiller, Paul Buhle, Phil Courter, Gay Courter, David Coulson, Jack DeWitt, Bob Fogarty, Michele Gordon, Mary Jo Graca, Frank Herron, Aileen LeBlanc, Layne Longfellow, Bill Phillips, Dan Nakamura, Philomene Offen, Bly Straube, and Mary Tom Watts.

For help with illustrations, thanks are due Richard Irvine-Brown, Bob Bryla, Lucy Carswell, Erica Flanagan, John Fleming, Mike Harding, Chris Kirtley, Courtney Loy, Kitty Munger, John Mustain, John Pantozzi, David Rose, Ira Seskin, Anna Smith, Steve Vogel, and Mort Walker.

My sons David and Scott gave me invaluable assistance at different stages of the project.

Daniela Rapp did a fine job of shepherding the book to publication as its editor. Editors Nichole Argyres and Ethan Friedman got it under way in the first place, as did agent Michelle Tessler who gave this project her usual good support. Adam Goldberger did a meticulous job of copyediting the manuscript.

Most of all, I would like to thank my wife, Muriel, whose help with this project went far beyond the call of duty. It always does.

# Notes

These notes are intended to cite sources of information noted in the text and provide guidance for readers who might wish to verify these sources or pursue further research of their own. The dates of newspaper articles I consulted are given following the names of the newspapers themselves. Magazine articles are referenced by the name and date of the publication in which they appeared as well as page numbers. (Where germane I've also included the title of such articles and their author.) The names of websites I've accessed are given along with their URLs and the date I accessed them. The editions of books I consulted are cited and page numbers from that edition along with the date of their original publication when the edition I consulted was a reprint. Miscellaneous unpublished papers, e-mails, and phone conversations are noted as well. A bibliography of sources I most relied on follows the notes.

## 1. Talking Retro

**Beloit Mindset Lists:** "The Beloit College Mindset List," Beloit College, http://www.beloit.edu/~pubaff/mindset/ (May 14, 2008).

**South Carolina high school teacher:** Sally Sue Garris, of Columbia, South Carolina, noted in *Brill's Content,* December 1999–January 2000, 36.

**Canton high school students:** Veronica Van Dress writing about students of Marc Bliss in the *Canton Repository,* December 30, 2004.

**Harvard graduate student:** Michele Gordon, "Whatcha Talkin' 'Bout?" unpublished paper, Harvard School of Education, December 5, 1994.

**Elderly New Yorker, "ka-ching":** *New York Times,* May 28, 2007.

**Tom Wolfe's lament:** Susan Stamberg, *Talk* (New York: Turtle Bay/Random House, 1993), 112.

**Florida teacher:** Lane DeGregory on unnamed teacher in *St. Petersburg Times,* November-26, 2006.

**Columnist, Mayberry:** Leonard Pitts, *Dayton Daily News,* April 29, 1998.

**Bryson, "unless we understand":** Bill Bryson, *Made in America* (New York: Morrow, 1994, Avon, 1996), xiii.

**Basil Hall and Noah Webster:** Page Smith, *The Nation Comes of Age: A People's History of the Ante-Bellum Years,* vol. 4 (New York: McGraw-Hill, 1981), 251–52.

## 2. Story Lines

**Thackeray, skeletons in closets:** William Makepeace Thackeray, *The Newcomes: Memoirs of a Most Respectable Family* (1855, London: Macmillan, 1923), 129.

**Miner, "axe to grind":** "Have an axe to grind," Phrase Finder, http://www.phrases.org.uk/meanings/174000.html (December 31, 2007).

**Ward: "A Hard Case":** Artemus Ward, *The Complete Works of Artemus Ward* (New York: G. W. Dillingham, 1901), 115–16.

**1914 book, "have you stopped beating":** Gus C. Edwards, *Legal Laughs: A Joke for Every Jury* (Detroit: Legal Publishing Company, 1914), 152.

**Star-Tribune reader:** *Minneapolis Star-Tribune,* March 2, 1998.

**Acheson, "only when I laugh":** Dean Acheson, *Present at the Creation: My Years in the State Department* (New York: Norton, 1969), 366.

## 3. The Name's Familiar

**Bales, Mrs. O'Leary's cow:** Richard F. Bales, *The Great Chicago Fire and the Myth of Mrs. O'Leary's Cow* (Jefferson, N.C.: McFarland, 2002), 3–7, 51–59, 77, 132.

**Emily Post told readers:** *New York Times,* September 27, 1960; Thinkexist.com., http://thinkexist.com/quotes/emily_post/ (April 30, 2008).

**Imelda Marcos:** Katherine Ellison, *Imelda: Steel Butterfly of the Philippines* (New York: McGraw-Hill, 1988), 6–7, 170; *The Wit and Wisdom of Imelda Marcos,* http://www.thewil-yfilipino.com/imelda.htm (September 14, 2006).

**Norman Rockwell, "I paint life":** *Philadelphia Inquirer,* November 12, 1978.

**Mata Hari:** Pat Shipman, *Femme Fatale: Love, Lies, and the Unknown Life of Mata Hari* (New York: Morrow / HarperCollins, 2007), 148, 364–68, 372–75; "Mata Hari," Wikipedia, http://en.wikipedia.org/wiki/Mata-Hari (May 8, 2008).

## 4. Fighting Words

**Kipling, "bite the bullet":** Rudyard Kipling, *The Light That Failed* (1891; Chicago: Rand McNally, 1925), 179.

**W. C. Fields, "looking for loopholes":** Ronald J. Fields, *W.C. Fields: A Life on Film* (New York: St. Martin's, 1984), 253.

**Ron Suskind:** *The Diane Rehm Show,* WAMU-FM, Washington, D.C., August 11, 2006.

**Army's surgeon general, basket cases:** Paul Dickson, *War Slang: American Fighting Words and Phrase from the Civil War to the Gulf War* (New York: Pocket / Simon & Schuster, 1994), 40.

**Evans Carlson and Rewi Alley:** "Gung Ho! According to Evans F. Carlson," *Gunny G's Globe and Anchor,* R.W. Gaines, www.angelfire.com/ca/dickg/gungho.html (January 12, 2008); Dickson, *War Slang,* 170–71, 243–44.

**boondoggle:** William Safire, *Safire's New Political Dictionary* (New York: Random House, 1993), 74–75; "Boondoggle," *World Wide Words,* http://www.worldwidewords.org/qa/qa-bro3.htm (August 12, 2008). *New York Times,* April 5, 1935.

## 5. Stump Speech

**Jefferson, "stump orators":** Thomas Jefferson letter to John Adams, June 27, 1813 in Andrew A. Lipscomb, ed., *The Writings of Thomas Jefferson,* vol. 13 (Washington, D.C.: Thomas Jefferson Memorial Association, 1903), 281.

**"Politics ain't beanbag":** Finley Peter Dunne, *Mr. Dooley in Peace and War,* in Robert Hutchinson, ed., *Mr. Dooley on Ivrything and Ivrybody* (New York: Dover, 1963), 3; Edward J. Bander, *Mr. Dooley and Mr. Dunne: The Literary Life of a Chicago Catholic* (Charlottesville, Va.: Michie, 1981), 169.

**"If you can't stand the heat":** "Remarks at the Wright Memorial Dinner of the Aero Club of Washington," December 17, 1952, *Public Papers of the Presidents of the United States: Harry S. Truman, 1952–53* (Washington, D.C.: United States Government Printing Office, 1966), 1085–86; Robert H. Ferrell, *Harry S. Truman: A Life* (Columbia: University of Missouri Press, 1994), 109.

**Unruh, "money is mother's milk":** T. George Harris, "Big Daddy's Big Drive," *Look,* September 25, 1962, 82; *Time,* December 14, 1962, 20; e-mail from T. George Harris, June 24, 2004.

***Washington Post* political editor:** John F. Harris, *The Diane Rehm Show,* WAMU-FM, Washington, D.C.; October 24, 2006.

**James Baird Weaver and waving the bloody shirt:** Fred Emory Haynes, *James Baird Weaver* (Iowa City: State Historical Society of Iowa, 1919), 24–25.

**Sherman statement:** *Harper's Weekly,* June 24, 1871; William Tecumseh Sherman, *Memoirs of Gen. W. T. Sherman, Written by Himself* (New York: Charles L. Webster, 1891), 466.

**John Sherman, "mending fences":** Robert Hendrickson, *The Facts on File Encyclopedia of Word and Phrase Origins* (New York: Checkmark / Facts on File, 2004), 257; Safire, *Safire's New Political Dictionary*, 243.

**Smoke-filled rooms:** *Cleveland Plain Dealer*, June 13, 1920; *New York Times*, June 13, 1920; *Evening Star* (Washington, D.C.), June 14, 1920; Mark Sullivan, *Our Times*, vol. 6 (New York: Scribner's, 1935), 37–38.

**Henry IV, "a chicken in every pot":** Henry F. Woods, *American Sayings: Famous Phrases, Slogans, and Aphorisms* (1945; New York: Perma Giants 1950), 104–5; Thomas Bailey, *Voices of America: The Nation's Story in Slogans, Sayings, and Songs* (New York: Free Press, 1976), 376; Safire, *Safire's New Political Dictionary*, 117.

**"Brains trust," *New York Times* reporter:** Charles Earle Funk, *2107 Curious Word Origins, Sayings & Expressions* (New York: Galahad, 1993), 99–100; Stuart Berg Flexner, *I Hear America Talking: An Illustrated History of American Words and Phrases* (1976; New York: Touchstone Simon & Schuster, 1979), 255.

**Robert Taft accused president:** Cabell Phillips, *The Truman Presidency: The History of a Triumphant Succession* (New York: Macmillan, 1966), 215; Margaret Truman, *Harry S. Truman* (New York: Morrow, 1973), 23.

**Truman on McCarthy:** Ralph Keyes, *The Wit and Wisdom of Harry Truman* (New York: HarperCollins, 1995), 12, 108, 156.

**Lee Atwater:** *New York Times*, May 30, 1988; Lee Atwater with Todd Brewster, "Lee Atwater's Last Campaign," *Life*, February 1991, 60–67.

**Sister Souljah:** *New York Times*, June 14, 1992, June 17, 1992.

## 6. From Levittown to Jonestown

**Levittown, Levitt:** *Time*, July 3, 1950, 67–72; *New York Times*, September 21, 1987; Jane Stern and Michael Stern, *Jane & Michael Stern's Encyclopedia of Popular Culture* (New York: HarperPerennial, 1992), 280–82.

**Richard Simon as cover model:** André Bernard, *Now All We Need Is a Title: Famous Book Titles and How They Got That Way* (New York: Norton, 1995), 121.

**Paint-by-numbers:** William L. Bird Jr., *Paint by Number* (New York: Princeton Architectural Press, 2001); Karal Ann Marling, *As Seen on TV: The Visual Culture of Everyday Life in the 1950s* (Cambridge, Mass.: Harvard University Press, 1994), 59–66; David Mamet, *True and False: Heresy and Common Sense for the Actor* (New York: Pantheon, 1997), 54.

**David Halberstam liked to call himself:** *New Yorker*, May 7, 2007, 29.

**Jack Weinberg, "can't trust anyone":** *San Francisco Chronicle*, November 15, 1964; *Washington Post*, March 23, 1970; *Bill of Rights Journal*, Winter 1988, 15; telephone interview with Jack Weinberg, December 5, 1990.

**Burning bras:** Judith Hole and Ellen Levine, *Rebirth of Feminism* (New York: Quadrangle, ·

1971), 123, 136, 229–30; Rick Perlstein, "Correction of Things Past," *Civilization*, December 1998–January 1999, 27.

**Irina Dunn, "fish needs a bicycle":** Sydney Ladensohn Stern, *Gloria Steinem: Her Passions, Politics, and Mystique* (New York: Birch Lane, 1997), 391–92, 398; *Time*, October 9, 2000, 20; David Sakrison, "A bit of Herstory: The Definitive Word on the Origin!" Fish and Bicycle Page, http://www.geocities.com/SiliconValley/Vista/3255/herstory.htm (January 4, 2005); Eoin Cameron, "Fish & Bicycle," ABC Perth, September 1, 2004, http://www.abc.net/au/perth/stories/s1189577.htm (January 4, 2005); Robert Anton Wilson, *Cosmic Trigger: Final Secret of the Illuminati* (Tempe, Ariz.: New Falcon, 1977), 98.

**Timothy Leary, "Turn On, Tune In":** *New York Times*, June 9, 1996; Timothy Leary, *Flashbacks: An Autobiography* (Los Angeles: Tarcher, 1983), 251–53, 257; Timothy Leary, *The Politics of Ecstasy* (New York: Putnam's, 1968),13–14, 28, 64, 67, 89–90, 104, 160, 223–25, 236, 253–62, 304–9, 332, 353–58; *Current Biography*, 1970, 246.

**"Radical chic":** Tom Wolfe, "Radical Chic: That Party at Lenny's," *New York*, June 8,1970, 26–56; "Who's Afraid of *The New Yorker* Now?" in Seymour Krim, *Shake It for the World, Smartass* (New York: Dial, 1970), 186.

**"Mau-Mauing":** Tom Wolfe, "Mau-Mauing the Flak Catchers," in Tom Wolfe, *Radical Chic & Mau-Mauing the Flak Catchers* (New York: Farrar, Straus & Giroux, 1970), 97–98.

**"Me decade":** Tom Wolfe, "The 'Me' Decade and the Third Great Awakening," *New York*, August 23, 1976, 26–40.

**Rosen, "That's the last word I ever invent":** *Playboy*, June 1978, 23.

**Jim Jones, Jonestown:** Paul Sann, *American Panorama* (New York: Crown, 1980), 194–96; Min S. Yee and Thomas N. Layton, *In My Father's House: The Story of the Layton Family and the Reverend Jim Jones* (New York: Holt, Rinehart & Winston, 1981); Deborah Layton, *Seductive Poison: A Jonestown Survivor's Story of Life and Death in the People's Temple* (New York: Anchor / Doubleday, 1998).

## 7. Law and Order

**Charles Lynch, "lynch law":** Thomas Walker Page, "The Real Judge Lynch," *Atlantic Monthly*, December 1901, 731–43; Christopher Waldrep, *The Many Faces of Judge Lynch: Extralegal Violence and Punishment in America* (New York: Palgrave / Macmillan, 2002); Mac McLean, "Who Was Charles Lynch?" *Register & Bee* (Danville, Va.), August 1, 2005.

**Allan Pinkerton:** Sigmund A. Lavine, *Allan Pinkerton—America's First Private Eye* (New York: Dodd, Mead, 1963).

**Arizona Bill:** Raymond Hatfield Gardner in collaboration with B. H. Monroe, *The Old Wild West: Adventures of Arizona Bill* (San Antonio, Tex.: Naylor, 1944); Sisela Barnes, "Medicine Shows Duped, Delighted," *Smithsonian*, January 1975, 51.

**Clark Stanley:** Clark Stanley, *The Life and Adventures of the American Cowboy* (Providence, R.I., 1897).

**Federal authorities tested Snake Oil Liniment:** Joe Nickell, "Snake Oil: A Guide for Connoisseurs," Investigative Files, Committee for Skeptical Inquiry, http://www.csicop.org/sb/ 2006-09/i-files.html, September 2006 (May 2, 2008).

**Bobbitt worm:** "Bobbit Worm," Vibrant Sea, http://www.vibrantsea.net/bobbitt7_ani-lao18.htm (January 31, 2006).

**Kitty Genovese:** *New York Times,* June 10, 1964; *New York Times,* February 8, 2004; "The Kitty Genovese Syndrome," Crime Library, www.crimelibrary.com/notorious_murders/ mass/work_homicide/4.html (January 31, 2006); "The Murder of Kitty Genovese: This Much Is Certain," A Picture History of Kew Gardens, N.Y., September 7, 2004, www.old-kewgardens.com/kitty_genovese-002.html (January 31, 2006).

**Patrick Henry Sherrill, "going postal":** *New York Times,* August 21, 1986; *New York Times* August 22, 1986; "Going Postal," Patrick Henry Sherrill, Crime Library, www.crimelibrary .com/notorious_murders/mass/work_homicide/4.html (November 30, 2006).

## 8. Good Sports

**Ham Fisher, Joe Palooka:** Judith O'Sullivan, *The Great American Comic Strip: One Hundred Years of Cartoon Art* (Boston: Bulfinch / Little, Brown, 1990), 164; Maurice Horn, ed., *100 Years of Comic Strips* (New York: Gramercy, 1996), 155; "Comics and Their Creators," *Literary Digest,* November 17, 1934, 11.

**Wally Pipp:** Jonathan Eig, *Luckiest Man: The Life and Death of Lou Gehrig* (New York: Simon & Schuster, 2005), 64–67.

**Barzun, "Whoever wants to know":** Jacques Barzun, *God's Country and Mine: A Declaration of Love Spiced with a Few Harsh Words* (Boston: Atlantic Monthly / Little, Brown, 1954), 159.

**Barber, "catbird seat":** Red Barber and Robert Creamer, *Rhubarb in the Catbird Seat* (Garden City, N.Y.: Doubleday, 1968), 29.

**Rockne, Gipp:** Jerry Brondfield, *Rockne* (New York: Random House, 1976), 97, 219–23; Francis Wallace, *Knute Rockne* (Garden City, N.Y.: Doubleday, 1960), 212–17; Knute K. Rockne, "Gipp the Great," *Collier's,* November 22, 1930, 64.

**"Winning isn't everything":** Steven J. Overman, " 'Winning Isn't Everything. It's the Only Thing': The Origin, Attributions, and Influence of a Famous Football Quote," *Football Studies* 2 (October 1999): 77–99; David Maraniss, *When Pride Still Mattered: A Life of Vince Lombardi* (New York: Simon & Schuster, 1999), 365–70; Joel Sayre, "He Flies on One Wing," *Sports Illustrated,* December 26, 1955, 29.

**Gorgeous George:** Joe Jares, *Whatever Happened to Gorgeous George?* (Englewood Cliffs, N.J.: Prentice-Hall, 1974); "George Wagner," Wikipedia, March 31, 2008, http://en .wikipedia.org/w/index.php?title=George_Wagner&printable=yes (May 2, 2008); *Dayton Daily News,* February 4, 2005.

## 9. Getting Around

Charles Dickens, "cut and run": Charles Dickens, *Great Expectations* (1861; New York: Holt, Rinehart & Winston, 1964), 32–33.

John Bright, flog a dead horse: E. Cobham Brewer, *The Dictionary of Phrase and Fable* (1894; New York: Avenel, 1978), 471.

D. L. Stewart, rolling down car window: *Dayton Daily News,* July 16, 2006.

Michael Quinion, "doozy": Michael Quinion, *Ballyhoo, Buckaroo, and Spuds: Ingenious Tales of Words and Their Origins* (Washington, D.C.: Smithsonian, 2004), 104.

## 10. Yes, Virginia, There Is a Casting Couch

Church, "Yes, Virginia": Frank M. O'Brien, *The Story of the Sun* (1928; Westport, Conn.: Greenwood, 1968), 236–39.

Transcontinental relay, yellow journalism: W. A. Swanberg, *Citizen Hearst* (New York: Scribner's, 1961), 88–89; Joyce Milton, *The Yellow Kids: Foreign Correspondents in the Heyday of Yellow Journalism* (New York: Harper & Row, 1989), 40–44; W. Joseph Campbell, *Yellow Journalism* (Westport, Conn.: Praeger, 2001), x, 5, 26–33, 38–41.

Cardoso, "gonzo": William McKeen, *Hunter S. Thompson* (Boston: Twayne / Hall, 1991), 11, 35.

"Cut to the chase": Mark Israel, "Cut to the Chase," alt.usage.english Home Page, http://alt-usage-english.org/excerpts/fxcuttot.html (July 30, 2005); Etymologies & Word Origins, http://www.wordorigins.org/wordorc.htm (July 30, 2005); William Safire, *Coming to Terms* (New York: Doubleday, 1991), 293–94; J. P. McEvoy, *Hollywood Girl* (New York: Grosset & Dunlap, 1929) 104–6.

Bryson, "circling the wagons": Bryson, *Made in America,* 124.

Soukhanov, "noirish": Anne H. Soukhanov, *Word Watch; The Stories Behind the Words of Our Lives* (New York: Holt, 1995), 390.

Zanucks, "casting couch": "The Zanucks: Reel Royalty," CBS News, CBSNews.com, July 10, 2005, http://www.cbsnews.com/stories/2005/07/08/sunday/main707725.shtml (August 12, 2008).

## 11. Movie Metaphors

Museum of Modern Art "Film and Faith" program: *New York Times,* December 7, 2003; *Times* (London), December 11, 2003.

Psychiatrist Philip McCullough: *New York Times,* February 18, 1979.

Creature from Black Lagoon, *Eucritta melanolimnetes*: Jennifer A. Clack, "A New Early Carboniferous Tetrapod with a *Mélange* of Crown-Group Characters," *Nature,* July 2, 1998, 66–69.

**Susan Faludi, "pod feminists":** Elinor Burkett, "In the Land of Conservative Women," *Atlantic Monthly*, September 1996, 24.

**Authors of *Suburban Nation*, Invasion of Body Snatchers:** Andres Duany, Elizabeth Plater-Zybere, Jeff Speck, *Suburban Nation: The Rise of Sprawl and the Decline of the American Dream* (New York: North Point, 2000), xiii.

**Greenfield referred:** Meg Greenfield, *Washington* (New York: Public Affairs / Perseus, 2001), 51.

**Gary Cooper, hernia operation:** Geraldine Fabrikant, "Grace on the Cutting Room Floor," *New York*, March 18, 1977, 53.

**Mike Nichols, Buck Henry, "plastics":** *Orlando Sentinel*, August 23, 1992; *The Record* (Bergen County, N.J.), February 11, 1997; *Washington Post*, December 7, 2003.

**In his book *Big Blues*:** Paul Carroll, *Big Blues* (New York: Crown, 1993), 16, 190.

**Nora Ephron, Billy Crystal, "I'll have what she's having":** "AFI's 100 Years . . . 100 Movie Quotes," Bravo, September 17, 2005.

**Safire traced that concept:** William Safire, *Watching My Language* (New York: Random House, 1997), 232–34.

**According to Sydney Ladensohn Stern:** Stern, *Gloria Steinem*, 227.

**American Film Institute's top fifty movie villains:** AFI's 100 Years . . . 100 Heroes and Villains, http://www.afi.com/tvevents/100years/handv.aspx (May 5, 2008); *Dayton Daily News*, June 4, 2003.

## 12. Home & Hearth

**Earmarking:** J. C. Furnas, *The Americans: A Social History of the United States, 1587–1914* (New York: Putnam's, 1969), 169; e-mail from Beverly Straube, April 25, 2008.

**Antebellum Georgia doctor:** Marvin Harris, *Good to Eat: Riddles of Food and Culture* (New York: Simon & Schuster, 1985), 116.

**Alice Roosevelt Longworth, "mush":** Joseph P. Lash, *Eleanor and Franklin* (New York: Norton, 1971, Signet, 1973), 802.

**Dickens, "straws of hints":** Charles Dickens, *Our Mutual Friend* (New York: Bounty, 1865), 522.

**Frederic Tudor, ice:** Daniel Boorstin, *The Americans: The National Experience* (New York: Random House, 1965), 11–16. Stuart Berg Flexner, *Listening to America: An Illustrated History of Words and Phrases from Our Lively and Splendid Past* (New York: Simon and Schuster, 1982), 317–20.

**Rees, belt and braces:** Nigel Rees, *Cassell's Dictionary of Word and Phrase Origins* (London: Cassell, 2002), 20.

**Yale students, "shoe":** Russell Lynes, "How Shoe Can You Get?" *Esquire*, September 1953, 59, 123.

**Jefferson, "silk stocking gentry":** Thomas Jefferson letter to Elbridge Gerry, June 11, 1812, in Andrew A. Lipscomb, ed., *The Writings of Thomas Jefferson,* vol. 3, 163. http://infomotions.com/etexts/gutenberg/dirs/1/6/7/8/16784/16784.htm (May 12, 2008).

## 13. Sizzling Widgets

**Widgets:** George S. Kaufman and Marc Connelly, *Beggar on Horseback: A Play in Two Parts* (New York: Liveright, 1924), 94–99, 104–111, 132–133.

**Edsel:** Lisa Grunwald and Stephen J. Adler, eds., *Letters of the Century: America; 1900–1999* (New York: Dial, 1999), 399; Donald McQuade and Robert Atwan, *Popular Writing in America* (New York: Oxford University Press, 1974), 40; Jan G. Deutsch, *Selling the People's Cadillac: The Edsel* (New Haven, Conn.: Yale University Press, 1976), 38.

**Pinto:** "Design Defects of the Ford Pinto Gas Tank," www.fordpinto.com/blowup.htm (August 22, 2006).

**Goizueta, New Coke:** David Greising, *I'd Like the World to Buy a Coke: The Life and Leadership of Roberto Goizueta* (New York: Wiley, 1998), 132.

**Gary Dahl, pet rocks:** Dale Dauten columns, *Dayton Daily News,* February 25, 2001, June 3, 2001; Stern and Stern, *Jane & Michael Stern's Encyclopedia of Popular Culture,* 379–81.

**According to Bill Bryson, cash registers:** Bryson, *Made in America,* 93–94.

**Stuart Berg Flexner, wooden nickels:** Stuart Berg Flexner, *Listening to America,* 195.

**Hendrickson, dime-a-dance:** Hendrickson, *The Facts on File Encyclopedia of Word and Phrase Origins,* 292.

**Moxie:** Frank N. Potter, *The Moxie Mystique* (Virginia Beach–Norfolk, Va.: Donning, 1981); "Moxie Facts," Marietta Soda Museum, www.mariettasodamuseum.com/moxie _facts.htm (March 31, 2006); "Moxie and a President," Moxie Collectors Page, http://www .metrocast.net/~moxieman/coolidge.html (May 5, 2008).

**Charles Atlas:** Charles Gaines, *Yours in Perfect Manhood, Charles Atlas* (New York: Fireside / Simon & Schuster, 1982).

**Herblock on Nixon:** *Washington Post,* October 9, 2001.

**Cliff Freeman, "Where's the beef?":** *New York Times,* February 11, 1984; *Philadelphia Inquirer,* March 10, 1984; *Philadelphia Daily News,* February 22, 1986.

## 14. On the Job

**John Scott Haldane, canary in the mine:** Walter S. Weeks, *Ventilation of Mines* (New York: McGraw-Hill, 1926), 151–52; George A. Burrell, "The Use of Mice and Birds for Detecting Carbon Monoxide After Mine Fires and Explosions," Technical Paper 11 (Washington, D.C.: Government Printing Office, 1912), revised July 4, 2001; Charles R. Anderson, *Puzzles and Essays from "the Exchange": Tricky Reference Questions* (New York: Haworth, 2003), 12.

**Luddites:** Malcolm L. Thomis, *The Luddites: Machine-Breaking in Regency England* (New York: Schocken, 1970) 11–12, 19–22; Kirkpatrick Sale, "The Achievements of 'General Ludd': A Brief History of the Luddites," *Ecologist,* August–September 1999, 310–13.

**Thomas Carlyle, "red tape":** Thomas Carlyle, "Three Downing Street," Latter Day Pamphlets, 1850, http://carlyle.classicauthors.net/LatterDayPamphlets/LatterDayPamthlets3 .html (March 1, 2007); Safire, *Safire's New Political Dictionary,* 654.

**Bette Nesmith, Liquid Paper:** *Wall Street Journal,* October 16, 1986.

**William Thayer, "be your own President":** William Roscoe Thayer, *Theodore Roosevelt, an Intimate Biography* (Boston: Houghton Mifflin, 1919), 334.

## 15. Over the Wires and in the Groove

**Western Union, Alexander Graham Bell:** Tom Standage, *The Victorian Internet: The Remarkable Story of the Telegraph and the Nineteenth Century's On-Line Pioneers* (New York: Walker, 1998), 197; James Meyers, *Egglants, Elevators, Etc.: An Uncommon History of Common Things* (New York: Hart, 1978), 268; Erick Schonfeld and Jeannette Borzo, "The Next Disruptors," *Business 2.0,* October 1, 2006.

**Lily Tomlin:** *Technology Review,* May 1980, 59.

**Almon Strowger, dial telephone:** "No Operator, Please," *Technology Review,* January–February 2000, 104; John Bray, *The Communications Miracle* (New York: Plenum, 1995), 57.

**Thomas Edison:** *Scientific American,* December 22, 1877, 384.

## 16. Kid Stuff

**Tulsa journalist David Jones, brass ring:** GTRNewsOnline, www.gtrnews.com/greater-tulsa-reporter/1705/gtr-editor-hopes-to-become-maytag-repairman (March 5, 2007).

**Theodore Roosevelt, 1899 letter:** Elting E. Morison, ed., *The Letters of Theodore Roosevelt,* vol. 2 (Cambridge, Mass.: Harvard University Press, 1951), 999; "Climb Onto the Bandwagon," Phrase Finder, www.phrases.org.uk/meanings/94500.html (February 22, 2007).

**John Sinnema, "play hookey":** John R. Sinnema, "The Dutch Origin of *Play Hookey,*" *American Speech,* Autumn–Winter 1970, 205–209; Mark Twain, *Tom Sawyer,* in Sinnema, ibid., 205.

**Secret decoder rings:** Gerald Nachman, *Raised on Radio* (New York: Pantheon, 1998), 268–70.

## 17. Stay Tuned!

**Lone Ranger:** David Rothel, *Who Was That Masked Man? The Story of the Lone Ranger* (San Diego: A. S. Barnes, 1981); James Van Hise, *Who Was That Masked Man? The Story of the Lone Ranger* (Las Vegas: Pioneer, 1990); Bruce Jackson, "Silver Bullets," *Antioch Review,* Winter 2006, 6–23.

Tonto, "kemo sabe": Martha Kendall, "Forget the Masked Man. Who Was His Indian Companion?" *Smithsonian*, September 1977, 113–120; "Kemo Sabe," Write101.com, www.write101.com/kemosabe.htm (March 9, 2007).

Chuck Barris, *The Gong Show*: Dwight Whitney, "Chuckie Baby Reigns as King Gong," *TV Guide*, April 15, 1978, 34–36; Frank Swertlow, "Gong Show's Barris: Where Will He Stop?" *US*, April 18, 1978, 11; Chuck Barris, *Confessions of a Dangerous Mind* (New York: Hyperion, 2002), 154–55, 159–61, 178–79.

Lucy and Ricky Ricardo, *I Love Lucy*: "I Love Lucy: Encyclopedia," AllExperts, http://experts.about.com/e/i/i/i_love-lucy.htm (December 29, 2006); Geoffrey Mark Fidelman, *The Lucy Book: A Complete Guide to Her Five Decades on Television* (Los Angeles: Renaissance, 1999, 70–71).

Victor De Costa, *Paladin*: *New York Times*, April 17, 1974; "The Controversy," *Have Gun Will Travel*, www.hgwt.com/hgwt8old.htm (August 30, 2006).

## 18. Seen in the Funny Papers

John Steinbeck, Al Capp: Al Capp, *The World of Li'l Abner*, introduction by John Steinbeck (New York: Farrar, Straus & Young, 1953), ii.

Carlos Fuentes, Rivera and Kahlo as Mutt and Jeff: Frida Kahlo, *The Diary of Frida Kahlo*, introduction by Carlos Fuentes (New York: Abradale / Harry N. Abrams, 2001), 10.

Arthur Momand, "Keeping Up with the Joneses": *New York Times*, December 5, 1987; Funk, *2107 Curious Word Origins, Sayings, & Expressions*, 647–48; "Keeping Up with the Joneses," Don Markstein's Toonopedia, www.toonopedia.com/joneses.htm (May 1, 2006).

Elzie Segar, Popeye: Bud Sagendorf, *Popeye: The First Fifty Years* (New York: Workman, 1979); Fred M. Grandinetti, *Popeye: An Illustrated Cultural History* (Jefferson, N.C.: McFarland, 2004); Horn, ed., *100 Years of Comic Strips*, 371–73; Brian Walker, *The Comics Before 1945* (New York: H. N. Abrams, 2004), 238.

Rube Goldberg: Clark Kinnaird, ed., *Rube Goldberg vs. the Machine Age: A Retrospective Exhibition of His Work with Memoirs and Annotations* (New York: Hastings, 1968); Peter C. Marzio, *Rube Goldberg: His Life and Work* (New York: Harper & Row, 1973); John Ciardi, *A Browser's Dictionary, and Native's of Guide to the Unknown English Language* (New York: Harper & Row, 1980), 155.

Schulz himself once said: Lee Mendelson in association with Charles M. Schulz, *Charlie Brown and Charlie Schulz* (New York: World, 1970), 75.

## 19. Between Covers

H. L. Mencken and George Jean Nathan: Donald Hall, ed., *The Oxford Book of American Literary Anecdotes* (New York: Oxford University Press, 1981), 203.

Sinclair Lewis: Mark Schorer, *Sinclair Lewis: An American Life* (New York: McGraw-Hill / Delta/Dell, 1961); Vance Bourjaily, "Red Lewis' Town Is Kinder to Him Than He Was to It," *Smithsonian*, December, 1985, 46–56; Bernard, *Now All We Need Is a Title*, 73, 75.

Erskine Caldwell, genesis of *Tobacco Road*: *New York Times,* December 1, 1982.

George Orwell, "doublethink": George Orwell, *1984* (New York: Harcourt, Brace, 1949), 215.

London reporter counted thirty-two cameras: *Evening Standard* (London), March 31, 2007.

*Catch-22, 18*: *New York Times,* February 16, 1994; CBS News Sunday Morning, March 2, 2008.

"no second acts": F. Scott Fitzgerald, *The Last Tycoon* (1941; New York: Bantam, 1976), 212.

Anthony Kennedy once said: *Newsweek,* January 30, 2006, 38.

*Lolita Midsleeper*: Reuters, February 1, 2008.

Jacqueline Susann on Philip Roth: *New York Times,* May 11, 1981.

## 20. Retro U

Stanely Milgram, "Six degrees": Stanley Milgram, "The Small World Problem," *Psychology Today,* May 1967, 61–67; Thomas Blass, *The Man Who Shocked the World: The Life and Legacy of Stanley Milgram* (New York: Basic / Perseus, 2004), 284–89.

Judith Kleinfeld: Judith Kleinfeld, "Six Degrees of Separation: Urban Myth?" *Psychology Today,* March–April 2002, 74.

Duncan Watts: Duncan Watts, *Six Degrees: The Science of a Connected Age* (New York: Norton, 2003), 135; Clive Thompson, "Is the Tipping Point Toast?" *Fast Company,* February 2008, 74.

Hawthorne effect: *New York Times,* December 15, 1983; *New York Times; December* 6, 1998; Stephen R. G. Jones, "Is There a Hawthorne Effect?" *American Journal of Sociology,* November 1992, 451–68.

Bermuda triangle debunked: "The Bermuda Triangle," Naval Historical Center, U.S. Department of the Navy, http://www.history.navy.mil/faqs/faq8-1.htm (May 6, 2008); "Bermuda Triangle," Wikipedia, http://en.wikipedia.org/w/index.php?title=Bermuda_Triangle&printable=yes (May 6, 2008).

Prince Charles, sister Anne: Nigel Dempster and Peter Evans, *Behind Palace Doors* (London: Orion, 1993), 36.

Mrs. Patrick Campbell, Judi Dench, "scare the horses": Alan Dent, *Mrs. Patrick Campbell* (1961; Westport, Conn.: Greenwood, 1973), 78; Margot Peters, *Mrs. Pat: The Life of Mrs. Patrick Campbell* (New York: Knopf, 1984), 211; *Newsweek,* January 9, 2006, 63.

Mae West, "gun in your pocket": Leslie Halliwell, *Halliwell's Filmgoer's Companion* (New York: Scribner's, 1984), 1065; Emily Morris Leider, *Becoming Mae West* (1997; New York: DaCapo, 2000); 289; Jill Watts, *Mae West: An Icon in Black and White* (New York: Oxford University Press, 2001), 219; John Kobal, "Mae West," *Films and Filming,* September 1983, 22.

Isaac D'Israeli, "angels can dance": "Did Medieval Scholars Argue over How Many Angels Could Dance on the Head of a Pin?" Straight Dope, December 23, 1988, www.straightcope .com/classics/a4_132.html (March 17, 2007).

Phil Schewe, angels on pin: *New York Times*, November 11, 1997.

Ralph Waldo Emerson, better mousetrap: Burton Stevenson, "The Mouse Trap," *Colophon*, December 1934, pages unnumbered; Burton Stevenson, "More About the Mouse Trap," *Colophon*, Summer 1935, 71–85.

## 21. Miscellany

Schjelderup-Ebbe, "pecking order": Porter G. Perrin, "Pecking Order' 1927–54," *American Speech*, December 1955, 265–68; John Price, "A Remembrance of Thorleif Schjelderup-Ebbe," *Human Ethology Bulletin*, March 1995, 1–7.

Lyman Bagg, "put on dog": L. H. Bagg, *Four Years at Yale, by a Graduate of '69* (New Haven, Conn.: Charles C. Chatfield, 1871), 44.

banana republics: O. Henry, *Cabbages and Kings* (Garden City, N.Y.: Doubleday, Page, 1904), 132.

Brownie points: "Brownie Points," CPRR Discussion Group, March 28, 2006, http://cprr .org/CPRR_Discussion_Group/2006/03/brownie-points.html (January 11, 2007); "Brownie Points," World Wide Words, http://www.worldwidewords.org/qa/qa-bro3.htm (January 11, 2007).

Mieder, "no tickee, no washee": Wolfgang Mieder, " 'No Tickee, No Washee': Subtleties of a Proverbial Slur," *Western Folklore,* Winter 1996, 1–40.

Robert Hendrickson on "Dutch" expressions: Hendrickson, *The Facts on File Encyclopedia of Word and Phrase Origins*, 228–29.

My favorite explanation of "Nosey Parkers": "Nosey Parker," World Wide Words, http:// www.worldwidewords.org/qa/qa-nos2.htm (May 7, 2008).

Pindar, "keep the pot boiling": Peter Pindar, *The Works of Peter Pindar, Esq.* (London: Goulding, 1812), 352.

Stuart Berg Flexner, AWOL: Flexner, *I Hear America Talking*, 88.

"Hurrah! for a new deal": Charles James Lever, *Roland Cashel* (Oxford, U.K.: Oxford University Press, 1858), 116.

Mark Twain, Theodore Roosevelt, "square deal": Mark Twain, *Life on the Mississippi* (New York: Heritage, 1944), 301; Theodore Roosevelt, *Presidential Addresses and State Papers*, vol. 8 (New York: Review of Reviews, 1910), 321.

## 22. The Future of Retrotalk

Beloit's 1999 list: Mindset List 2003, http://www.beloit.edu/~pubaff/mindset/2003.php (May 7, 2008).

**Theodora Smafield, Lily Wuebel, bake-off:** "Pillsbury Bake-Off Contest," http://food.ya-hoo.com/pillsbury-bakeoff/, http://food.yahoo.com/recipes/pillsbury-bakeoff/13708/no-knead-water-rising-twists, http://food.yahoo.com/recipes/pillsbury-bakeoff/13662/orange-kiss-me-cake (May 6, 2008).

**"Truman Show Delusion":** *National Post*, August 20, 2008.

**A study of rats, "Pac-Man":** *Dayton Daily News,* November 2, 1999.

# Bibliography

The following bibliography cites sources consulted overall for material in this book. It is divided between sources of general interest and those related specifically to language.

## General

Anderson, Ann. *Snake Oil, Hustlers and Hambones: The American Medicine Show.* Jefferson, N.C.: McFarland, 2000.

Bailey, Thomas. *Voices of America: The Nation's Story in Slogans, Sayings, and Songs.* New York: Free Press, 1976.

Beck, Ken, and Jim Clark. *The Andy Griffith Show Book.* New York: St. Martin's, 2000.

Bell, Robert R. *The Philadelphia Lawyer: A History, 1735–1945.* London: Associated University Presses, 1992.

Berger, Arthur Asa. *The Comic-Stripped American: What Dick Tracy, Blondie, Daddy Warbucks, and Charlie Brown Tell Us About Ourselves.* New York: Penguin, 1974. First published 1973 by Walker.

———. *Li'l Abner: A Study in American Satire.* Jackson: University of Mississippi Press, 1994. First published 1969 by Twayne.

Boyer, Paul, and Steve Nissenbaum. *Salem Possessed: The Social Origins of Witchcraft.* Cambridge, Mass.: Harvard University Press, 1974.

Bray, John. *The Communication Miracle.* New York: Plenum Press, 1995.

Bruce, Scott. *Cereal Box Bonanza: The 1950's.* Paducah, Ky.: Collector Books / Schroeder, 1995.

Bruce, Scott, and Bill Crawford. *Cerealizing America.* Boston: Faber & Faber, 1995.

Cantwell, Robert. *The Real McCoy.* Princeton, N.J.: Auerbach, 1971.

Capp, Al. *My Well-Balanced Life on a Wooden Leg: Memoirs.* Santa Barbara, Calif.: John Daniel, 1991.

Churchill, Alan. *Remember When.* New York: Ridge / Golden, 1967.

Clark, Charles L., and Earle Edward Eubank. *Lockstep and Corridor: Thirty Five Years of Prison Life.* Cincinnati: University of Cincinnati Press, 1927.

Coupri, Pierre, and Maurice C. Horn. *A History of the Comic Strip.* Translated by Eileen B. Hennessy. New York: Crown, 1968.

Cummings, Richard. *The American and His Food: A History of Food Habits in the United States.* Chicago: University of Chicago Press, 1940.

Daniels, Les. *Comix: A History of Comic Books in America.* New York: Bonanza / Crown, 1971.

Davis, Stephen. *Say Kids! What Time Is It? Notes from the Peanut Gallery.* Boston: Little, Brown, 1987.

de Madariaga, Isabel. *Russia in the Age of Catherine the Great.* New Haven, Conn.: Yale University Press, 1981.

Editors of *ben is dead* magazine. *Retrohell: Life in the '70s and '80s, from Afros to Zotz.* New York: Little, Brown, 1997.

Fletcher, Jennifer. *Peter Paul Rubens.* London, New York: Phaidon, 1968.

Fried, Frederich. *A Pictorial History of the Carousel.* New York: A. S. Barnes, 1964.

Furnas, J. C. The *Americans: A Social History of the United States, 1587–1914.* New York: Putnam, 1969.

Fussell, Paul. *The Great War and Modern Memory.* New York: Oxford University Press, 1975.

Gelatt, Roland. *The Fabulous Phonograph.* Philadelphia: Lippincott, 1955.

Gill, Brendan. *Here at the* New Yorker. New York: Random House, 1975.

Grandinetti, Fred M. *Popeye: An Illustrated Cultural History.* Jefferson, N.C.: McFarland, 2004.

Greenfield, Jeff. *Television: The First Fifty Years.* New York: Crescent, 1981.

Griffin, Al. *"Step Right Up, Folks!"* Chicago: Regnery, 1974.

Halliwell, Leslie. *Halliwell's Filmgoer's Companion.* New York: Scribner's, 1984.

Harris, Marvin. *Good to Eat: Riddles of Food and Culture.* New York: Simon & Schuster, 1985.

Harmon, Jim. *Radio & TV Premiums: A Guide to the History and Value of Radio and TV Premiums.* Iola, Wis.: Krause, 1997.

Heide, Robert, and John Gilman. *Dime-Store Dream Parade: Popular Culture, 1925–1955.* New York: Dutton, 1979.

Higgins, Kathleen M., and Robert C. Solomon. *A Short History of Philosophy*. New York: Oxford University Press, 1996.

Hinds, Anne Dion. *Grab the Brass Ring: The American Carousel*. New York: Crown, 1990.

Hoffmann, Frank W., and Bill Bailey. *Arts & Entertainment Fads*. Binghamton, N.Y.: Harrington / Haworth, 1990.

Horn, Maurice, ed. *100 Years of Comic Strips*. New York: Gramercy, 1996.

Hossent, Harry. *Gangster Movies*. London: Octopus, 1974.

Jasen, David A. *Tin Pan Alley: An Encyclopedia of the Golden Age of American Song*. New York: Routledge, 2003.

Johnson, Richard A. *American Fads*. New York: Beech Tree / Quill, 1985.

Jonas, Susan, and Marilyn Nissenson. *Going, Going, Gone: Vanishing America*. San Francisco: Chronicle, 1994.

Jones, James H. *Alfred C. Kinsey: A Public/Private Life*. New York: Norton, 1997.

Kael, Pauline. *The Citizen Kane Book*. Boston: Little, Brown, 1971.

Kinnaird, Clark, ed. *Rube Goldberg vs. the Machine Age: A Retrospective Exhibition of His Work with Memoirs and Annotations*. New York: Hastings, 1968.

Kurlansky, Mark. *Salt: A World History*. New York: Walker, 2002.

Lahue, Kaltan C. *Bound and Gagged: The Story of the Silent Serials*. New York: Castle, 1968.

Lee, Laura. *The Name's Familiar: Mr. Leotard, Barbie, and Chef Boyardee*. Gretna, La.: Pelican, 1999.

Liu, Aimee, and Meg Rottman. *Shoe Time*. New York: Arbor House, 1986.

Marling, Karal Ann. *As Seen on TV: The Visual Culture of Everyday Life in the 1950s*. Cambridge, Mass.: Harvard University Press, 1994.

Marum, Andrew, and Frank Parise. *Follies and Foibles*. New York: Facts on File, 1984.

Marzio, Peter C. *Rube Goldberg: His Life and Work*. New York: Harper & Row, 1973.

Meyers, James. *Eggplants, Elevators, Etc.: An Uncommon History of Common Things*. New York: Hart, 1978.

Mingo, Jack, and John Javna. *The Whole Pop Catalog*. New York: Avon, 1991.

Nachman, Gerald. *Raised on Radio*. New York: Pantheon, 1998.

Norton, Mary Beth. *In the Devil's Snare: The Salem Witchcraft Crisis of 1692*. New York: Knopf, 2003.

O'Sullivan, Judith. *The Great American Comic Strip: One Hundred Years of Cartoon Art*. Boston: Bulfinch / Little, Brown, 1990.

Panati, Charles. *Browser's Books of Beginnings: Origins of Everything Under, and Including, the Sun*. Boston: Houghton Mifflin, 1984.

————. *Extraordinary Origins of Everyday Things.* New York: Perennial / Harper & Row, 1987.

Perrin, Noel. *Dr. Bowdler's Legacy: A History of Expurgated Books in England and America.* New York: Atheneum, 1969.

Plunkett-Powell, Karen. *Remembering Woolworth's: A Nostalgic History of the World's Most Famous Five-and-Dime.* New York: Griffin / St. Martin's, 1999.

Polley, Jane, ed. *Stories Behind Everyday Things.* Pleasantville, N.Y.: Reader's Digest, 1980.

Proudfoot, W. B. *The Origin of Stencil Duplicating.* London: Hutchinson, 1972.

Read, Oliver, and Walter L. Welch. *From Tinfoil to Stereo: The Acoustic Years of the Recording Industry, 1877–1929.* Gainesville, Fla.: University of Florida Press, 1994.

Reitberger, Reinhold, and Wolfgang Fuchs. *Comics: An Anatomy of a Mass Medium.* Translated by Nadia Fowler. Boston: Little, Brown, 1972.

Rothel, David. *Who Was That Masked Man? The Story of the Lone Ranger.* San Diego: A. S. Barnes, 1976.

Sagendorf, Bud. *Popeye: The First Fifty Years.* New York: Workman, 1979.

Sann, Paul. *American Panorama.* New York: Crown, 1980.

Schein, M. W., ed. *Social Hierarchy and Dominance.* Stroudsburg, Pa.: Dowden, Hutchinson & Ross, 1975.

Sheed, Wilfrid. *Muhammad Ali.* New York: New American, 1976.

Smith, Bruce. *The History of Little Orphan Annie.* New York: Ballantine, 1982.

Soloveytchik, George. *Potemkin: Soldier, Statesman, Lover, and Consort of Catherine of Russia.* New York: Norton, 1947.

Stern, Jane, and Michael Stern. *The Encyclopedia of Bad Taste.* New York: HarperCollins, 1990.

————. *Jane & Michael Stern's Encyclopedia of Popular Culture.* New York: HarperPerennial, 1992.

Stern, Sydney Ladensohn. *Gloria Steinem: Her Passions, Politics, and Mystique.* New York: Birch Lane, 1997.

Theroux, Alexander. *The Enigma of Al Capp.* Seattle, Wash.: Fantagraphics, 1999.

Thompson, E. A. *A History of Attila and the Huns.* Westport, Conn.: Greenwood, 1975. First published 1948 by Oxford University Press.

Thompson, Hunter S. *The Proud Highway.* New York: Villard, 1997.

Trask, Richard B. *The Devil Hath Been Raised: A Documentary History of the Salem Village Witchcraft Outbreak of March 1692.* Danvers, Mass.:Yeoman, 1997. First published 1992 by Phoenix.

Tuleja, Tad. *The New York Public Library Book of Popular Americana.* New York: Macmillan, 1994.

Van Hise, James. *Who Was That Masked Man? The Story of the Lone Ranger,* Las Vegas: Pioneer, 1990.

Waldrep, Christopher. *The Many Faces of Judge Lynch: Extralegal Violence and Punishment in America.* New York: Palgrave / Macmillan, 2002.

Walker, Brian. *The Comics Before 1945.* New York: H. N. Abrams, 2004.

Walker, Mort. *Backstage at the Strips.* New York: Mason / Charter, 1975.

———. *The Lexicon of Comicana.* Port Chester, N.Y.: Comicana Books, 1980.

Walker, Samuel Americus. *Sneakers.* New York: Workman, 1978.

Waller, Altina L. *Feud: Hatfield, McCoys, and Social Change in Appalachia, 1860–1900.* Chapel Hill: University of North Carolina Press, 1988.

Watts, Jill. *Mae West: An Icon in Black and White.* New York: Oxford University Press, 2001.

Webster, H. T. *The Best of H. T. Webster.* New York: Simon & Schuster, 1953.

———. *The Timid Soul.* New York: Simon & Schuster, 1931.

Weltman, Manuel, and Raymond Lee. *Pearl White: The Peerless Fearless Girl.* South Brunswick, N.J.: A. S. Barnes, 1969.

White, Gordon. *John Caples: Adman.* Chicago: Crain, 1977.

White, Pearl. *Just Me.* New York: George H. Doran, 1919.

Zimmerman, Caroline A. *The Super Sneaker Book.* Garden City, N.Y.: Dolphin Books, 1978.

## Language

Algeo, John, ed. *Fifty Years Among the New Words.* Cambridge, U.K.: Cambridge University Press, 1991.

Ammer, Christine. *The American Heritage Dictionary of Idioms.* Boston: Houghton Mifflin, 1997.

American Heritage editors. *Word Histories and Mysteries: From Abracadrabra to Zeus.* Boston: Houghton Mifflin, 1986.

Ayto, John, ed. *Twentieth Century Words.* New York: Oxford University Press, 1999.

Barnhart, David K. *Neo-Words: A Dictionary of the Newest and Most Unusual Words of Our Times.* New York: Collier / Macmillan, 1991.

Barnhart, David K., and Allan A. Metcalf. *America in So Many Words.* Boston: Houghton Mifflin, 1997.

Baron, Naomi S. *Alphabet to E-Mail: How Written English Evolved and Where It's Heading.* London: Routledge, 2000.

Beale, Paul, ed. *A Concise Dictionary of Slang and Unconventional English, from* A Dictionary of Slang and Unconventional English *by Eric Partridge.* New York: Macmillan, 1989.

Brewer, E. Cobham. *The Dictionary of Phrase and Fable.* New York: Avenel, 1978. A facsimile of the 1894 edition.

Bryson, Bill. *Made in America: An Informal History of the English Language in the United States.* New York: Avon, 1996. First published 1994 by Morrow.

———. *The Mother Tongue: English and How It Got That Way.* New York: Morrow, 1990.

Carver, Craig M. *A History of English in Our Own Words.* New York: HarperCollins, 1991.

Chapman, Robert L. ed. *New Dictionary of American Slang.* New York: Harper & Row, 1986.

Ciardi, John. *A Browser's Dictionary: And Native's Guide to the Unknown American Language.* New York: Harper & Row, 1980.

———. *Good Words to You: An All-New Browser's Dictionary and Native's Guide to the Unknown American Language.* New York: Harper & Row, 1987.

Claiborne, Robert. *Loose Cannons and Red Herrings: A Book of Lost Metaphors.* New York: Norton, 1998.

Clark, Gregory R. *Words of the Vietnam War.* Jefferson, N.C.: McFarland, 1990.

Cole, Sylvia, and Abraham H. Lass. *The Facts on File Dictionary of Modern Allusions.* New York: Checkmark / Facts on File, 2001.

Daizell, Tom, and Terry Victor, eds. *The New Partridge Dictionary of Slang and Unconventional English.* London: Routledge, 2006.

Delahunty, Sheila Dignen, and Penny Stock. *The Oxford Dictionary of Allusions.* Oxford, U.K.: Oxford University Press, 2001.

Dickson, Paul. *Baseball's Greatest Creations.* New York: HarperCollins, 1991.

———. *Slang: The Topical Dictionary of Americanisms.* New York: Walker, 2006.

———. *War Slang: American Fighting Words and Phrases from the Civil War to the Gulf War.* New York: Pocket / Simon & Schuster, 1994.

Dillard, J. L. *All-American English: A History of the English Language in America.* New York: Random House, 1975.

———. *American Talk: Where Our Words Came From.* New York: Vintage, 1977. First published 1976 by Random House.

Dohan, Mary Helen. *Our Own Words,* New York: Penguin, 1975. First published 1974 by Knopf.

Effros, William C., ed. *Quotations, Vietnam: 1945–1970.* New York: Random House, 1970.

Ehrlich, Eugene. *What's in a Name? How Proper Names Became Everyday Words.* New York: Holt, 1999.

Ewart, Neil. *Everyday Phrases: Their Origins and Meanings.* Poole, Dorset, U.K.: Blandford, 1983.

Farkas, Anna, ed. *The Oxford Dictionary of Catchphrases.* Oxford, U.K.: Oxford University Press, 2002.

Flavell, Linda, and Roger Flavell. *The Chronology of Words and Phrases: A Thousand Years in the History of English.* Enderby, Leicester, U.K.: Silverdale / Bookmart, 1999.

Flexner, Stuart Berg. *I Hear America Talking: An Illustrated History of American Words and Phrases.* New York: Touchstone, 1979. First published 1976 by Simon & Schuster.

———. *Listening to America: An Illustrated History of Words and Phrases from Our Lively and Splendid Past.* New York: Simon & Schuster, 1982.

Fraser, Edward, and John Gibbons. *Soldier and Sailor Words and Phrases.* London: Routledge, 1925.

Freeman, Morton S. *Even-Steven and Fair and Square: More Stories Behind the Words.* New York: Plume / Penguin, 1993.

Funk, Charles Earle. *2107 Curious Word Origins, Sayings, & Expressions.* New York: Galahad, 1993.

Garrison, Webb. *Why You Say It.* New York: Routledge / MJF, 1992.

Gooden, Philip. *Name Dropping: An A to Z Guide to the Use of Names in Everyday Language.* New York: St. Martin's, 2008.

Hendrickson, Robert. *American Talk: The Words and Ways of American Dialects.* New York: Viking, 1986.

———, ed. *The Facts on File Encyclopedia of Word and Phrase Origins,* New York: Checkmark Facts on File, 2004.

Hirsch, E. D., Jr., Joseph F. Kett, and James Trefil. *The New Dictionary of Cultural Literacy.* Boston: Houghton Mifflin, 2002.

Kirkpatrick, E. M., and C. M. Schwarz. *The Wordsworth Dictionary of Idioms,* Ware, Hertfordshire, U.K.: Wordsworth, 1993.

Knowles, Elizabeth, ed. *The Oxford Dictionary of Phrase, Saying, and Quotation.* Oxford, U.K.: Oxford University Press, 1997.

Korach, Myron. *Common Phrases and Where They Come From.* Guilford, Conn.: Lyons Globe Pequot, 2002.

Lighter, J. E., ed. *Random House Dictionary of American Slang.* Vol. 1. New York: Random House, 1994.

———, ed. *Random House Dictionary of American Slang.* Vol. 2. New York: Random House, 1997.

Makkai, Adam, Maxine T. Boatner, and John E. Gates. *Handbook of Commonly Used American Idioms.* Hauppauge, N.Y.: Barron's, 1995.

Mann, Leonard. *A Bird in the Hand, and the Stories Behind 250 Other Common Expressions.* New York: Prentice-Hall, 1994.

Mathews, Mitford M., ed. *A Dictionary of Americanisms: On Historical Principles.* 2 vols. Chicago: University of Chicago Press, 1951.

McBride, Joseph. *High and Inside: An A-to-Z Guide to the Language of Baseball.* Chicago: NTL, 1997.

McQuain, Jeffrey. *Never Enough Words: How Americans Invented Expressions As Ingenious, Ornery, and Colorful As Themselves.* New York: Random House, 1999.

Mencken, H. L. *The American Language.* New York: Knopf, 1936.

Metcalf, Allan. *Predicting New Words.* Boston: Houghton Mifflin, 2002.

Mieder, Wolfgang, ed. *The Prentice-Hall Encyclopedia of World Proverbs.* New York: MJF, 1986.

Morris, Evan. *From Altoids to Zima.* New York: Fireside / Simon & Schuster, 2004.

———. *The Word Detective: Solving the Mysteries Behind Those Pesky Words and Phrases.* New York: Plume/Penguin, 2001.

Morris, William, and Mary Morris. *Harper Dictionary of Contemporary Usage.* New York: Harper & Row, 1985.

———. *Morris Dictionary of Word and Phrase Origins.* New York: HarperCollins, 1988.

Nunberg, Geoffrey. *The Way We Talk Now: Commentaries on Language and Culture.* Boston: Houghton Mifflin, 2001.

Palmatier, Robert A., and Harold L. Ray. *Dictionary of Sports Idioms.* Chicago: NTC, 1993.

Partridge, Eric. *A Dictionary of Catch Phrases.* Edited by Paul Beale. New York: Dorset Press, 1988.

———. *A Dictionary of Slang and Unconventional English.* New York: Macmillan, 1961.

———. *Origins: A Short Etymological Dictionary of Modern English.* New York: Macmillan, 1958.

Quinion, Michael. *Ballyhoo, Buckaroo, and Spuds: Ingenious Tales of Words and Their Origins.* Washington, D.C.: Smithsonian, 2004.

———. *Gallimaufry: A Hodgepodge of Vocabulary.* Oxford, U.K.: Oxford University Press, 2006.

Rees, Nigel. *Cassell's Dictionary of Word and Phrase Origins.* London: Cassell, 2002.

———. *Dictionary of Popular Phrases.* London: Bloomsbury, 1990.

Reinberg, Linda. *In the Field: The Language of the Vietnam War.* New York: Facts on File, 1991.

Rogers, John. *Origins of Sea Terms.* Mystic, Conn.: Mystic Seaport Museum, 1985.

Safire, William. *Safire's New Political Dictionary.* New York: Random House, 1993.

Smith, Logan Pearsall. *Words and Idioms: Studies in the English Language.* Boston: Houghton Mifflin, 1925.

Smith, Stephanie A. *Household Words: Bloomers, Sucker, Bombshell, Scab, Nigger, Cyber.* Minneapolis: University of Minnesota Press, 2006.

Soukhanov, Anne H. *Word Watch: The Stories Behind the Words of Our Lives.* New York: Holt, 1995.

Standage, Tom. *The Victorian Internet: The Remarkable Story of the Telegraph and the Nineteenth Century's On-Line Pioneers.* New York: Walker, 1998.

Steinmetz, Sol. *Semantic Antics: How and Why Words Change Meaning.* New York: Random House, 2008.

Steinmetz, Sol, and Barbara Ann Kipfer. *The Life of Language: The Fascinating Ways Words Are Born, Live, and Die.* New York: Random House, 2006.

Taylor, Anna Marjorie. *The Language of World War II: Abbreviations, Captions, Quotations, Slogans, Titles, and Other Terms and Phrases.* New York, Wilson, 1948.

Titelman, Gregory. *America's Popular Sayings.* New York: Random House, 2000.

Tuleja, Tad. *Marvelous Monikers: People Behind More Than 400 Words and Expressions.* New York: Harmony, 1990. First published 1987 by McGraw-Hill.

Urdang, Laurence. *A Fine Kettle of Fish, and Other Figurative Phrases.* Detroit: Visible Ink / Gale, 1991.

———. *The Whole Ball of Wax and Other Colloquial Phrases: What They Mean & How They Started.* New York: Perigree / Putnam, 1988.

Vanoni, Marvin. *Great Expressions: How Our Favorite Words and Phrases Have Come to Mean What They Mean.* New York: Morrow, 1989.

Webber, Elizabeth, and Mike Feinsilber. *Merriman-Webster's Dictionary of Allusions.* Springfield, Mass.: Merriman-Webster, 1999.

Woods, Henry F. *American Sayings: Famous Phrases, Slogans, and Aphorisms.* New York: Perma Giants, 1950. First published 1945 by Duell, Sloan & Pearce.

## Online

About.com: Urban Legends

Linguist List: Archives of ADS-L (American Dialect Society)

Merriam-Webster Online

NewspaperArchive.com

Online Etymological Dictionary

Oxford English Dictionary Online

Phrase Finder

Project Wombat

Questia

Snopes.com

Wikipedia

Wordorigins.org

World Wide Words

# Index of Retroterms

This index lists the principal retroterms discussed in the book. Most are alphabetized by the first letters of the word or phrase cited (e.g., "according to Hoyle"). When a key word within a phrase is the one most likely to be looked up, however (e.g., "tenterhooks, on"), or where several retroterms follow from a key word (e.g., "duck: dead, sitting"), the key word is the one alphabetized. Proper names that double as retroterms are alphabetized by the first letter of the first name (e.g., "Norman Rockwell"). For the sake of brevity, some retroterms are abbreviated (e.g., "coulda been contender").